Aspects of Language Variation in Arabic Political Speech-Making

Aspects of Language Variation in Arabic Political Speech-Making

Nathalie Mazraani

Routledge
Taylor & Francis Group
LONDON AND NEW YORK

First published 1997 by Routledge

2 Park Square, Milton Park, Abingdon, Oxon OX14 4RN
711 Third Avenue, New York, NY 10017, USA

Routledge is an imprint of the Taylor & Francis Group, an informa business

First issued in paperback 2016

Transferred to Digital Printing 2009

Typeset in Palatino by LaserScript, Mitcham, Surrey

British Library Cataloguing in Publication Data
A catalogue record for this book is available from the British Library

Library of Congress in Publication Data
A catalogue record for this book has been requested

ISBN 0–7007–0673–9

Publisher's Note
The publisher has gone to great lengths to ensure the quality of this reprint but points out that some imperfections in the original may be apparent.

ISBN 978-0-7007-0673-0 (hbk)
ISBN 978-1-138-96399-3 (pbk)

This book is dedicated to my parents,
to Mazen and his family.

Contents

Acknowledgements

This book is a revised and updated version of my PhD thesis submitted to Cambridge University in 1993. I wish to thank Professor Clive Holes for his invaluable comments and suggestions throughout my original research. Any mistakes are of course my own.

I am deeply grateful to Fondation Wiener Anspach and to the British Academy for their financial support.

Transliteration conventions and abbreviations

Phonology

č	voiceless alveolar affricate
ẓ	emphatic interdental sibilant
Z	emphatic dental sibilant
ḍ	emphatic dental plosive

a, i, u	short vowels
ā, ī, ū, ē, ō	long vowels

Abbreviations

adj	adjective
BGI	Baghdadi Arabic
C	Consonant
CA	Cairene Arabic
f	feminine
L	Lexicon
L-S	Lexico-semantic status
m	masculine
MSA	Modern Standard Arabic
MPP	Morphophonology
n	noun
OA	Old Arabic
P	Phonology
pass	passive
pl	plural
prep	preposition
S	Syntax
sg	singular
subj	subjuntive

TA	Tripoli Arabic
v	vowel
vb	verb

1 The sociolinguistic framework

1.1 INTRODUCTION

This sociolinguistic study of Arabic political discourse attempts to explore the relationship of language forms to language functions, through the speeches of Gamal Abdel Nasser, Saddam Hussein and Muammar Al Gaddafi. Each chapter concerned with the study is dedicated to a linguistic analysis of language variation and to observations of how language variation is used for communicational purposes by the politician.

The first part of this introductory chapter is concerned with positioning the work in general trends of sociolinguistics with a critical survey of related works. Basic concepts such as language and varieties within their social context and speech communities will be discussed, and mechanisms of code-switching and code-mixing will be looked at.

The second part of the chapter tackles the western approach to the linguistic description of Arabic: the concept of diglossia and the development of this notion into a theory of "multilectal" language system and the concept of a continuum. Finally, I will examine functional strategies in Arabic discourse and present the study and its objectives.

The sociolinguistic studies which are considered examine the interaction between language and society and more precisely, the linguistic patterns motivated by social and rhetorical roles. In order to deal with this sociolinguistic interrelation, I define some basic concepts: what kind of language one is dealing with, and what the social and geographical factors are which might affect the use of a language, in other words, the sociolinguistic framework.

1.1.1 Defining Language

Sociolinguistic studies look at social structures and how these are reflected in language use in a speech community. The basic linguistic system of a community is described by the linguist in terms of the formal rules (phonological, syntactic) and the situations in which these rules are used and interpreted. According to Fishman,[1] a situation is defined by the cooccurrence of two or more interlocutors related to each other in a particular way, communicating about a particular topic, in a particular setting.

Languages are broken down into "varieties", a neutral term, or defined as "standards" versus "dialects", in order to refer to linguistic systems used in specific situations or associated with particular functions. Gumperz,[2] for instance, in his study of the Hindi speaking area in North India, distinguishes: (a) village dialects which vary from village to village, (b) regional dialects which avoid local features and are relatively uniform over a large area, and, (c) standard Hindi, used in large cities.

1.1.2 The speech community and social factors

Although individuals have linguistic idiosyncrasies, a group of people from the same society will share similar linguistic rules and patterns of use. Hence we talk of the speech community which "refers to any human aggregate characterized by regular and frequent interaction by means of a shared body of verbal signs and set off from similar aggregates by significant differences in language usage".[3] Recurrent patterns have been observed in individuals' speech which are related to their particular society, similarities that are patterned and socially determined.[4]

Numerous linguistic studies have dealt with variability within speech communities. Labov[5] developed the concept of the sociolinguistic variable where the linguistic variable correlates with other linguistic elements as well as with extralinguistic factors such as speaker, addressee, setting, audience, socioeconomic status, ethnic origin or age group, etc. Communities can be defined according to various criteria and people's speech can be influenced by one or several of these interacting social variables, with the number and relevance of these criteria differing from one community to another. Sociolinguistic frameworks vary according to the country and area, with noticeable regional differences.

When selecting variables for study, it is important to ensure that the variables and the language varieties have the same value for all members of the concerned community, and that they are normatively associated with particular types of activity.[6] Sociolinguistic studies of different speech communities have taken into consideration parameters such as:

a) Literacy: Gumperz,[7] for instance, in his study of a north Indian village, concentrates on the village dialect of a group of illiterate men.

b) Gender: People's ability to use the varieties of language available in their society at large depends upon their being exposed to situations where those varieties are normally used. Bakir's case study[8] shows that in the southern Iraqi city of Basrah, men, because of their wider social networks, can use non-standard and standard forms, whereas women, being restricted to domestic chores and each others' company, have a narrower social network and do not have the opportunity or need to use the standard forms. The study shows moreover that women are reluctant to use standard forms, which have come to be associated with men, and thereby risk losing their female identity.

Al Khatib[9] looks at the influence of the speaker's sex on his or her use of language in the case of Jordanian Arabic. Here, women again tend to use the standard prestigious forms less than men, but women were also found to favour the urban variants more often than men.

Milroy's[10] study of phonological variation shows that, in Ballymacarrett, a working class enclave of Protestant east Belfast in northern Ireland, men retain their working class variants while women adapt to standard speech usage. This is related to differences in male/ female occupation patterns, with men working mainly within the area and women outside it. Milroy[11] investigated the inhabitants' social networks (a concept elaborated by Gal[12]), i.e. how people's relationships with each other in terms of kinship, religion, occupation, etc, affect their speech habits. Milroy observed, as in the case of Ballymacarrett, that the denser the social network, the greater the number of vernacular realizations.

c) Age: Age is another parameter that proved relevant in Milroy's study since younger women, in comparison to younger men of the community, have a broader social network and consequently are "innovators of linguistic change in the district".[13] Labov's[14] work in New York City shows that some variables are correlated to social class and even more so to age, with, for instance, the [ei] occurrence that has become stigmatized and found recurrently in the speech of those over sixty and not realized at all in the speech of younger persons.

d) Religion: the case of Bahrain[15] shows how religion and sect-membership, together with literacy and urban / rural origin, are related to different patterns of language variation. In Iraq, one finds that, broadly speaking, Sunnis in the north and Shi'is in the south of the country speak separate dialects. This distinction however is not true in Baghdad where Baghdadi Arabic is spoken by everybody throughout the capital: Shi'is and Sunnis share the dominant gelet dialect, although some minority groups such as Jews and Christians have the qeltu dialect (see chapter 4 for a discussion of Iraqi dialects).

e) Social class: In his Norwich study, Trudgill[16] related the realization of phonological variables to social class. For instance, the Lower Middle class and the Upper Working class are the most socially mobile and ambitious, and show a concomitant tendency to drop stigmatised and adopt prestige forms in the realizations of phonemes.

f) Geographical region – urban versus rural contrast: The urban rural divide underlines the existence of a geographical dimension in any approach to the analysis of synchronic variation, and many authors[17] have dealt with this issue in the case of Arabic. Ingham[18] for instance, looked at regional (and occupational – nomad versus settled) factors that correlate with dialect differences in southern Iraq and Khuzistan. The socio-cultural character of the different communities, (ḥaḍar) settled people and ('arab) Bedouin Arabs tend to coincide with differences in vocabulary, morphology and phonology.

Several linguistic studies concentrate on phonological variables rather than lexical ones because phonemes are non-referential, and are consequently more resistant to conscious suppression or change; they are part of the inherent system of a speaker who has less control over them than on other lexical items. As Gumperz[19] says, phonological features are automatic and more closely embedded in our speech habits than lexical items, and Ingham,[20] in his study of southern Iraqi Arabic, concentrated on phonology since "phonological variation showed the greatest patterning and better correlation with extra-linguistic factors". This debate on which linguistic variable to choose, belongs to studies involving variable rules, where phonological variables are preferred because they carry no referential meaning, whereas syntactic variants for instance, can seldom with complete confidence, be assumed to be referring to "the same thing" in the way different phonological realisations do. Lavendera,[21] in her article, questions the validity of the variable rule analysis in the study of syntactic variation. She gives an example of a passive construction, and shows how difficult the task is in establishing similarity of referential meanings, since it has been agreed that for the definition of a non-phonological linguistic variable the referential meaning of all the variants of a variable must necessarily be the same.[22] The present work is concerned with language shifts in the Arabic discourse and will consider the behaviour of phonological, morphophonological, syntactic and lexical features, to see how and why level-shifting affects elements at each of these linguistic levels of phonology (P), morphophonology (MPP), syntax (S) and lexicon (L).

1.1.3 Functions of language

As well as analyzing and describing variables affected by social and linguistic constraints, sociolinguists are also concerned with relating linguistic variation to functional factors in language use.

Dittmar[23] gives a general sociolinguistic agenda with parameters in the context of which, a socially-based descriptive study of language variation could be conducted. According to him, socio-linguistic theory aims to explain how, and in what functions, language systems are divided (regional, social, functional language varieties); how speech realizations are evaluated (privileged versus stigmatized status of speech norms; how they change on the basis of such evaluations (revaluation / devaluation of standards, dialects, speech behaviour of minority groups); to what extent language systems interfere with one another on the phonological, syntactic and semantic levels; how they are acquired, conserved and modified on these levels and, finally, in which relationships they coexist and / or conflict.

Ferguson,[24] building on the earlier work of the French Arabist William Marçais, developed the concept of diglossia, a stable situation in which two varieties of what its speakers regard as one language exist side-by-side; he refers to these as the High (H) and Low (L) varieties, formally different and used for different functions. In the case of Arabic, for instance, the literary language, the H variety, is the code for religion, official activities, and most broadcasting, whereas the dialect, the L variety, is the language of everyday conversation. In Ferguson's diglossia, there are nine aspects in which H and L are distinct: function, prestige, literary heritage, acquisition, standardization, stability, grammar, lexicon and phonology.

Ferguson's article, despite the criticisms that followed, in terms of the unsuitability of diglossia to match reality and variation,[25] was in its time seen as an improvement in the description of a number of languages – Arabic, Swiss German, Creole, Greek – and provided predictions as to the sociolinguistic factors that would destabilize a diglossic situation.[26] As was said, such a classification into H and L does not match reality and appears too idealistic. Even if a diglossic situation to describe the Arabic case for instance was appropriate 30 years ago, progress in terms of literacy and diffusion of broadcasting power have contributed to a change in diglossic situations or rather a redistribution of the functions of the different varieties. One has seen a blurring of different linguistic levels of the population as a result of the spread of education and literacy, and the influence of the electronic media. It appears for instance that the two supposedly independent codes are not kept separate but can be used within the "same" discourse. Ferguson[27] initially attributed this mixing to randomness. But if one attributes a function to each code, then what is or are the function(s) of mixed codes ? Rather, mixing should be seen as an additional part of the linguistic repertoire of an individual.[28]

In what follows, I will refer to some studies on language variation related to function and then to phenomena of code-switching, code-mixing, and cases of metaphorical and situational switchings.

1.1.4 Code-switching and code-mixing

Gumperz's article[29] on the use of Hindi and Punjabi in Delhi, was the first of a long series of works on code-switching. This work is particularly interesting in the context of this study because sociolinguistic studies are generally based on linguistic patterns of a speech community or a large group of informants; Gumperz's article and the present book are based on individual informants. Gumperz analyzed the discourse of an informant fluent in Hindi and Punjabi. Although historically related, Hindi and Punjabi are felt by speakers to be mutually unintelligible, and kept as separate codes. While Punjabi is used inside and outside the home, Hindi, or rather varieties of Hindi, predominate in commerce. Gumperz looked at phonological, morphemic and lexical features which are recognized as basic properties of language, and observed a mix of elements from different codes, as if the two languages were gradually merging. He also noticed a resistance of some linguistic elements to borrowing, and this phenomenon will also appear in our data: "at the extremes of the stylistic continuum, [...] the Punjabi verbal suffix -nd- and the Punjabi question word k-ii ("what") do not seem to be subject to borrowing".[30] Although Hindi is promoted as the standard, unifying language of India,[31] code-switching is associated with lack of prestige for native Hindi and Punjabi speakers. Reasons for this code-switching seem "uncertain" for Gumperz[32] apart from the attempt at reducing distance between speakers, since linguistic overlap is greatest in those situations which favour intergroup contact.

In Gumperz's later works, the discourse strategies behind code-switchings become more apparent. Code-switchings within a conversation can serve various functions such as quoting, specifying the addressee, interjecting, reiterating, qualifying the message.[33] The interpersonal objectives behind such code-switching aims at showing solidarity with the interlocutor or establishing some kind of distance, or implying the speaker's involvement with his discourse and the audience (see section 2.5 for a discussion on Involvement). Different codes are used to contrast "talk about action" versus "talk as action".[34] I will refer to these terms in the functional analyses of the speech extracts.

Blom and Gumperz[35] look at the social meanings of speech patterns in a community in Hemnesberget, a small town in northern Norway. The speech community is seen in diglossic terms with the coexistence of Ranamål and Bokmål. Ranamål is the local dialect which has great prestige and is recognized as a hallmark of local identity and pride in the community. Bokmål is the standard language of official transactions, religion, and the mass media, originally the language of the landowning commercial and administrative elite who despised locals for their lack of education and sophistication. Both languages are part of the community linguistic repertoire and felt to be mutually exclusive because of the differentiation of their functions. The authors observed however cases of code-switchings in the informants' discourse, as well as instances of cooccurrences from the phonological, morphological and lexical variables. The authors pointed out that, since the informants spoke both varieties perfectly, choice of linguistic features was not linked to concerns of intelligibility but to contextual constraints and social factors. The concept of the social meaning emerged to refer to the social value implied when an utterance is used in a certain context. A speaker may wish to play different roles in a conversation and as a consequence, the verbal messages vary and the codes are different. Blom and Gumperz distinguished situational switching which "assumes a direct relationship between language and the social situation", and metaphorical switching where the unexpected use of a code is meant to symbolize the situation, activities, and connotations associated with it. This switching relates to changes in topic or subject matter rather than to changes in social situation. Together with the sociolinguistic features, suprasegmental elements such as intonation contours play a part in the communication of meaning in the exchange.

Still within this investigation on code-switching, Gal[36] analyzed Hungarian-German shifting in Oberwart, a small Austrian village on the Hungarian border. She observed that German was used in conversation for rhetorical effects, to strengthen commands and to assert expertise and authoritativeness about an issue or about a technical speciality; Opinions and judgements appear to gain credibility and stature when uttered in German, the language associated in Oberwart with work, knowledge and sophistication.

The notion of code-switching thus appears as a much more subtle theoretical construct than diglossia. Initially, varieties were portrayed as strictly divided and used for different functions, in different settings, with different types of people, and where one code was employed at any one time.[37] Code-switching is a recognition of linguistic reality and the complex relationship between different codes, and it relies on the meaningful juxtaposition of what speakers must consciously or subconsciously process as strings formed according to the internal rules of two distinct grammatical systems.[38] Metaphorical code-switching which can be an unconscious mechanism, has an affective dimension to it: you change the code as you redefine the situation – formal to informal, official to personal, serious to humorous, and politeness to solidarity.[39]

While code-switching – where sections in one code are followed by sections in another one in the same conversation – affects the discourse at most linguistic levels (phonological, morphophonological, syntactical and lexical) and is functionally related, code-mixing, i.e. the mixing of different varieties within a single utterance or even within a single word, is linguistically determined, the mixing is more "local", i.e. limited to a word, and need not affect all linguistic levels (see Methodology Chapter for examples).

Code-mixing can occur without any change in topic or function involved.

Conversational code-switching is defined as the juxtaposition within the same speech exchange of passages of speech belonging to two different grammatical systems or subsystems.[40] Conversational code-switching is mentioned in Pfaff and Labov[41] in an example of discourse of a New York Puerto Rican speaker where two languages are mixed in rapid alternation, and Labov concludes that it must be described as the irregular mixture of two distinct systems, without suggesting however any reason for this mixing.

Although I have been referring to the works of Gumperz, and Blom and Gumperz mainly, there are other authors who have dealt with the concept of code-switching such as Poplack[42] and his study of code-switching among Puerto Ricans in Spanish Harlem, language choice in Montreal,[43] in Hong Kong[44] and Hindi English code-switching[45] for instance.

In what follows, I will be looking at Arabic linguistic studies which have dealt with these matters. This section is developed separately so as to concentrate on aspects specific to the Arabic language and Arab society, and to trace the progress made from diglossia to the concepts of functional code-switching over a continuum dimension.

1.2 ARABIC AND THE FERGUSONIAN DICHOTOMY

The Arabic linguistic situation is a particularly fruitful and complex phenomenon. Most Arabs as a matter of fact define their language in terms of a diglossic split. The Classical, literary Arabic (al-'arabiyya l-fuṣḥa) is the holy language, used for religious, intellectual and legal purposes and, according to Ferguson's article on diglossia, any deviation from it in formal situations would occasion scorn. The colloquial (al-'āmmiyya) on the contrary, devoid of any literary authority, is thought of as "imperfect", "wrong" or "bad" Arabic. Arabs feel uneasy in giving it the status of a language even though it is used in ordinary daily conversation.

Marçais in 1930 and Ferguson in 1959 were the first to describe the Arabic situation in terms of diglossia. As we have noted, Ferguson's simplistic classification of the Arabic language into H and L varieties does not match the reality now, if it ever did in the past. El Hassan[46] criticizes this two-valued system. A sermon in a mosque is categorized as a typically H situation according to Ferguson but El Hassan gives an extract from a sermon by Sheikh

Abderrahim Ibrahim in a mosque in Egypt and describes much of the language used as Educated Spoken Arabic (ESA). Some sentences fit Ferguson's linguistic criteria for H while others are plainly L and yet, there is a residue of sentences that do not belong to H or L. This example amongst others, illustrates the need to redefine Ferguson's division from both the formal and functional points of view. Many authors considered here, have attempted to illustrate the range of levels, intermediate between H and L, variously labelled al-wusṭā, Educated Spoken Arabic (ESA), etc. From those differing developments has emerged the concept of an Arabic language continuum in which the language is perceived as a seamless whole, and any changes from one part of the continuum to another proceed gradually rather than suddenly. Even if a variationist approach is now accepted, a comprehensive explanation of the social and extralinguistic factors which trigger these variations in Arabic has not been offered to date. One of the targets of this study will be to suggest hypotheses explaining the link between variation in Arabic with extralinguistic context and functions of the language.

1.2.1 Blanc and interdialectal studies

Blanc's[47] pioneering work is a study of interdialectal conversational Arabic: four Arabic informants, speaking different dialects (two Baghdadis, one Jerusalemite and one Syrian) are gathered in a language school in Monterey, California and are asked to discuss the Arabic language. Their conversation, of twenty minutes approximately, is recorded. Blanc's objective is to see what are the salient linguistic features when the informants of different origin converse: what specific strategies are used by the speakers to communicate with each other across dialectal differences, to make their dialects more understandable to one another. Blanc assigns particular features of dialect or standard to different parts of a continuum and distinguishes five discrete levels:

- standard classical
- modified classical
- semi-literary or elevated colloquial
- koineized colloquial
- plain colloquial

Speakers's speech movements from one level to another are the result of levelling and classicizing devices. Levelling involves replacing a local item by another one which is more well-known, though not necessarily Classical, as for instance the use by Iraqis of the Classical /ma'a/, /?āxar/ and /kalb/ instead of the Baghdadi /wiyya/ "with", /lāx/ "other" and /čalb/ "dog" respectively. These are the mechanisms that the informants mainly resorted to among themselves. Classicizing is a tendency found in a more formal speech context or when the topic itself demands a formal style, and, according to Blanc,[48] is only at the disposal of educated speakers, [it] will lend the speech an elevated or semi-literary tone. By classicizing is meant, for instance, the use of/bilād/, /ma'a/ and /?āxar/ instead of the dialectal forms /blād/ "country", /wiyya/ and /lāx/ respectively. The last two examples were pointed out by Blanc and by El Hassan[49] as cases of overlapping between levelling devices which apply in the "koineized colloquial" and classicizing devices found in "modified classical" Arabic. Boundaries between levels and levelling and classicizing devices are however vague since a given feature may appear under both headings, and the three middle levels can hardly, if at all, be verified.[50]

Blanc's chart seems to be too rigid and provokes uneasiness amongst native speakers:[51] the chart is perceived as artificial, with the examples being selected to match preconceived concepts. The limitations of Blanc's procedures (only four Arabic speakers, employed at the language school and talking about the "language of the educated") although already recognized by Blanc himself, are criticized by El Hassan[52] as is his analysis of Educated Spoken Arabic. El Hassan compares Blanc's general linguistic statements against a sizeable corpus of Educated Spoken Arabic that he himself collected in Egypt, Syria, Jordan and Kuweit. After analyzing features of ?i'rāb, negation, passive forms and word order, El Hassan concludes that Blanc's findings are inadequate and fall short of approaching the status of general tendencies, let alone rules, of Educated Spoken Arabic.

1.2.2 The emergence of Educated Spoken Arabic as a concept

In contrast to Blanc, El Hassan's study,[53] as said previously, is based on a large-scale data base of mainly unprepared conversations. The informants are men and women – aged between seventeen to sixty – and whose professions are representative of the population: students, teachers, civil servants, media personnel, barristers, accountants, translators, book-agents, diplomats, editors and housewives. El Hassan's object is to discover whether there is a "grammar" of ESA shared by speakers in all Arab countries. His large body of data provides many counterexamples to Blanc's theories, which he says have no validity outside the small and rather artificial study from which they emerge. El Hassan[54] randomly selects some features at the level of morphology and syntax to show that Blanc's system is inadequate because it generalises.

Following Blanc, many authors have explored the distinguishing linguistic differences which exist between dialects and standard Arabic. Cowan looked at Modern Standard Arabic (MSA), Bishai defined Modern Inter-Arabic (MIA), and Cadora[55] showed three different coexisting spoken languages, Modern Standard Arabic (MSA), Intercommon Spoken Arabic (ISA) and Dialectal Arabic (DA). In all these cases, the researchers assume the existence of named separate varieties without their discreteness being clearly indicated or justified by patterning in the data. Diem on the other hand in his study on standard language and dialect in Arabic, defines the relation between the standard and the dialect not as competitive but as complementary.

These studies however are symptomatic of the uneasiness with, and unsuitability of the diglossic theory and the need to provide a better description of reality. The spread of literacy saw the emergence of a new elite that felt unhappy about MSA as an expressive tool, inadequate for many aspects of modern life, while the dialect, suitable for mundane needs, was deemed equally inadequate.[56] The urge to develop a modern spoken idiom which could be understood at all levels of the population, resulted in the emergence of Educated Spoken Arabic, which has been given different names by different observers. ESA was, moreover, officialized and legitimised in the fifties and sixties through the speeches of politicians such as Gamal Abdel Nasser.[57]

Going back to the traditional Arabic linguistic debate, we should note Jack Fellman's[58] work, which brought a new and systematic technique in Arabic sociolinguistics. Fellman was able to enrich the sociolinguistic framework by stressing the importance of geographical, socioeconomic and religious features, in the makeup of individual linguistic competence. Each speaker, according to Fellman, is endowed with an idiosyncratic array of social features which not only identify him as a member of various overlapping speech communities but highlights his uniqueness too. Fellman agrees that Blanc made a start on the elaboration of such an approach in his work on Baghdadi Arabic,[59] where the three religious groups of Muslims, Christians and Jews speak three different dialects. The Muslims, settled more recently than the other groups, are influenced by their nomadic Bedouin origins, while the Jews and the Christians speak older urban dialects. Abu Haidar[60] also looked at the Muslim dialect of Baghdad, and more precisely at the "urban" versus "rural" contrast in Iraqi dialects. Abu Haidar acknowledged Blanc's work[61] on the communal dialects in Baghdad, but observed that over more than twenty years, the social factors that characterized the Baghdadi Arabic, in 1964, have been levelled and other linguistic features have been introduced to the dialect, due to urbanisation on a large scale.

Studies in the 1960's and 1970's introduced major refinements on Ferguson's simplistic division into High and Low, though these developments left some questions unanswered and posed others. Among the main improvements, as far as the linguistic theories are concerned, are:

- the dichotomy High and Low was shown to be too crude and idealistic in explaining the facts of actual usage;
- it was conclusively shown that a multiplicity of nonlinguistic factors intersect in any community or individual, each of which may have a linguistic reflex;
- from the methodological point of view, these studies attempted to grapple with the complexity of overwhelming amounts of data.

As to the drawbacks:

- the explanatory theories that were proposed present a static rather than a dynamic model of variation – given his socio-linguistic approach, Badawi would be the first to present an attempt at a dynamic model;
- there is no real attempt to handle the "multi-style" nature of actual conversation, and explain variation as, for example, a function of changing rhetorical intent;
- methodological drawbacks are still a major hindrance to proposed theories: data collection techniques are unsystematic and doubts arise as to the representativeness of the data.

1.2.3 Badawi and new sociolinguistic approaches

Badawi's[62] book is a major contribution to Arabic sociolinguistics. The author aims at defining the Arabic spoken in Cairo in terms of a continuum and he analyses in depth the "colloquial of the educated", the third level in his chart, mainly through the language of the media, e.g. language as spoken on television. Badawi identifies five levels of language in contemporary Egypt and analyses each of them according to phonological, morphological and syntactic features, and signals the level and occasion of respective use.

1 fuṣḥa t-turāth: "Heritage" Arabic, traditional Classical Arabic, uninfluenced by any colloquial or external influences.
2 fuṣḥa l-'aṣr: contemporary classical, literary Arabic influenced by contemporary civilisation.
3 'āmmiyyat al-muthaqqafīn: vernacular of the highly educated influenced by classical Arabic and contemporary civilisation together.
4 'āmmiyyat al-mutanawwirīn: vernacular of the semi-educated influenced by contemporary civilisation.
5 'āmmiyyat al-?ummiyyīn: vernacular of the illiterate not influenced by either classical or contemporary civilisation.[63]

Badawi's levels, clearly influenced by Blanc's five-fold classification, constitute a major improvement on Ferguson's H and L. Levels are described as affecting each other to a certain extent, the pivotal level being the rich and maximally flexible and variegated level three ('āmmiyyat al-muthaqqafīn). Badawi conceives of the lower three levels (i.e. those which have a dialectal morpho-syntactic base) as defined as collections of co-occurrent probabilities. There are very few variables, in other words, which always or never occur in any of these three levels. Badawi is determined to introduce a sociolinguistic dimension to his concepts: according to him, Blanc's levels are established on the basis of linguistic criteria alone, while his are based on sociolinguistic factors. Hence each individual (apart from the illiterates) is influenced by his education, family, and social background, but is nonetheless able to use more than one level in the same conversation or on different occasions, varying from sentence to sentence in order to match language with topic for instance.[64]

While Blanc posited levelling and classicizing devices that would determine the change from one level to another, Badawi resorts to "integrating" and "fragmenting" factors over the five levels, i.e. factors that determine the interaction of these levels within each other. Among the "integrating" factors, one notes that:

- despite all their peculiarities, these levels come from the same historical source (al-'arabiyya), which leaves the door for interaction wide open between them;
- all levels mix within Egyptian society. These levels exist within a single integrated community, which makes it possible for an individual to move from one to another whenever the psychological and social contexts concur;
- as said before, each individual (except for the illiterate) is able to use more than one level because of education. However, across the strata of society, there is a gap between ability to receive information and ability to perform in all of these levels;
- there is some overlapping between factors which means that many linguistic features are interchangeable or shared between some levels: they occur "more or less" and not in an "all or nothing" level specific manner.

The fragmenting factors will differentiate one individual from another as his speech is determined by a multitude of different factors. As much as the Egyptian society is extremely complex, the "language" used in that society is equally complex in its phenomena and components. It is therefore difficult to characterize an individual's linguistic behaviour and to pinpoint a single level of language on the ladder of formality which he occupies. Elements influencing a person's speech are education, area of residence (which may be different from the region worked in), age and gender.[65] Even if we take one factor, say, education, there are still so many different nuances: students come from private or public schools, religious or secular ones, from Egyptian and foreign universities, etc. Occupation is an important factor that influences speech, and engineers, businessmen, carpenters, bus drivers, teachers, etc, all having a way of talking at work which is different from the one spoken at home. Thus, says Badawi, the "us" of the Cairene society is an entity of numerous, varied factors.

Although several authors have criticized the ambiguity of such descriptions, Badawi is precisely making use of it to explain the distribution of items over more than one level. He resorts to a metaphor of a rainbow to illustrate this concept: there are areas of bright colour, which represent the "core" of a level, and marginal areas where colours merge, which are linguistically "border" areas between levels. The following examples show that vagueness applies to the limits of content of each level:

1 The aspectual particle bi-, prefixed to certain verbs to indicate non-past time, belongs to the fifth (lowest) level, because it is purely a colloquial feature used by all including the illiterate. bi- is however found in the fourth and third levels as well, mixing with features which are not found in the fifth level.
2 The third level is the most complex of all phonologically, as it is influenced by literary, colloquial and foreign languages and can, for example, have three different phonological realisations for the same word:
/t͟haqab/ /saqab/ /ta?ab/ "to perforate"

However, as each of these items "belongs" to other levels as well, the selected pronunciation will be seen as a move in the direction of the level with which it is normally associated: MSA at level 2 for /t͟haqab/, and levels 4 and 5 for /ta?ab/. /sa?ab/ is the only one of the three which is a "core" level 3 realisation.

The third level, after being described as a bridge with a two-way traffic, is further on presented as a "door" through which pass ideas and expressions of foreign origin or of Egyptian origin but from another (higher or lower) level.

One is removed from Ferguson's mere dual division where, for instance, a university lecture is said to be given in H. According to Badawi, the university professor writes in fuṣḥa l-'aṣr but gives his lecture in 'āmmiyyat al-mut͟haqqafīn. Thus the third level borrows from the fuṣḥa its terminology, expressions and abstract modes of signification, and from the vernacular, its basic sentence structure. The "vernacular of the educated" says Badawi is then born as a necessity or a mirror of civilisation. This image is too idealized according to El Hassan[66] who criticizes the vagueness of Badawi's chart, and the considerable overlapping between the levels. If a classification is established, each level should at least have some independent common core, some particular items which distinguish one level from another, and linguistic elements should be clearly defined as either continuous or discrete variables.

Furthermore, Badawi introduces a psychological factor, i.e. the consciousness or unconsciousness of a speaker whenever he is delivering his message: he may be aware of the different connotations conveyed by some lexical items and deliberately use them in order to make the "right" impression. One can imagine a politician delivering his speech in front of a large audience and for one reason or another – this audience consisting mainly of villagers rather than journalists for instance – he may wish to keep the speech at a lower level of formality and deliberately, or unconsciously, resort to certain phonological, morphological and syntactic features which he perceives as appropriate to his audience.

Badawi's features are based mainly on radio speeches and observations of native speakers of Cairo. Classifications and descriptions therefore cannot be representative of contemporary Egyptian Arabic as a whole.

El Hassan

El Hassan[67] uses creolist terminology in his attempt to define language varieties. MSA is identified with acrolect (prestige level), ESA with mesolect and colloquial Arabic (CA) is identified with basilect (standard level). According to El Hassan, ESA and CA are not discrete and constitute a continuum.

El Hassan's material consists of unprepared discussions between different combinations of Jordanians, Egyptians, Syrians and Lebanese. Some of his observations on the differential effect of variation between nationalities can be exemplified. Jordanian educated speakers tend, more than other nationalities, to use items endowed with formality when they are in formal situations. Conversely, in informal situations, the tendency is to use more non-prestigious forms.[68] Also, educated Jordanians tend to use more prestigious demonstrative tokens when talking to educated persons from their own country than when talking to educated persons from another Arab country. On the other hand, educated Egyptians when conversing with other educated Egyptians or with non-Egyptians tend to use far more stigmatized forms than prestigious demonstrative tokens,[69] showing maybe a desire for those educated Egyptians to sound "Egyptian", or that they enjoy a high degree of linguistic security and they can "afford" to talk more colloquially in a relatively formal context.

Meiseles

Meiseles[70] defines four levels of language and refines the Fergusonian dichotomy H/L, here literary and vernacular Arabic, within his varieties of contemporary Arabic: Literary Arabic (LA); Sub-standard Arabic (SsA); Educated Spoken Arabic (ESA); basic or plain vernaculars (VA). He further defines Oral Literary Arabic (OLA) as "the language used for oral expression, on all formal occasions, and many a time also on semi-formal ones", and

Informal Written Arabic, the written counterpart of OLA, which is "largely open to deviations from LA norms and receptive to the infiltration of lexical and structural elements from the vernacular".[71]

Like several authors cited previously, Meiseles agrees that the basic distinction between LA and the vernaculars is the absence of ?i'rāb, i.e. case and mood endings, in the vernaculars.

Meiseles's classification is somehow misleading because he defines the Arabic continuum as LA - SsA - ESA - VA whereas his personal contributions apply to the OLA - ESA - VA chart. Literary and dialectal influences are as follows: OLA lexical features influence ESA, and VA syntactic, morphological and phonological factors can be found in ESA.

Thus, at a phonological level, the phoneme /q/ is part of OLA whereas VA has /?/. Nothing is said about ESA apart from the fact that phonological features from above and below influence it. No account is given of hybrid forms (if this is really to tally with Badawi's third level). Secondly, interdental fricative /ẓ/ is found in OLA and in ESA as well: /ẓ/ and /Z - ḍ/ are found merging at the ESA level as a "reflection of the vernaculars". From this plethora of acronyms, we are left wondering what actually occurs and is realized at the VA and ESA levels.

Syntactically, the conjunctions /?an/ and /?anna/ are found at the level of OLA whereas ESA and VA show asyndeton. Meiseles's[72] example is the following:

/nardjū mina l-?ustāz ?uṣman ?an yataḥaddath lana/
"we'll ask Mr Osman to speak to us"

and the Egyptian ESA would have instead:

/nardjū mina l-?ustāz ?uṣmān yikkallim lana/

Meiseles however does not mention the cases where /?an/ can be found in ESA. The distribution of elements seems to be:

OLA	complementiser/?an,?anna/	/q/	interdental /ẓ/
ESA	asyndeton	/q - ?/	/dh/ and /Z - ḍ/
VA	asyndeton	/?/	/Z - ḍ/

Meiseles's refusal to pinpoint systematically salient elements for each level is justified seemingly by the difficulty of the process, and he concludes somewhat lamely that although the linguistic situation of contemporary Arabic as a language continuum, indivisible in any finite number of varieties is quite clear, its problems of description are too complex to lend themselves to an easy solution.[73]

Mitchell

Mitchell's[74] articles encourage the avoidance of prescriptivism and show refinement in definition. Mitchell[75] defines Educated Spoken Arabic that would be created and maintained by the interplay between written Arabic and vernacular Arabic(s). A shared standard arising from a modern literary tradition has to be supported by a wide educated public and appear in their speech as well as in their writing. Mitchell quadriglottic chart refers to LA - MSA - ESA - VA. MSA is the language used in journalism, television and radio news broadcasts, and is influenced morphologically and syntactically by classical Arabic. Where Mitchell recognizes MSA and ESA, Meiseles speaks of OLA and ESA, OLA being closer to MSA and ESA to the vernacular. The borderlines between ESA and MSA are kept somehow vague, apart from the fact that the hallmark of ESA is the lack of /?iʿrāb/ - case and mood endings. ESA is however characterized by vernacular negative particles, and numerals for instance, whereas MSA is influenced by the classical equivalents of these items.

Mitchell[76] gives a brief survey of the different positions held towards diglossia and the typology of levels.[77] His major contributions provide a richer sociolinguistic framework for the study of Arabic linguistics as he introduces the notions of stigmatized and unstigmatized forms as well as formality and informality.

Stigmatized versus unstigmatized forms

Mitchell argues that even if the pan-Arabic ESA is meant to be understood everywhere, differences will appear regionally. Geographical diversities, which are not evenly distributed and accepted, will exist on a stigmatized / unstigmatized axis. A grammar of ESA should then take stigmatized and unstigmatized forms into account since they are the most salient aspects. In the examples given by Mitchell, Jordanians, in contrast to Lebanese and Palestinians, tend to derive amusement from such exclusively Syrian forms of pronunciation as /ftāḥ/ "open!" or /ktōb/ "write!". Syrians are in turn strongly motivated not to use them, at least in conversation with Jordanians, to avoid the ridicule occasioned by the use of stridently local forms, and at the same time to proclaim oneself well able to handle the forms of pan or inter-Arabic.[78]

Moreover some forms may be stigmatized in one region and not in another. Ingham[79] talks of the multivalency of dialectal features: given a social (for example sect-based, Sunni versus Shi'i, or occupational, sedentary versus Bedouin) and geographical (southern Iraq versus Kuwait/ Gulf states) framework, the relevance and significance of a contrast (/dj/ versus /y/) as a reflex of standard Arabic /dj/ may be different from place to place, and "the valency of the contrast is stated for a particular subregion of the total area".

Standard Arabic /dj/ has an analogue /y/ in southern Iraq and is particular to the Shi'is, whereas /dj/ is particular to the Sunnis in the same area. However, the urban Sunni population of Zubair in southern Iraq and of Kuweit city use the pronunciation /y/. In Bahrain, the distinction /dj/ versus /y/ is also found but it has the opposite social distribution: /y/ is the local "prestige" form and is used by the Sunni population, while /dj/ is typical of Baharna (Shi'i) speech.[80]

The concept of stigmatized versus unstigmatized forms mentioned earlier is part of a long standing debate on the "prestige" attached to a form or dialect. Prestige was already a criterion distinguishing Ferguson's H from L. Over the years, with a better knowledge of language varieties, linguists have nuanced and refined the notion, terminology varying according to authors and to the object of study.

This debate is reminiscent of what Labov and Trudgill[81] called overt prestige of a variety, in the sense that positive, status-linked characteristics are ascribed to it, and covert prestige of non-standard varieties, in that, for their speakers, they function as symbols of group solidarity and personal identity.[82]

Tradition used to equate prestige to the standard form, MSA in the case of Arabic. The "real" picture however is more complex. In the case of Bahrain for instance,[83] Shi'is have some MSA-like phonological elements which are stigmatized compared to the dominant Sunni speech, resulting in a "non-standard standard" according to Holes, i.e. " a locally recognized standard of prestige [that] exists apart from the standard H variety".[84] Yet, Shi'is would abandon their MSA-like "standards" elements (for instance [dj] < OA /dj/) and adopt prestigious and non-MSA features, such as [y] from OA /dj/[85] in some lexical items in particular contexts. Thus, "it appears that the two forces of social prestige and linguistic "correctness" are pulling in opposite directions".[86]

Formality

Furthering the Fergusonian dichotomy, Mitchell[87] attempts at distinguishing degrees of formality within one variety, the unstigmatized ESA divided into Formal F and informal -F, -F being further split into Careful -Fa and Casual -Fb. According to Mitchell, these distinctions are applicable to phonological forms, morphological elements, syntactic structures and lexical items. As a matter of fact, the formal level is defined strictly phonologically and any failure to maintain the orthoepic standards will automatically transfer the item into Informal -F. Some forms, still within ESA, are subject to "fluctuation" between Formal (F), Informal Careful -Fa and Informal Casual -Fb. Such fluctuation is seen in the Syrian form for "she wrote":

/katabat/ F /katabit/ -Fa /katbit/ -Fb

Another example of threefold fluctuation is seen in Cairene Arabic, with the definite article assimilated to the noun beginning by a velar plosive (k, g), which is then doubled in -Fb:

/?alkitāb/ F /?ilkitāb/ -Fa /?ikkitāb/ -Fb
"the book"

Mitchell[88] tackles the problematic issue on variation in a descriptive way, and attempts at some explanatory comments.[89] A syntactic analysis enables Mitchell to define the style of the following sentence:

/yastaṭī' al-mudarris ?an yudjahhiz mā yalzamu min wasā?il ta'limiyya/
"the professor can prepare what he needs by way of teaching aids"

First, the /u/ of yudhahhiz, the /mā/ instead of the dialectal /illi/ and the /a/ of the preformative of /yalzamu/ determine the sentence as of "higher" level within ESA. Secondly, the sequential order of verb-subject is characteristic of formal level, written language, hence the characterization of the style of this sentence as "high flown". Yet, it must be noted that a subject-verb order, unmarked in informal speech, will be a means of topicalizing at the formal level: /?il mudarris yastaṭī'/ is marked in formal speech compared to /yastaṭī' ?il mudarris/.

This particular F vs. -F distinction, according to Mitchell, may be an over simplification, since there seems to be an increasing tendency for the subject-verb order to occur in formal contexts, especially in radio and television news bulletin, possibly as a result of the influence of western languages.

Mitchell resorts to an example already given by Meiseles, and adapts it to his own system and demonstrates the existence of a stylistic fulcrum and crossover features within it,[90] i.e. the possibility of two levels within a word, as well as the mechanism that allows variation within a sentence:

/mā fīsh 'andi ḥāga ?uḍifha ?ila mā qālahu l-ginirāl/
"I have nothing to add to what the general said"

/u/ in /?uḍifha/ is the "correct" vowel in the formal form of the verb, but the phonology of the shortened second syllable /ḍif/ is Cairene colloquial. In keeping with what precedes ?uḍifha, the suffix /-ha/ is a "returning" or "resumptive" form says Meiseles, which refers back to /ḥāga/. ?uḍifha is a hybrid form combining colloquial and MSA features, and introduces what follows syntactically and formally as high-flown.

There is no doubt that a skilled speaker is able to make use of the different levels and degrees of formality in Arabic, to meet his communicative needs, and topic of conversation. He may even resort to stigmatized forms in order to make his speech clear and intelligible to an illiterate audience, for instance.

In the case of intra-dialectal understanding where uneasiness is felt towards a "careful" form, i.e. where a speaker lacks confidence regarding the communicative and authoritative values of his dialect, the tendency will be to become more formal, and to use "pan-Arabic" forms.

1.3 CONCLUSION

The writers cited so far have provided important contributions to the study of Arabic linguistics and have presented, in some cases, excellent descriptions of varieties in different dialects. Most of the studies are however of limited direct relevance to this study of political discourse; some deal with intradialectal studies, whilst the concerns of this study are firstly, to examine individual speech communities (Iraqi, Libyan, Egyptian), and secondly, to compare shared tendencies in the relationship between language form and functions in a single, well-defined context across the three communities.

Other authors have established the existence of several layers/ lects/ varieties of language, showing even "free" boundaries between them and discrete features without explaining how these differences occur.

Several authors have acknowledged the importance of variation in Arabic but generally they have failed to adequately define and explain the wealth of data. Badawi[91] says that the registers do not have clear, permanent boundaries between one and another, whereas for Meiseles,[92] the interplay between the different varieties of Arabic depends upon factors so difficult to control that it seems impossible to determine predictability of any kind as to their use. Mitchell has been however, the most daring in attempting to introduce cross-dialectal and psychological factors in explaining stigmatized and unstigmatized forms.

In considering language function, and its relation to formal differences, some studies have been published on the phenomenon of code-switching.[93] In Eid's study for instance, code-switching is analyzed mechanically, i.e. to see where and how it occurs ("switch positions" are determined by syntactic conditions), without any answer to why code-switching occurs in conversation, and what function(s) it is fulfilling if any. Heath's book[94] is a thorough analysis of the Moroccan Arabic dialect: he looks at the various influences, adaptations and borrowings which come from Classical Arabic, other Arabic dialects and even European languages. In the process, he considers code-switching in so far as it functions as an avenue for more complete integration.[95] Heath presents a few cases of textual passages and shows how language choice can be related to topic of discourse and how borrowing is lexically determined; he does not look however at discourse strategies which are of interest here. Owens and Bani-Yasin's work[96] provides a careful study of language variation in the agreement system determined by lexical items, without however referring to the "full image" of language variation in discourse of which lexical determination is but one aspect. Reference is also made to the types of functions that linguistic variation achieves in Abd El Jawad's article.[97] Theoretical points are often enlightening, yet practical, linguistic examples are missing of how solidarity or distance for instance is actually achieved in casual conversation in Arabic.

1.4 OBJECTIVES OF THIS BOOK

This book is a contribution to Arabic sociolinguistics and hopes to "fill the gap" of relating function of discourse to form in language. Most of the works cited before have been dealing with an analysis of the language based on a group of informants. This work on the other hand deals with one speaker at a time for each of three sets of data. El Hassan[98] analyzed a sermon given by Sheikh Abderrahim Ibrahim and yet, his main aim seems to prove the existence of ESA and destroy the Fergusonian dichotomy, rather than looking at the subtle shifting back and forth between levels, and how this relates to shifts in speech functions.

This study examines variation in the speeches of three Arab politicians (Gamal Abdel Nasser, Saddam Hussein, Muammar Al Gaddafi) from three different areas of the Arab world. Firstly, I will look at the language in each data analytically, to see the mechanisms of the language used. For clarity's sake, I will take into account the various linguistic levels of the phonology, morphophonology, syntax and lexicon, so as to have a comprehensive perception of the structure of the language of the speeches. I will divide the vocabulary into MSA, mixed and dialectal sets of vocabulary, and verbs for instance will be characterized morphophonologically as (a) MSA, (b) close-to-MSA, (c) multivalent, (d) close-to-dialect, and (e) dialectal cases with two "extra" categories of hybrid and symbiotic verbs. This should not be seen as yet another listing of terminologies since it is not an end in itself but rather a tool for clarifying my perception of the language used in these speeches.

During this analytical process, I will refer to notions such as phonological convergence, communicative competence, and together with mechanisms of code-switching and code-mixing.

Secondly, in order to have the "full image" of what is going on in those speeches and what is being achieved, some extracts will be presented to illustrate various functions aimed at by the speaker, and correlate them with the language being used, with a discussion of the concept of "involvement" in Arabic political speech-making.

Of course, the three dialects have their individual structures and therefore cannot be directly compared at the formal level. However, one needs to look at dialectal flexibility and at any shared tendencies, and see the way MSA and dialectal features mix; from this angle, parallels can be drawn between the three dialects.

Subsequently having shown how variation operates in the three dialects, I will compare functions of discourse across dialects. I will hypothesize as to the "universality" of these language strategies; distancing for instance may be expressed through MSA passages while establishing solidarity and explaining a difficult concept may be expressed through the dialect. I will question whether these phenomena hold in other Arab countries and outside the Arab scene as well: speeches in English for example show linguistic and extralinguistic changes with varying functions, as in the case of the Black American political speech discussed by Gumperz[99] with the use of slang and "Black" code-switching and extralinguistic factors such as intonation and stress.

I believe this distinctive language form and function is valid and perceptible not only in the political arena but seems to be true of discourse and conversation in general: whether we want to give authority to a conversational point or whether we are explaining a concept, linguistic and extralinguisitc elements vary accordingly.

Although the obvious limitations of this work reside in the fact that data consist of a small number of speech extracts spoken by one informant from each country, this study is nonetheless a first attempt to examine political discourse in any depth across a range of Arab speech communities. Whatever similarities are revealed about the ways political leaders make use of level variation as a rhetorical strategy are very likely to reflect the "rules of use" of the wider communities in which political leaders function, whether local or pan-Arab.

NOTES

1 Fishman 1969: 48.
2 Gumperz 1958: 27.
3 Gumperz 1968 quoted in Giglioli 1972: 219.
4 Gumperz 1958: 25.
5 Labov 1972b: 237.
6 Blom and Gumperz 1971: 433; Bakir 1986: 5.
7 Gumperz 1958: 29.
8 Bakir 1986.
9 Al Khatib 1995; see also Abu Haidar's article (1991) and Benrabah (1994).
10 Milroy 1976.
11 Milroy 1980.
12 Gal 1979: 131–51.
13 Chambers and Trudgill 1980: 171.
14 Labov 1966.
15 Holes 1983a.
16 Trudgill 1974.
17 among them Palva 1969, Ingham 1973, 1976, Holes 1983a, b, Abu Haidar 1988.
18 Ingham 1976.
19 Gumperz 1958: 27.
20 Ingham 1976: 65–6.

21 Lavendera 1978.
22 Lavendera 1978: 175.
23 Dittmar 1976: 104–5.
24 Ferguson 1959; Marçais 1930.
25 see Landsman 1989: 31–7; El Hassan 1977, 1978.
26 Mahmoud 1986: 239.
27 Ferguson 1963: 169.
28 Heller 1988: 1.
29 Gumperz 1964.
30 Gumperz 1964: 217.
31 see Wardhaugh 1986: 347.
32 Gumperz 1964: 208.
33 see Gumperz 1982: 75.
34 see Gumperz 1982: 80 and the concept of text versus exegesis in Holes 1993.
35 Blom and Gumperz 1971.
36 Gal 1978: 236.
37 Gumperz 1982: 60.
38 Gumperz 1982: 66.
39 Wardhaugh 1986: 103.
40 Gumperz 1982: 59.
41 Pfaff 1979; Labov 1971: 457.
42 Poplack 1980.
43 Heller 1982.
44 Gibbons 1987.
45 Pandit 1986.
46 El Hassan 1977: 119.
47 Blanc 1960.
48 Blanc 1960: 84.
49 El Hassan 1977: 119.
50 see note 49 above.
51 see note 49 above.
52 El Hassan 1977: 120.
53 El Hassan 1977.
54 El Hassan 1977: 120–5.
55 Cowan 1968; Bishai 1966; Cadora 1965.
56 Mahmoud 1986: 245.
57 see El Hassan 1977: 115; Mahmoud 1986: 246; Abd el Jawad 1986:24; Holes 1993.
58 Fellman 1973.
59 Blanc 1964.
60 Abu Haidar 1988.
61 see note 60 above.
62 Badawi 1973.
63 Badawi 1973: 89.
64 Badawi 1973: 93.
65 Badawi 1973: 92.
66 El Hassan 1977: 126.
67 El Hassan 1978.
68 El Hassan 1978: 36.

69 El Hassan 1978: 42.
70 Meiseles 1980: 125.
71 see note 70 above.
72 Meiseles 1980: 130.
73 Meiseles 1980: 134.
74 Mitchell 1980, 1986.
75 Mitchell 1986: 8.
76 Mitchell 1986: 11.
77 Ferguson 1959, Blanc 1960; Badawi 1973.
78 Mitchell 1986: 27.
79 Ingham 1982: 31.
80 Holes 1983b: 437–47.
81 Labov 1966, 1972b; Trudgill 1972.
82 Kerswill 1985: 8.
83 see Holes 1986: 19.
84 Ibrahim 1986: 118.
85 OA, Old Arabic, is the putative ancestor of MSA and of which the correct pronunciation is not known.
86 Holes 1980: 81; Abd El Jawad 1987.
87 Mitchell 1986: 17.
88 Mitchell 1986: 23.
89 as seen in the section "syntactico-stylistic variation" Mitchell 1986: 21–7.
90 see Mitchell 1980: 102.
91 Badawi 1973: 95.
92 Meiseles 1980: 180.
93 see Eid 1988, Heath 1989, Suleiman 1993.
94 Heath 1989.
95 Heath 1989: 23.
96 Owens and Bani-Yasin 1987.
97 Abd El Jawad 1986.
98 El Hassan 1977.
99 Gumperz 1982: 198–200.

2 Methodology

The first chapter dealt with a study of the concept of diglossia and recent research in Arabic sociolinguistics. In that chapter, I explained the objective of this study – examining variation and relating it to speech function in Arabic political discourse – and positioned the study within current Arabic sociolinguistic research.

As was stated, this research deals with three dialects, Cairene (CA), Tripoli (TA) and Baghdadi Arabic (BGI), and is based on speeches delivered by Gamal Abdel Nasser, Saddam Hussein and Muammar Al Gaddafi. My initial objective is to analyse the three sets of data individually at different linguistic levels (phonology (P), morphophonology (MPP), syntax (S) and lexicon (L)) in order to describe the structure of the language of public speaking and to observe variation within one speaker's production and also between speakers. Ultimately the study will compare the three sets of data and make observations on any shared relationships between language functions and forms across the data as a whole. Chapter three deals with the Egyptian study and is based on two speech extracts from 1957 and 1962 delivered by Nasser. Chapter four is concerned with the Iraqi corpus, consisting of a lengthy press conference given by Saddam Hussein in 1980. Chapter five is based on two speeches: a religious sermon (1978) and a political speech (1981) delivered by Muammar Al Gaddafi. In chapter six, I will summarise and discuss the similarities in the data from the three different countries, bearing in mind that each has its own history, that the speeches were delivered at different points in time, and that the leaders come from different sociolinguistic and political backgrounds.

This chapter will deal with the methodology of the linguistic analysis and define a number of terms used throughout the study. A discussion on the concept of involvement will also be introduced in view of the functional and communicative interpretation of the speech extracts.

2.1 THE STUDY

The material in this study consists of video and audio recordings of the speeches which were obtained from cultural attachés and press officers at the Libyan and Iraqi embassies in Brussels and in London in 1988, and at the Radio and Television Centre in Cairo in 1989, for Nasser's speeches. Since I am concerned with registers and variation in public speaking across Modern Standard Arabic and dialects, the study is based on video and audio tapes, transcribed phonemically. The quality of the tape recording is generally good and the transcription is as accurate as possible apart from three short sequences in the Libyan data which were difficult to grasp, even with the aid of native speakers, due to the speed of delivery. I enlisted the help of native speakers to check the transcriptions of the speeches. The selected speeches represent a variety of contextual factors which provide a suitable framework for variation studies in Arabic. In all three sets of data, I will look at variation and at the language level(s) used by the speaker.

2.2 PRESENTATION OF ANALYSIS

This study is based on three individuals' use of language in three different countries and does not deal with the language variation of a community as such. Some social variables (discrete and continuous) such as education, gender, age, religion, occupation, social class are usually set as parameters in sociolinguistic studies. In this work however, I am concerned with the discourse of an individual and the social variables will not be dealt with systematically except in so far as they impinge on individual performance. At the beginning of each descriptive section of chapters 3, 4 and 5, I refer to the sociolinguistic background of the country and of the speaker so as to provide a contextualising framework for the analysis which follows it. In the last chapter however, although I have been dealing up to that point with individual language use, I will attempt to see the implications and extent of generalisations from the results that can be made on other forms of discourse outside the realm of politics.

Chapters three, four and five consist of a descriptive analysis of different types of variable in the speeches:

1 Phonology: choice of phonemes from Modern Standard Arabic (MSA) or the dialects in different types of lexical items.
2 Morphophonology of verb formation: taking account of (a) inflectional affixes, (b) combinatorial rules, (c) the lexical status of the item.
3 Phrasal syntax: combinatorial rules between words. In particular, I will be looking at the inclusion or omission of verb complementiser ?an, "verb strings", and the negative system.
4 Lexicon: occurrence of dialectalisms, analysis of collocations, and the agreement system of noun-adjective phrases involving different types of lexical items.

Of course, there are many other linguistic features that could also be analyzed but the selected aspects occur frequently and thus provide a fruitful site for the examination of variation processes.

2.3 TECHNICAL TERMINOLOGY USED IN THIS STUDY

This section clarifies terms used throughout the study and explains the methodology of the analysis and the assumptions being made. Much of this work consists of a description of code-switching in different data, involving a change between "codes", i.e. Modern Standard Arabic (MSA), the dialect and a third form of language which is neither dialect nor MSA. Ultimately we will refer to the MSA, the dialectal and the "shared" sets of vocabulary.

2.3.1 MSA

MSA, the descendant of medieval Classical Arabic (fuṣḥa), is respected as such since it is a modern continuation of the language of the Quran, the vast literary heritage and the legal system. It is generally considered by Arabs "beautiful" and unquestionably superior to the different dialects: studies[1] have shown in a matched guise test that speakers of literary Arabic are highly valued in terms of "intelligence, likeability, religiousness and leadership" compared to those speakers of dialectal Arabic. This MSA form of language, or something approximating it, is expected in formal settings, in religious, political and academic gatherings, in administration and diplomacy. It is considered more "appropriate" than any dialect in such circumstances, the aesthetic aspect of the language sometimes predominating over intelligibility. This impact of public opinion in favour of MSA is surprising since there are few people who can actually use this level without feeling ill at ease. MSA formalizes communicative channels and is felt inappropriate for the expression of emotions and ill-suited to the material and concrete aspects of modern life.[2] In addition to the literary vocabulary inherited from Classical Arabic, MSA contains many newly-coined lexical items referring to modern abstract concepts, and political matters. MSA phonology corresponds to Classical Arabic phonology as far as we know from the descriptions of the mediaeval grammarians, and its morphophonology tallies largely with the grammatical rules of Classical Arabic.[3]

2.3.2 Dialect

The dialect, being the first, natively learnt form of the language, is the natural one compared to the learned, literary MSA; it is used in ordinary conversational situations as the medium for discussing and arranging the concrete, everyday aspects of life and is the only medium used in normal social intercourse to express emotions. The purely dialectal vocabulary consists of items which refer to concepts and entities of everyday, domestic concern only. Dialectal phonology, morphophonology, syntax and lexicon differ from one place to another and will be dealt with separately in the next three chapters.

2.3.3 A third, intermediate level

As was stated in the first chapter, a third, intermediate level is found as well, which is neither MSA nor a dialect but a combination of the two to some degree, depending on subject matter and communicative aims. It seems to be produced by MSA-dialect combinatorial rules which limit particular rule combinations, although the resulting intermediate form of language cannot, yet, be defined comprehensively. In each country, it should be seen as part of a continuum with one end closer to MSA and the other end closer to the local dialect. Ideationally, this third level is associated with relatively formal settings, e.g. political speeches, university lectures, but tempered by overriding contextual and interpersonal factors which tend to "pull" the language in the direction of the colloquial. Consequently, this level includes some purely dialectal features from the phonology, morphophonology, syntax and lexicon, and also produces "hybrid" forms, i.e. combinations of MSA and dialectal elements which are part of neither code.

Interestingly, it is by means of this third level that much of the purely MSA discourse is organised, and through which "involvement" rather than "detachment" is signalled; a discussion on involvement will be introduced below. In the shared set of vocabulary, items, which are common to both MSA and the dialect, often belong lexically to MSA while their morphophonological realizations can be dialectal. This will be illustrated in the morphophonology section below. Verbs belonging to this third "shared" set can be subdivided on the basis of their morphophonology, into close-to-MSA, multivalent and close-to-dialect. Shifts between MSA and dialect have been observed in previous studies.[4] Principally, one notes the flexibility of the continuum which will be illustrated in the sections dealing with verbs. Some lexically shared items are closer to the MSA end, with for instance t͟hawra "revolution", quwwāt "forces", qimma "summit", qā?id "leader" which could be said to belong to political – hence more specialized, and abstract – terminology. But because of the widespread use of these terms, appearing in daily news bulletins and potentially part of everyday conversation, they can be considered part of the "shared" set of MSA-dialectal vocabulary and keep MSA characteristics, such as phoneme q < OA /q/, e.g. qimma, in the sense of political summit, mu?tamar qimma "summit conference", OA being the putative ancestor of MSA, and of which the correct pronunciation is not known. The etymon ?imma exists as well in Egyptian dialect but with the concrete meaning of "top". Similarly, quwwāt "forces", as part of a "military" collocation, always has /q/ e.g. quwwāt musallaḥa "armed forces", quwwāt ir-rad'"deterrent forces", while ?iwwa has the meaning "strength" in non-military contexts and is found in non-literary idioms.

In nouns, morphophonological variation is quite limited: to phonemes (qimma-?imma) or to feminine endings in cases of noun-pronoun complexes, as will be described in the dialectal descriptions later with, for example, quwwatuhu (MSA), quwwathu (hybrid) and quwwitu (dialect) "its force". Verb morphophonology varies to a greater degree since verbs are formed of a greater number of components which are susceptible to variability.

Since we are dealing with three different dialects, verbal morphophonological rules vary. The variable components, for instance vowel patterning, will be different in these three dialects and hence the content of actual rules will sometimes be different: for instance, resyllabication is a factor in Iraqi and Libyan examples where it is not one in Egyptian equivalents. However general relations of form to speech function are at a higher level of abstraction and might be expected to affect the dialects equally, regardless of local rule differences, e.g. distancing moves expressed in MSA, specification, explaining in dialect, see chapters six and seven.

2.3.4 Communicative competence

Before illustrating notions such as lexico-semantic status, morpho-phonological shape and "sequences", a brief outline of the notion of individual communicative competence as it might apply to Arabic.[5] This consists of:

(a) grammatical knowledge;
(b) sociocultural knowledge, i.e., knowing what level to use in what context;
(c) individual skills of the speaker to use (a) according to (b) to serve his communicative purposes.

As to this grammatical knowledge, speakers have a knowledge of MSA rules (which are formalised and consciously learnt) and of dialectal rules (which are unconsciously controlled and not formalised). They also, to judge by their behaviour, have a tacit knowledge of mixed, hybrid forms (which are again nowhere formalised as such) and of the combinatorial rules as to how to combine elements from the same or different levels. MSA rules apply to elements from the phonology, morphophonology, syntax and lexicon that are likely to occur in MSA "sequences" (see below), while dialectal elements are found in non-MSA sequences. Mixed level passages that are neither MSA nor dialectal occur as well, and are presumably rule-governed in some way.

2.3.5 Lexico-semantic and morphophonological statuses

In the following chapters, items are analysed according to their lexico-semantic (L-S) status and morphophonological (MPP) shape. The lexico-semantic status of a word refers to its *sociocultural status*[6] and *use*. Lexical items, from the point of view of their root-meaning relationships, belong to different sets of vocabulary, MSA, dialectal and shared as explained above. The sets are respectively associated with the literate pan-Arab culture (MSA), local, domestic, pure and simple contexts (dialect), or, in a significant part of their meaning, overlap the two (hence shared).

The morphophonological section will be concerned with verbs in terms of their triliteral root, superimposed vowel patterning, syllable structure, quality of stem vowel and of preformative vowel, lexical enclitics, ?i'rāb (mood endings) and occasionally, for some dialectal verbs, resyllabication rules. Verb formation and combinatorial rules are obviously different between MSA and each dialect. Hence in each data study, we will illustrate the MSA and dialectal rules and the possible influences between the two in mixed forms. The following examples illustrate cases of what is meant by L-S and MPP status:

- the root f-h-m meaning "to understand" is part of the "shared" set of vocabulary, and words derived from it can be found in MSA and dialectal settings and sequences, hence the L-S status of the words derived from it is shared. The morphophonological realisations however can vary, and a L-S shared verb can have a close-to-MSA, close-to-dialect and multivalent morphophonology (see below for a description of verbal categories). Examples of close-to-MSA and close-to-dialect morphophonological realisations for the same shared lexical item follow. From now on, in the case of a shared verb we will use the term "close-to-MSA" MPP to differentiate it from the MSA morphophonological realisation of an MSA verb, and "close-to-dialect" MPP to differentiate it from the dialectal morphophonological realisation of a dialectal verb:

shared L-S status		*f-h-m*		*"to understand"*
stem vowel	MSA	-a-	BGI	-a-
preformative	MSA	-a-	BGI	-i-
person/mood ending	MSA	-ūna (indic) -ū(subj/juss)	BGI	-ūn
	MSA realisation (called close-to-MSA) yafhamūna/yafhamū		BGI realisation (called close-to-BGI) yifhamūn	

Each dialect has its own rules which differ from MSA and from those of other dialects. For example, in the Iraqi and Libyan data, we find cases of resyllabication as in yiḥimlūn (MSA yaḥmilūna) but not in Cairene; in BGI, deletion and prosthetisation of vowel as in inḥawwal; and in CA and BGI, deletion of unstressed syllable as in yiṣṣawwar but there is no example of this phenomenon in our Libyan data. The aspectual non-past prefix bi- is found in CA and in TA (binisma') but not in BGI. As to verb endings, for the plural of the non-past tense form, BGI has -ūn while CA and TA have -ū. An approximation to MSA ?i'rāb can also be found with close-to-MSA verbs in very formal passages within a less formal overall context, hence yafhamūn above.

?i'rāb

?i'rāb refers to case and mood endings. There are three moods in MSA, indicative, subjunctive, jussive and the cases are nominative, accusative and genitive. ?i'rāb is practically non-existent in the dialects, except in a few "frozen" forms found in Arabic nomadic-type dialects and in some other fixed forms such as adverbs, as in dā?iman "always", ṭab'an "naturally", ḥālan "immediately", ?aḥyānan "sometimes", taqrīban "nearly", ra<u>gh</u>man "in spite of".[7] Apart from these fixed expressions, ?i'rāb is very rare in our study, except for a few verb endings -ūna found with MSA MPP of a verb in an MSA sequence. ?i'rāb is therefore an extramarker: it adds an extra flavour of formality and is more likely to occur in religious contexts and obligatorily in quotations from the Quran. Most of the verbs in the data can have a stem which has an MSA MPP, yet also a dialectal verb ending, e.g. for the non-past tense -ūn in BGI and -ū in CA and TA. These dialectal endings have infiltrated so much into various levels of formality that they have become acceptable with MSA forms, and verbs such as yuḥāwilūn in BGI and yuḥāwilū in CA and TA are classified in this study as "close-to-MSA" for a lexically shared verb. A lexically MSA verb will have an MSA MPP.

Description of verbal categories

To go back to the issue of L-S and MPP statuses, verbs from the three sets of data will be divided into five categories:

L-S / MPP verbal categories chart

(1) L-S: MSA	MPP: MSA	MSA level
(2) L-S: shared	MPP: close-to-MSA	Third, intermediate level
(3) L-S: shared	MPP: multivalent	between
(4) L-S: shared	MPP: close-to-dialect	MSA and dialect
(5) L-S: dialect	MPP: dialect	Dialectal level

and we can make the following observations:

a) An MSA verb is a verb that belongs to the MSA set of vocabulary described earlier and its MPP reflects the MSA rules of verb formation and inflection. For instance, in the CA data, yumsika (subjunctive) has an MSA L-S status (?-m-s-k) and its MPP is also MSA (vowel patterning, preformative and ending).

b) Verbs with a shared L-S status, given the flexibility of the continuum, can have, hypothetically, various morphophonological forms: close-to-MSA, multivalent and close-to-dialect.

continuum

⟵⟶

		Third level			
Category:	1	**2**	**3**	**4**	5
L-S:	MSA	**shared**	**shared**	**shared**	dialect
MPP:	MSA	**close-to-MSA**	**multivalent**	**close-to-dialect**	dialect

Thus different realisations for shared verbs are possible although it does not mean that they always occur since some verbs by their own "nature", sociocultural status and use, would tend to be found nearer the MSA end with a close-to-MSA MPP while others are nearer the dialectal end, with a close-to-dialect MPP.

c) Shared verbs with a close-to-MSA morphophonology (category 2 above) tend to be referentially abstract, part of the political and journalistic terminology. These verbs are found at the third intermediate level, between MSA and the dialect. The triconsonantal root with the same meaning but a different vowel patterning can be found in the dialect, contrarily to lexically MSA verbs which cannot be found with a dialectal MPP vowel patterning. Together with their lexico-semantic status and their use, these verbs have an MSA MPP sometimes allowing a slight dialectal influence which will be shown in the respective sections.

d) Multivalent verbs are lexically not identifiable with one particular level, and because of their common and widespread use, they are found at all levels. They are shared lexically but also morphophonologically. Overall, in the data, such cases are quite rare and occur in common verbs such as kān or ?iḥtafal which are shared lexically and morphophonologically between MSA and the dialect. Sometimes, the close-to-MSA form is so widespread that it can be found as such in dialect as in ya'ni. The close-to-dialect yi'ni is found in the dialect but not in the data, whereas ya'ni is multilevel, i.e. found at various levels of formality. Similar concepts were expressed by other authors:[8] for Eid, multivalent forms are forms ambiguous between the dialect and MSA, hybrids being intermediate between them, neither in one category nor another.

e) Shared verbs with a close-to-dialect morphophonology also belong to the third, intermediate level between MSA and the dialect. Because of this L-S status (part of the ordinary conversational vocabulary, without being solely the "property" of the dialect), and their dialectal MPP shape, these close-to-dialect verbs, unlike close-to-MSA verbs, tend to be used in casual conversation and are found in the dialectal passages of a discourse. Some of these verbs can be found in mixed sequences (see below); however, because of their widespread use in dialect, they have become firmly associated with it.

The following examples show the various realisations of lexically shared verbs with the number of occurrences actually found in the data:

(i) in CA, shared L-S status, "to celebrate"

	ḥ-t-f-l	
yaḥtafil	?iḥtafal	yiḥtifil
close-to-MSA	multivalent	close-to-dialect
(7 occurences)	(1)	(no occurrence)

Symbiotic forms such as binaḥtafil, 1 occurrence, will be discussed below and preformative yi-, more than any other feature, constitutes a marker of dialectalness and will allow us to cast the form into the close-to-dialect category)

(ii) in BGI, shared L-S status, "to master"

	?-ḥ-s-n	
yuḥsinūn		yiḥsinūn
close-to-MSA (5)		close-to-BGI (1)

(iii) in TA, shared L-S status, "to say"

	q-w-l	
?aqūl		yigūl
close-to-MSA (9)		close-to-TA (28)

f) Dialectal verbs belong to that set of vocabulary as seen earlier, i.e. they have a dialectal L-S status, and obligatorily follow the dialectal morphophonological rules, e.g.:

in CA, dialectal L-S status, "to see", b-ṣṣ, with a dialectal MPP in binbuṣṣu (4).

Symbiotic and hybrid verbs

Going back to the L-S / MPP verb category chart seen earlier, we have, in addition to the lexically MSA and shared verbs, occasional cases of morphophonological hybrid and symbiotic verbs. Symbiotic verbs consist of aspectual bi- prefixed to a verb with a shared L-S status and close-to-MSA MPP, such as binaḥtafil and byastaṭī' in CA and bitudīru in TA, i.e. in the Egyptian and Libyan data only since BGI does not have prefix bi-.

Hybrid verbs consist generally of a dialectal element within a "usually" MSA structure. Cases consist of:

(a) BGI lexical enclitic -it plus close-to-MSA MPP of a lexically shared verb as in hybrid baḥathit which results from MSA baḥathtu + BGI biḥathit "I looked for";
(b) TA resyllabication cooccurring with MSA phoneme q and MSA MPP as in taqublu "you (pl.) accept" in the TA data, from MSA taqbalūna and TA tigiblu;
(c) A verb with an MSA L-S status, an MSA phoneme q and dialectal preformative as in tinṭaliq in the BGI data. Although preformative yi- is a very strong dialectal marker, its effect is alleviated in this case since it occurs in a lexically MSA verb.

Observation of the data shows that (i) symbiotic forms occur in the Egyptian and Libyan data and not in the Iraqi one, and, (ii) whereas symbiotic forms are morphophonological realisations of shared verbs only, hybrid forms in the data are morphophonological realisations of lexically MSA and shared verbs.

As will be discussed in chapter six, hybrid forms are interesting as they show the persistence of some dialectal elements into higher levels of formality.

All these categories will be illustrated at length within each chapter. It must be stressed however that these categories are not meant to be strictly defined entities, since there is a morphophonological overlap between them. Verbs are strictly defined lexically but they can fluctuate morphophonologically in the case of shared verbs. Rather, they should be seen within the frame of a continuum. The verb categories outlined above are an attempt to "formalize the chaos", i.e. to represent one aspect of the language of public speaking and political discourse which combines MSA, mixed and dialectal elements.

2.4 DEFINING SEQUENCES

Sequences play a part in indicating the sociocultural status of an item, since they show its typical use. We have discussed how to formally classify an individual language item as MSA, dialectal or shared, but passages are also categorizable as MSA, dialectal and, mixed. The "MSAness" or "colloquialness" of a passage is related to the cooccurrence of MSA or dialectal elements from the phonology, morphophonology, syntax and lexicon occurring in its component sequences: a sequence is the speech between two pauses (we do not make a distinction between pauses and silences), the beginning and end of a sequence being indicated in the transcription (see appendices) by a single slash "/". The analysis refers to the cooccurrence of elements, e.g. preformative, vowel patterning, phonemes, in a sequence but we do not consider the raw number of dialectal or MSA elements within the sequences (say, 3 dialectal features and 1 MSA feature) as crucial. Simply counting MSA, dialectal or mixed features within a sequence is a crude procedure and would be erroneous since sequences are of varying lengths. We judge the character of a sequence by the presence and combination of elements from the P, MPP, S and L and look at the overall picture of the choices that the speaker is making, i.e. towards the MSA or the dialectal systems. Various ways of analyzing data and dividing it into sequences were considered: grammar-based (verb-subject-complement), number of words (every ten words) but these classifications seem unnatural given the nature of the data. The division according to pauses, is the most appropriate given this study on variation since, most of the time and there cannot be any 100% likelihood in this assessment just because the speaker is no ideal speaker, pauses seem to coincide with four different factors:

1 the ideational structure of the text, one idea per flow and, hence
2 a syntactic string, i.e. an idea expressed in a syntactic structure that is complete. This is important in a study on variation, since code-switching points tend to correspond to sequence boundaries, which often correspond to phrasal and clausal boundaries.[9] Pauses also correspond to
3 paralinguistic factors (see below), and finally,
4 elements within a sequence, as defined, tend, on inspection, to be of the same level of formality, either MSA or dialectal.

As this study will show, many sequences are however mixed, i.e. with elements from MSA and the dialect. We witness cases of (a) code-mixing which are determined linguistically within a sequence as in (TA) mā ?a'taqdsh "I don't believe" syntactically determined in this case, where sh is automatically uttered as part of the discontinuous negation mā -sh, together with a close-to-MSA verb.

(b) Cases of code-switching from one sequence to the next which is determined functionally, i.e. a particular function of the language requires a particular language level, for instance, a speaker recounts a historical fact in MSA but jokes in dialect.

In this attempt to determine the MSA content or colloquialness of a sequence, I will also refer to paralinguistic factors such as speed of delivery (fast versus slow pace and number of words per second); rhythm and intonation; conversational versus oratorical delivery and intonation which are paralinguistic features associated with formal (MSA) versus non-formal (dialectal) linguistic forms, and also correspond to pauses in speech and hence sequences. Paralinguistic factors will reinforce our perception and classification of elements into various levels of formality. In cases of code-switching, paralinguistic factors, such as a different pace, rhythm, intonation, tell the audience that a change occurred and catch their attention (see discussion on involvement below).

To go back to the issue of defining sequences, it must be said, however, that there are some limitations when dealing with the pausal sequencing:

(a) sequences can be very short, consisting of a few words and sometimes even one. The following sequence from the BGI data, for example, is short (*SH1 l.5*)[10] /mā yifhamūn il-ʻilim/ and is classified as BGI since all components are dialectal.
(b) Occasionally, there can be an overlap of labelling for similar items: for example in CA /ṭalīʻa thawriyya/ is a fixed expression, a collocation, and the sequence is categorized MSA, whereas a similar expression (with intermediate phoneme s < OA /th/) in the following sequence is not accorded any "MSA" weight: (*1962 l.63*) /wa ?innamā ba?ūl ṭalīʻa sawriyya/.[11] MSA collocations, because of their widespread use, are found in the dialect and this sequence as a whole is categorized as "dialectal". Hence, to establish the level of a sequence, one does not judge isolated elements but their combination.
(c) some mixed sequences (i.e. combining MSA and dialectal elements) produce a stylistic fulcrum and crossover features[12] where a sudden change in language level occurs, within a sequence, as a result of:
    (i) linguistic influence: the use of a frozen, stilted expression has induced the speaker to level up his speech, as in CA (*1962 l.126*) /marḍish yiskut ʻala ẓ-ẓulm walākinnu qāma

wa qātal/ where there is a levelling up from dialect to MSA after the MSA term ẓulm; or

(ii) functional influence: an idea or function of the language being better expressed in a different style (a conversation in reported speech is in dialect), hence language variation occurs not just at the beginning and end of the sequence but within the sequence as well.

Some sequences in the data, however, are found mixed with no apparent reason, as in the BGI data (*SH3 l.39*)

> /wa ?aẓunn ?anna ṭ-ṭā?irat il-'arabiyya il-waḥīda ?illi siqṭat 'ala l-?arḍ ?illi yuqām 'alēh il-kiyān iṣ-ṣahyūni hiya l-'irāqiyya/ which shows the combination of MSA elements such as MPP of verb (?aẓunn), collocation (il-kiyān iṣ-ṣahyūnī) passive verb (yuqām) and phoneme [q] < OA /q/, and BGI elements such as ?illi, long vowel ē for MSA diphthong ay, and MPP of verb (siqṭat).

Hence, for a sequence to be classified as MSA, it would have to contain combinations of purely MSA characteristics, such as, MSA phonemes, MPP of verb with complementiser ?an + subjunctive, MSA negative particles, MSA abstract lexicon, word order (verb-subject), long nominal clauses, collocations and occasionally ?i'rāb. And, of course, it would have to be free of dialectal characteristics.

Conversely, a sequence is dialectal when it combines some of the following elements: dialectal phonology with consonant and long vowels instead of diphthongs, dialectal MPP of verbs with elements such as preformative, vowel patterning, asyndetic verb strings, aspectual prefix bi- (in CA and TA), non-MSA negative particles, dialectal lexicon, word order such as the demonstrative after the noun in CA.

A sequence will be mixed when it has a combination of MSA and dialectal elements, or symbiotic and hybrid forms.

These elements, within the MSA and dialectal sequences, need not be automatically present in every sequence, but rather we should see which choices the speaker makes towards the dialectal system or the MSA level. There follow some examples of various types of sequence:

1 an MSA sequence in the BGI data (*SH1 l.54*)
/?an yudriku ?inna l-?umma l-'arabiyya bada?at tanhaḍ wa laysa hunālik man huwa qādir 'ala ?īqāf nuhūḍha/ which combines MSA elements such as phoneme q, complementiser

?an, verb patterning of a derived form (yudriku), MSA collocation (l-?umma l-'arabiyya), negation (laysa), long nominal clause (man ... nuhūḍha)).

2 a dialectal sequence in CA (*1962 l.68*)
/mā kānitsh ti?dar ta'mil ḥāga ?abadan/ which combines dialectal features such as [?] < OA /q/, MPP of verb with lexical enclitic -it (kānit) and preformative ti- (ti?dar), discontinuous negative particle mā -sh, lexical item ḥāga and, adverbs such as ?abadan can be found with ?i'rāb in the dialect without adding any MSA weight to the sequence.

3 a mixed sequence in TA (*1981 l.142*)
/zēn al-?ān lā yumkin njī ngūl/ where dialectal elements such as long vowel ē (zēn), verb string (njī ngūl) combine with MSA features such as negative particle lā + a non-past tense verb with an MSA MPP (yumkin).

There are problems occasionally in classifying sequences due to the internal dialectal characteristics, as in the following example from the Egyptian text:

/?aw min ?agli maṣlaḥatin zātiyya/ (*1957 l.89*) where sibilant [z] is an intermediate form between MSA realization [dh] < OA /dh/ and dialectal realization [d]. [z] is a minor downgrading from MSA /dh/ and hence the sequence, with the presence of extramarker ?i'rāb in maṣlaḥatin, is categorized as MSA. A similar problem occurs in:
/'ala d-duwal al-kubra wa d-duwal al-'uZma/ (CA *1957 l.102*)

[Z] is also a slight downgrading from MSA [ẓ] < OA /ẓ/ and an intermediate form between MSA [ẓ] and dialectal [ḍ], and the sequence consisting of two collocations, is categorized as MSA. These examples illustrate already the possibilities of close cooccurrence between even highly marked MSA features and non-MSA features which however are not plain dialect. In each data chapter, we will refer to the dialectal rules and give examples of sequences since dialectal elements and their combination vary to a certain degree within dialects.

This section aimed at explaining the terminology used in the linguistic analysis of variation. I will now refer to the concept of involvement which as we will see is crucial in the functional analysis of political speeches.

It appears from the speeches that the politicians are at times using MSA linguistic forms and sometimes dialectal and mixed forms. Switches between passages marked as MSA, dialectal or mixed can be described as changes in *register* which is determined by three situational variables, referred to as field, tenor and mode (what is going on, who is taking part, and what role the language is playing), and three semantic components which are the ideational, interpersonal and textual aspects.[13] The speaker's aim is to get the audience involved in, and committed to the goals of his discourse through the manipulation of functional and semantic components.

2.5 INVOLVEMENT

This concept of *involvement* was introduced in studies of oral versus written discourse; spoken mode was characterized as "involved" while written mode was described as "detached", terminology varying with authors.[14] Since the linguistic analysis is based on the audio version of the speeches, this study is concerned with the oral mode, although the speaker can be using a written text at least as a point of departure. It is worth looking at current discussions on oral versus written discourse since many factors characterizing the written mode hold in Arabic for some MSA spoken passages, or at least provide useful insights and terminologies to distinguish not only between various levels of language but also between other speech styles.

Several authors have considered the oral-written discourse in terms of a dichotomy: Kay[15] defended the idea that written language is decontextualized and autonomous, while spoken language is context-bound. Ochs[16] contrasted planned written versus unplanned spoken. Chafe[17] developed a discoursal theory of Detachment vs Involvement and a syntactic theory of Integration vs Fragmentation. Involvement was seen as the product of the following factors:[18]

(a) devices by which the speaker monitors the communication channel (rising intonation, pauses, requests for back-channel responses)
(b) concreteness and imageability through specific details
(c) a more personal quality: use of 1st person pronouns
(d) emphasis on people and their relationships
(e) emphasis on actions and agents rather than states and objects
(f) direct quotation
(g) reports of speaker's mental processes
(h) fuzziness
(i) emphatic particles (really, just)

Detachment[19] on the other hand is characterized in writing by:

(a) a higher degree of abstractness
(b) as the writer has more time, he will have an integrated text and deal with more thoughts at once
(c) emphasis on states and objects having things done to them
(d) impersonal aspect of the written mode
(e) while involvement deals with events in an "experiential" and detailed manner, detachment gives a more abbreviated report.

Halliday[20] puts forward the concept of lexical density: speech has a low lexical density (fewer high content words and more clauses) while written discourse has a higher lexical density (more high content words but fewer clauses). However, it appears that this oral versus written dichotomy is a false one[21] and oral-written discourse should be seen in terms of a continuum. Involvement strategies cannot be limited to the oral discourse only since authors acknowledged the fact that there are different kinds of oral discourse but also that involvement can be found in the written mode as well. According to Murray,[22] literacy and orality are not dichotomous nor do they represent ends of a continuum along which various types of literate and oral modes can be placed, as a result of their specific characteristics. Together with this concept of a continuum, authors stress the importance of a register[23] of which "interpersonal involvement is but one aspect of a taxonomy of characteristics that contribute to choice of mode and/or medium".[24] Tannen,[25] moreover, adds a different dimension to the oral/written polemic by suggesting that integration (vs. fragmentation) is a surface feature of linguistic structure while involvement (vs detachment) is a deeper dimension and reflects the interpersonal relations of the writer or speaker to his audience. Part of the mode component, textual cohesion is achieved in orality through paralinguistic and non-verbal channels (prosody, facial expression and gesture) while cohesion in writing is established through lexicalization and complex syntactic structures. These cohesive patterns reveal the speaker's attitude towards his discourse and audience. Stylistics, in the sense of rhetorical ornamentation, is also part of the cohesive devices and aims at interpersonal involvement and emotional impact on the audience. The primary aim of the discourse is communicative and, says Chafe,[26] the speaker is aware of the impact of speech as he is monitoring communicative channels. In the case of Nasser's speeches, there can be a certain degree of audience involvement in the MSA passages because of the influence of traditional rhetoric on the audience: having prepared, "planned" his speech, the speaker is of course aware of the audience and of ways of mesmerizing it. Traditional Arabic public speaking strategies, with features such as repetition, assonance, paranomasia, etc., add an emotional dimension to the discourse: they are a way of fixing key elements onto the audience's mind, keeping the attention of the listener and it is highly appreciated in the Arab culture. Various styles such as saj' (rhyming prose) and xuṭba (oration) with devices such as parallelism and repetition, are engrained in Arabic writing.[27] Rhetorical ornamentation then induces involvement and emotion by arousing the audience's feelings and poetic senses.

Patterns of intonation contribute to discourse organisation. Words such as ?innahardā "today" and dilwa?ti "now" in Cairene Arabic, produced at the beginning of a passage with a rising intonation and followed by a pause, are time change markers[28] indicative of a change occurring at different levels, change in person, time, subject-matter. Reported speech or constructed dialogue is a way of making the discourse livelier, more vivid by imitating an everyday chit-chat. Besides time change markers and reported speech, discourse organizing strategies may also include story telling. These three devices are invariably accompanied by a code-switch from MSA to dialect (P, MPP, S, L) and a change in prosody; a rapid tempo, a conversation-like contour for instance will be the first indications to the audience that a change is occurring at other levels as well (linguistic, subject-matter, function of the language). Murray and Kay[29] discuss the interrelation of variables and of simultaneous transmission: when one participant mode-switches, that change is an indicator to the listener that there is likely to be some associated change occurring in field, speaker/hearer, and/or setting. In this organic model, change in one dimension results in change in other areas.

As the speaker expresses his feelings and attempts to get the audience committed to his discourse, one way for hearers to display their involvement is through feedback (clapping, singing, repeating key words). This response is very important to the speaker as it tells him how his speech is received and the impact he is having on his audience. Havelock[30] and his study on Plato, has often been quoted in works dealing with involvement. Plato stressed the power of the poet/ minstrel/ skilled orator over his audience and argued that poets should be banned from political functions in the Republic: "The audience listened, repeated and recalled and so absorbed it....[The performer] sank his personality in his performance. His audience in turn would remember only as they entered effectively and sympathetically into what he was saying and this in turn meant that they became his servants and submitted to his spell. ...Psychologically it is an act of personal commitment, of total engagement and of emotional identification".[31] In her research on involvement, Tannen discusses discourse strategies that "create involvement by requiring audience participation in sense-making" such as repetition and constructed dialogue as well as imagery and detail and other aspects "intertwined in story telling".[32] By repeating a sequence with an abstract content in MSA on a different linguistic level, the dialectal, or by telling a personal story to illustrate more general points, and using concrete detailed examples in so doing, the speaker allows his listeners to relate more directly to the subject-matter in terms of their own experience, and identify with the issue under discussion. Tannen[33] comments that the accurate representation of the particular communicates universality, whereas direct attempts to represent universality often communicate nothing. Particularity allows the audience to imagine a scene, and this participation in sense-making is emotionally moving. Generality does not trigger this process and therefore leaves audiences unmoved.

As said earlier, one of the objectives of this study is to look at form and function through Arabic political discourse. It must be mentioned however that there are cases where it is difficult to observe any particular functional significance to a passage; such cases concern mainly mixed sequences where elements from various levels are combined without any functional meaning either to be claimed or analysed.

NOTES

1 see, e.g. El Dash and Tucker 1975: 33–54.
2 see Shouby 1951: 286.
3 see Wright 1962 and Cantarino 1974.
4 not necessarily dealing with political speeches, e.g. Blanc 1960.
5 Hymes 1971a: 7 and Widdowson 1979: 90. See also Chen & Starosta 1996: 356 for a discussion on Communicative Competence.
6 see Holes 1983b: 441 and Abd El Jawad and Awwad 1987: 94–5.
7 Heath 1989: 225–6.
8 Eid 1988: 55; Ingham 1982: 31.
9 Heath 1989: 23.

10 The Iraqi material consists of five questions and answers. SH1 refers to Saddam Hussein's first answer; see appendix C.
11 1962 refers to the year the speech was uttered and l.67 refers to the line where the example is taken from, see appendices.
12 see Mitchell 1980: 102.
13 see Halliday 1978: 31–5, 116–7 and which Fairclough relates to representations, relations and identities 1995: 17.
14 see Chafe 1979, 1982; Ochs 1979; Tannen 1982a.
15 Kay 1977.
16 Ochs 1979.
17 Chafe 1979.
18 see Tannen 1982a: 8.
19 Chafe 1983: 1099.
20 Halliday 1978.
21 Lakoff 1979.
22 Murray 1988: 370.
23 Tannen 1982a: 3, Beaman 1984: 51.
24 Murray 1988: 370.
25 Tannen 1982a: 2.
26 Chafe 1983: 1099.
27 Beeston 1983: 184.
28 van Dijk 1981: 181.
29 Murray 1988: 371; Kay 1977.
30 Havelock 1963.
31 Havelock 1963: 159–60, quoted in Tannen 1989: 195.
32 Tannen 1988: 90.
33 Tannen 1988: 92.

3 Form and Function in the Egyptian data

This chapter[1] is concerned with some variational aspects of Egyptian Arabic analysed through the political discourse of Gamal Abdel Nasser. The first part of this chapter attempts to define registers and describe linguistic features from phonology (P), morphophonology (MPP), syntax (S) and lexicon (L). Some of the selected variables are different from the Iraqi ones for instance, being marked in Cairene Arabic (CA) as non-standard whereas in Baghdadi Arabic (BGI), they have "standard"-like reflexes. In the phonological system, CA has the realisations [th], [s], [t] < OA /th/ whereas BGI has only [th] < OA /th/. Hence, for Iraqis, /th/ is not, potentially, a stylistic marker in the same way as it is for Cairenes. The second part of the chapter relates language form and language function and highlights the relationship between the speaker's use of the language and the subject of his discourse.

3.1 THE DATA AND MACRO-LEVEL CONTEXTUAL FACTORS

This chapter is based on two speech extracts delivered by Nasser, one lasting thirty minutes in Port Said on 23 December 1957 and the second, twenty-five minutes, given on 22 July 1962 in Cairo. In the 1957 speech, Nasser appeals to different nations to make all possible efforts to put behind them the spectre of Port Said, some twelve months after the Anglo-French invasion. The speech marks the anniversary of the departure of English and French military forces from Egypt. However, Nasser reminds his audience that this celebration is marred by the continuing Israeli occupation of the Sinai. As for the 1962 speech, which coincides with the tenth anniversary of the 1952 revolution, Nasser is looking forward rather than back, and tells his audience that, "we should raise our head with honour and faith" and "we have the right to look ahead and we should have confidence in ourselves and in our future". That tenth anniversary of the revolution is symbolic according to Nasser as "this generation has an appointment with destiny".

3.1.1 Micro-level contextual factors

The themes of the speeches are country-centered: Egypt's role in history, its achievement in becoming a non-aligned nation, and its freedom from any external colonizing influence. The immediate contextual factors of these speeches are different from the Iraqi ones, for instance, which consist of a press-conference with a question/answer type of discourse (see Chapter four). Here, Nasser addresses a very large crowd of Egyptians (the Iraqi audience consists of Arab and foreign journalists) who occasionally interrupt and participate in the speech by cheering, chanting and clapping. This feedback is important to the speaker and allows him to measure the impact of the speech. The Iraqi, Libyan and Egyptian speeches, as examples of political discourse, all aim to convince an audience, and thus constitute a persuasive discourse as opposed to an ordinary conversation.[2] Moreover, Nasser's speeches here should be seen in the context of the aim of his speeches in general, which are quite didactic in nature, his ambition being to convert the Egyptians to his view and many of his speeches took the form of lectures on his conception of Arab nationalism in the tradition of Egyptian paternalism.[3]

Nasser's background

Although government publications used to give Nasser's birthplace as Bani Murr, a village in Upper Egypt, he was born in a district of Alexandria.[4] During his youth Nasser had to move frequently between Alexandria and Cairo and then went to the Cairo Royal Military Academy. It is difficult to say if Nasser was influenced at all by Alexandrian linguistic features, since no evidence of them is found in the data, and thus it can be assumed for all intents and purposes that his native speech is Cairene Arabic. The Cairene sociolinguistic situation is subtly different from the one described later in the section dealing with Saddam Hussein: Nasser's native speech is Cairene Arabic, and when he is not using MSA forms, he switches to non-MSA, Cairene forms, which are shared by his audience or, at least, understood by the majority of the population. He is not faced with a potential choice between his own and another colloquial when not using MSA, as (as we shall see) Saddam Hussein is.

After a brief discussion of the sociolinguistic situation in Egypt, the predominance of Cairene Arabic in the country and its prestigious status in Egypt, as well as in some other Arab countries, I will question the relevance of the concept of *convergence* (a process by which a speaker adapts his linguistic habits to those of his interlocutor(s) in crossdialectal discourse, in intercommunal situations) to the Egyptian data, as well as discuss different levels of formality.

3.2 THE SOCIOLINGUISTIC SITUATION IN EGYPT

Egypt has a population of 51.9 million,[5] most of it crammed along the Nile valley. The linguistic situation of the country can be viewed diametrically, Lower vs. Upper Egypt, Cairo vs. the rest of the country, nomad vs. settled, urban vs. rural. Some research has been carried out on the country's various dialects. In 1969, Khalafallah wrote a grammar of Sa'īdi Arabic, a variety of Egyptian Arabic spoken along the Nile between Cairo and Aswan, in which he distinguished Northern Sa'īdi (between Giza and Asyut) from Southern Sa'īdi (between Asyut and Aswan). Behnstedt and Woidich provide detailed analyses of dialects along the Nile up to Aswan and of the Western Desert group (aṣ-ṣaḥrā l-g̱harbiyya). The Nile stands as a linguistic frontier between the Bedouin dialects of the Eastern Desert (aṣ-ṣaḥrā s̱h-s̱harqiyya)[6] which are related to the Syro-Palestinian dialects, and those of the western desert (aṣ-ṣaḥrā l-g̱harbiyya) which are akin to the Libyan ones. Variation also occurs in the Nile delta, Alexandria having different features from Cairene Arabic, and along the Maryut coast.[7]

3.2.1 Predominance of Cairene Arabic

Cairo derives its importance in the country from its position as political, administrative, economic, cultural and symbolic heart. Egypt has a strong tradition of powerful, centralised authority[8] and constitutes the largest educational centre in the Arab world[9] with students coming from all over the Arab world. In 1980, 528,751 students were enrolled at Cairene universities and among them were 21,751 foreign students.[10] Cairene Arabic is perceived as a non-standard standard[11] language and understood by the majority of Arab countries as a result of the widespread circulation of Egyptian television programmes, the popularity of Egyptian films, and the large expatriate Egyptian population in most Arab countries. The impact made by the broadcasting of Cairene dialect is certainly a factor in its comprehension and its prestige compared with both the other Egyptian dialects and other Arabic dialects, in Egyptian and other Arab eyes. In cross-dialectal conversations, Egyptians very often keep to their own dialect while other Arabic speakers tend to converge towards Cairene Arabic.[12] In the discourse under consideration, we do not have cases of variation caused by *convergence* since, Nasser, in addressing the Cairene crowd, uses MSA and CA, his own native speech. The majority of his audience either shares CA as L1, the first language, or will be so familiar with it that no allowance need be made by Nasser. Ferguson[13] claims that the Arabic of Cairo serves as a standard L for Egypt, and educated individuals from Upper Egypt must learn not only H but also, for conversational purposes, an approximation to Cairo L. Hence, the following dialectal divisions appear in Egypt:

- outside Cairo, non-prestigious, non-standard dialects;
- in Cairo, a minority non-standard Cairene as used by native Cairene Jews;[14]
- Muslim / Christian Cairene Arabic with various degrees of formality which have been found typical by various writers of different contexts and different social backgrounds.[15]

Contrarily to the Iraqi scene discussed in chapter four, the linguistic situation in Cairo is one of minor differentiation[16] since variation occurs geographically and is not closely related to religious adherence or other superordinate social factors. By Cairene Arabic, one should understand the dialect spoken in Cairo, including religious groups: 93% of the population is estimated to be Sunni Muslim and minorities include Coptic Christians, Greek Orthodox, Greek Catholics, Armenian Orthodox, Melchites, Jacobites, Maronites, Anglicans, Protestants. However it would be foolish to assume that Cairene Arabic is one homogeneous and static variety and factors such as education, degree of urbanization, exposure to the mass media, the mosque and foreign cultures, contribute to the linguistic differentiation of the population.[17]

3.3 ANALYSIS OF THE DATA: SOME PRELIMINARY COMMENTS

The two speeches of 1957 and 1962 were transcribed phonemically and analysed. It became clear that variation was present throughout the data and that the speaker was switching between MSA and different levels of Cairene Arabic. This switching does not appear randomly but occurs to some degree, predictably throughout. Although the general aim of the speeches is to persuade the audience of Egypt's new position in the world, the speeches can be subdivided into sections which have more specific communicative aims:

- whenever Nasser tries to inform his audience or presents historical facts, he usually favours use of MSA as will be described below. Although such discourse focuses essentially on Egypt, it is intended for general appeal of Arabs and to their aspirations for il-?umma l-'arabiyya;
- when Nasser is explaining or clarifying points which he feels may not be fully understood, or when he is stressing narrowly Egyptian nationalistic feelings, or attempting to establish a sense of communion or solidarity, he favours Cairene Arabic. Such discourse seems to be particularly directed at Egyptians, although, as has been pointed out, Cairene Arabic is widely understood throughout the Arab world.

The notions of MSA, dialect and an intermediate level were described earlier in the Methodology Chapter. Using their communicative competence, speakers are able to produce appropriate (formalised) MSA and (tacit) dialectal and mixed forms dependent on combinatorial rules.

This communicative competence frame is not shared by a whole community since few Egyptians are actually able to use MSA for instance.[18] This competence holds for Nasser in the context of Egypt and of the Cairene dialect: as said earlier, Cairo is a densely populated capital city with high rates of illiteracy, Cairene dialect in the 1950's and 60's was probably the only language which would be understood by a majority. The situation is different today with increased literacy[19] and the output of the media, using MSA mainly, impinges on all classes of the population throughout the country. Cairene has always had a privileged position, both in Egypt and beyond, and this explains why Nasser's deliberate use of dialect in "normally" MSA set political speeches was so popular and welcomed. Dialect however is not found overwhelmingly throughout the speeches. In fact, there are few passages that are fully dialectal and many are in the intermediate "third" level. As to the personal aspect of communicative competence, Nasser was an outstanding orator who was able to juggle with MSA, dialect and the third level; by breaking the (then) rules of Arabic public speaking and introducing dialect into speeches, he opened the way for other speakers as well.

The following examples show what is meant by the different possible distributions of lexico-semantic status and morphophonological shapes in the CA verb system (shared, MSA only, dialect only). These examples are, of course, not exhaustive. The lexico-semantic status refers to the meaning of the word together with its use.

a) "shared"

q-w-l has a shared L-S status, meaning "to say"

MSA	CA	
q-w-l	?-w-l	underlying consonant skeleton
a-ū-u	i-ū-u	vowel patterning of the non-past tense
yaqūl(u)	yi?ūl	non-past tense
close-to-MSA MPP		close-to-dialect MPP

b) "MSA only"

t-ṭ-ll-'	has an MSA L-S status, meaning "to look out"
a-a-a-a-ū(na)	MSA vowel patterning of the non-past tense
yataṭalla'u	MSA realisation of the non-past tense
	(the case of ?i'rāb was discussed in Chapter two)

c) "dialect only"

b-ṣṣ	dialectal status, meaning "to see"
u-u-	CA vowel patterning of the non-past tense
nubuṣṣ	dialectal MPP
binbuṣṣ	zdeletion of vowel and aspectual prefix b-

Below follow some examples of sequences from the Egyptian data:

a) MSA sequence

The following MSA sequences display cooccurrence of MSA phoneme [q] and [th], close-to-MSA MPP of verb (?istaṭā'a, yaqdiru), ?i'rāb (yamlika, makānan) and complementiser ?an:

> *1962 l.22* /ḥatta ?istaṭā'a hādha l-gīl/ ?an yamlika li nafsih/ makānan/ yaqdiru minhu thawriyyan 'ala taghyīri ḥayātina wa ?i'ādati ṣun'iha min gadīd/

b) Dialectal sequence

The following example shows the cooccurrence of dialectal features such as phoneme [?] < OA/q/, [t] < OA /th/, MPP of verbs, deletion of vowel, prefix b-, lexically marked pronoun ?illi and verb nshūf.

> *1962 l.105* /binshūf ?ēh il-'ashra sinīn ?illi ?abli s-sana tnēn u xamsīn/

c) Mixed sequences

Mixed sequences consist of the cooccurrence of MSA and dialectal elements as in:

> *1962 l.83* /lam tutaḥ lahum il-furṣa 'alashān yashtarikū fī talāta wa 'ishrīn yulyu?/ where MSA elements such as negative particle lam, particle la, MPP of verb (tutah) cooccur with dialectal lexical item 'alashān and phoneme [t] < OA /th/. Symbiotic forms such as biyastaṭī' are also found in mixed sequences:
> *1957 l.47* /kān kulli wāḥad fīkum biyastaṭī' ?an yuqābil al-mu'tadīn waghan li wagh/

In the following passage, although we have [z] for OA /dh/, the sequence will be classified MSA because of ?i'rāb which is an MSA extramarker. As will be seen later, intermediate phoneme [z] is found at higher levels of formality:

> *1957 l.89* /?aw min ?agli maṣlaḥatin zātiyya/

3.3.1 Phonology

Phonological variants are viewed in terms of their socio-cultural and lexical status and the morphophonological shape of the forms in which they occur. These phonological variants, together with the morphological ones, are part of lexical items whose occurrence is related to the subject matter of discourse: a more abstract topic is presented via MSA lexical realisations and a more concrete one is realized in dialectal analogues. Although the phonological realisation is "sometimes lexically marked", there is a strong correlation between the style of speaking and the realization of the interdentals.[20]

The aim of this section, following the descriptive analysis, is to see how variation works on a public, political scene and compare elements from the phonology and morphophonology which are affected with those which are less so.

Analysis of the data reveals that Nasser follows the MSA phonological system,[21] except in a few instances, such as OA /q/,

/th/, /dh/, /ẓ/ and /dj/. Briefly, it appears that the realisation of any given phoneme is related to subject matter[22] and combines with the occurrence of other phonological realisations, but also, as will be seen later, cooccurs with particular MPP, S and L elements.

From the phonemes observed in the data, interdentals yield interesting results: OA /th/, /dh/ and /ẓ/ are realized in the data as MSA [th], CA [s] and [t], MSA [dh], CA [z] and [d], and MSA [ẓ], CA [Z] and [ḍ] respectively. Interdentals appear in lexical items with MSA L-S status, and the stops appear in dialectal lexical items while the sibilants yield the most varied results and appear at dialectal and MSA levels. In the next section, I intend to discuss the general tendencies of the various realizations. These observations are similar to those of Abd El Jawad and Awwad where interdentals in Amman are analyzed historically and synchronically. The Jordanian data is based on recordings and questionnaires collected in urban centers and observations on interdentals were compared to similar changes in Cairo and Damascus, with particular attention to sibilization. Much of Abd El Jawad and Awwad's work concerns historical phonological changes which are beyond the scope of this study.

OA /th/

1. OA /th/ > [th]

The data show 94 occurrences of reflexes of OA /th/ realised as:

- MSA [th] only — 6 tokens (5 items)
- CA [s] only — 14 tokens (10 items)
- CA [t] only — 36 tokens (6 items)
- [th] - [s] variably — 38 tokens (2 items)

MSA [th] occurs in MSA lexical items, in MSA sequences (2 occurrences) and in mixed level sequences (4 occurrences). Items include: ḥaythu "since, as", thā?ira "tumultuous", ?inba'athat "it originated", muthaqqafīn "educated", nuthbit "we establish". [th] occurs in MSA sequences as in:

> *1962 l.28* /lam tastaṭi' ?an tuwāfi? l-qadara ḥaythu ?ashāra laha/ where [th] cooccurs with MSA particles lam + jussive and ?an + subjunctive, close-to-MSA verb morphophonology (tuwāfi), ?i'rāb (?ashāra), MSA particle (la), and the MSA lexical item (tastaṭi') after MSA particle lam (*lam ti?dar could not occur). MSA [th] occurs as well in mixed sequences as in:

1962 l.126 /wa nuthbit li l-?agyāl il-qādima ?in il-gīl ?illi kān ʻāyish fī sanat itnēn u xamsīn/ [th] cooccurs with MSA phoneme /q/, close-to-MSA MPP (nuthbit), preposition li, and with some dialectal elements such as CA relative pronoun (?illi), present participle (ʻāyish), CA phoneme [t] < OA /th/ and connective u. This mixed sequence is an example of stylistic fulcrum where there is a level change after a certain element; in this case, there is a level downgrading after the particle ?in. The first half of the sequence is MSA, the second, (from ?in onwards), is dialectal and the end result is a mixed style.

2. OA /th/ > CA [s]

CA [s] is a high-level variant of OA /th/ competing with MSA [th] and found in MSA and mixed sequences as a result of the lexico-semantic status of the item in which it occurs. This phonetic downgrading, from /th/ to [s], does not necessarily affect the morphophonology of the word in which it occurs, nor the syntactic structure of the rest of the sequence. Occurrences with [s] consist of: tasbīt "stabilization", siqa "faith", ta?sīr "influence", ?asiq "I trust". In the following MSA sequence, high-level sibilant [s] cooccurs with MSA phoneme [q] (?asiq, qādima) and ?iʻrāb (?agyālan):

1962 l.59 /?asiq ?anna ?agyālan qādima/

3. OA /th/ > [th] - [s]

In 2 items only, thawra and thumma, [th] and [s] occur variably as reflexes of OA /th/, the MSA realisation cooccurring with other MSA elements in the sequence and [s] combining with non-MSA elements. The most common occurrence is with thawra/sawra, 16 and 19 realisations respectively. thawra is found in MSA sequences and sawra occasionally in mixed sequences and particularly in dialectal ones. Although thawra "revolution" is typical of journalistic political jargon, Nasser's treatment of topic makes it possible for it to occur even in dialectal sequences, where, for instance, he is functioning in "exegetical" mode, see the example below, part 2. The following passage shows how variable /th/ adapts itself to cooccurring elements from MSA or the dialect:

1962 l.63 /kāna ṭalīʻatan thawriyyatan fī ḥayāti l-?umma/ wa ?innamā ba?ūl ṭalīʻa sawriyya/ In the first part, MSA elements cooccur such as ?iʻrāb (accusative endings) and phoneme [th], while in the second part, dialectal features combine: aspectual prefix b-, phoneme [?] for OA /q/ and [s] for OA /th/. sawra is a hybrid form[23] since one has the cooccurrence of an MSA element (diphtong -aw-) and a levelling down in the phoneme s < OA /th/.

4. OA /th/ > CA [t]

The dental stop [t] is limited to dialectally marked items. [t] represents a much stronger levelling down than sibilant [s] and cooccurs with same-level MPP of the item in which it occurs, and the syntax of the sequence, both of which would be dialectal. In the data, the 36 tokens derive from 6 items only (all numbers: talāta, itnēn, tāniya, tultumiya, tnāshar and tamantāshar) which are always realized in this colloquial shape. Numerals, because of their complex declension rules, tend to be found in the simplified colloquial forms[24] even in formal settings such as this one. There are 6 cases of [t] in mixed level as in:

> *1962 l.83* /lam tutaḥ lahum il-furṣa 'alashān yashtarikū fī talāta wa 'ishrīn yulyu/ where MSA negative particle lam occurs with close-to-MSA MPP of verb and dialectal lexical item 'alashān and phoneme [t]. Otherwise, [t] occurs in colloquial sequences:
> *1962 l.105* /binshūf ?ēh il-'ashra sinīn illi ?abli s-sana tnēn u xamsīn/ In this passage, [t] is found with dialectal features such as prefix b- and vowel patterning (binshūf), CA [?] < OA/q/, connective u for wa, lexically marked item (nshūf), relative pronoun illi, and long vowel [ē] for diphtong [ay].

OA /dh/

The data show 100 tokens of reflexes of OA /dh/, distributed among 16 items:

- MSA [dh] only — 10 tokens (5 items)
- CA [z] only — 13 tokens (6 items)
- CA [d] only — 2 tokens (1 item)
- [dh] - [z] variably — 75 tokens (4 items) (40 dh and 35 z)

Interdental /dh/ behaves in the same way as th in that MSA [dh] is found in lexically MSA items in MSA sequences; stop [d] is found in dialectal items while the sibilant varies more freely between MSA, mixed and dialectal levels, generally competing with MSA /dh/. Some examples:

1. OA /dh/ > MSA [dh]

There are 10 tokens of MSA [dh] with the items limādha "why", alladhi "who", dhālika "that". These forms are frozen "high-flown" MSA items which exhibit no variation and only occur in MSA sequences. Their dialectal analogues, by contrast lēsh, illi, and di respectively, are found in mixed as well as in dialectal levels. [dh] can however cooccur with dialectal elements such as prefix b- as in batadhakkar "I remember", a symbiotic form, and CA lexical enclitic badhalit "she exerted efforts" (a hybrid form), but most often occurs in MSA sequences as in:

> *1962 l.31* /limādha lam naltaqi ma'a l-qadar fī hādhihi l-?ayyām/ where MSA /dh/ cooccurs with MSA phoneme [q] (naltaqi, qadar), close-to-MSA MPP (naltaqi), and MSA particle lam + jussive.

2. OA /dh/ > CA [z]

As it was the case for sibilant [s]-[th], it is possible for [z] to vary with [dh] in some items associated with MSA vocabulary without a concomitant change in the morphophonological pattern. In such words, [z] < OA /dh/ is only a very minor stylistic downgrading from MSA [dh]. Items include:

?izā'a	"proclamation"	nufūz	"influence"
?izlalna	"our humiliation"	zātiyya	"personal"
zikrayāt	"reminiscences"	?izan	"then"

[z] reflexes of OA /dh/ are also found in MSA sequences as in:

> *1962 l.16* /wa ?an nadhkur ?ayḍan az-zikrayāt al-?alīma l-bākiya/ where sibilant [z] is juxtaposed to MSA phoneme [dh], MSA complementiser ?an + subjunctive and a long high-flown noun phrase.

3. OA /dh/ > [dh] - [z] variation

This section concerns 75 tokens of the following items: 36 occurrences of hādha, hādhihi vs. 34 of hāza, hāzihi, and 4 occurrences of ?adhkur vs. one of azkur. As said earlier of [s] < OA /th/, [z] is found in dialectal levels higher than "pure" dialect, i.e. in MSA sequences, and in mixed sequences. [s] and [z] seem more resistant to replacement than are lexical items when the style shifts upwards: hāza, for instance, is less likely to be changed into hādha than ni?dar into nastaṭī'u. Moreover, hāza occurs in MSA sequences while its dialect analogue in CA sequences is post-nominal da (feminine dī, plural dōl), as in (*1962 l.72*) /lēh ish-shi'arāt dī/. The [dh] variant is used with MSA items or with items where other MSA phonological choices have been made, e.g.:

> *1962 l.102* /... hādhihi l-?ummati th-thā?irati l-munāḍila/ where dh is paired with MSA elements such as phoneme [th], ?i'rāb and a long high-flown noun phrase.

The [z] variant, although a slight downgrading from OA /dh/, competes with the MSA variant: [z] varies with [dh] in certain expressions strongly associated with MSA, but often without a concomitant change in the morpho-phonological pattern. That is, [z] < OA /dh/ in such words is only a very minor stylistic downgrading from MSA [dh]. [z] combines with MSA elements, MSA phoneme [q], long noun phrase in:

> *1957 l.87* /ṭalī'ati l-ma'raka fī hāza l-qitāl l-marīr/

4. OA /dh/ > CA /d/

There are only two occurrences of CA [d] < OA /dh/, biyaxud and yaxud, both in dialectal sequences. This verb is of course part of the common, everyday vocabulary of CA. Although the following sequence is short, it displays several indicators of its dialectal status: use of lāzim as a modal expression in a non-MSA syntactic structure; the glottal in ya?xudhu is dropped and vowel lengthened, as it also is in ra?s:

> *1957 l.112* /lāzim yāxud rās gisr/

OA /ẓ/

OA /ẓ/ has 26 tokens, distributed as follows:

- MSA [ẓ] only — 5 tokens (3 items)
- CA [ḍ] only — 2 tokens (1 item)
- CA [Z] only — 8 tokens (4 items)
- [ẓ] - [Z] variably — 11 tokens (3 items)

Although there are few occurrences of OA /ẓ/ in the data, it behaves similarly to /th/ and /dh/ since MSA [ẓ] is found only in MSA lexical items. Stop [ḍ] is found in dialectal collocation while the sibilant [Z], as previously for [s] and [z], represents a minor stylistic downgrading from MSA /ẓ/.

1. OA /ẓ/ > MSA /ẓ/

There are 5 occurrences of MSA lexically marked items such as 'aẓīm "sublime", ẓurūf "circumstances", ẓulm "tyranny", in MSA sequences as in:

1962 l.98 /min dhālika l-yawm al-'aẓīm/

2. OA /ẓ/ > CA [Z]

There are three tokens of CA [Z] as in miZallāt "parachutes", Zaharat "it appeared" and lahaZāt "moments" in MSA sequences, and five symbiotic forms as binantaZir "we are waiting", all in dialectal sequences, e.g.

1957 l.138 /kunna barḍū binantaZir/

3. OA /ẓ/ > [ẓ] - [Z] variation

The eleven occurrences include ẓallām / Zallām "oppressor", 'uẓma / 'uZma "greatest", nanẓura / nanZur "we contemplate" where [ẓ] is found in MSA sequences and [Z] in MSA mainly:

1962 l.100 /?innanā l-yawm nastaṭī'u ?an nanẓura ?ila hādhihi s-sanawāt al-'ashr/ This is a completely MSA sequence: MSA phoneme [ẓ] cooccurs with MSA elements such as phoneme [dh], ?i'rāb (nastaṭī'u), complementiser ?an + subjunctive (nanẓura). Sibilant [Z], a slight downgrading from MSA [ẓ], is found in MSA sequences as in:

1962 l.39 /wa lam yataqabbal 'uhūd aZ-Zalām bi ?ayyi ḥālin min al-?aḥwāl/. Here [Z] cooccurs with MSA particle lam + jussive and ?i'rāb (ḥālin).

4. OA /ẓ/ > CA /ḍ/

As to the CA stop [ḍ], it occurs in the following dialectal sequence:

1962 l.133 /iḍ-ḍuhr ?igtama'na u ba'da ḍ-ḍuhr ?igtama'it il-qiyāda/ where CA [ḍ] as part of dialectal phrases and collocations (iḍ-ḍuhr and ba'da ḍ-ḍuhr) cooccurs with the dialectal lexical enclitic -it (?igtama'it) and connective u for MSA wa. Note however the "frozen" [q] in qiyāda "(political) leadership which is a good illustration of the fact that this phoneme does not always betoken a raising of style. Its significance depends on the lexical status of the word in which it occurs (see next section).

OA /q/

Phoneme /q/ behaves differently from the interdentals seen previously: its dialectal realization, CA [?], although not confined to dialectal items only, is found in dialectal sequences and there are few cases in the data of CA [?] occurring in an MSA sequence. Abd El Jawad,[25] in his Jordanian data, found that the non-standard variants of OA /q/, i.e. [?], [g] or [k], are rarely used in the high formal styles, while the standard variant [q] is used almost invariably in these contexts. The same divisions (MSA phonemes versus CA phonemes) apply to the Cairene example where items with [?] tend to be clearly identified with the dialectal context and there is no case of a third phoneme like [s], [z], and [Z] considered in the immediately preceding section, which is displacing the MSA phoneme:

OA /q/ is realized in the data as [q], [?] and the [q]-[?] variable:

- MSA and CA [q] only — 96 tokens (82 items)
- CA [?] only — 11 tokens (6 items)
- [?]- [q] variably — 68 tokens (14 items) (38 [?] and 30 [q])

1. OA /q/ > MSA [q]

There are 175 tokens of [q] < OA /q/ occurring in the two speeches, and of which follow some examples:

naltaqi	"we encounter"	qanābil	"bombs"
yuqāsi	"he suffers"	ṭāqithum	"their ability'
qawā'idha	"its foundations"	yataqabbal	"he receives"
'aqabāt	"obstacles"	ṭarīq	"method"
mawqif	"position"	mu<u>th</u>aqqafīn	"educated"
tanaqqulāt	"transfers"	muqtaḥima	"invading"
qitalkum	"your fight"	?istiqlālna	"our independence"

We observe from our data that these elements occur in mixed sequences and in purely MSA sequences, as in:

1957 l.1 /laqad kāna l-liqā? il-?axīr/

Interestingly, some of the items from the list can be found with phoneme [?] but they appear with [q] only in the data. This list consists of specialized and non-specialized items. It is important to point out that even the non-specialized, more general terms (such as mawqif, ṭarīq) appear with q and not ? in our data, as said above.

Other political-military items such as quwwāt (military) "forces", qawmiyya "nationalism", qiyāda "leadership", qā?id "leader", qanāl "canal", qarn "century" as well as qur?ān "Quran" and qāhira "Cairo" are semantically shared by MSA and the dialect, yet they are only found with [q] and would appear as such in the dialect. As said in Schmidt,[26] words such as qur?ān, and terms associated with religious tradition and other "learned words" tend not to undergo a dialectal influence. Phoneme [q] seems to be a strong MSA marker and demands co-occurrent MSA MPP such as vowel patterning (yuqāsi), ?i'rāb occasionally (yuḥaqqiqa), ya- preformative, and full personal pronoun (qudratihi). In MSA sequences, as in the example below, [q] cooccurs with MSA features of verb morphology, phoneme <u>dh</u>, complementiser ?an + subjunctive, demonstrative alla<u>dh</u>ī (not dialectal ?illi) and MSA lexical verb yataṭalla'a:

> *1962 l.7* /alla<u>dh</u>ī wā'adahu l-qadar/ ?an yataṭalla'a warā?ahu ?ila mā qāma bihi min ?a'māl/

There are a few instances of [q] occurring in a symbiotic form (see below in the morphophonology section) in a mixed sequence such as bituqatlu, biyuqātil, baltaqi realized with dialectal aspectual prefix b- and the deletion of unstressed vowels, and taqaddamit, where a dialectal lexical enclitic is used with a close-to-MSA MPP. Some of the MSA items are found in frozen expressions, fixed collocations such as, mawqif salbī "a negative position", al-quwwāt al-musallaḥa "the armed forces", qawmiyya 'arabiyya "Arab nationalism".

2. OA /q/> [?] - [q] variation

There are a few semantically shared items which have the variant [?] - [q]. [q] as in ḥaqq "right", mustaqbal "future", waqt "time", qabla "before", qāma "he stood up", yaqūlūna "they say") tends to be found in MSA sequences:

> *1962 l.95* /<u>th</u>ummā yaqūlūna fī yaqīn/ hā<u>dh</u>a bad?u tārīxin gadīd/

while [?] as in ḥa??, musta?bal, wa?t, ?abl, ?ām, ?āl is found in dialectal sequences:

> *1962 l.75* /yi?ūlak bittikallim fī ?ē sa'd bā<u>sh</u>a ?āl mā fī<u>sh</u> fayda/

3. OA /q/ > CA [?]

Occurrences of CA [?] tend to occur in dialectal sequences. Lexically, these items are associated with the everyday, conversational vocabulary (dilwa?t "now") or the dialectal lexical choice for common words (ti?dar "you can" instead of tastaṭī'u). [?] occurs with MPP elements such as prefix b- and dialectal vowel patterning, verb strings (as in ni?dar nu?ūm, ?a?dar ?a?ūl), discontinuous negative particle (mā ba?sud<u>sh</u> and /mā kān<u>itsh</u> ti?dar ta'mil ḥāga ?abadan/ and [?] cooccurs with lexical items belonging to the dialectal core such as ?izzay "how", binbuṣṣu "we look", ni<u>sh</u>ūf "we see", ?illi "which" and 'ala<u>sh</u>ān (so that, because) as in:

1962 l.103 /'ala<u>sh</u>ān ni?dar ni'raf/

OA /d̲j̲/ as CA [g]

Although Upper Egypt Arabic has occurrences of [d̲j̲] and [d] as realisations of OA /d̲j̲/ , Cairene Arabic has [g], "even in readings of Classical Arabic" and [d̲j̲] occurs only very rarely in "highly dignified or serious speech, as for instance in /d̲j̲ā?a/ instead of /gā?a/ "to come".[27] The Cairene pronunciation of MSA and CA share [g] from OA /d̲j̲/, so use of /g/ is not in itself associated with any particular level. The following examples show the consistent realisation of OA /d̲j̲/ as [g]:

gīl	"generation"	mugābihan	"facing"
guhūd	"efforts"	rag'iyya	"reactionism"
xaragū	"they left"	?igtama'na	"we gathered"
?agli	"for my sake"	magmū'	"sum"
gunūd	"soldiers"		

To conclude this phonological section, one can make the following observations:

- In the case of interdentals OA /th/, /dh/, and /ẓ/, the Egyptian data shows an intermediate, third phoneme (sibilants s, z and Z respectively) to fill the gap between the MSA and the dialectal phonemes. The sibilants, which are stylistically only a slight downgrading from the MSA realisations, emerged as a substitute for two stylistically more marked choices, and are common in both MSA and mixed sequences.
- The case of OA /q/ is different; there is no third phoneme between the MSA [q] and dialectal [?]. Phoneme [?] however is found combining occasionally with MSA elements in mixed sequences. As will be discussed in chapter six, the persistence of dialectal phoneme [?] is related to the fact that [?] is so widespread that it is "acceptable" even with MSA elements in mixed sequences as in:

1957 l.91 /kullu wāḥad fīkum ?ām yuqātil/

where [?] cooccurs with MSA elements such as phoneme q < OA /q/ and MPP (yuqātil). [q], on the other hand, while it cannot be substituted for [?] in dialectal items (like dilwa?ti) to "style raise", is quite common in dialectal sequences because of the importation of frozen MSA phrases and collocations into such sequences, for which no dialectal equivalents exist.

3.3.2 Morphophonology

This section is concerned with an analysis of the verb system and the description of variation in it in terms of lexico-semantic status and morphophonological shape. As said earlier, some passages of the discourse are "formal", MSA, in their linguistic form and in their ideational value: they refer to abstract concepts and "serious" matters as discussed in official settings. Other passages are informal, dialectal at various linguistic levels and ideationally refer to everyday, concrete matters, or to serious matters dealt with in a more personalised, ordinary way. These two tendencies are clearly differentiated and accompanied by paralinguistic and stylistic elements (see below) and verbs in these passages can be easily identified as MSA on the one hand or dialectal on the other. Yet, some sequences in the discourse are neither strictly MSA nor dialectal but constitute an intermediate, third level and verbs from this level consist of a mixture of MSA and dialectal features to varying degrees producing close-to-MSA, close-to-dialect, and multivalent verbs with occasional hybrid and symbiotic forms. Hence, the speech continuum should be seen in these terms: MSA and dialect at each end and the third level in between, one side closer to MSA, the other closer to dialect, with in the middle, multivalent forms (see Methodology Chapter).

Verbs will be classified according to one of these 5 categories. There are 2 "extra" categories (hybrid and symbiotic) that apply in the case of the Egyptian dialect. These categories, with examples from the data, are illustrated below.

1	MSA (L-S and MPP) verbs	22 tokens (12 items)
2	Shared L-S and close-to-MSA MPP verbs	177 tokens (116 items)
3	Shared L-S and multivalent	72 tokens (11 items)
4	Shared L-S and close-to-dial. MPP verbs	116 tokens (45 items)
5	Dialect (L-S and MPP) verbs	16 tokens (9 items)

Hybrid verbs show 8 tokens (6 items) and symbiotic verbs 21 tokens (13 items).

MSA verbs

A verb form is identified as MSA, when its lexico-semantic status together with its morphophonology conform to canonical dictionary/ grammar descriptions, and thereby make it suitable for uses, such as the "official" circumstances of political discourse. Such verbs belong to the formal, literary lexicon and will not be found at the dialectal level. For instance, the MSA verb tamakkana "he was able" is used in MSA sequences and would not be found in the dialectal ones (where ?idir would be used). Its MPP cannot be changed into a dialectal one, but rather, style lowering requires wholesale lexical substitution. These MSA verbs conform to the MSA formation rules (of derived forms, lexical enclitics of past and non-past tenses) as, for instance, in the MSA vowel patterning of tubā'idu, the lexical enclitic -at of rāwadat, the subjunctive ending of yumsika and (occasionally) the full final ?i'rāb of tamakkana. ?i'rāb, as said in Chapter two, is an optional MSA extramarker and does not need to occur to define the verb as MSA or close-to-MSA morphophonologically.

	Past tense	*Non-past tense*
I	CaCaCa(a)	yaCCaC(u)
	CaCiC(a)	yaCCiC(u)
	CaCuC(a)	yaCCuC(u)
II	CaCCaC(a)	yuCaCCiC(u)
III	CāCaC(a)	yuCāCiC(u)
IV	?aCCaC(a)	yuCCiC(u)
V	taCaCCaC(a)	yataCaCCaC(u)
VI	taCāCaC(a)	yataCāCaC(u)
VII	?inCaCaC(a)	yanCaCiC(u)
VIII	?iCtaCaC(a)	yaCtaCiC(u)
IX	?iCCaCC(a)	yaCCaCC(u)
X	?istaCCaC(a)	yastaCCiC(u)

Lexical enclitics of the first form:

	Past tense	*Non-past tense*
1 sg	-tu	?a-stem-(u)
2 m sg	-ta	ta-stem-(u)
2 f sg	-ti	ta-stem-ī(na)
3 m sg	-a	ya-stem-(u)

3 f sg	-at	ta-stem-(u)
1 pl	-nā	na-stem-(u)
2 m pl	-tum	ta-stem-ū(na)
2 f pl	-tunna	ta-stem-na
3 m pl	-ū	ya-stem-ū(na)
3 f pl	-na	ya-stem-na

Data show 22 occurrences of MSA verbs in MSA sequences:

tahāwat	"it collapsed"	rāwadathum	"she tempted them"
yatagāwab	"he converses"	?aflatat	"it escaped"
yataṭalla'u	"they look out"	yata?ahhabu	"they are ready"
tamakkana	"he was able"	tubā'idu	"you cause a separation"

MSA verbs and dialectal influence

This list presents verbs with ?i'rāb and others without ?i'rāb, all of them considered lexically and morphophonologically MSA. Non-past tense plural ending u/ū instead of ūna, as well as shortening of long vowels u for ū, is a consistent concession towards dialect that is made because of the widespread and penetrating use of the dialectal endings that became acceptable in formal contexts. These verbs are considered MSA because of their lexico-semantic status and their morphophonology, i.e. MPP of the verb stem, the MSA stem vowels and preformative ya-. ?i'rāb is then an MSA extramarker: it is not indispensable in categorizing the item as MSA, and its presence would position the sequence one step higher in the MSA end of the continuum but its absence is tolerated in MSA sequences as well. ?i'rāb adds an extra tinge of MSAness to the item/sequence and has a stylistic function: found in religious texts, it will add authority to the message. Because of their MSA L-S status, verbs of the above chart, rule out the cooccurrence of non-MSA morphophonological elements such as:

(a) preformative yi- (*tibā'idu).
(b) shortening of long vowel (*yatagawabu).
(c) deletion and prosthetisation of vowel (*ithāwat).
(d) ?i'rāb, being the stylistically highest MSA marker, cannot co-occur with CA dialectal markers (*tmakkina).
(e) the glottal stops are not deleted and the vowel lengthened as they would be if dialectal rules were applied (*yatāhhabu), e.g. compare CA yāxud / MSA ya?xudhu.
(f) The dialectal past tense lexical enclitic is not found with an MSA verb as *tahāwit.

(g) dialectal aspectual prefix b- is not found with purely MSA verbs (*btubā'idu) (but see below for symbiotic forms).

Dialectal verbs

Verbs are categorized as purely dialectal when they do not appear in standard MSA dictionaries. Their L-S status associates them ideationally with the concrete, ordinary, common events occurring in everyday life. They tend to be verbs of perception or speech, such as binbuṣṣu "we are looking", fādit "she replied', nishūf "we see". Semantically, these verbs have their MSA analogues: nanẓuru "we look", narā "we see", ?agābat "she replied". Morphophonologically, such lexically dialectal verbs invariably conform to the dialectal morphophonological rules. The dialectal verb forms are:

	Past tense	*Non-past tense*
I	CaCaC	yuCCuC / yiCCiC / yiCCaC
	CiCiC	yiCCiC / yiCCaC
II	CaCCiC	yiCaCCiC
	CaCCaC	yiCaCCaC
III	CāCiC	yiCāCiC
IV	?aCCaC	yiCCiC (as form I)
V	?itCaCCaC/iC	yitCaCCaC/iC
	itCaCaC(pass.)	yitCiCiC
VI	?itCāCiC	yitCāCiC
VII	?inCaCaC	yinCiCiC
VIII	?iCtaCaC	yiCtiCiC
IX	?iCCaCC	yiCCaCC
X	?istaCCaC/iC	yistaCCiC/aC

Lexical enclitics of the first form:

	Past	*Non-past tense*
1 sg	-t	?a-stem
2 m sg	-t	ti-stem
2 f sg	-ti	ti-stem-i
3 m sg		yi-stem
3 f sg	-it	ti-stem
1 pl	-na	ni-stem
2 pl	-tum	ti-stem-u
3 pl	-u	yi-stem-u

Verbs with a dialectal morphophonology display dialectal characteristics such as: lexical enclitic (fādit), prefix b- (binbuṣṣu), deletion of vowel (nshūf). There are other dialectal features that will be illustrated in the close-to-CA section. Dialectal verbs are rare in the data, and only occur in dialectal sequences which combine other dialectal features as in:

> *1962 l.8* /izzayyi mā binbuṣṣu warāna winshūf ?ēh il-?a'māl illi 'amalnāha/ where the dialectal verbs (binbuṣṣu, nshūf) combine with the dialectal items izzayyi, ?ēh and illi, negative particle mā + non-past tense of a dialectal verb.

The third, intermediate level

In the data, pure MSA and dialectal passages are, on the whole, few. Most of the data is set in this third, intermediate level, i.e. neither MSA nor dialectal but a combination of the two levels to some degree; strict boundaries cannot be established between the levels. What happens along the continuum is, at times, passages with a high incidence of dialectal features which tend towards the dialectal end and other passages with numerous MSA features, close to the MSA end. Sequences of this third level are political in content, relatively impersonal, but delivered in a more or less relaxed style. Nasser is speaking for a long time, 30 minutes or more in contrast with the very short, concise statements typical of television "sound-bites" for instance.

Morphophonologically, some of these verbs, cooccurring with other linguistic elements, adapt to the general trend of the sequence (close-to-MSA, close-to-dialect). Some other verbs are multivalent, i.e. they are semantically and morphophonologically the same or very similar in MSA/CA while other verbs have hybrid/ symbiotic forms (see chapter two for a description of verbal categories).

Shared verbs with a "close-to-MSA" MPP

Some verbs, because of their L-S status and their typical contexts of use, tend to remain close to the MSA end of the continuum morphophonologically and undergo hardly any dialectal influence. These verbs are mainly associated with more formal discourse. The list is very long (116 items) and includes:

yaḥtafil	"he celebrates"	nuḍaḥḥi	"we make a sacrifice"
nuthbit	"we certify"	yuḥaqqiqa	"he fulfils"
naltaqi	"we encounter"	yuḥāwilu	"they try"
?āmanu	"they believed"	yasta'idd	"he gets ready"
yanṭaliqu	"he releases"	yughādru	"they abandon"

These verbs are not classified as MSA from the L-S perspective because a dialectal analogue of the same root and similar meaning exists. Thus the lexico-semantic status is shared. A choice has been made to realise these verbs through MSA morphophonological patterns. Now compare the verbs above with the following:

?ista'raḍna	"we considered"	?ishtaraku	"they contributed"
?iḥtafal	"he celebrated"	?iḥtall	"he occupied"
?intaha	"he finished"	?istamarr	"he continued"
?istaṭā'a	"he was able"	?intaṣarna	"we triumphed"
?inṭalaqu	"they left"		

These verbs, in this particular morphophonological form, can be found in an elevated variety of the dialect; as can be seen from the list, they are identical (without ?i'rāb) to the close-to-MSA and close-to-CA morphophonological realisations. Because of their L-S status, these tokens are classified as "shared" with a close-to-MSA MPP, and not as "multivalent" (although in the 3rd person singular and plural and the 1st person plural of the past tense, the verbal form is the same in the dialectal realisation). An easier way to decide on overall stylistic choice being made (between competing MSA and dialect forms) is therefore to examine forms which have other lexical enclitics, and specifically, at the non-past tense since such forms are clearly marked as either CA or MSA, with, for instance, the obligatory choice of preformative yi- (dialectal) or ya- (MSA). Frequently, Nasser takes the MSA option for verbs of this type found in the data. For example, although niḥtifil exists in CA, we find in the discourse its MSA-like analogue naḥtafil; for CA ?istamarrit, we find ?istamarrat "it continues" with an MSA lexical enclitic; for ?inba'asit (CA [s] < OA /th/ and -it enclitic), ?inba'athat "it was sent out"; instead of nistaṭī', the MSA option nastaṭī' is taken. MSA features do however occur in these verbs, such as ?i'rāb occasionally (namuddu), passive voice (bullighat), vowel patterning of derived forms (nuthbit, yuḥāwilu), subjunctive (yuḥaqqiqa, yashuqqa, yughayyira), preformative ya- (yaḥtafil). The concessions to dialect in these examples seem to be the lack of ?i'rāb, and occasionally deletion of unstressed vowel as in yughādru for yughādiru. On the other hand, these "close-to-MSA" verbs do not seem to occur with dialectal morphophonological features such as: prefix b- (*bnuthbit), lexical enclitic -it (*bullighit), preformative yi- (*yighayyira), and dialectal phonemes as CA [?] for OA /q/ (*yashu??a, *yanṭali?u). [?] as in ?inṭala?a (MSA ?inṭalaqa) is of course possible but would cooccur with other dialectal factors such as vowel patterning (nilti?i vs naltaqi). This may of course be an artefact of the limited data base; however it is striking that such forms do not occur. These "close-to-MSA options" are found in mixed and MSA sequences appearing with other MSA features as in:

> *1962 l.31* /limādha lam naltaqi ma'a l-qadar fī hādhihi l-?ayyām/ where lam + jussive, phonemes /q/ and /dh/, and the lexical choice of limādha, hādhihi cooccur with naltaqi.

As was stated, lexically shared verbs can have various morphophonological realisations (close-to-MSA, close-to-dialect, multivalent, symbiotic and hybrid). One notices from the data that some verbs because of their sociocultural status tend to be associated with formal settings and found towards the end of the continuum, while others, often more semantically "concrete", are found towards the dialectal end. Still, as the chart below indicates, shared verbs can be found with various morphophonological realisations. These verbs should not be disregarded as random cases but are an evidence of the flexibility of the continuum and of the possible verbal combinations.

Close-to-MSA	*symbiotic forms*	*close-to-dialect*
na'mal (2)		ni'mil (4)
nuwāgih (5)		binwāgih (1)
?istaxdamat (2)		bitistaxdim (2)
qāma (4)		?ām (4)
yaqdiru (1)		?a?dar (3)
na'īshu (3)		bin'īsh (1)
ḍarabat (1)		niḍrab (1)
yumkin (1)		yimkin (5)
qālu (3)		?āl (28)
na'rif (1)	bna'raf (2)	bni'raf (2)
?intaṣarna (4)	binantaṣir (1)	
	ḥanantaṣir (1)	
yuqātil (4)	biyuqātil (6)	
yantaẓiru (1)	binantaZir (4)	
yuḥāwil (1)	biḥawlu (1)	

Thus some verbs can belong to different morphophonological charts but their lexico-semantic status remains the same, i.e. shared (a shared verb counts as one item with different types of morphophonological tokens).

Shared verbs with a "close-to-dialect" MPP

This section is concerned with verbs that belong lexico-semantically both to MSA and dialect but, given their use, are strongly associated with the colloquial and the dialectal morphophonology is mostly chosen. Lexically, these verbs are less associated with formal discourse than the ones from the previous list and very close to the dialect although MSA morphophonological options can occur (na'mal instead of ni'mil). Examples:

ni?dar	"we can"	fātit	"it passed by"
yiqūm	"he stands up"	yi'gib	"he pleased"
nunZur	"we look"	niḍrab	"we hit"
rig'it	"she returned"	binisma'	"we hear"
fiḍil	"it was left"	yiskut	"he keeps silent"
ksibna	"we won"	bn'īsh	"we live"

From the point of view of their meaning and patterns of use outside political discourse, these verbs are much more concrete, simple and direct than the "close-to-MSA" ones and have dialectal MPP characteristics such as preformative yi- (yiqūm), vowel patterning (ṭil'u, yi'gib), lexical enclitic -it (rig'it), CA [?] for OA /q/ (ni?dar), prefix b- + morphophonologically dialectal verb (bini?dar, bi-nisma'), future tense prefix ḥa- + morphophonologically dialectal verb (ḥati'mil). These verbs are found in dialectal sequences as in:

> *1962 l.121* /law kunna nu?'ud nihṣib il-'amaliyya bi wara? u ?alam/
> *1957 l.58* /walākin mā kunnāsh bini?dar niḍrab iḍ-ḍarba bi ḍarba/ where they cooccur with dialectal elements such as: close-to-CA MPP of verbs (bini?dar, niḍrab), phonemes [?], verb strings, discontinuous dialectal negation mā -sh and prefix b-.

?āl/ yi?ūl "to say" is an interesting case; it is clearly lexically shared, but in its MPP, [?] for OA /q/ acts as a knock-out factor and rules out cooccurring MSA morphophonological features: for example ?i'rāb and preformative yi- (*yi?ūlūna), phoneme [q] and enclitic -it (*qālit). However, this verb is extremely common and widespread. A marker of a more conversational style, it is found in dialectal sequences as in:

> *1957 l.128* /wa ti?ūl ?innaha ḥati'mil bulīs/ where ti?ūl cooccurs with future tense prefix ḥa-, MPP of verb (ti'mil) and dialectal lexical item (bulīs).

There are only three occurrences of the verb in its MSA shape (yaqūlūna); otherwise the verb is realised with the dialectal morphophonology. ?āl is also a marker of reported speech. Because of its widespread use, ?āl occasionally penetrates into what are otherwise MSA sequences. It seems to work like prefix bi-, in that it is clearly a dialectal feature of high frequency which, as a result, has lost some of its saliency and has begun to spread into more formal contexts. Such is perhaps also the case with a few other items occurring with [?]. The verb ?ām is found combining with MSA features as in: *1957 l.91* /kullu wāḥad fīkum ?ām yuqātil/. As will be discussed in chapter six, the presence of dialectal [?] < OA /q/ is due to the fact that [?] is well accepted pan-Arabically to the point of slightly losing its dialectal markedness and appearing with MSA elements.

Shared verbs with a multivalent MPP

These verbs are semantically and morphophonologically shared by MSA and the dialect and are flexible as to their use since they are acceptable at practically all levels in this context of official settings and political speech. Inevitably, some examples of shared forms invoke the first person plural, third singular and plural of past tense. These forms are different from the "close-to-dialect" verbs in that their MPP is not marked as exclusively dialectal, and lexically, they are not the exclusive "property" of the dialect either. Examples:

daxalna	"we entered"	ḥadas	"it occurred"
kān	"he was"	zāl	"he ceased"
xaragū	"they left"	ḥaṣal	"it happened"
'ishna	"we lived"	ya'ni	"it means"

These verbs can be found in MSA, mixed and dialectal sequences as in:

> *1962 l.65* /magmū'it ish-shabāb ?illi xaragū yōm talāta wa 'ishrīn yulyu/ where multivalent xaragū combines with dialectal features such as feminine ending -it (magmū'it), lexical item (?illi), long vowel ō (yōm), phoneme [t] < OA /th/ and numerals.

Some observations on multivalent verbs:

ḥadas is realized with the intermediate phoneme [s] which is a slight (and acceptable at all levels) downgrading from MSA [th]

< OA /t͟h/. kān may be seen as a borderline case: it is a flexible, multivalent form that occurs very often in the data (57 times), and adapts itself according to the sequence. The root k-w-n can be realised as multivalent kān, found in all types of sequences, and can have a close-to-MSA realisation (kāna, yakūn) in MSA sequences, or a close-to-dialect realisation (yikūn) in mixed and dialectal sequences:

close-to-MSA	multivalent	close-to-dialect
kāna/yakūn	kān	yikūn

Only kān is a multivalent form since kāna, yakūn and yikūn all contain MSA or dialectal markers that would cast the forms into different categories: ?i'rāb and preformative ya- in kāna/ yakūnu, hence close-to-MSA forms, preformative yi- in yikūn, hence close-to-dialect form.

Prefix b- and symbiotic verbs

As seen earlier, aspectual prefix b- as a dialectal marker is found with a dialectal verb in a dialectal sequence. Part of the Cairene dialect, it is used to express habitual, durative, continuous or repetitive aspects of the verb. Prefix b- + non-past tense verb generally indicates a fact as opposed to a notional possibility (expressed by the subjunctive, i.e. non-past tense verb form without prefix b-). Doss[28] describes prefix b- as one of the dialectal features which is most widespread in Spoken Literary Arabic (SLA), an elevated style of dialect used by the Egyptian media. Prefix b-, as used in SLA, fulfills functions different from those in CA: it is used (a) in the expression of the optative, (b) with verbs in subordinate clauses, (c) with verbs of evaluation and perception and, (d) with impersonal verbs (in CA we would not have biyumkin). The limitations of Doss's findings should however be pointed out since her data was gathered from TV programmes of a cultural or technical nature, some thirty years after Nasser's time. As Doss mentions herself, use of bi- in SLA was not consistent, and subject to "language control policies" on medias. In the two speeches, from the 43 occurrences of bi + verb, the forms are mainly cases of perception such as binataṭalla' "we look", bni'raf "we know", bnisma' "we hear", kuntu bas͟h'ur "I was feeling", or signal a state of mind batad͟hakkar "I remember", mā ba?sud͟sh "I don't mean". Data show 22 uses of bi- with a morphophonologically dialectal verb and 21 cases of bi- with symbiotic forms. As a dialectal marker, prefix b- cooccurs with the dialectal elements mentioned above: lack of ?i'rāb, ū/u ending for MSA ūna, colloquial vowel patterning (bni'raf, bini?dar), long vowel reduction in closed syllable (bi?ulkum), deletion of glottal (bāxud), preformative yi-, which can be elided and the vowel shortened so one can have biyi?ūl > byi?ūl > bī?ūl > bi?ūl, deletion and prosthetisation of vowel (bin'īsh, binshūf, binbuṣṣ) and bi- occurs within the discontinuous dialectal negation (mā ba?sudsh).

While prefix bi- cooccurs regularly with dialectal features, it can also be commonly found with MSA elements (i.e. with shared verbs and a close-to-MSA MPP). Such forms are symbiotic as explained by Meiseles,[29] i.e. "produced by the co-occurrence of elements belonging to every one of the languages involved, with each retaining its identity", the languages in this case being MSA and CA. The Egyptian data show many examples of prefix bi- + derived forms which have an MSA flavour, and "which are universally felt to belong to Literary Arabic",[30] as one of the cases of symbiosis. The other symbiotic forms are bi- + verb with an MSA MPP and a plural ending in ūn,[31] and b- with a passive verb (byu'tabar). The following examples show bi- combined with ?i'rāb-less MSA forms and a few dialectal features such as deletion of unstressed vowel (biḥāwlu for biḥāwilu) and preformative yi-:

baltaqi	"I am meeting"	binantaṣir	"we are victorious"
biyuqātil	"he is fighting"	biyudāfi'	"he is resisting"
bnuwaggih	"we are facing"	binataṭalla'	"we are looking"
batadhakkar	"I remember"	biḥāwlū	"they are attempting"

Prefix bi- + derived verb form, as a symbiotic feature, can combine syntagmatically with MSA complementiser ?an (biyastaṭī' ?an yuqābil), and occurs in mixed sequences as in the following example where the symbiotic form cooccurs with MSA elements (phoneme dh) and dialectal features (phoneme [s] < OA /th/ and lexical item ?innahardā):

> *1962 l.56* /wa ana innahardā wa ana batadhakkar hādhihi l-?aḥdās/

Prefix ḥa- + non-past tense (shared) verb with a close-to-MSA MPP indicating futurity is another symbiotic form: ḥayashtariku "they will cooperate", ḥanantaṣir "we will triumph". As is the case for multilevel prefix bi-, ḥa- does not occur with ?i'rāb which is too "high-level" and would be stylistically incompatible.

Meiseles makes the further observation that such symbiotic forms tend to be carried over into written Arabic as well and this point will be mentioned later on with a discussion on the differences between the "live" and written versions of Nasser's speeches. These symbiotic forms, besides being an indication of a "mixed" language "neither clearly Literary Arabic nor clearly vernacular",[32] suggest a change of status for prefix bi-. As mentioned above, bi- has come to fulfill different functions in SLA and at the same time is losing its markedness for colloquialness: the presence of bi- will not automatically confer a dialectal MPP to the verb and bi- becomes a multilevel feature. This "multilevelness" inheres in a few CA elements of very high frequency (?illi, prefix bi-, lexical enclitic -it, nominal feminine ending -it, lexical item 'alashān "so that", numerals) that infiltrate higher levels (see chapter six).

Hybrid forms

As opposed to symbiotic forms, Meiseles[33] contrasts hybrid constructions which are "offsprings of crossing between features of different languages; their salient feature is that they are new, intermediate forms, not identifiable in any one of the languages involved", as in MSA 'arafa and CA 'irif yielding the hybrid 'arif "he knew". Our data show the following cases: dialectal phoneme with close-to-MSA MPP and lexical enclitic (samarat for OA thamarat); multilevel lexical enclitic -it cooccurs with MSA features such as MSA phoneme (badhalit), MSA derived verb form (ta'arradit, taqaddamit, taḥarrakit) or with a form I verb (ṭal'it for MSA ṭala'at, CA ṭil'it).

Hybridization occurs in nouns as well with the feminine ending -at in noun-pronoun constructions. Ending -at is a hybrid between the MSA atu/a/i and the dialectal ending.

Noun-pronoun constructions can be realized as:

MSA system	*hybrid forms*	*dialectal system*
-atu/a/i (6)	-at (2)	-it (10)
ex. siyāsatuna	siyāsatna	siyāsitna

This case shows the recurrence of dialectal forms (with the number of occurrences) that are pervasive throughout the data and penetrate higher levels of formality. MSA forms include ḥarakatuhu, hybrid forms xiṭaṭna, maṣlaḥathum and dialectal forms siyāsitna, natīgitha.

To conclude this morphophonological section, I would like to point to an important phenomenon that was noticed throughout the data. In this analysis of the interaction between MSA, dialectal and mixed forms, one observed that some dialectal elements pervade higher levels of formality and combine with MSA elements in mixed sequences. These elements seem to be losing their dialectal markedness, changing status and becoming multivalent. Such is the case of:

(a) non-past tense ending ū (instead of MSA extramarker -ūna) accepted even with lexically MSA verbs (yataṭalla'ū)
(b) deletion of unstressed short vowel in close-to-MSA verbs (as in yug<u>h</u>ādru)
(c) relative pronoun ?illi instead of the MSA choice of alla<u>dh</u>ī, allatī, alla<u>dh</u>īna
(d) lexical enclitic -it with close-to-MSA verbs in hybrid verbs (ba<u>dh</u>alit)
(e) aspectual prefix bi- with close-to-MSA verbs in symbiotic verbs (as in binantaZir) as well as future tense prefix ḥa + close-to-MSA verb in ḥaya<u>sh</u>tariku
(f) as far as feminine endings are concerned, we see the emergence of the hybrid ending -at as well as the recurrent realisation of dialectal endings throughout the data in noun-pronoun constructions.

3.3.3 Some syntactic features

The previous section was concerned with describing verbs according to their lexico-semantic and morphophonological statuses in terms of their use, i.e. whether a verb is used mainly in a stylistically formal type of sequence, a dialectal or a mixed one. As said earlier, the degree of formality of a sequence is defined by the cooccurrence of various linguistic elements from the MSA or the dialectal level. However, within a sequence, some syntactic elements have a strongly syntagmatically "style-raising" or "style-lowering" effect on the elements which follow. This is the case for the negative particles, the complementiser ?an + verb at the MSA level and the complementiserless verbs, asyndetic verb strings, at the dialectal level.

The negative system

This section consists of a description of the cooccurrence of syntactic and morphophonological factors. The following summarises the systems potentially at Nasser's disposal for expressing negative propositions using an overt negative marker:

The negation system

MSA	*Dialect*
1) *Completed past action*	
lam + jussive	mā + past tense vb + sh
mā + past tense	mā + kānsh + participle/ b)non-past verb/adverb
2) *Present action*	
lā + non-past tense	mā + (b)non-past verb +sh
3) *equational sentences*	
laysa + n/adj/prep.phrase	mā + prep/pronoun +sh
ghayr + adj/n	mish + participle/prep cl./ adj/noun/pronoun
mā + prep phrase	
lā + n/adj/prep	
4) *Negation of the future*	
lan + subj	mish + ḥa + non-past tense vb
5) *Negative command*	
lā + jussive	lā + non-past tense vb
	mā + non-past tense vb + sh

Examples from the data (Nasser's actual use of the negative (MSA/ dialect) system) illustrate the cooccurrence of various elements from the P, MPP, S and L. We find the unsurprising results that MSA particles tend to occur with MSA and close-to-MSA verbs in MSA and occasionally mixed sequences while dialectal particles occur with morphophonologically dialectal verbs in dialectal and mixed level sequences. Hence, there is a strong degree of predictability between the particle and the verb and a stronger link between the two than with what precedes the particle, for instance.

The negative system in the Egyptian material is as follows:

A. The MSA system

Particles lam, lan, laysa, lā and mā (+past tense) cooccur with MSA elements from the P, MPP, S, and L in an MSA type of sequence.

1 completed past action: In the following sequence, MSA particle lam (21 occurrences) is followed by an MSA or shared (with a close-to-MSA) verb (yataqabbal), and cooccurs with ?i'rāb (ḥālin), lexically marked 'uhūd aẓ-ẓalām (where we have intermediate [Z] for OA /ẓ/):

1962 l.39 /wa lam yataqabbal 'uhūd a Z-Zalām bi ?ayyi ḥālin mina l-?aḥwāl/

There are some cases of MSA particle lam followed by a passive verb cooccuring with a dialectal lexical item ('alashān) and CA phoneme [t] for OA /th/ in a mixed sequence as in:

1962 l.83 /lam tutaḥ lahum il-furṣa 'alashān yashtarikū fī talāta wa 'ishrīn yulyu/

However, here it is clear that 'alashān acts as switching point between the first half of the sentence in MSA, and the second, which is mixed. There are 3 occurrences of particle mā + past tense where mā as in /mā zālat il-?ān/ occurs in a fixed expression, with the MSA lexical enclitic (zālat) and ?ān which is the only possible MSA lexical choice (dialect would have ?innahardā).

2 Equational sentences: The following MSA sequence shows the only case of laysa occurring with adj. (with MSA q), complementiser ?an and MSA verb in a fixed MSA expression:

1962 l.125 /fa laysa ?aqall min ?an nuḍaḥḥi/

Particle lā (8 occurrences) occurs in fixed expressions (as in lā yazāl) with MSA phoneme q < OA /q/ and MPP verbs (yazāl, yuqāsi):

1957 l.13 /lā yazāl yuqāsi min al-?iḥtilāl/

Particle lā also occurs with nouns (8 occurrences) and ?i'rāb (fā?ida):

1962 l.71 /bi ?annahu lā fā?ida wa lā ?amal/

3 Negation of the future: There are two occurrences of lan cooccurring in MSA sequences with MSA MPP verbs (takūn, naxḍa') and ?i'rāb (manṭiqati, nufūzi):

1957 l.25 /wa ?innanā lan naxḍa' li manṭiqati nufūzi ?aḥad wa lan naxḍa' li sulṭān ?aḥad/

B. The dialectal system

Particles mā + non-past tense, discontinuous particle mā -sh and mish cooccur with dialectal elements from the P, MPP, S and L. In our data, dialectal mā +-sh is normally applied to verbs (past and non-past tenses) which have dialectal features such as deletion of glottal and shortening of the vowel, deletion of vowel in unstressed syllables (mā sma'nāsh, māstaṭa'nāsh), and yi preformative, or is followed in asyndetic verb strings similarly marked for "dialectalness". Dialectal particles occur in mixed and dialectal sequences.

1 Completed past action: mā -sh combines (11 occurrences) with multivalent verb fakkarna, connective u for MSA wa and collocation (ad-duwal al-kubra) in a mixed sequence:

1957 l.127 /u mā fakkarnāsh ?in ad-duwal al-kubra/

In the following sequences, mā combines with kān (4 occurrences), dialectal enclitic -it, an asyndetic verb string, lexically marked ḥāga and ?abadan:

1962 l.68 /mā kānitsh ti?dar ta'mil ḥāga ?abadan/

2 Present action: Dialectal discontinuous particle mā -sh cooccurs once with prefix b-, phoneme [?] for OA /q/, [z] for OA /dh/, [t] for OA /th/, relative pronoun illi (for alladhi), and long vowel [ō] for diphthong [aw] in:

1962 l.64 /?ana mā ba?sudsh bi hāza illi ṭil'u l-yōm talāta wa 'ishrīn yulyu/

3 Equational sentences: Discontinuous mā -sh cooccurs (3 times) with dialectal preposition fī, long vowel reduction, deletion of glottal, epenthetic y in fayda, and phoneme z for OA /dh/:

1962 l.76 /mā fīsh fayda fī hāza l-kalām/

Particle mish is realized (4 times) with a particle as in the following dialectal sequence where in (a) mish combines with dialectally marked genitive particle bita', and dialectal lexical enclitic -it, and in (b) mush (allophone of mish) combines with multivalent mumkin, and yi- preformative:

(a) *1957 l.72* /mish bita'it nās ma'dūdīn/ mish bita'it il-xidēwi/
(b) *1962 l.76* /l-?inglīz mush mumkin yiṭla'u min maṣr/

Hybrid negative structures

There are only a few examples of hybrid negative expressions occurring in the data, e.g. a dialectal particle in an MSA structure. Particle mā + non-past tense is potentially the most productive point for crisscrossing between the two levels: it is an unlikely structure in MSA, although it existed in Classical Arabic. On the other hand, in Cairene Arabic, mā would not occur on its own (i.e. without -sh) except as part of some idiomatic expressions such as 'umri mā + (verb in past or non-past tense) "never", or in yarēt mā

(+ verb in past or non-past tense) "I wish" or, ya rabb mā (+verb in the subjunctive) "I hope". Most commonly mā occurs in the discontinuous negation mā + (past or non-past tense) verb-sh. Data show only a few examples of a mixed, hybrid form as in mā nikkallim "we don't talk" and mā niṭla' "we don't go up", where dialectal mā (b-) nikkallimsh and mā (b) niṭla'sh might have been expected. Thus we have cases of mā + close-to-CA verb without sh and cases of mā + close-to-MSA verb + sh as in mā staṭa'nāsh. In general, it can be said that there is little in the way of a merger going between the MSA and dialectal negative systems in the Egyptian data. Compared to prefixes bi- and ḥa-, the mā -sh discontinuous negative is less common at higher levels; and there are no examples at all of lam and lan being used with anything other than MSA or close-to-MSA verbs.

Complementiser ?an + verb

As mentioned earlier, the morphophonology of a verb is predictable after a negative particle and also after complementiser ?an + subjunctive. ?an is an MSA marker and the verb might have the subjunctive ending -a (sg) or -ū (pl) or no ?i'rāb. Verbs with ?an, however, always have preformative ya- and the MSA vowel patterning; unstressed vowels are not deleted and verbs are MSA or close-to-MSA (yataṭalla'u, yaḥtafil, yuḥbiṭa). 30 out of the 34 ?an occurrences consist of ?an + MSA and shared / close-to-MSA verbs in MSA and mixed sequences. As seen in the following extract, ?an cooccurs with MSA features such as negative particle lam, the lexical choice (tastaṭī') rather than the dialectal (ti?dar), ?i'rāb in qadara, phoneme [th] in ḥaythu "since, as" (CA has hēs) and MSA preposition lā

1962 l.28 /lam tastaṭi' ?an tuwāfi l-qadara ḥaythu ?ashāra laha/

There are 4 mixed sequences where ?an cooccurs with a symbiotic form as in:

1957 l.47 /kān kulli wāḥad fīkum biyastaṭī' ?an yuqābil al-mu'tadīn waghan li wagh/

Here yastaṭī' and ?an represent a switching point from a dialectal level to a higher one.

In the 1957 speech, many sequences show complementiser ?an + verb occurring in a fixed form (?istaṭā'a + ?an) with a generally literary type of lexis: kunna nastaṭī' ?an nuwāgihha "we were able to face", ?an nuqābil "to confront", lam ?akun ?astaṭī' ?an ?aḥtafila ma'akum "I could not celebrate with you", ?istaṭā'at ?ingiltira ?an tu?ammin "England was able to guarantee", although compare ?istaṭa'na ?an nuwa??if "we were able to stop", in which the verb has [?] instead of [q] where the meaning is somewhat more concrete and the verb more associated with the "everyday".

Asyndetic verb strings

While complementiser ?an + verb is found in MSA sequences mostly, dialectal (and mixed) sequences have asyndetic verb strings, i.e. complementiserless verbs. Some verbs because of their lexical and morphophonological statuses will be complementiserless and followed by another dialectal verb. Asyndetic verb strings occur mainly in dialectal sequences and cooccur with other dialectal factors such as preformative yi-, dialectal vowel patterning, prefix b-, discontinuous negative particle mā -sh, lexical enclitic -it, phoneme [?] for OA /q/, and dialectally marked lexicon as in:

1962 l.68 /mā kānitsh ti?dar ta'mil ḥāga ?abadan/ and,
1962 l.103 /'alashān ni?dar ni'raf/

There are however occasional mixed sequences such as:

1962 l.126 /marḍish yiskut 'ala ẓ-ẓulm walākinnu qāma wa qātal/ marḍish yiskut would be lam yarḍa ?an yaskuta in MSA; ẓulm however is uttered with OA phoneme /ẓ/ and, because of its lexical status as an abstract concept, it has a formalising effect on the rest of the sequence, hence one has ?i'rāb and MSA phoneme [q]. This is another case of a stylistic fulcrum as described in Mitchell,[34] i.e. where a (lexical and morphophonological) change occurs in an item and style-raises the rest of the sequence.

In the syntactic features analyzed, one observes a similar phenomenon as the one observed in phonology and MPP, i.e. the persistence (and acceptability) of dialectal elements in mixed sequences with MSA features. Such is the case of the dialectal negative particle mā which is occasionally found occurring with MSA features and close-to-MSA verbs (māstaṭa'nāsh). MSA complementiser ?an however is overwhelmingly followed by a verb with MSA characteristics, even though it can occur with dialectal elements in a mixed sequence. This suggests that the link between ?an and the following verb is very strong compared to the link between other items, say a subject noun and a predicate verb. Asyndetic verb strings are found occurring mainly in dialectal and mixed sequences, and combining with dialectal and close-to-CA verbs.

3.3.4 MSA and dialectal lexicon

As illustrated earlier, sequences consist of the concurrence of phonological, morphophonological and syntactical elements; lexical features are involved as well, an MSA choice being favoured in a MSA sequence and a dialectal one in a conversational-type sequence. Some items are associated with the abstract level of discourse and a political, journalistic lexicon is used in this kind of official setting while ordinary, straight dialectal vocabulary is found in the conversational passages of the discourse. It appears however that, when comparing the audio and written versions of the same speech (i.e. the audio tapes and the written text as found in "ḥadīth al-baṭal al-za'īm gamāl 'abdunnāṣir ?ilā l-?umma" in 4 volumes), adjustments in the written text have been made to some elements, which clearly belong to the dialect and which are replaced by items with a higher L-S status, while other aspects are given simply the MSA morphophonology. These adjustments allow one to see for instance, which items are felt by editors to be "too" dialectal to appear in a written text. The list on the left consists of the most recurring dialectal elements in the audio version while the list on the right shows the changes being made in the written text with the page reference (2 referring to the second volume and 3 to the third):

Dialectal core	*written version*	*meaning*
'alashān	li/likay (407/3)	"in order to"
dilwa?ti	dhālik al-waqt (408/3)	"now"
?innahardā	al-yawm (406/3)	"today"
lēsh/lēh	limādha (639/2)	"why"
?izzay	kayfa (408/3)	"how"
dī	hādhihi (407/3)	"this"
dōl	ha?ulā?i (407/3)	"those"
'āyiz/'āwiz	yurīd (641/2)	"he wants"
barḍū	lā yazāl (641/2)	"still, also"
il[li]	allati/dhī/ (406/3)	"that"
lāzim nunZur	lā budda ?an nanẓura(408/3)	"we should see"
lāzim yāxud	yagib ?an ya?xudha (641/2)	"he must take"

Dialectal prefix b- is dropped in the written version as in:

ba?ūlkum	?aqūlu lakum (406/3)	"I say to you"
biḥāwlū	yuḥāwilūna (407/3)	"they try"
bash'ur	?ash'uru (638/2)	"I feel"
bin'īsh	na'īshu (639/2)	"we live"
btuqātlu	tuqātilūna (640/2)	"you fight" (pl)

In other cases, a syntactic adjustment is made, *verb strings* are replaced by verb and complementiser ?an + verb as in:

?a?dar ?a?ūl ?astaṭī' ?an ?aqūl (406/3) "I can say"
'alashān ni?dar ni'raf likay nastaṭī' ?an na'rif (408/3)
"so that we are able to know"

and dialectal negative particles are replaced by MSA ones:

mā fīsh fāyda	lā fā?ida (407/3)	"there is no point"
mā kan shi	lam yakun (639/2)	"it wasn't"
mā fakkarnash	lam nufakkir (641/2)	"we did not think"

lēh mā kunnāsh binantaṣir limādha lam nakun nantaṣir (639/2)
"why did we not gain a victory"

al-?inglīz mush mumkin yiṭla'u min maṣr is in the written text:

al-?inglīz laysa mina l-mumkin ?an yaxrugū min maṣr (407/3)
"It is not possible for the English to leave Egypt"

This left-hand list includes the most recurrent lexical items in dialectal sequences, to which could be added verbs of action, feeling and physical pain (basma' "I listen", bash'ur "I feel", nubuṣṣu "we look", nshūf "we see", ni?dar "we can", nizlu "they went down", ti'mil "you make", ṭil'it "it appeared"). Present participles ('āyish "living", 'āyiz/'āwiz "wanting") are often found in the data instead of verbs which appear in the written text. Emphatic expressions such as ṭab'an "of course" and ?abadan "never" are also found in dialectal sequences and form part of the involvement strategies as discussed in the following section (see 3.4). Although these emphatic particles can be found in MSA, they are commonly used in conversational style to give more emphasis to the point and, in our data, they are found in dialectal sequences, as in:

1957 l.42 /?intu kuntu 'arfīnhum ṭab'an hinā fī bōr sa'īd/
1962 l.68 /mā kānitsh ti?dar ta'mil ḥāga ?abadan/

Some syntactic and lexical dialectal elements, however, are preserved in the written text. The reason for this might be that convention allows the infiltration of some common, widespread dialectal elements to pervade in the written text[35] as they become multilevel. These elements include prefix b- (bi?ūl "he says" (408/3), bitakallam "you speak" (407/3)), a discontinuous negative structure (mā fīsh fayda "there is no point" (407/3)), a verb string (mā kunnāsh ni?dar nu?ūm bi ?ay 'amal "we could not undertake any action" (406/3)), and a lexical item (?innahardā "today" (406/3)). Dialectal phonemes such as CA [?] < OA /q/ are, as a matter of convention, not realised as such and are written with the MSA (OA ?) phoneme. Of course these inconsistencies may simply be a reflection of an inconsistent editorial policy; or it may be that in some cases the editors were working from the MSA version of the text which Nasser, no doubt, had in front of him, whilst in others they were working from a combination of the text and a recording which showed marked deviations from the text, and which they have attempted to catch the dialectal flavour of. There is no way of knowing.

While the dialectal lexicon comprises items used in everyday conversation referring to definite actions and events, temporal and logical connectors, the MSA lexicon consists primarily of jargon used in politics, national and international affairs generally. Some phrases however, although associated with politics, inevitably do occur in mixed and dialectal sequences; this is the case for MSA collocations which are fixed, frozen forms of language with no equivalents in the dialect. They occur as such in a dialectal discourse, without necessarily being seen as raising the stylistic level. Here are some examples from the speeches.

al-'ahdi al-'uthmāni	"the Ottoman era"
ad-duwal al-?isti'māriyya	"the imperialistic countries"
al-mu?amarāt al-?isti'māriyya	"the imperialistic conspiracies"
al-xiyānati al-mutaḥālifati	"the allied treachery"
taghyīran ḥāsiman	"a decisive change"
ṭalī'a thawriyya	"a revolutionary vanguard"
shi'ārāt ?inhizāmiyya	"defeatist slogans"
shi'ārāt thawriyya	"revolutionary slogans"
al-quwwāt al-musallaḥa	"the armed forces"
al-qawmiya l-'arabiyya	'Arab nationalism"

Such fixed collocations are found at all levels of formality, cooccurring with MSA and dialectal features as in the following sequences where the collocation combines with MSA features such as an MSA verb MPP (bada?at), or with dialectal elements such as lexical enclitic (kānit) and the intermediate phoneme z < OA dh (hāzihi):

1957 l.30 /bada?at ma'ārik muttaṣila/
1957 l.50 /kānit hāzihi l-ma'raka ma'raka muxtalifa/

The agreement system

As said before, the data conform to the general pattern according to which MSA linguistic features cooccur in an MSA sequence and dialectal items in a dialectal one. We saw above that some elements (such as negative particles, complementiser ?an + subjunctive and the first element in an asyndetic verb string) trigger a "complement" that belongs to their own level. This formal / informal influence holds also for the agreement system between nouns and adjectives. MSA or dialectal agreement rules are "conditioned"[36] by the lexical status of the item: an MSA status noun (i.e. literary, abstract, or complex concept) triggers an MSA agreement with its adjective, while a dialectal noun follows the dialectal rules of agreement. Throughout the data, given the "seriousness" and formality of the setting, noun adjective agreement conforms to the MSA rules in MSA and also in dialectal passages. With a singular noun the adjective agrees in gender and in number (m.sg.noun + m.sg.adjective al-'ahdi al-'uthmāni "the Ottoman era", f.sg.noun + f.sg.adjective fatra ṭawīla "a long period"), with a plural noun referring to human beings the adjective agrees in number as al-?ixwatu al-muwāṭinūn "the compatriot brothers", with a plural noun not referring to human beings the adjective is in the feminine singular (l-mu?amarāt l-?isti'māriyya "the imperialist conspiracies"). In the dialectal system, non-human plural nouns can be followed by plural adjectives or feminine singular adjectives. McGuirk[37] gives the following example, il-buyūt il-kubār, while Owens and Bani-Yasin[38] mention lērāt kulliyyātin "all the dinars" from their Jordanian data. Our data show only cases of the MSA noun adjective agreement system, as in the following example of non-human plural noun and a feminine singular adjective 'anāṣiri aṭ-ṭufayliyya "intrusive elements". Data show plural nouns in -āt ending belonging to the abstract MSA set of vocabulary, and which trigger only feminine singular agreement: adh-dhikrayāt "the reminiscences", al-mas?ūliyyāt "the responsibilities", aṣ-ṣu'ubāt "the difficulties", al-mu?amarāt "the conspiracies", al-?imkaniyāt "the possibilities", al-quwwāt "the forces" but also broken plurals, as-sinīn "the years", ad-duwal "countries", al-?a'māl "the operations", al-bilād "the countries", al-?ayyām "the days". Broken plurals have, potentially, a higher degree of variability since they can take feminine singular or broken plural agreement.[39] The data give MSA examples only.

The results of this lexical section are different from the phenomena observed in the P, MPP and S sections where some dialectal features became multilevel and penetrated higher levels of formality. This time, things go in the opposite direction: collocations which are originally fixed MSA expressions (although with a dialectal ending -a to the noun) are mixed with dialectal elements and can lose their MSA markedness. Secondly, presumably because of the formality of the setting, the noun adjective agreement system conforms to the MSA rules: agreement is lexically conditioned and dialectal rules would be too marked in this kind of discourse. Hence, while dialectal elements from the P, MPP, and S ascend the ladder of formality, MSA lexical elements lose their markedness and move downwards.

3.4 LANGUAGE FORM AND LANGUAGE FUNCTION

This chapter so far has consisted of a descriptive analysis of the Egyptian data and the present aim is to relate results from this analysis to the subject matter of the discourse and the function(s) of the language. What is the aim of the speaker, what is he actually attempting to convey in his speech and how would this affect the linguistic choices he makes? One has to be careful in using a cause effect terminology, since most of the discourse actions were probably taken at the level of the unconscious. As said earlier, Nasser is concerned with local issues in these speeches and is trying to restore a sense of "honour and dignity" among Egyptians, as well as leading them to appreciate Egypt's new position in the world in contact with its colonized past. The aims of the discourse are of course varied: as Abd El Jawad[40] claims, speakers through language usage desire to express one or more of a set of overlapping communicative functions such as expressing solidarity, intimacy, to signal unity and integration, showing respect to others and achieve practical purposes, and expressing local, group or ethnic identification and membership. Section 2.5 introduced a discussion on register and involvement strategies, that could be used in political discourses.

3.4.1 Register and the Egyptian data

The Egyptian data consist of two speeches in which Nasser addresses a very large crowd assembled in Port Said (1957) and Cairo (1962). The occasion marks the departure of foreign armies from Port Said, he reminds the audience of the Egyptian position amongst international powers and summarises the local political activities of the last years. The speeches are prepared, if not fully written, with some key words that the speaker repeats and develops.

Observation of the variation of levels, from MSA to CA, leads us to relate language form and function in terms of mode, ideational and interpersonal components as introduced in section 2.5. Broadly speaking, when the speech is meant to inform the audience of policies, remind them of depersonalised historical facts, it is expository and the discourse is characterized ideationally by abstractness, compactness, formality, detachment, planning, and integration. The interpersonal relation is one of distance, the pronouns "we" and "they" in this case tend to refer to an abstract impersonal entity, Egypt as a nation among others. At the linguistic level, such expository passages are characterized by:

- MSA phonology (OA [q], [th], [dh], [ẓ])
- MSA morphophonology of verbs, passive verbs, complementiser ?an + subjunctive, sa/sawfa verb to indicate future tense, ?i'rāb (but not systematically as MSA passages are also compatible with an absence of ?i'rāb which should be seen as an MSA extra marker);
- long sentences with subordinate clauses, long noun phrases, maṣdars, word order (verb and subject), and MSA negative particles;
- abstract vocabulary (journalistic, political), frozen collocations, high lexical density (many content words), and MSA lexical choices triggering MSA noun-adjective agreement patterns.

At the paralinguistic level, we found in such passages a predominance of sentence-end falling tones (giving a statement-like contour to many clauses), a rhythmic and slow tempo (1.25 words per second on average) with occasional pauses after key words so as to give them full emphasis. Prosodic and stylistic elements (such as repetition, assonance, paranomasia) are also found and are evidence of a deliberate use of involvement strategies via an appeal to people's auditory and poetic senses.

On the other hand, Cairene Arabic is used when Nasser is stressing narrow Egyptian nationalistic feelings, when the discourse is meant to explain or specify detail which the speaker feels may not be fully understood, when it is used to illustrate text,[41] to establish contact or solidarity, to personalise the speech, or be provocative. Briefly, when the speaker hopes to engage the audience, his performance is characterized on the ideational level by personalisation of argument. Here the discourse has the appearance of being spontaneous, unplanned, extemporaneous. At the interpersonal level, the discourse is characterized by familiarity: the use of "we", "you" and "I" pronouns is more frequent, and is calculated to create a sense of closeness, a one-of-us feeling of audience and speaker. Interpersonal involvement is established through rhetorical questions, discourse-organizing, time change markers, reported speech, "constructed dialogue"[42] and story telling with specific examples. These situational and semantic elements are accompanied on the linguistic levels by the cooccurence of the following dialectal elements:

- Phonologically, the colloquial (and "intermediate" sibilants) phonemes [?] < OA /q/; [s],[t] < OA /th/; [z],[d] < OA /dh/; [Z], [ḍ] < OA /ẓ/.
- Morphophonologically, absence of ?i'rāb, preformative yi-, MPP of verbs, prefixes bi- and ḥa- + verbs, hybrid constructions, deletion of hamza, deletion of vowel in unstressed syllables, u/ū third person plural ending instead of ūna.
- Syntactically, asyndetic verb strings, short sentences (hardly any subordinate clauses), subject-verb word order, colloquial negative and interrogative particles.
- Lexically, everyday Cairene vocabulary, an absence of abstract nouns and a low lexical density (fewer content words).

Paralinguistically, textual cohesion is achieved in dialectal passages through imitation of an ordinary, conversational, Cairene prosody, a variable pitch and a faster tempo (2.5 words per second on average). The Cairene intonation adds a feeling of spontaneity to the speech and gives the impression of sincerity, natural which in turn ("he is one of us", "he speaks like us").

3.4.2 Extracts

The 1957 and 1962 speeches have many dialectal passages and examples of variation between MSA and dialectal passages that can be described in terms of the functional and semantic components discussed above.

Extract 1 *1962 l.69 to 76*

> 1 iṭ-ṭalī'a s-sawriyya/ fī ra?yi/ hiya kulli n-nās ?illi ?amnum bi ?imkāniyyāt it-taghyīr/ kull ?illi ṭaraḥū sh-shi'arāt il-?inhizāmiyya s-sābiqa bi ?annahu lā fā?ida wa lā ?amal/ 2 ?iḥna ṭli'na wa kunna bnisma' ?ēh/ kunna ?amma nikkallim fī ?ayyi ḥāga ?alūlina sa'd bāsha ?āl mā fīsh fā?ida/ lēh ish-shi'arāt dī/ shi'arāt ?inhizāmiyya kānū biḥāwlu bihā ?innuhum/ 3 yabussu fī nufusna l-ya?s/ wa yaqḍū 'ala l-?imān fī qulubna/ 4 ?anā ?azkur min ?awwil ?ayyām iṭ-ṭufūla/ kullama nikkallim fī ?ayyi ḥāga/ yi?ūlak bittikallim fī ?ē sa'd bāsha ?āl mā fīsh fayda/ mā fīsh fayda fī hāza l-kalām/
> The revolutionary vanguard, in my opinion, consisted of all the people who hoped for a possible change, all those who rejected the defeatist slogans according to which there is no point and no hope. When we went out what did we hear? Whenever we talked about anything people would say Saad Pasha said: "there is no use". Why those slogans? Those defeatist slogans, they tried by them to spread desperation in our spirits and kill off faith in our hearts. As I recall, in my childhood days, whenever we were talking about anything, they said to you Saad Pasha said that there is no use, there's no use in that kind of talk. (Nasser is referring to Saad Zaghlūl, the first leader of Egyptian nationalism).

Passage 1 starts with Nasser's general axiomatic definition (fī ra?yi) of the "revolutionary vanguard" and expands on the defeatist attitude of some people, lā fā?ida wa lā ?amal, uttered as a statement with a low falling tone on ?amal. There is then a pause. In part 2, the intonation changes to a Cairene conversational one and a fast tempo (3 words per second) as the content becomes anecdotal and amplifies in a more personal and conversational way the same message.

Using code-mixing to enhance his communicative purposes, the speaker is organizing his discourse, with story-telling and constructed conversation (?alūlina). He displays his feelings and uses rhetorical questions "why those defeatist slogans?". By using the first person plural, he creates a sense of rapport, of unity with the audience, making the concept of "revolutionary vanguard" more approachable and understandable. In part 3, to give more authority and more distance to his point, Nasser uses poetic abstraction, switches to MSA and utters his next statement as a reported quotation and proverb-like type of discourse, neutral and abstract ("to spread desperation in our spirits and kill off faith in our hearts"). Tempo is slower (1.4 words per second) so that full attention can be paid to words, and rhythm is extremely important in this passage with stressed syllables at regular intervals, long vowels (in nufūsna and ?imān) and the repetition of -s- sound in the first part:

/yabússu fī nufūsna l-yá?s/ wa yáqḍū 'ala l-?imān fī qulúbna/

This rhetorically balanced, "poetic" statement is contrasted in 4 with a levelling down in the formality: a shift towards concreteness occurs with childhood reminiscences of words familiar to all Egyptians, of the defeatist paternalism of Saad Zaghlūl. As Nasser is speech-reporting and story telling to render the discourse livelier, tempo gets faster (2.3 words per second) although the message is exactly the same as in the beginning of the section, lā fā?ida [MSA] turns into mā fīsh fayda [CA].

Linguistically, parts 2 and 4 share the following colloquial characteristics: phoneme [?] < OA /q/ (?alūlina), dialectal morphophonology of verbs (ṭli'na, nikkallim), preformative yi- (yi?ūlak), prefix bi- + verb (bittikallam and bnisma'), third person ending ū; colloquial interrogative particles such as lēh, ?ēh at the end of the sentence; negative particles mā + prep-sh (mā fīsh); demonstrative after the noun shi'arāt di, Cairene lexicon (ḥāga).

Extract 2 *1957 l.10 to 16*

1 /fīlwa?t/ ?illi kuntu bash'ur fī bi mashā'irkum/ wa basma' fī l-?izā'a/ il-?iḥtifalāt wa l-hutāfāt wa ?aghāni n-naṣr/ wa r-rūḥ il-'āliya ba'da xurug il-?inglīz min maṣr/ 2 kuntu ?ash'ur ?inni bēnkum/ walākinni fī hāza l-waqt lam ?akun ?astaṭī'/ ?an ?aḥtafila ma'akum/ li?an/ kān fī guz?i/ min ?arḍ al-waṭan/ lā yazāl yuqāsi min al-?iḥtilāl/ fī sīna/ kāna l-yahūd yaḥtallu guz?i min sinā?/ wa ghazza kānat tuqāsi min al-?iḥtilāl al-yahūdi wa mā kānsh in-naṣr bi n-nisba li maṣr yu'tabar naṣr kāmil/

At that precise moment during which I was sharing these feelings with you and hearing on the radio the celebrations, the acclamations and the songs of victory, the high spirits after the departure of the British from Egypt, I wanted to share all these feelings with you but at the same time I could not celebrate it with you because a piece of the home-land was still suffering from occupation in the Sinai. The Jews were occupying a part of Sinai and Gaza was suffering from Jewish occupation, and the victory as far as Egypt was concerned could not be considered a complete one.

In this passage, variation again seems to be a conscious ploy in the discourse organizing tactics. In part 1, Nasser draws attention to himself and the language level is dialectal (prefix bi- + verb, 1st person singular) and seems to express solidarity with the crowd. In part 2, as they are all gathered in the celebration of the victory, he distances himself from the crowd by expressing his frustated, angry feelings because of the occupied territories. In this distancing process, as the speech becomes more stilted, MSA elements are better suited to express serious facts and committed leadership. Hence, the use of MSA phoneme [q] < OA /q/ (yuqāsi), MSA MPP of verbs (yazāl), complementiser ?an + subj (?an ?aḥtafila), MSA lexical choice (?astaṭī'), ?i'rāb (guz?i) and passive form (yu'tabar). There is however, a levelling down at the end with the colloquial negative form mā kānsh. The key words are "feelings and sufferings"; land is personified as "suffering" and Nasser wishes to share his concern about the situation: "although we are celebrating this new freedom, I cannot share this feeling with you since some land is still suffering from Israeli occupation". This distancing move allows the speaker to patronize his audience somewhat for its seeming lack of concern, in order to trigger their reaction and commitment.

Extract 3 *1957 l.63 to 69*
As to "discourse organizing", the 1957 speech has several occurrences of time change markers (?innahardā, dilwa?ti, ba'da kida) which, together with contrastive stress and rising intonation followed by a pause, indicate a change in person or an emphasis on the person, or on subject matter and function of the language:

1 wa ?intaṣarna ?ayḍan fī hāzihi l-ma'raka/ (clapping)/ ?innahardā/ (clapping)/ wa ?ana baltaqi bīkum fī bōr sa'īd/ wa naḥnu nash'ur bi n-naṣr/ wa naḥmadu llāh 'ala hāza n-naṣr/ wa naḥtafil bi hāza n-naṣr/ in-naṣr fī l-ḥarb il-musallaḥa ḍiddi d-duwal il-kubra/ in-naṣr 'ala l-'udwān/ in-naṣr 'ala l-quwwa l-ghāshima/ in-naṣr 'ala siyāsati l-quwwa/ 2 nubuṣṣu li nafsina/ winshūf lēh ?intaṣarna/ fī hāzihi l-fatra wa lēh mā kunnāsh

binantaṣir fī l-māḍī/ 3 ?intaṣarna ?innahardā li?anna maṣr/ milki li?abnāha/ mish milki lifi?a minna n-nās/
And we won that battle as well. Today, as I meet you in Port Said and all together we are aware of our victory, and we praise God for this victory and we celebrate this victory, this victory of armed battle against the big powers, victory over aggression, over a tyrannical force, over the policy of force, we look at ourselves and try to see why we triumphed during that time and we could not win in the past; we won today because Egypt is the property of its sons and does not belong to a handful of people.

In the first passage, the discourse organizing time marker (?innahardā) helps to redefine the situation and interlocutors ("as *I* am meeting you today for *us* to celebrate this victory"). The aim is to emphasize the fact of victory and to praise the audience for it. There is no new information and the discourse becomes full of redundant material and bombast with the repetition of "naṣr" and parallelism in construction:

in-naṣr 'ala l-'udwān
in-naṣr 'ala l-quwwa l-ghāshima
in-naṣr 'ala siyāsati l-quwwa

Much of these seem to be a parenthetical insertion, a backgrounding of the main message which starts with /?innahardā/ "today" and then, after the insertion, is resumed at 2 nubuṣṣu … "we see ..". 2 comes as a contrast with a fast tempo (2 words per second) and the stressed tone unit nubuṣṣu li nafsina. The speaker is questioning, challenging, stimulating his audience with a constructed dialogue for a lively speech: "we ask ourselves why /lēh/" and the answer comes with /li?anna/. CA is used to make speech natural. In speaking of past defeats, one gives the impression of solidarity. Rhetorically, he asks for audience's fulsome support. Textually, 2 is characterized by a colloquial MPP of verbs (nubuṣṣu), a dialectal phoneme [z] < OA /dh/ (hāzihi), CA lexicon (nshūf), CA interrogatives lēh, discontinuous negative particle mā -sh (mā kunnāsh), prefix bi + verb (binantaṣir). The last section introduced by ?innahardā comes as a redefinition of the subject matter, it reinforces the concept of national concern and communion and the audience is told "Egypt is your property, belongs to all of you". Following this passage the idea of property is repeated over and over, but with the colloquial lexical choice bita' instead of milki.

Extract 4 *1957 l.122 to l.128*

> 1/ ?iḥna kunna binantaZir/ al-'udwān min bōr sa'īd/ kunna binantaZir il-'udwān min ?iskindiriya/ kunna binantaZir il-'udwān min lībyā/ u kānat xiṭaṭna l-'askariyya/ ?in niḥna nastaṭī'/ ?an nattagih/ ?ila l-'udwān/ fī l-makān ?illi yō?a' fīh/ walākin ḥaṣal il-ghadr wa l-xiyāna/ hagamit ?isra?īl/ wa kān/ taqdīrna ?inna l-ma'raka r-ra?īsiyya ma'raka ma'a ?isra?īl/ 2 u mā fakkarnāsh ?in ad-duwal al-kubrā/ tighishsh ar-ra?yi l-'ām il-'ālami wa ti?ūl ?innaha ḥati'mil bulīs/ bēn maṣr wa ?isra?īl/ 'ashān tuhāgim maṣr/
>
> We expected aggression from Port Said, from Alexandria, from Libya, and our military plan was that we could face the aggressor whenever it occurred. But trickery and treachery appeared. Israel attacked us. We thought the chief battle would be with Israel but how on earth could we guess that the big powers would deceive world public opinion and say they would march in and lay down the law between Egypt and Israel so as to attack Egypt.

This passage illustrates yet again the change from ideational abstractness to specifics, which correlates with a shift in language level, from mixed to CA level. This change from a planned military tactic to an unexpected reversal of situation is conveyed in the form of reported speech and military history turned into an anecdote. The beginning of the section is mixed, with the multilevel prefix bi- + verb and the third person feminine ending -it and with the cooccurrence of complementiser ?an + verb (?an nattagih), the occurrence of [Z] from OA /ẓ/, the lexical choice of nastaṭī', the long clause ?inna l-ma'raka r-ra?īsiyya ma'raka ma'a ?isra?īl. Stylistically, the repetition of parallel structures adds to the image of a military schedule and builds up tension, which is then punctured by the colloquial of 2:

> kunna binantaZir il-'udwān min bōr sa'īd
> kunna binantaZir il-'udwān min ?iskindiriya
> kunna binantaZir il-'udwān min lībyā

In part 2, linguistic and paralinguistic features change: as there is a fast tempo (2.6 words per second), a conversational tone and accompanying dialectal characteristics: [?] < OA /q/ (ti?ūl), prefix ḥa- + verb (ḥati'mil), colloquial MPP (tighishsh) and lexicon ('ashān, ti'mil bulīs), negative particle mā -sh (mā fakkarnāsh), connective u for ?aw, long vowel ē instead of diphtong ay (bēn).

This is followed up by an anecdote, again the preserve of the dialect, in the following paragraph (*l.129*) with the reported speech of General Ketley:

/il-d̲jinirāl kitli ... ?āl ?innu kān 'āyiz/ yuhāgim maṣr min libyā/

Such concretisation makes the discourse and the great affairs of state more vivid and accessible to the audience; it triggers their indignation and involvement with the speaker.

Extract 5 *1957 l.36-43*

1 /fa naḥnu ?ayḍan/ naḥtafil/ bi n-naṣr fī ma'rakati l-?a'ṣāb/ wa fī ma'rakati ḍ-ḍag̲h̲ṭ al-?iqtiṣādi/ wa fī ma'rakati t-tagwī'/ wa fī l-ma'raka llati kānu yahdifūn biha ?ixḍā'na wa ?izlālna/ [...]/ 2 ?ayyuha l-?ixwa/ fī far?i kbīr/ bēna l-ma'raktēn/ ma'rakat il-'udwān/ wa ma'rakat il-'azl wa l-?ixḍā'/ ma'rakat il-'udwān kānat bitistaxdim/ al-qanābil/ iṭ-ṭayārāt/ ?asāṭīl ad-duwal al-'uZma/ brīṭāniya u faransa/ rigāl il-muZallāt/ 3 ?intu kuntu 'arfīnhum ṭab'an hinā fī bōr sa'īd/ wa is̲h̲-s̲h̲ayāṭīn il-ḥumr willa l-'afarīt al-ḥumr/ barḍu ?intu s̲h̲uftuhum hina fī bōr sa'īd/
We celebrate as well the victory of the war of nerves, and the battle against economic pressure and starvation, and the battle in which they were aiming to subjugate and humiliate us.[...] Dear countrymen, there is a big difference between the two battles, the battle of (physical) aggression and the battle of isolation and subjugation; the aggressive battle was using bombs, planes, fleets of the super powers, Britain and France, (and) paratroopers. Of course you know them in Port Said, the red devils and the red satans and you saw them also in Port Said.

This passage shows a gradual levelling down in the language as the discourse becomes exegetical. Nasser switches from MSA, to mixed and then to CA as he clarifies, concretises and finally anecdotalises. This long extract is presented in three parts with a levelling down of style: the third part explains the second one which in turns explains the first part. In 1, the speaker lists victories in abstract terms such as ma'rakati l-?a'ṣāb "war of nerves", ma'rakati ḍ-ḍag̲h̲ṭ al-?iqtiṣādi "battle against economic tension", ma'rakati t-tagwī' "starvation battle", ?ixḍā'na "our subjugation", ?izlālna "our humiliation". The linguistic level is MSA, with the use of ?i'rāb (ma'rakati), MPP of verbs (naḥtafil, yahdufūn), maṣdars (?izlāl, ?ixḍā') and long nominal phrases. In 2, the level goes down (phoneme [?] for OA /q/ (far?i), deletion of unstressed vowel (kbīr), long vowel ē for diphtong ay (ma'raktēn), use of CA fī. The speaker addresses the audience directly and explains the difference between the physical battle with bombs, etc., and the battle against isolation and humiliation. The difference established, Nasser illustrates the two examples, and language level is close to dialect (prefix bi- and dialectal vowel patterning (bitistaxdim)), followed by a means list used. In part 3, Nasser keeps his audience interested by implicating them in the action on the ground and addressing them directly: of course you remember them, of course you saw them. Ideationally, there is a repetition of ?intu to reinforce the directness and involvement of the conversational style and textually, a dialectal MPP of verbs and lexical items (shuftuhum), and emphatic particles (ṭab'an, barḍu).

Extract 6 *1962 l.6 to 8*

A sudden shift from "high form" MSA to "plain" CA is found in several places. At the beginning of the 1962 speech, after a series of parallel constructions with a concurrence of MSA features, the level is suddenly dropped, and the argument is repeated and "explained" in plain language.

> 1 min ḥaqqi kulli shābb/ min ḥaqqi hādha l-gīl/ kulluh/ alladhī wā'adahu l-qadar/ ?an yataṭalla'a warā?ahu ?ila mā qāma bihi min ?a'māl/ 2 izzayi mā binbuṣṣu warāna winshūf ?ēh il-?a'māl illi 'amalnāha/
> Every young man has the right, this generation has the right, everybody, who has an appointment with destiny, has the right to look back at what he has done. Just as we look behind us and see the actions we carried out.

In 1, several MSA elements cooccur, with phoneme [q] < OA /q/ (ḥaqq), OA /dh/ (hādha), relative pronoun alladhī, complementiser ?an + verb (?an yataṭalla'a) and paralinguistic elements (a slow tempo of 1.05 words per second). In 2, the tempo abruptly changes and becomes faster (2.2 words per second), and the same idea is paraphrased into pure dialect. Ideationally, the "generation" that is looking behind (as a neutral and impersonal concept) is changed into personal "we" (we look behind us and see what we accomplished).

Extract 7 *1962 l.62-68*

> /1 hādha l-gīl ?ayyuha l-?ixwatu l-muwātinūn/ alladhi na'īshu/ kāna ṭalī'atan thawriyyatan fī ḥayāti ?umma/ 2 wa ?innamā

> ba?ūl ṭalī'a sawriyya/ ?ana mā ba?sudsh bi hāza ?illi ṭil'u l-yōm talāta wa 'ishrīn yulyu/ magmū'it ish-shabāb ?illi xaragū yōm talāta wa 'ishrīn yulyu/ 3 li yaruddū 'ala nidā?i sh-sha'bi l-muliḥḥi min ?agli t-taghyīr/ hādhihi l-magmū'āt min ash-shabāb/ lam takun tastaṭī' shay?an/ 4 magmū'āt ish-shabāb ?illi ṭil'it fī sawra yōm talāta wa 'ishrīn yulyu sana tnēn u xamsīn/ 5 mā kānitsh ti?dar ta'mil ḥāga ?abadan/
> This era, dear countrymen, that we live, was the revolutionary vanguard in the life of the nation. And when I say revolutionary vanguard, I don't mean by this those who came out on 23 July: the group of young men that went out on 23 July to echo the insistent call of the people in the cause of change. This group of young men could not do anything; the group of young men that came out in the revolution on 23 July in 1952 couldn't do anything at all.

This extract shows a shift from MSA to CA: passage 1 is bombastic, sounds impersonal and MSA elements cooccur with ?i'rāb (ṭalī'atan thawriyyatan) and phoneme OA /dh/. In passage 2, level drops to CA with a faster tempo (from 1.3 words per second in 1 to 2.3 words per second in 2) as Nasser explains the meaning of ṭalī'a sawriyya (and when I say the revolutionary vanguard, I don't mean by this...). Textually, CA elements cooccur such as phoneme [?] for /q/, [t] for OA /th/ (talāta), long vowel ō for diphthong aw (yōm), prefix bi-, discontinuous negative particle mā -sh (mā ba?sudsh), phoneme z for OA /dh/ (hāza), MPP of verbs (ṭil'u) and CA feminine ending -it. In 3, there is a style raising with abstract concepts (nidā?i sh-sha'bi l-muliḥḥi "the insistent call of the people") and MSA elements such as ?i'rāb (sha'bi muliḥḥi), MPP of verb (yaruddū, tastaṭī'), negative particle lam and particle li + verb (instead of 'ashān). Passage 4 shows a levelling down in style into a mixed sequence with dialectal elements such as long vowel ō for diphthong aw (yōm), verb MPP (ṭil'it) and relative pronoun (?illi). The same concept as in passage 3 is repeated in 5 in a conversational style, and dialectal features cooccur in a faster tempo (3 words per second): negative particle mā -sh and lexical enclitic (mā kānitsh), MPP of verbs and asyndetic verb strings (ti?dar ta'mil) and lexically marked items (ḥāga and ?abadan): /lam takun tastaṭī' shay?an/ in 3 becomes /mā kānitsh ti?dar ta'mil ḥāga ?abadan/. The issue becomes specific, approachable, seemingly more detailed as the speaker uses the audience's way of describing things. As said in the discussion on involvement (see section 2.5), the resort to detail and to the audience's imagination via storytelling appeals to people's senses and taps into their emotion. Tannen[43] argues that by involving imagery, the audience participates in understanding and becomes more readily involved. The moves from MSA to CA in this last extract illustrate the use of code-switching for clarifying in CA abstract, complex terms. MSA terms ("text") are explained and repeated in the dialect (i.e. "exegesis") to make sure that the audience understood the point and registered the message.

This section has attempted to show that variation in language form is related closely to variations in the function of language and the objective of the discourse. When the speaker switches from MSA to dialect he is generally aiming at involving the audience in his discourse by co-opting their emotions and explaining his meaning. He approaches them with simple vocabulary, and his speech content varies widely. Involvement is established through the combination of dialectal linguistic characteristics, easily understood, the ideational (concreteness) and interpersonal (personalisation) functions, conversational prosody (fast tempo, stressed time markers) and involvement strategies (dialogue, conversational and reported speech types of discourse).

NOTES

1 A presentation of an earlier version of this chapter was made at the AIDA conference on Arabic Dialectology in Cambridge, September 1995.
2 Lakoff 1981: 26.
3 Mansfield 1982: 64.
4 see Woodward 1992, Mansfield 1969: 3.
5 in 1988, Unesco: Statistical Yearbook 1990: 1–5.
6 see Abul Fadl 1961.
7 Hartmann 1899, Matar 1967.
8 Mansfield 1982: 140.
9 Meiseles 1980: 140.
10 Unesco: Statistical Yearbook 1990: 68.
11 Holes 1986: 19.
12 see Grotzfeld 1983: 87, Mitchell 1986: 27–8.
13 Ferguson 1959: 10.
14 Blanc 1974: 207.
15 Badawi 1973, as seen earlier, describes three levels of 'āmmiyya; see also Harrell, 1960, variation in Egyptian Radio Arabic; Doss, 1987, colloquial influence on "Spoken Literary Arabic".
16 Blanc 1964: 14–6.
17 see El Hassan 1977: 117.
18 the level of illiteracy in Egypt in 1960 was of 79.5 %, see Statistical Pocket Year Book Egypt 1962: 2, 14.

19 51.6 % in 1990, see Unesco: Statistical Yearbook 1990: 1–14.
20 Abd El Jawad and Awwad 1987: 80.
21 see Harrell 1957 and Selim 1967.
22 see Owens and Bani-Yasin 1987: 720, 726; Holes 1995.
23 see Schmidt 1974: 158.
24 see Blanc 1960: 107, 1964: 91 and Badawi 1973: 144.
25 Abd El Jawad 1981 quoted in Abd El Jawad and Awwad 1987: 82.
26 Schmidt 1974: 83.
27 Harrell 1960: 15–6.
28 Doss 1987: 94.
29 Meiseles 1981: 1077.
30 Meiseles 1981: 1084.
31 as bta'taqidūn "you consider" the example given by Meiseles 1981: 1084, but there are no such cases in the Egyptian data.
32 Meiseles 1980: 132.
33 see note 29 above.
34 Mitchell 1986: 24–5.
35 see Meiseles 1980: 133.
36 Owens and Bani-Yasin 1987: 717.
37 McGuirk 1986: 20.
38 Owens and Bani-Yasin 1987: 718.
39 see Owens and Bani-Yasin 1987: 712.
40 Abd El Jawad 1986: 23–4.
41 e.g. the National Charter, see Holes 1993.
42 see Tannen 1989: 25.
43 Tannen 1988: 109.

4 Form and Function in the Iraqi data

This chapter[1] describes variation in Iraqi Arabic political discourse. I will attempt to see how variation works and which linguistic features from the phonology (P), morphophonology (MPP), syntax (S) and lexicon (L) are affected in a speech of Saddam Hussein. It will appear that variation is not random but largely predictable. As in chapter three, language functions will be analyzed vis-à-vis language forms used by the speaker.

4.1 THE DATA AND MACRO-LEVEL CONTEXTUAL FACTORS

The data of the study is based on a sixty minute taped press conference, delivered by the Iraqi president Saddam Hussein in Baghdad on 20 July 1980, to mark the twelfth anniversary of the July 1968 Revolution in Iraq. This press conference was attended by Arab and foreign journalists, and questions covered local, Arab and international affairs including: the Iraqi nuclear programme, the security of the Arabian Gulf, the Arab economic relations and the Arab summit conference, the situation in Lebanon and the Iraqi position, relations between Iraq and the then USSR, friendly relations and cooperation between Iraq and countries of the world. The macro-level contextual factors of this political discourse are different from those of the Egyptian data and consist of: a press conference (as to setting) with a question-answer type of discourse, where Saddam Hussein addresses Arab and foreign journalists (as to participants). The discourse however, as the Egyptian one, deals with Arab and international affairs. These parameters would be sufficient to set the language level as formal or High, to use Ferguson's word. When variation occurs, we will see which linguistic features are kept as Modern Standard Arabic, and which as dialectal.

4.1.1 Micro-level contextual factors

As with most political speeches, this discourse is meant to persuade[2] the audience of Iraqi policies, inform them on the state of affairs, nationally and internationally. Saddam Hussein may have had it in mind to unify Iraqis before a political crisis, at a time of worsening of relations between Iran and Iraq and two months before the Iraq-Iran war. The press conference is addressed to both foreigners and all Iraqis, and was covered by the Iraqi media. As expected in a formal setting, Saddam Hussein uses MSA but also resorts to Baghdadi Arabic, the dialect of the largest urban centre in Iraq, and for Iraqis, an embryonic "non-standard standard" in the sense already explained, in the context of the discourse of the function of Cairene Arabic in Egypt.

After describing the sociolinguistic situation in Iraq, I shall discuss the concept of convergence which is one explanation of variation and then describe linguistic significant features from the data. The second stage is an analysis of the data preceded by a description of significant features of the three codes concerned, i.e. Modern Standard Arabic (MSA), Baghdadi Arabic (BGI) and Tikriti Arabic (TKI) as noted in the literature. The data is studied in terms of phonology (OA /q/ and OA /k/ phonemes), morphophonology of verbs, syntactic variables (negation system, complementiser ?an and asyndetic verb strings) and some lexical examples (with the agreement system); the last section consists of an analysis of some selected passages where the linguistic levels are likely to display variational cooccurrence. The same procedure, in other words is followed as in chapter three.

4.2 THE SOCIOLINGUISTIC SITUATION IN IRAQ

For clarity, I must mention the sociolinguistic background of Saddam Hussein. He is a native of Tikrit,[3] in the north of Iraq, born and educated there through primary cycle. He went to secondary school in Baghdad where he lived with Tikritis, and took a degree in Law in Cairo.

Tikriti Arabic

Tikriti Arabic (TKI) is a northern Iraqi dialect and contrasts with the southern Iraqi dialects. It is one of the so-called "qeltu" dialects in contrast to the "gelet" types defined by Blanc.[4] TKI Arabic is associated with the ruling party for political, economical and religious reasons: politically, northern Iraq and Tikrit in particular can be contrasted with the south, as several northern towns have provided some powerful and influential families, active in government. Those families[5] "were the decision-makers or the holders of positions of responsibility in the government, the army, the bureaucracy, and the Ba'th party machine". Tikrit, Saddam Hussein's native town, originated the "Tikriti Connection", whose members, besides being politically significant in the Ba'thist constitution, all belonged to the same tribe (the Albu Nasir), and maintained strong family links. Similarly, northern Iraq is relatively rich: the northern towns, Baghdad included, traditionally are the most industrialised: towns like Mosul, Erbil, Tikrit, and Kirkuk are centres for agriculture, oil and textile industries, dates, cement, tobacco, marble and sugar plants. The economy of the south and Basra in particular is weaker: it relies on date cultivation, agriculture and Basra port. The "Marsh Arabs" of the area north of Basra are engaged in buffalo breeding.

Iraq's population is 76% Arab, 19% Kurd and 5% other minorities (Turkomans, Assyrians, Armenians, Yazidis etc).[6] Arabic is the first language of four fifths of the population, Kurdish and Turkic are the most widely spoken minority languages. Although there are minority religions (Muslim Shi'is, Sunnis, Christians, Jews) the majority of the population is Shi'i Muslim, with an estimate of 60% Shi'is, 20% Sunnis and 20% other religions). However, while the Sunnis are inferior in number, they form the "economic, political, social and intellectual elite" and the Sunni group as a whole, feels superior to the rest of the community.[7]

Within the Mesopotamian dialect area, Blanc[8] distinguishes the qeltu and gelet dialects, "qeltu" and "gelet" are different pronunciations of the first person singular of the past tense of "to say". The qeltu types are spoken by the non-Muslim population of Lower Iraq and the sedentary population (Muslim and non-Muslim) in the rest of the country. Jastrow[9] investigated the qeltu dialects and divided them into three major groups, Anatolian, Tigris and Euphrates, TKI being part of the Tigris group. The gelet dialects are spoken by the Muslim population (sedentary and non-sedentary) of Lower Iraq, and by the non-sedentaries in the rest of the country. The gelet form of Arabic, as spoken in Baghdad, is the pervading dialect, the non-standard standard, as a result of the centralization of the administrative state and the growing impact of Baghdad, as the all powerful centre for a number of reasons. Firstly, conscious efforts were made to encourage culture and education (compulsory education to the secondary level) and to revive the national Arab character through arts and literature making a full use of the media. Secondly, although MSA is mostly used in broadcasting, lighter programmes, plays and discussions are performed in BGI and have reached the population throughout the country, while the capital is expanding due to constant immigration. "The gelet dialect of Baghdad", says Abu Haidar,[10] is the language used in business transactions, government offices, schools and colleges. As a result, BGI is accepted as a kind of national dialect, although not all the population shares features inherent in the gelet type.

Although Saddam Hussein is originally from Tikrit, it is interesting to note that MSA and BGI features from the P, MPP, S and L cooccur in the data. One interpretation might be that after so many years spent in Baghdad, his dialect has become BGI. Given the relatively small size of our data, it is difficult to reach any conclusion and this question remains an open one. In the following sections, we will point out some TKI rules and the difficulty of recognizing such forms since they can be very close to MSA features.[11]

In a study of community and dialect in Baghdad, Blanc[12] distinguished cases of minor and major differentiation and classified the contrasts between Muslims and non-Muslims (Christians and Jews) of Baghdad as examples of major differentiation, i.e.: "it permeates the whole phonology and grammar of the dialects, and correlates fully with community membership". When Baghdadi Arabic (of the gelet type) is mentioned, it should be understood to be Muslim BGI Arabic, as there are two other communities in Baghdad, the Christians and the Jews, both qeltu minorities in contrast to the gelet (majority) dialect. As for Muslim speech, Blanc[13] found no difference between Sunnis and Shi'is in Baghdad.

4.2.1 Variation within gelet and qeltu types

As said earlier, Iraq can be described according to the gelet and qeltu dialect areas. Within these areas however, there can be some variation:

qeltu variation

Christian Arabic (C), Jewish Arabic (J), Mosul Arabic and Tikriti Arabic (the last two being Sunni areas) are all qeltu dialects, closely related but with differences. There follow some examples of local variation within the qeltu dialect:

- Phonologically, qeltu has the phoneme [gh] < OA /r/ while gelet has [r]. This phoneme is a salient feature distinguishing qeltu from gelet. In the following examples, qeltu [gh] is found with a varying morphological shape: for MSA raqaba "neck", Mosul has ghaqqabi, C has gheqbi and TKI has ghuqba. Variation affecting qeltu [gh] < /r/ can occur as well: TKI has ?aghub'a, but C has ?arba'a and Mosul ?ōba'a[14] where MSA has ?arba'a "four".
- Morphophonologically, the qeltu dialect is distinguished from the gelet one, by the first person singular lexical enclitic for the past tense -tu, whereas gelet has -it. TKI, C and J have lexical enclitic -tu as expected but verb morphophonology vary for C, and where TKI and J have ktabtu "I wrote", C has katabtu. A similar vowel deletion occurs for the second person masculine singular of the past tense, with TKI ktabit "you wrote" and J ktabt while C has katabit.[15]

gelet variation

Within the gelet speech, phonological variation occurs as well: for OA /q/, gelet dialect has mainly [g], a few examples of [q] in lexically marked items such as qur?ān, and al-'irāq, [dj] and [k]. [dj] and [k], however, are felt "provincial" with [dj] occurring mainly in rural dialects within the gelet area as in [rfīdj] "friend";[16] [k] is found in items such as [wakit] "time" and [kital] "he killed".

Morphophonologically, there is a variation in the gelet speech of southern Iraq, related to occupation and geographical region. Ingham[17] analysed some differences between nomads and settled people; in this study, Ingham refers to the nomads of the south and west of the Euphrates and to town dwellers and palm cultivators of southern Mesopotamia. Among the selected points of contrast between nomadic and sedentary of the gelet type, there is notably a case of resyllabication in the nomadic dialects when a guttural closes a non-final syllable (nomadic y'arif versus sedentary yi'rif "he knows", nomadic bghadād versus sedentary baghdād). Different rules of resyllabication apply when the vowel-initial lexical enclitics are suffixed: nomadic has CCvCat as in nshidat "she asked" and sedentary has CvCCat as in nishdat.

Lexically, the gelet type displays variation and, for instance, the Shatt al 'arab has hassit "there is" and yamta "when", whereas the rest of the gelet area has ?aku and shwakit respectively.[18]

4.2.2 Variation and convergence

The differences within the gelet and qeltu types show variation in the speech of members of the same religion, in different areas, (Sunnis in Baghdad speak the gelet variety whereas Sunnis in Mosul speak the qeltu form of language). Variation here is analyzed across dialects. One has to say now that variation might result from the inability of the speaker to maintain a formal, standard level, or from a deliberate choice in selecting standard or non-standard level forms, to suit changing communicative needs. One sees in the section 4.4 below that whenever Saddam Hussein is making a move to get closer to his audience, he uses BGI features from the phonology, morphophonology, syntax and lexicon.

Iraq is certainly an interesting place to observe convergence. By convergence, one means the process by which a speaker adapts his linguistic habits to those of his interlocutor(s) in crossdialectal discourse, in intercommunal situations. This is often the case for speakers of minority or non-standard dialects, who adapt to the majority or standard dialect. In Baghdad for instance, J or C (qeltu) speakers adapt to the M (gelet) dialect, when in conversation with Muslim speakers. As mentioned by Al Ani,[19] people from Tikrit and Mosul feel strongly about their dialect and tend to "converge" less easily or less often than people from Hiit for instance, when addressing gelet speakers.

Another aspect of convergence is, that speakers of non-standard dialects sometimes adapt their linguistic habits to those of the standard dialect, even if this process implies abandoning forms closer to MSA. Ibrahim[20] notes that "some equivalent features" to Classical Arabic "are in fact stigmatized" in the colloquial. This aspect has been observed in different dialects: Grotzfeld[21] mentions the case of Druzes who have [q] representation for OA /q/ and who converge using the standard Lebanese /?/, when addressing non-Druze speakers. In Bahrain, Holes[22] observed that Shi'is, when dealing with Sunnis, switch, for instance, from their /d̲j/ < OA /d̲j/, which is MSA-like, to the dialectal /y/ as pronounced by the dominant Sunnis. The same phenomenon occurs in Iraq, where natives of Hiit (of the qeltu-type), switch from their MSA but non-dominant [q] and [k] to the standard, dominant BGI [g] < OA /q/, and [č] < OA /k/ respectively, when in conversation with a BGI speaker, "but not in Mosul and Tikrit where retention of [q] seems to have a much stronger foothold".[23]

During this process of accommodation, as Trudgill[24] calls it, some features are modified and some are not (see the agreement system later). Hence some aspects are more resistant to change than others; in the Muslim dialect of Baghdad, it is ordinarily overtly rural features that are modified. These often include substituting /k/ for the more rural /č/ in comparable environments, and eliminating the 2nd and 3rd persons feminine plural pronouns affixes, since urban Baghdadi Arabic shows no 2nd and 3rd persons plural gender distinction".[25]

As said earlier, forms closer to MSA can come to be stigmatised in the dialect. Classical Arabic, however, is still theoretically preferred to all dialects[26] and praised for its "pan-Arab character, its glorious literature, its supposed intrinsic beauty and logic".[27] There does not seem to be an equivalent to what people claim to prefer and use in language.

The reason for dialect convergence is usually that the minority group wants to associate itself with the dominant group. In our case, however, we are talking of one individual who, as will be seen later, wants to associate himself with the BGI dialect and the Iraqis in general: politicians, claims Abd El Jawad,[28] use code-switching to gain more favorable attitudes, fuller understanding and more emotional support from their audience. Code-switching and style-shifting serve functions such as group identification, solidarity, intimacy, to signal unity and integration – a technique in which, as one saw, Nasser started in the 1950's and 60's.

4.3 ANALYSIS OF THE DATA

The aim of this section, after the descriptive analysis, is to see how variation works on a public, political scene, which linguistic elements are affected and which elements are less amenable to change.

4.3.1 Phonology

I will deal here with phonological variation in the data, and with the distribution of salient phonemes. These phonological forms, together with morphological ones, realise the lexical items which express the subject matter. As in the Egyptian case, more abstract topics are expressed in MSA lexical items and more specific discourse is realized in dialectal ones. Although in some lexical items the phonological realisation is unequivocally stylistically marked, there is no general one-to-one correspondence between the formal realisation and the subject matter, but rather a very strong correlation between the style of speaking and the realisation of the phonemes.[29]

MSA, BGI and TKI are similar consonantally apart from three salient differences:

1 OA /r/ is realised as MSA [r], BGI (gelet dialect) [r] and TKI (qeltu dialect) [gh] (of which there are no examples in the data);
2 OA /q/ is realised as MSA [q], BGI [q], [g], [k] and [dj] and TKI [q] and;
3 OA /k/ is MSA [k], BGI [k] and [č] and TKI [k].

Since phoneme /q/ proved to be the most fruitful source of phonological variation, this section deals essentially with OA /q/ and with a few interesting cases of OA /k/.

As will be seen from the examples, Saddam Hussein uses MSA and BGI variants but not, it seems, the marked features of TKI. To determine if TKI is used at all in the data, one has to look at dialectal and non-dialectal passages and see which colloquial elements are used and from which dialect. It appears that there is no evidence of saliently TKI forms in the data (see below for aspects of TKI dialect).

OA /q/

There is a conflict between the linguistic prestige of [q] which has a high-status because it is MSA and, on the other hand, the pervasiveness of BGI [g], part of the non-standard standard. The following chart illustrates the high occurrence of [q] as opposed to BGI [g] < OA /q/ in the present data, and it will be shown that the distribution of phonemes [q] and [g] conforms to rules of lexical conditioning,[30] with BGI [g] being found in dialectal items and sequences, while [q] is found in MSA and "shared" items and in mixed and MSA sequences. The absence of other TKI features and the cooccurrence of other unambiguously MSA elements point to this [q] being an "MSA [q]", rather than a TKI [q].

1. OA /q/ > q

• [q] only	269 tokens	(131 items)
• [g] only	3 tokens	(2 items)
• [q] - [g] variably	59 tokens	(6 items)
• [q] - [k] variably	8 tokens	(2 items)

Phoneme OA /q/ tends to be realized overwhelmingly in our data as [q]. Among the items realized with [q], we distinguish the following phenomena:

a) q in MSA items: items with /q/ that are lexically marked as MSA, i.e. belong to the MSA set of vocabulary. These items tend to be associated with the abstract, formal political vocabulary, but, because of their widespread use and the present subject matter (a press conference) they can be found in dialectal passages of the speech as well. MSA phoneme [q] is invariably retained and the whole item does not show any downgrading to the dialect apart from the absence of ?i'rāb. Items in this category include:

mu<u>th</u>aqqafīn	"educated"	mustaqbal	"future"
muwāfaqa	"agreement"	?iltiqā?	"meeting"
mawqif	"situation"	?istiqlāl	"independence"
?iqtiṣādī	"economic"	muqarrarāt	"decisions'
qaḍāya	"problems"	qimma	"summit"
niṭāq	"extent"	muqaddamāt	"vanguard"
qawā'id	"bases"	qisma	"division"
wāqi'iyya	"real"	tafawwuq	"supremacy"
?inqaḍa	"it was concluded"	muwaqqi'	"signatory"
taṭwīq	"encirclement"	?irtiqā?	"progress"

Items from this list tend to cooccur with other MSA elements in MSA sequences (apart from 4 items occurring in mixed sentences) as in:

> *SH1 l.15* /il-'irāq muwaqqi' 'ala 'adam ?inti<u>sh</u>ār il-?asliḥa n-nawawiyya/ This MSA long nominal clause combines phoneme [q] (muwaqqi'), maṣdar (?inti<u>sh</u>ār) and frozen MSA collocation (l-?asliḥa n-nawawiyya).

Occasionally, items such as country names and collocations with the phoneme q are realised in a BGI sequence:

> *SH1 l.11* /likay itgūl ?inna l-'irāq garrab yinti<u>dj</u> qunbula nawawiyya/ MSA [q], in a collocation, cooccurs with BGI elements: phoneme [g] (itgūl, garrab); MPP of verb (yinti<u>dj</u>); preformative yi- and deletion and prosthetisation of vowel (itgūl); and verb string (garrab yinti<u>dj</u>).

b) q with BGI features: We now look at [q] combining with BGI features within the same item. Such cases concern verbs mainly such as: yit'āqad, tit'allaq, yiṣādiqna, yiqātil (17 tokens, 13 items). It is interesting to notice that although q is an MSA feature, it can combine with dialectal preformative yi- as seen from these verbs. The persistence of q with dialectal features may be explained by the fact that q is the only phoneme possible here, in this kind of discourse, as the variant [g] would be too dialectally marked. It is interesting to point out also that preformative ya- and the stem vowel are downgraded (to yi- and -i-) more easily than phoneme q to g. As will be discussed later in the MPP section, preformative yi- is of a particular status: it is widespread, found at higher levels of formality, and has become multilevel. Now, if I consider in the Egyptian data examples of q combining with dialectal features within the same item, one obtains the following cases: baltaqi, biyuqātil, bituqatlu (8 tokens, 3 items). Although there are few cases, one observes a similar phenomenon to the one discussed above: [q] combines with multilevel aspectual prefix bi-, that is, given their inherent dialectal differences, the CA and BGI data show cases of the persistence of a multilevel element (yi- in BGI, bi- in CA) at higher levels of formality, combining with MSA elements such as phoneme q. This phenomenon of persistence of dialectal elements into higher levels of formality will be discussed below with MPP, syntactic and lexical features, and summarized in chapter six.

2. OA /q/ > [g]
Lexical items in which [g] is the sole reflex occur in close-to-BGI verbs (see below) and BGI items and are very scarce in the data. The two items with [g] exclusively (yilgāha "he meets her" and ga'na "our land") are part of the everyday vocabulary and occur in BGI sequences. This gives some indication of the rather non-dialectal "feel" of the whole speech, and is less than the equivalent figure for Nasser in chapter three, though the difference is probably not statistically significant.

3. OA /q/ > [q] - [g] variably
Here one is concerned with items that are variably realized as [q] or [g], generally more often as the latter. The items include yigūl "he says" (and other persons of the verb), gawmi "national", wugaf "he stopped", nigdar "we can", garrab "he got near", gādir "able". All these items tend to occur, often together, in dialectal sequences as in:

> *SH2 l.57* /... yigulūn ?innu niḥin shū nigdar insawwi/ where [g] cooccurs with dialectal features: niḥin "we", lexical items (shū, insawwi), deletion and prosthetisation of a vowel (insawwi) and

close-to-BGI MPP of verb (nigdar). The use of the verb gāl/ yigūl at higher stylistic levels will be discussed below in the morphophonology section.

4. OA /q/ > [q] - [k]
Items with [k] are few but heavily marked as BGI, specifically – wakit "time" and kital "to kill". They occur in BGI sequences as in:

> *SH4 l.46* /tara ?ittifāq il-'irāq il-?īrān il-mu'arruḍ ?ila ?an yinfi<u>dj</u>ir fī ?ay wakit/ where [k] in wakit cooccurs with BGI MPP (yinfi<u>dj</u>ir) and the lexical item tara.

As said earlier, the frequent occurrence of MSA realisations of OA /q/ is linked to the lexico-semantic status of the words and to the general non-dialectal feel of the speech.

OA /k/

OA /k/ is realised as [k] and [č] in BGI. In the data, however, only [k] occurs apart from two realisations of č, both, significantly, non-content words, in hīč "like this", in a BGI aside *SH4 l.24* (mā hīč yā duktūr "not so, doctor?"), and in čam "a few" in a BGI sequence:

> *SH5 l.12* /?innu ṣ-ṣumūd wa t-taṣaddi mā ṣār ?ila čam sana/

The reason why we have so few (2) occurrences of BGI [č] from OA /k/ in comparison to phoneme g < OA /q/ is due to the fact that [č] is more heavily marked for the dialect and would be inappropriate in a press conference. The speaker is naturally drawn to use features suited to his audience, avoid localisms, and prefer pan-Arabic elements to dialectal ones. In chapter six, I will argue that Egyptian phoneme [?] < OA /q/ occuring together with MSA features is more acceptable from a pan-Arab audience's point of view compared to the BGI marked [g] < OA /q/ and [č] < OA /k/. BGI [g] has a low frequency of occurrence with MSA elements, while [č] is practically non-existent in the data, as both phonemes are too "local" to pervade higher levels of formality. Moreover, to go back to the predominance of CA [?] < OA /q/, as discussed in chapters one and six, Egyptians feel very confident using their dialect which, as pan-Arabic, is prestigious.

Contrary to chapters on Libya and Egypt, I do not analyze interdentals in this chapter simply because <u>th</u>, <u>dh</u> and ẓ are normal BGI phonemes, and combine with MSA and BGI elements. Thus, unlike the situation in Cairene Arabic, interdentals are multilevel in Baghdadi Arabic. The realisation of these phonemes is close to Old Arabic and can be seen as well in Southern Iraq and other Bedouin-type dialects due to the isolation of the areas compared to urban ones such as Cairo.[31]

4.3.2 Morphophonology

Verbs are analyzed, as before, according to their lexico-semantic status and morphophonological shape. Examples from the data allow us once again to place these verbs into five categories:

			Third level		
L-S:	MSA	**shared**	**shared**	**shared**	BGI
MPP:	MSA	**close-to-MSA**	**multivalent**	**close-to-BGI**	BGI

MSA and BGI are at the two ends of the continuum. MSA verbs tend to deal with abstract concepts and conform to the MSA rules. BGI verbs are part of the everyday, conversational vocabulary and show a BGI MPP. In between, there is the third, intermediate level, made of lexically shared (between MSA and BGI) items which can vary morphophonologically, one end close-to-MSA, another close-to-BGI and in the middle, multivalent verbs. One finds some hybrid verbs but no symbiotic verbs this time since aspectual prefix bi- does not exist in BGI. Moreover, data show no other type of symbiosis peculiar to BGI (for instance, a dialectal prefix combined with MSA features). These different categories are explained and illustrated below (see also section 2.3 for a description of verbal categories). The general image of the verb system in the data is that there are few purely MSA (18) or BGI (19) verbs, the vast majority being part of this third level (436 verbs).

Verbal categories

(1) L-S and MPP MSA verbs	18 tokens (7 items)
(2) L-S shared and close-to-MSA MPP	205 tokens (105 items)
(3) L-S shared and multivalent MPP	51 tokens (14 items)
(4) L-S shared and close-to-BGI MPP	180 tokens (91 items)
(5) L-S and MPP BGI verbs	19 tokens (6 items)

MSA verbs

MSA verbs are part of the abstract, formal vocabulary and appear in MSA sequences. These verbs, with their MSA lexico-semantic status and morphophonological shape, are not part of the dialectal lexicon. The data show 18 occurrences of MSA verbs (7 items) which conform to the MSA rules of lexical enclitics for the past and non-past tenses for the first and derived forms. MSA verbs include:

satamtalik	"you will acquire"	tanṭaliqu	"you leave"
tanhaḍ	"it rises"	yantahik	"he desacrates"
yuṭawwaq	"it is surrounded"	?alḥaqa	"he annexed"

These verbs show MSA morphophonological characteristics such as preformative ya- (yantahik), vowel patterning in a derived form (yuṭawwaq), ?i'rāb (?alḥaqa), future tense prefix sa- (satamtalik), and occur in MSA sequences as in:

> *SH1 l.54* /?an yudriku ?inna l-?umma l-'arabiyya bada?at tanḥad wa laysa hunālik man huwa qādir 'ala ?īqāf nuhūḍha/ where MSA elements combine such as phoneme q (qādir), verb MPP (bada?at), multilevel complementiser ?an + verb, lexical item (laysa, hunālik, tanhaḍ), collocation (l-?umma l-'arabiyya) and maṣdar (?īqāf).

MSA verbs and dialectal influence

Some of the MSA verbs presented in the list do not have ?i'rāb (e.g. yantahik). Absence of ?i'rāb is the only concession to dialect encountered in the above list but it does not imply a levelling down of the lexical status of the item. An MSA item without ?i'rāb is still considered MSA. The presence of ?i'rāb, on the contrary, is considered as an extramarker.

-ūna, the MSA plural ending for non-past tense in the 2 and 3 masc. forms, is not found as such in this Iraqi data whereas the singular endings occur occasionally. Instead of ūna, the BGI ending ūn, itself quite close to "correct" MSA, is used. This -ūn ending is multilevel, and its use is so widespread that it has become acceptable at higher levels than pure BGI, even with MSA verbs. TKI has the -awn ending but there is no sign of it in the data.

The following examples show that cooccurrence restrictions are tight and that many theoretical MSA-BGI combinations of elements are impossible, such as phoneme [g] < OA /q/ with ?i'rāb (*tanguṣu), BGI [g] < OA /q/ with MSA MPP (*yuṭawwag), yi-preformative with sa- future marker (*satimtilik). The case of BGI/multilevel -ūn is different from the dialectal ending in Egyptian and Libyan dialects where we have -ū ending, being marked for the dialect but accepted as such at higher levels of formality. In these dialects, -ūna is an MSA extramarker which does not occur in our data, apart from very occasional cases.

As expected, MSA verbs tend to appear in MSA sequences i.e. in cooccurrence with other MSA features from other levels. In one rare case, however, a lexically MSA verb appear with a BGI MPP, tinṭaliq "it emanates", a hybrid construction (see hybrid forms below).

Dialectal verbs

Dialectal verbs are part of the everyday vocabulary, conversational style and deal with common, specific matters. These verbs are not found in the MSA lexicon (or if they are, e.g. sawwa/ yisawwi, they have a different meaning). As might be expected in the context of a press conference, such verbs are relatively scarce. These verbs conform to the BGI MPP rules as to the lexical enclitics of the past and non-past tenses:

	Past tense	*Non-past tense*
I	CaCaC	yiCCaC / yuCCaC
	CiCaC	yiCCiC
	CuCaC	yuCCiC / yuCCuC
II	CaCCaC	yCiCCuC/ yCaCCiC
III	CāCaC	yiCāCiC
IV	?aCCac	yiCCiC/ yuCCuC
V	tCaCCaC	yitCaCCaC
VI	tCāCaC	yitCāCaC
VII	nCiCaC/uCaC	yinCiCiC/yinCuCuC
VIII	CtiCaC/uCaC	yiCtiCiC/yiCtuCuC
IX	CCaCC	yiCCaCC
X	staCCaC	yistaCCiC/yistaCCuC

Lexical enclitics of the first form:

	Past	*Non-past tense*
1 sg	stem-it	?a-stem
2 m sg	stem-it	ti-stem
2 f sg	stem-ti	ti-stem-īn
3 m sg	stem	yi-stem
3 f sg	stem-at	ti-stem
1 pl	stem-na	ni-stem
2 pl	stem-tu	ti-stem-ūn
3 pl	stem-aw	yi-stem-ūn

The data shows 19 tokens (6 items) of BGI verbs which include insawwi "we do", yirūḥ "he goes", tithāwa<u>sh</u>ūn "you fight each other", yishūf "he sees", xallih "let him" and tunṭūnhum "you give them". These BGI verbs show the cooccurrence of the following BGI features:

(a) preformative yi- and the MPP of verb (yishūf),
(b) deletion and prosthetisation of vowel (insawwi),
(c) deletion of unstressed short vowel (tithāwashūn).
(d) tunṭūnhum "you give them" is a BGI localism, with consonant n instead of ', the MSA form being tu'ṭūnahum. More BGI characteristics will be illustrated with examples from the data in the close-to-BGI verbs section. The following BGI typical characteristics are illustrated with lexically shared verbs with a close-to-BGI MPP:
(e) long vowel ō instead of ū (for the 3rd person plural past tense of bilghōh for instance) where the form is suffixed (by regular phonological rule).
(f) stem vowel is dropped when the 3rd f.sg. or 3rd pl. lexical enclitic is added, as in si?lat "she asked", si?law "they asked" and kitbat "she wrote".

These BGI verbs occur with other dialectal elements in dialectal sequences as in:

SH2 l.57 /li?annu bi s-sābiq kānu yigūlūn ?innu niḥin shū nigdar insawwi/

MSA phoneme [q] occurs here but the item in which [q] occurs is commonly found as such in BGI. In this sequence BGI elements cooccur such as phonome [g] < OA /q/, preformative yi-, close-to-BGI MPP, BGI ending -ūn (yigūlūn), pronoun niḥin, deletion and prosthetisation of vowel (insawwi), asyndetic verb string (nigdar insawwi) and localism shū.

Switches in the discourse vary between MSA, BGI and intermediate levels located between MSA and BGI. Tikriti morphology differs from the BGI one in the lexical enclitics of the past and non-past tenses:

Lexical enclitics of the past and non-past tenses in TKI

	Past tense	*Non-past tense*
1 sg	CCaC-tu	?a-CCvC
2 m sg	CCaC-it	t-CCvC
2 f sg	CCaC-ti	t-CiCC-ayn
3 m sg	CaCaC	y-CCvC
3 f sg	CaCC-at	t-CCvC

1 pl	CCaC-na	n-CCvC
2 pl	CCaC-tim	t-CvCC-awn
3 pl	CaCC-u	y-CvCC-awn

As can be seen from this chart, TKI has some very distinctive features. The examples given here are from Johnstone and Jastrow[32] since there are no TKI verbal cases in the data. TKI characteristics include for the past tense:

(a) -tu ending (1st sg) which is a salient feature of the qeltu dialects, "not only in contrast to the gelet-types, but as against Arabic dialects as a whole, since all but these have lost the final /u/".[33]
(b) the -tim ending for the second person plural,
(c) u ending for the 3rd person plural (BGI has -aw),
(d) the vowel in unstressed open syllables is elided as in ktabtu "I wrote"
(e) as for BGI verbs, the stem vowel is dropped when the 3rd f. sg. or 3rd pl. lexical enclitic is added as in katbat "she wrote".
(f) the non-past tense has -ayn ending for the 2nd f. sg., -awn as a plural ending, and resyllabication occurs as a general rule for the 2nd f. sg. and the 2nd and 3rd person plural, while in BGI, resyllabication is optional rule.
(g) preformatives of the non-past tense show ya-, yi- and sometimes deletion of vowel, y-.[34]

Shared verbs with a close-to-MSA MPP

As seen in the preceding sections, there are few MSA and dialectal verbs. Most of the verbs in the data belong to the third intermediate level where items are lexically shared between MSA and the dialect. Some verbs however are closer to MSA and have a "close-to-MSA" MPP. These shared, close-to-MSA verbs sometimes allow a slight dialectal influence. ?aḥsan "he mastered" for example, is shared lexically in MSA and BGI. However, when the verb is used in the imperfect, the MSA MPP is generally adopted, as in yuḥsinūn(a) "they master". For the non-past tense, BGI has one morphophonological shape for the first and the fourth forms, yiḥsinūn. yinbighī exists in BGI, but the data show only occurrençes of the verb in its close-to-MSA shape, yanbaghī "he should".

While MSA verbs make a concession to ?i'rāb, shared verbs with a close-to-MSA MPP, a slight downgrading from MSA verbs, have a further concession which is the unstressed vowel deletion, as in yat'āmal where the close-to-BGI is yit'āmal, preformative yi- being a marker of dialectalness.

This way of classifying verbs (into MSA, BGI, and threefold third level) seems satisfactory since it allows five distinctions to be made in the stylistic classification of verbs which are realized according to linguistic rules of cooccurrence and to subject matter. In other words, some items will always be MSA and found in MSA sequences dealing with abstract concepts in formal situations, other items are BGI and found in BGI sequences concerned with concrete matters in a casual style. But most of the data belongs to the continuum in between MSA and BGI. A verb may be shared between MSA and BGI with a close-to-MSA MPP and would tend to appear in MSA sequences and cooccur with other MSA elements. However, occasionally, the same verb appears in a less formal sequence: morphophonological adjustments are then made for the verb to combine with dialectal elements. The following sequence shows how the repeated shared verb yuḥāwilūn/ yiḥawlūn changes from close-to-MSA to close-to-BGI to conform to the other elements of the level-switched sequence which the speaker, after a hesitation, inserts:

> *SH1 l.23* /wa li dhālik yuḥāwilūn kull 'ēn 'arabiyya tkūn imfatḥa yiḥāwlūn yiṭfūnha/ yuḥāwilūn has a close-to-MSA MPP even with the lack of ?i'rāb but yiḥāwlūn has a close-to-BGI MPP with yi- preformative and the deletion of unstressed vowel.

Our Iraqi data consist of a very long list (205 tokens) of lexically shared and morphophonologically close-to-MSA verbs (105 items) of which some examples follow:

yat'āmal	"he trades"	yuḥsinūn	"they master"
tuhzam	"it is defeated"	yuḥāwilūn	"they try"
tustaxdam	"it is used"	yaḥtādjūn	"they need"
yatḥaddathu	"he speaks"	yanbaghi	"he should"
yudriku	"he understands"	turattib	"you arrange"
yataxarradj	"he is trained"	yufshilu	"he disappoints"
yuntidju	"he produces"	yuḥtaram	"he is respected"
na'tamid	"we rely"	nuṣādiq	"we befriend"
naktashif	"we find out"	na'taqid	"we believe"
tarfuḍ	"you reject"	ḍuminat	"it was guaranteed"
yaqbalūn	"they accept"	yuwaffir	"he increases"
yatadhakkar	"he remembers"	yaqtaḍi	"he requires"
ṭuriḥat	'it was held"	yaxtalif	"he differs"

These verbs conform to the MSA rules of MPP apart from a few concessions to dialect: the lack of ?i'rāb, the non-past BGI ending -ūn (MSA -ūna) being found with a close-to-MSA MPP (yuḥsinūn, yuḥāwilūn) and occasionally, deletion of unstressed short vowel as in yatḥaddathu, yat'āmal. These verbs have distinctive MSA elements, as in yuntidju which is a true MSA IV form (BGI has a merger with the first form yintidj), and in tustaxdam and ḍuminat which are passive forms (7 passive verbs in the data). The passive voice has disappeared from BGI and from most Arabic dialects; rather, reflexive forms such as tCaCCaC, ?inCiCaC and iCtiCaC would be used.[35] These close-to-MSA verbs occur in mixed and MSA sequences mainly as in:

> *SH1 l.27* /idh-dharra ?il-?ān tustaxdam 'ala niṭāq wāsi' wa bi l-?asās li l-?aghrāḍ is-silmiyya/ This typical sequence combines MSA elements such as passive voice and close-to-MSA MPP (tustaxdam), phoneme q (niṭāq) and MSA collocations (l-?aghrāḍ is-silmiyya), and:
> *SH1 l.41* /yanbaghī ?an yuwadjdjah hādha s-su?āl min qibalkum ?ilā kull il-muta'āṭifīn ma'a l-kiyān iṣ-ṣahyūniy/ where MSA elements cooccur such as phoneme q (qibal) in the agent passive structure, close-to-MSA MPP of verb (yanbaghi), internal passive (yuwadjdjah), MSA collocation (l-kiyān iṣ-ṣahyūniy) and multi-level complementiser ?an.

These close-to-MSA verbs are however too "formal" to combine with dialectal elements such as phoneme [g] < OA /q/ (*nuṣādig, *yagtaḍi).

This section was concerned with lexically shared verbs with a close-to-MSA MPP. As we said earlier, lexically shared verbs can have various morphophonological realisations (close-to-MSA MPP as discussed above, close-to-BGI and multivalent MPP in the sections below). The following chart shows the variability of the morphophonological realisations of lexically shared verbs.

Flexibility of the lexically shared verbs

close-to-MSA	*multivalent*	*close-to-BGI*
yuḥsinūn (5)		yiḥsinūn (1)
yuwādjih (9)		inwādjih (1)
yuḥāwlūn (1)		yiḥāwlūn (2)
ya'rifūn (3)		ti'arfūn (2)
yurīd (3)		yirīd (4)
naḥrus (1)		yiḥris (3)
yaqbalūn (1)		yiqbal (1)

yakūn (23)	kān (11)	yikūn (11)
ṣārat (8)	ṣār (6)	yiṣīr (2)
zālat (2)	zāl (4)	
yuqāl (3)		yigūl (27)

Shared verbs with a close-to-BGI MPP

Close-to-BGI verbs belong to the third, intermediate level. Because of their L-S status, part of the ordinary conversational vocabulary, without being solely the "property" of BGI, and their BGI MPP shape, these close-to-BGI verbs tend to be used in less formal contexts than close-to-MSA verbs and are found in the dialectal passages of the discourse. Some of these verbs could be found in mixed sequences; however, because of their widespread use in the dialect they have become associated with it. There are 180 close-to-BGI verbs (91 items) in the data among which:

yifhamūn	"they understand"	yidirkūn	"they understand"
yiḥāwlūn	"they try"	tish'urūn	"you realize"
yitwaqqa'	"he expects"	tsahhilūn	"you facilitate"
yiḥris	"he guards"	ti'arfūn	"you know"
yiṭraḥa	"he rejects it"	yiṣṣawwar	"he imagines"
yifattish	"he looks for"	tit'allaq	"it relates"
inḥawwal	"we change"	nlōm	"we blame"
yiḥimlūn	"they carry"	tighumzūlu	"you wink at him"
siqṭat	"it fell"	yinfidjir	"it explodes"
zurit	"I visited"	tigūl	"you say"
bilghōh	"they reached it"	yilgāha	"he meets her"
yirafḍūn	"they reject"	siktaw	"they kept silent"
wugaf	"he stopped"		

Some of these verbs display very marked BGI features. However, they are not categorised as BGI verbs lexico-semantically because they are from this point of view shared between MSA and BGI, even if for some of them the actual data show only close-to-BGI MPP realisations and some are highly marked for BGI: ti'arfūn is highly marked but ya'rifūn, i.e. its close-to-MSA counterpart, occurs also in the data (see the chart of the variability in shared verbs). BGI characteristics in these close-to-BGI verbs include:

1 phoneme [g] < OA /q/ (tigūl, yilgāha) which is [q] in shared verbs with a close-to-MSA MPP (naqūl);
2 preformative yi- and MPP of verb (nigdar);

3 deletion of glottal stop (xa<u>dh</u>na);
4 deletion and prosthetisation of vowel (inḥawwal);
5 there are a few cases of resyllabication as in yidirkūn, ti'arfūn, yiḥimlūn, ti<u>gh</u>umzūlu, yirafḍūn. As an optional rule, there may be a stem change when the lexical enclitic begins with a vowel, or with a suffixed object enclitic, hence for the 2nd person f. sg. and the 2nd and 3rd plural of the non-past tenses.[36] This resyllabication represents a further stylistic downgrading of the verb paradigm:

   y-CCvC - v(C) → y-CvCC - v(C)

   yis?al "he asks", for instance, becomes ysi?la "he asks him" with an object enclitic;
6 assimilation of t into a double consonant ṣṣ (yiṣṣawwar);
7 deletion of unstressed vowel (tsahhilūn);
8 BGI MPP and endings (wugaf, yuskut, yinfi<u>dj</u>ir, siktaw, yifhamūn).

The form g-w-l "to say" is heavily used in the data and in reported speeches which have a dialectal morphophonology ("I said this and he said that" type of discourse), and because of its frequent use, close-to-BGI yigūl occasionally cooccurs in sequences with MSA elements. The speaker often shifts levels, so that where historical facts are simply being recounted, a more formal style is used, but where he plays a more active role, or depicts himself as such, the tone becomes personal and the level dialectal. Such issues of discourse strategies will be illustrated in the section on language form and language function.

The root k-w-n adapts to the sequence level, close-to-MSA with yakūn and close-to-BGI with yikūn. The form kān, however, is multivalent and discussed below. kān, yikūn and yakūn are all part of the same (shared) lexical item whose MPP is variable.

Shared verbs with a close-to-BGI MPP occur in dialectal and mixed sequences, i.e. sequences where MSA and BGI elements cooccur. Example of BGI sequences:

> *SH1 l.5* /mā yifhamūn il-'ilim/ where dialectal elements combine such as negative particle mā and a non-past tense verb, close-to-BGI MPP (yifhamūn), phonology of the noun 'ilim not MSA 'ilm.
>
> *SH1 l.97* /wa ?illi yirīd yi'ādīna xallih yitwaqqa'/ where vowel deletion (yitwaqqa') combines with relative pronoun ?illi, close-to-BGI MPP of verb (yirīd), verb string (yirīd yi'ādīna).

SH2 l.68 /bass tighumzūlu bi ṭaraf ʻaynku yidji wara fatra/ which shows cooccurrence of BGI resyllabication (tighumzūlu), close-to-BGI MPP of verb (yidji) and lexical items (bass, wara).

The following mixed sequence shows the combination of MSA elements such as close-to-MSA MPP of verb (?aẓunn), collocation (il-kiyān iṣ-ṣahyūnī), passive verb (yuqām) and phoneme [q] < OA /q/ and BGI elements such as ?illi, long vowel ē for MSA diphtong ay, and close-to-BGI MPP of verb (siqṭat):

SH3 l.39 /wa ?aẓunn ?anna ṭ-ṭā?irat il-ʻarabiyya il-waḥīda ?illi siqṭat ʻala l-?arḍ ?illi yuqām ʻalēh il-kiyān aṣ-ṣahyūni hiya l-ʻirāqiyya/

Shared verbs with a multivalent MPP

Earlier on, I dealt with verbs whose lexico-semantic status was shared by MSA and BGI but, because of their use, their MPP was either close-to-MSA or close-to-BGI. This time, shared verbs have a MPP acceptable both in MSA and BGI, which we call multivalent: lexically, they are not identifiable with one particular level, and because of their common and widespread use, they are found at all levels. Forms which can be similar in BGI and MSA are limited and concern the 3rd masculine singular and the 1st person plural. Data has 51 occurrences of multivalent verbs (14 items) which include:

kān	"he was"	yaʻni	"it means"
wāfaq	"he agreed"	?akkadnāh	"we confirmed it"
ṣār	"he became"	mā zāl	"still"
waḍḍahna	"we explained"	nāqash	"he argued"
ʻāladj	"he treated"	kaththar	"he increased"
zawwadkum	"he provided you"	ḥawwalna	"we changed"
yumkin	"it is possible"	tara	"you see"

Some of these verbs display MSA characteristics (yumkin) but their use is so widespread that they are accepted as such even in the dialect. kān "he was" is multivalent, i.e. found in MSA and BGI. BGI, however, also has čān with BGI phoneme [č] as a realisation of OA /k/. čān is marked for BGI but there is no occurrence of it in the data. Although BGI has [č] in čān for the past tense, it has [k] for the non-past tense, as in yikūn.[37] kān without ?iʻrāb can be found at all levels, whereas yakūn and yikūn are morphophonologically marked, being close-to-MSA and close-to BGI respectively.

ya'ni "that is, in other words" is another multivalent term. Its L-S status is shared by MSA and BGI and its close-to-MSA MPP is found in MSA and BGI sequences.With the same root, '-n-y, BGI has the dialectal MPP yi'ni but with the meaning "to concern". ya'ni is a multilevel item and can be found in scientific texts as well as in conversational style, although it tends to be associated with the dialect because it functions often as a means of temporising in spoken discourse. The same point can be made about tara "you see" and yumkin "it is possible".

Although the forms are morphophonologically close-to-MSA and the lexical status is shared in MSA and BGI, they are however associated with the conversational style and found in dialectal passages of the data. Multivalent verbs occur in MSA, mixed and dialectal sequences as in:

> *SH2 l.72* /kaththar ?allah xayrhum/ This frozen MSA sequence has a religious connotation, the verb kaththar is multivalent but xayr is MSA as BGI has xēr.
>
> *SH4 l.18* /fa huwwa nāqash niqāsh ṭawīl 'ala l-djuzur il-'arabiyya th-thalātha u gāl ?innuh/ This sequence is mixed: nāqash is multivalent and the beginning of the sequence is MSA with conjunction fa, phoneme [q] < OA /q/ (niqāsh). The level drops with connective u instead of wa and close-to-BGI verb gāl to rephrase nāqash. Unlike Cairene data which systematically show phoneme [t] from OA /th/ in numerals, BGI keeps th as here in thalātha.

Hybrid verbs

Hybrid verbs combine MSA and BGI elements within the same verbal form but they are not defined as close-to-BGI for the following reasons: (1) we have a hybrid form from a L-S MSA verb (tinṭaliq "you leave") and not from a shared one. (2) In shared verbs, hybrid forms imply a dialectal element where a full close-to-MSA MPP would have been expected (see 2a and 2b). Preformative yi- is a dialectal marker and would cast the form as close-to-BGI for a shared verb (and hybrid for an MSA verb). The hybrid cases in the data concern:

(2a) a shared verb with normally a close-to-MSA MPP with a dialectal phonological element as in ?iltaqēt "I met" which has a long vowel ē instead of MSA diphtong ay;

(2b) other items include BGI lexical enclitic -it with an otherwise close-to-MSA MPP as in ?a'lanit which is a hybrid between MSA

?a'lantu and BGI 'ilanit "I revealed", and also in baḥathit, a hybrid form between MSA baḥathtu and BGI biḥathit "I studied".

Although I have been dealing with verbs in this MPP section, I would like to look at MPP cases of hybridization concerning nouns. In the Egyptian and Libyan data, we analyse the hybridization of nouns, i.e. the hybrid endings -at in noun-pronoun constructions. As discussed in chapter six, one sees that despite the emergence of a hybrid ending, the dialectal endings usually pervade higher levels of formality. The Iraqi data present a very interesting phenomenon in that the dialectal ending for the noun-pronoun construction is -at,[38] i.e. the same ending that has emerged in the other two dialects as hybrid. Thus dialectal ending -at is already acceptable as such and there is no need for a further hybrid form to emerge. As the following examples will show, the BGI dialectal endings are pervasive throughout the data.

noun-pronoun construction

MSA	*hybrid*	*dialect*
-atu/a/i(1)←————		-at (7)

Dialectal cases concern karāmatha "her prestige", siyādatha "its supremacy", ṣadāqatna "our friendship", 'ilāqathum "their relation", rāḥathum "their rest".

To conclude on the morphophonological aspects of the Iraqi data, I would like to point out some dialectal features that mix with MSA elements and pervade higher levels of stylistic formality. Through this process, these dialectal features seem to have lost their markedness and become multivalent. Such is the case of:

(a) BGI/multilevel ending -ūn for the non-past tense verb (yuḥsinūn) instead of MSA -ūna;
(b) feminine ending -at in noun-pronoun constuctions as discussed above;
(c) deletion of vowel in unstressed syllables in close-to-MSA verbs (yat'āmal);
(d) still in verbs, the lexical enclitic -it which in BGI is common for the 1st and 2nd m. sg.('alanit);
(e) relative pronoun ?illi instead of its MSA counterparts;
(f) preformative yi- pervading higher levels of formality.

4.3.3 Syntax

The previous section was concerned with the analysis of phonological and morphophonological aspects of the data. The level of an item was defined according to the cooccurrence of phonological and morphophonological elements together with its lexical status and use. A certain degree of dependency is observable between P and MPP, i.e. phoneme [g] < OA /q/ cooccurs with a close-to-BGI MPP as in yigūl but [q] < OA /q/ cooccurs with MSA MPP as in yuṭawwaq "it was surrounded" and with close-to-BGI MPP features as in siqṭat "it fell". There is a stronger degree of dependency between syntactic elements such as negative particles and their "component", the following verb and its MPP, than between P and MPP for instance and, syntactic elements have a style-raising and style-lowering effect on their complement. This section deals with the negative system, complementiser ?an + verb and the dialectal complementiserless verbs, i.e. asyndetic verb strings.

The negative system

The following chart presents the BGI negative system (TKI sharing the same system) at the disposal of the speaker:

BGI

1) *completed past action*
   mā + past tense
2) *present action*
   mā + non-past tense
3) *verbless equational sentences*
   mū + adj./prep phrase
   ghēr + adj/noun
   mā + prep.phrase
4) *negation of future*
   mā + rāḥ+ non-past tense
5) *negative command*
   lā + non-past tense

Examples from the data show that Saddam Hussein switches between, and does not hybridise the two systems: MSA particles occur with MSA MPP of verbs in MSA and mixed sequences, and BGI particles with BGI MPP of verbs in mixed and dialectal sequences. A similar phenomenon of predictability between the particle and the verb was observed in the Egyptian data.

A. The MSA system

The MSA system was introduced in the preceding chapter (see 3.3.3). The MSA particles (lam, lā, mā (+ past tense), laysa, ghayr) are used with an MSA complement in MSA sequences. Examples:

1 completed past action: there are two occurrences of lam + jussive in MSA verbs in MSA sequences, as in:

SH3 l.10 /ṭab'an ba'ḍa l-?aqṭār il-'arabiyya lam tuṣādiq 'ala hā<u>dh</u>a l-muqarrarāt/ where lam cooccurs with MSA phoneme [q] and close-to-MSA MPP of verb (tuṣādiq) and MSA collocation (l-?aqṭār il-'arabiyya). lam is a particularly stylistically marked feature, and hardly ever cooccurs with non-MSA elements in sequences.

There are 12 occurrences of mā + past tense in close-to-MSA and multivalent verbs in a few mixed sequences and mainly MSA sequences as in:

SH4 l.5 /?i<u>dh</u>a mā kān taṣarrufak ?i'tidā?i ḍidd ?ayy 'arabī fī l-xalī<u>dj</u>/ where mā occurs with multivalent kān, and masdar (taṣarruf).

On the other hand, mā + non-past tense is a theoretically "acceptable" MSA form. This construction, however, is avoided in written and hence formal Arabic because mā has become stigmatised and associated with the dialect.[39] As a result, mā + non-past tense is found in the data but as part of the dialectal system, with close-to-BGI verbs, in BGI and mixed sequences. Conversely, lā + non-past verb, like the lam negative, cooccurs with close-to-MSA verbs in MSA sequences.

2 present action: the 22 occurrences of lā + non-past tense are found with close-to-MSA verbs in a few mixed sequences and MSA sequences mainly, as in:

SH1 l.34 /limā<u>dh</u>ā n-nās il-'uqqāl fī hā<u>dh</u>ā l-kiyān lā yaḥsibūn ḥisābāt daqīqa li l-mustaqbal/ lā cooccurs with MSA elements such as close-to-MSA MPP (yaḥsibūn), phoneme [q], MSA collocations (n-nās il-'uqqāl, ḥisābāt daqīqa) and MSA lexical choices (limā<u>dh</u>a for BGI lē<u>sh</u>).

3 equational sentences: unsurprisingly, laysa, associated with a high-flown style is found in MSA sequences. There are ten occurrences of laysa (6 with prepositional phrases and four with nouns) combining with MSA features, as in the following where laysa negates the rest of the clause and cooccurs with complementiser ?an and close-to-MSA MPP of verbs (yudriku), phoneme [q], MSA collocations (l-?umma l-'arabiyya) and MSA lexical choices (tanhaḍ, laysa):

SH1 l.54 /?an yudriku ?inna l-?umma l-'arabiyya bada?at tanhaḍ wa laysa hunālik man huwa qādir 'ala ?īqāf nuhūḍha/

Other MSA negative particles include g̲h̲ayr + noun (3 occurrences in MSA sequences) as in:

SH2 l.5 /daradjat ṣadāqati faransa g̲h̲ayr daradjat ṣadāqat il-?axarīn fī ?ūrubbā/ which contains a long nominal phrase. lā occurs with prepositions and nouns mainly (10 occurrences in MSA sequences) as in:

SH2 l.43 /?iḥna lā na?mal ?an lā yakūn fī l-?umma l-'arabiyya taba' lā li l-?amerikān wa lā li s-sūfyēt wa lā li firansi wa lā li l-?inglīz/ which combines MSA elements such as lā + non-past tense in close-to-MSA MPP (na?mal), lā + preposition, lexical collocation (l-?umma l-'arabiyya) and multilevel complementiser ?an.

B. The dialectal system
In the BGI system, negative dialectal particles occur with BGI and close-to-BGI verbs in BGI and mixed sequences.

1 completed past action: there are 5 occurrences of mā + past tense with close-to-BGI verbs in BGI occurrences as in:

SH1 l.15 /wa ma'a d̲h̲ālika tis'atās̲h̲ sana wa 'abdunnāṣir ?allah yirḥamah mā gdar yintidj qunbula nawawiyya/ where mā cooccurs with phoneme [g], close-to-BGI MPP of verb yirḥamah and a verb string (gdar yintidj).

2 present action: there are 20 occurrences of mā + non-past tense with close-to-BGI and BGI verbs in BGI sequences mainly with a few mixed ones as in:

SH2 l.75 /xāridj ?arḍna mā nigdar nuwādjih il-djays̲h̲ il-?amirikī/ in which mā cooccurs with BGI elements such as phoneme [g] < OA /q/, close-to-BGI MPP (nigdar) and verb string (nigdar nuwādjih) and MSA elements such as close-to-MSA MPP (nuwādjih).

In the following sequence, mā cooccurs with BGI elements such as close-to-BGI MPP (nidji), deletion and prosthetisation of vowel (ns̲h̲ūf):

SH3 l.45 /lākin mā nidjī musabbaqan nitraddad nigūl xalli ns̲h̲ūf ?awwil marra/

Adverbs, however, such as musabbaqan, found in the dialect with a full ending, do not confer an MSA flavour to the sequence;

according to Heath,[40] adverbs with suffix -an are a Classical Arabic borrowing into the dialect.

3 Equational sentences: There are 6 occurrences of dialectally marked mū + nominal clause in BGI sequences:

SH1 l.77 /mū ḍiddi n-nās ?illi yistaxdimūn i<u>dh</u>-<u>dh</u>arra li l-?a<u>gh</u>rād is-silmiyya/ where mū cooccurs with ?illi and the close-to-BGI MPP of the verb (yistaxdamūn). As said previously, interdental <u>dh</u> is BGI and not an MSA realisation as would be the case in CA.

There are 3 occurrences of mā + preposition 'idna used to convey the idea of possession:

SH2 l.29 /lākin bi <u>sh</u>akil 'ām mā 'idna ṣu'ūbāt ni<u>sh</u>kū minha fī mawḍū'/ which combine dialectal features such as close-to-BGI MPP (ni<u>sh</u>kū) and dialectal localism ('idna).

4 negative command: there are 2 occurrences of lā + non-past tense in BGI sequences as negative commands:

SH2 l.58 /gulnā lkum lā ti<u>dj</u>ibūn ?ilna l-?amrikān tunṭūnhum il-qawā'id l-?a<u>dj</u>nabiyya/ This sequence shows BGI cooccurrences such as phoneme [g], close-to-BGI MPP of verbs (ti<u>dj</u>ibūn), preposition ?ilna instead of MSA ?ilaynā, and localism tunṭūn.

Hybrid negative structures
There are a few exemples of hybrid negative structures:

1 MSA particle lam + close-to-BGI MPP of a non-past tense verb in a BGI sequence (1 occurrence):

SH4 l.45 /wa gulnā lah bi wuḍūḥ mā lam yit'āla<u>dj</u>/

2 MSA particle lā + close-to-BGI MPP of a non-past tense verb in mixed and BGI sequences (6 occurrences):

SH1 l.11 /fā n-nās ?illi lā yiḥsinūn ?illā rukūb il-<u>dj</u>imāl kēf mumkin ?innu yinti<u>dj</u> qunbula nawawiyya/

3 BGI particle mū + MSA complement (faqaṭ instead of BGI bass) where the level changes within the correlative coordination (MSA has laysa...faqaṭ wa ?innamā, 1 occurrence):

SH2 l.26 /mū <u>dj</u>ay<u>sh</u> 'irāqī faqaṭ wa ?innamā <u>dj</u>ay<u>sh</u> il-?umma l-'arabiyya/

Other aspects of hybridization will be discussed below.

Complementiser ?an

In the BGI dialect, complementiser ?an has a status different from what one observes in the Egyptian and Libyan data where ?an is an MSA marker (CA and TA using the dialectal counterparts ?inn and asyndetic verb strings). Our Iraqi data show that ?an is multilevel and shared between MSA and BGI; lack of ?an is, in most cases, a dialect marker, but its use is not necessarily an MSA marker. Hence ?an can be followed by MSA and BGI features: in the Iraqi data, there are 31 MSA sequences with ?an plus MSA or close-to-MSA verbs. ?an cooccurs with MSA features such as preformative ya- and MPP of verb, usually without ?i'rāb, e.g. ?an yuwadjdjih, ?an yuntidj, MSA phoneme q (?an tafqudhu), passive voice (?an yuḥtaram). There is one rare case of a subjunctive ending (?an nuwaffira). ?an cooccurs with other MSA features in MSA sequences as in:

> *SH1 l.21* /qābila ?an tuhzam ?akthar min il-?umma l-mutamakkina 'ilmiyyan/ where ?an cooccurs with close-to-MSA verb and passive voice (tuhzam), phoneme q (qābila) and ?i'rāb ('ilmiyyan).

Among these 31 occurrences of ?an in MSA sequences, there are 7 occurrences of the fixed expression yanbaghī ?an + verb in a close-to-MSA MPP. The dialect, however, uses a different collocation, the expression lāzim + verb and a close-to-BGI MPP as in lāzim yikūn 'indak taṣawwur and, lāzim tisḥab quwwātik, to express this idea of obligation.

There are, however, 14 mixed sequences with ?an and close-to-BGI verbs. This combination of ?an and dialectal features is found in BGI and not in CA or TA.

> *SH4 l.39* /dūn ?an yis?alūn nafishum ?innu lēsh siktaw humma sab'a sinīn il-'irāq yiṣtari' ma'a shāh ?īrān/ In this BGI sequence, ?an cooccurs here with close-to-BGI MPP (yis?alūn), BGI morphology of nouns CvCvC (for MSA CvCC) as in nafis for MSA nafs, interrogative particle (lēsh), BGI suffix and MPP of verb (siktaw).

Asyndetic verb strings

BGI sequences have characteristic asyndetic verb strings (16 occurrences in dialectal sequences) from which complementiser

?an has disappeared. These complementiserless verb strings contain dialectal and "shared" verbs with a close-to-BGI MPP, e.g. garrab yintidj, yiḥāwlūn yiṭfūnha, nigdar insawwi and nrīd nḥuṭṭ, BGI elements cooccur such as preformative yi- and MPP of verb (yintidj), BGI ending ūn (yiṭfūn), deletion of unstressed vowel (yiḥāwlūn), phoneme [g] < OA /q/ (garrab), deletion and prosthetisation of vowel (insawwi), dialectal lexicon (nḥuṭṭ). There are 16 occurrences of asyndetic verb strings in dialectal sequences, e.g.:

> *SH2 l.30* /wa ba'ḍ il-ḥalaqāt ?illi l-?ittiḥād is-sūfyētī yigul mā 'indi ?aw mā ?agdar ?azawwidkum biha nrūḥ nāxidhha min id-duwal/

The Iraqi data also show a few cases (5) of the future particle rāḥ (MSA equivalent sa-) where rāḥ is followed by a non-past tense verb, as in:

> *SH1 l.97* /?inna l-?umma ?illi yi'ādīha rāḥ yishūfha l-yōm bi shakil/

gādrīn inwādjih is an asyndetic participle string whereas the MSA participle, when the speaker uses it, is followed by a preposition (qādir 'ala):

contrast: *SH2 l.73* /tara ?iḥna gādrīn inwādjih il-?adjnabī ḥatta lō kān/
with: *SH1 l.45* /...?inna l-?umma l-'arabiyya sataṣbaḥ qādira 'ala t-ta'āmul ma'a l-'ilm../

From the three syntactic features examined (the negative system, complementiser ?an and the asyndetic verb strings), one observes that negative particle mā + non-past tense is found to cooccur with BGI and close-to-BGI verbs only. The most recurrent hybrid forms is MSA particle lā + close-to-BGI verb which is explained by the fact that preformative yi- may penetrate higher levels of formality. Complementiser ?an is multivalent between MSA and the BGI dialect and can be followed by a verb with MSA or BGI features. Asyndetic verb strings, on the other hand, combine with dialectal elements mainly and occur in dialectal and mixed sequences.

4.3.4 Lexical features

The present section is concerned with the lexicon in MSA and BGI passages.

A. MSA sequences

In MSA sequences, lexicon contains many abstract concepts and is of a political, journalistic nature as expected in a press conference, with many occurrences of fixed collocations such as:

qunbula nawawiyya	"atomic bomb"
ḥisābāt daqīqa	"accurate calculations"
nās 'uqqāl	"sensible people"
minṭaqa dimuqrāṭiyya	"democratic region"
ḥāla mutaqaddima	"forward situation"
qanā'a qawmiyya	"national satisfaction"
qawanīn dawliyya	"international laws"

These expressions appear as frozen "chunks" of language and could be heard on the news on TV as well as in an informal conversation; they do not confer a formalising effect on any passage in which they occur although clearly they are more likely to occur in educated than uneducated speakers' speech.

B. BGI sequences

BGI passages are characterized, as expected, by BGI lexicon such as:

- the BGI verbs seen earlier, which combine BGI MPP elements and occur frequently in verb strings, insawwi "we do", yirūḥ "he goes", yishūf "he sees", yunṭēna "you give us";
- items with BGI phoneme ō as in dōl "those", bilghōh "they reached it", nō' "sort", yōm "day", nlōm "we blame", lō "if";
- items with dialectal phoneme ē as in bēn "between", ?iltaqēt "I met", ghēr "other", lēsh "why";
- where MSA has waqt "time", BGI has wakit with BGI phoneme [k] < OA /q/ and the application of a no final consonant cluster rule. This "no final consonant cluster rule" applies to many items throughout the lexicon: where MSA has CvCC as in 'ilm "knowledge", ?ism "name", BGI has CiCiC morphology as in 'ilim, ?isim.
- Other items include localisms wiyyāhum "with them", ?aku "there is", shwakit "when", and various dialectal items such as shi "thing", niḥin "we", hnāk "there is", bass "only", 'idna and 'inna "we have", hīč "like this", ?illi "that"; this last element ?illi is multilevel because of its widespread use in formal contexts and mixed sequences as in:

SH1 l.31 /wa lā yaḥtādjūn ?ilā l-waṣiyy ?illi yaḍrubhum bi l-'aṣā/ where relative pronoun ?illi cooccurs with MSA elements such as close-to-MSA MPP of verbs (yahtādjūn), negative particle lā and connective wa.

The agreement system
The lexicon, moreover, plays a major role in influencing the noun-adjective agreement system: because of its MSA lexical status, an abstract noun with the adjective following it triggers MSA agreement patterns.[41] A BGI item (in a more concrete, conversational style) should, in theory, induce a dialectal agreement rule with the adjective. Reasons for this consistent MSA agreement system are due to the subject-matter and setting of the discourse (a press conference on international policies and international affairs) which involves a complex, abstract, non-specific political jargon. However, throughout the data, even in dialectal passages, the noun-adjective agreement system applied corresponds to grammar-book MSA rules. BGI rules allow (1) a plural adjective following an impersonal plural noun, as in byūt ?ikbār "big houses",[42] and (2) a feminine plural human noun with a masculine plural adjective as in l-banāt kullish mashghulīn "the girls are very busy".[43] However, there are no such BGI examples in the data. All cases show MSA rules: impersonal plural noun and a feminine singular adjective (qaḍāya ?asāsiyya, l-mabādi? l-wāḍiha), and no case in our data of feminine plural human noun and feminine plural adjective. There are some cases of plural in -āt, and these take only MSA agreement, i.e. feminine singular adjective[44] as in ḥisābāt daqīqa, ṭā?irāt 'arabiyya, 'ilaqāt thunā?iyya; in BGI, broken plurals are possible in such noun-adjective combinations.

It is interesting to see that the agreement system conforms to the MSA rules throughout the data, with no case of hybridization for instance, i.e. a crossing between features from different levels.[45] Hybridization is an important aspect of variation as it is produced by cooccurrence rules which are part of one's communicative competence and tacit knowledge, and not recorded in any grammar. Hybridization shows the flexibility of the internal system of a language: in morphophonology for instance, verbs show a few hybrids between MSA and BGI. In syntax, there are a few cases of negative hybrid constructions (8 occurrences in the data). Multivalent complementiser ?an combines with MSA and BGI elements such as preformative yi- and close-to-BGI verbs in 14 sequences, while the agreement system, which is lexically determined, remains MSA throughout the discourse and does not produce any hybrid forms.[46] These results suggest that the cooccurrence rules have different degrees of flexibility and feasibility, and some parts of the linguistic system, such as the agreement rules, are less amenable to variation than others.

4.4 LANGUAGE FORM AND LANGUAGE FUNCTION

The previous sections were concerned with the analytical description of linguistic elements from the data. It appears that Saddam Hussein uses MSA, BGI and mixed forms in different parts of his speech. Variation, it will be argued, does not occur randomly but according to some tacit "rules" and this section is concerned with relating language form and language function. What is Saddam Hussein trying to achieve through his discourse, what is the aim of his speech and how is this affecting the way he speaks?

I have already distinguished between the ideational, interpersonal and textual aspects of discourse.[47] As in most political speeches, the speaker is trying to involve his audience. Saddam Hussein switches between MSA and BGI, it would appear, because dialectal Arabic and MSA have different symbolic and interpersonal values; besides, as in most speeches, the nature of the content which he wishes to mediate to the audience(s) is not always the same. As in the Egyptian discourse, it is possible to subdivide the speech and identify its aims.

At the ideational level, whenever Saddam Hussein is making political points, or when he is recalling historical events, exposing and setting Iraq's position among international powers, he uses MSA. Referring to the issues discussed earlier on involvement vs. detachment, the MSA discourse is characterized by abstractness, compactness, formality, detachment, planning and integration. Interpersonally, Saddam Hussein is at the same time distancing himself from the audience as he is preaching to the crowd, Europeans and Arabs included. He distances himself by using the third person ("he" or "they"). He adds weight to his words by giving a moral to his story, through general abstract statements, proverbs and philosophy; he organises and plans his discourse through more complex syntax (e.g. using more subordinate clauses, nominalised structures, passives).

Formally, such discourse is expressed by:

- MSA phonology, notably [q] < OA /q/ and [k] < OA /k/;
- MSA morphophonology of verbs, future tense prefix sa- + non-past tense verb, and ?i'rāb occasionally;
- long nominal phrases, MSA negative particles, maṣdars, long sentences with subordinate clauses and word order (verb and subject);
- Lexically, abstract vocabulary, and an MSA lexicon triggering an MSA noun-adjective agreement.

The tempo tends to be slow, with an average of 1.5 words per second, falling tonal nuclei and long pauses. Stylistic features and rhetorical ornamentation in the form of repetitive routines, paranomasia and assonance are used to appeal to the audience's aesthetic sense, though the usages are not particularly original. The MSA sections of the speech are apparently based on a written text, or at least a written plan, despite the fact that the answers are supposedly in response to "unprepared" questions.

Functions of the BGI dialect, on the other hand, parallel functions of CA and Tripoli Arabic (TA). BGI dialect is used when the speech becomes more specific: Saddam Hussein explains and in particular repeats some concepts uttered in MSA to emphasise them, and make sure they are understandable to the audience. The discourse here becomes exegetical. Interpersonally, the BGI discourse is characterized by speaker involvement, apparent spontaneity, a greater degree of personalisation, and in general these sequences sound unplanned and more natural. The use of 1st and 2nd persons pronouns ("you and me", "us") becomes more frequent as the speaker explains the Iraqi position vis-à-vis foreign powers. As the speaker tries to get closer to his audience, sound friendly and get the discourse livelier, he consciously imitates the conversational style ideationally: very often, he transforms political issues into an anecdotal, everyday conversation, personifying countries, recounting in simple words discussions between leaders and the position he defended so as to gain audience rapport and support. BGI Arabic occurs also in certain particular discourse moves: asides, story telling, rhetorical questions, and in "organisational discourse". Saddam Hussein uses a lot of reported speech which is a way of making the discourse more vivid by imitating an ordinary chat. All of these points are illustrated in the extracts section below.

BGI passages are characterized linguistically by the following features:

- Phonologically, BGI phoneme [g] < OA /q/ and a few cases of [č] < OA /k/.
- Morphophonologically, preformative yi-, the BGI MPP of verbs, lack of ?i'rāb, multilevel -ūn ending for the 3rd plural non-past tense, deletion and prosthetisation of vowels, deletion of unstressed vowels and of the glottal stop with a lengthening of the vowel, resyllabication.
- Syntactically, BGI negative particles, asyndetic verb strings, shorter sentences, subject-verb word order.
- Lexically, BGI passages are characterized by localisms, concrete, everyday vocabulary, phatic words and low lexical density (fewer content words per clause).

Paralinguistically, BGI passages have a conversational, extempore style with hesitations and repetitions, a fast tempo (with an average of 2.9 words per second), and BGI intonation occasionally. At times, an argumentative tone of voice or one of protest is used to display publicly the speaker's commitment and to unify the audience in its indignation at the criticisms uttered, and a more friendly and conversational style to trigger solidarity and communion. There follows a series of extracts which display the various level shifts.

4.4.1 Extracts

Extract 1 *SH1 l.4 to 9*
The press conference began with a journalist's questions on the development of the Iraqi nuclear technology and whether Israel had been undermining the Iraqi efforts to reach that goal. Although Saddam Hussein's answer is at first formal, BGI elements appear afterwards in the following passage under analysis.

> 1 /tigūl ?inna l-'arab <u>dh</u>ōl nās mutaxallifīn/ mā yifhamūn il-'ilim/ mā hum mu<u>th</u>aqqafīn/ mā yidirkūn mas?uliyāthum tidjāh nafishum/ 2 wa li<u>dh</u>ālik/ maṭlūb ?an yikūn 'alēhum waṣiyy u hā<u>dh</u>a l-waṣiyy lam/ (pause)/ yat'āmal wiyyāhum bi l-'aṣa l-<u>gh</u>alīẓa/ wa ?innu <u>dh</u>ōl il-'arab nās lā yuḥsinūn ?illā rukūb il-<u>dj</u>imāl/ wa l-bukā? 'ala l-?aṭlāl/ wa n-nawm bi l-xiyām/ 3 ?alaysa hā<u>dh</u>a ṣaḥīḥ/
> [Zionist quarters] say that Arabs are backward people, who do not understand science nor culture and do not realize their

responsibility toward themselves. And this is why a governor has to be appointed (pause) who would use a cudgel to deal with them since after all these Arabs are people who can only ride camels, weep upon ruins and sleep under tents. Isn't that true?

Variation occurs in three stages from BGI to mixed style to MSA. In 1, the speaker levels down his style to BGI as he recounts and lists criticisms made by the Zionist quarters towards the Arabs; by shifting to BGI, Saddam Hussein puts himself on the same level as all Iraqis, talking as one of them "this is what they say about us, that we are all backward, uneducated people". The offence of the criticism is conveyed more effectively through BGI than if it would have been in abstract, distant MSA terms. The speaker wants to provoke the audience and trigger their indignation vis-à-vis this accusation. He hopes to create a sense of involvement, solidarity and unity among Iraqis in front of this foreign interference on national policies. Paralinguistically, the stylistic repetition in 1 of the mā + non past tense structure creates an effect of listing the different faults of the Arabs.

In 2, there is a change to a mixed style and a distancing in the discourse as Saddam Hussein acts as a witness, a spokesman of the discussions held between foreign countries about the Arabs and of the decisions taken on their behalf since "they do not realize their responsibility toward themselves, a governor has to be appointed". 1 and 2 are contrasted by MSA 3: "isn't that true?" an MSA rhetorical question which challenges the audience, stimulates them and begs them for a reaction. To achieve this, the speaker uses this spurious, deliberatly ironical question which sounds very formal, too formal even (compared to the BGI mū hīč that might have been expected and that Saddam Hussein uses on another occasion when talking to his assistant on the platform, see mā hīč in extract 9). Arabs are said to be backward people, so how come they can speak in such a formal way? is an implication of the passage at another level.

Textually, 1 is BGI with the concurrence of elements such as phoneme [g] < OA /q/ (tigūl), noun morphology CiCiC ('ilim), close-to-BGI MPP of the verb with -ūn ending (yifhamūn), negative particle mā and non past tense verb, resyllabication of the verb (yidirkūn) as well as form I of the verb instead of IV (MSA yudrikūn), lexical item with BGI phoneme ō (<u>dh</u>ōl). In 2, there is a slight levelling up with MSA elements such as preformative ya- and close-to-MSA MPP of the verb (yuḥsinūn). BGI elements occur as preformative yi- (yikūn), deletion of unstressed vowel (yat'āmal), connective u for MSA wa, lexical element such as dhōl (interdental dh is BGI) and localism wiyyāhum (MSA has ma'ahum). The last sequences in 2 are already MSA, and the statement in 3 adds a formal, ironical note to the passage.

Extract 2 *SH1 l.33-37*
In this passage, Saddam Hussein addresses the Zionist quarters and questions their actions and reasoning:

> /?idhā kānat l-kiyān iṣ-ṣahyūniy yuqaddir ?inna l-?umma l-'arabiyya bada?at marḥalat in-nuhūḍ/ limādhā n-nās il-'uqqāl fī hādhā l-kiyān lā yaḥsibūn ḥisābāt daqīqa li l-mustaqbal/ kayfa mumkin ?an yitaṣawwarū ?innu mumkin ?an ya'īshū fī/ dāxil l-?umma/ tanhaḍ 'ilmiyyan ?ilā l-ḥaddi ?illi ṣāru yatḥaddathu 'anhā/ bi?annaha satamtalik l-qunbula dh-dharriyya fī wakit qaṣīr/
> If the Zionist entity realizes that the Arab nation is in a phase of renaissance, why do not the sensible people of that entity draw precise calculations for the future? How can they conceive that it is possible for them to live in the midst of a nation in such a state of scientific awakening that they are talking about whether it might possess the atomic bomb in the near future.

The extract is in a MSA high-flown style with abstract concepts such as marḥalat in-nuhūḍ "phase of renaissance". The initiators of the action are impersonal terms: the "Zionist entity", "the Arab nation". As it questions the Zionist position, the passage is meant too for the foreign journalists who are the "link" between Iraq and foreign powers "do not listen to them, we cannot be that backward if we are about to manufacture the atomic bomb", he seems to be saying. Throughout the MSA passage, the speaker is organising his discourse by the use of conditionals (?idhā) and rhetorical questions (limādhā and kayfa mumkin "how is it possible") to present his case and challenge the audience. As the speaker is building his argument, he organizes his discourse so that the audience can follow the development of his thought (if ... then why ... and how is it possible that ...). This discourse organizing adds logic and reasoning to the argument and gives it credibility.

Linguistically, MSA elements combine: phoneme [q] (yuqaddir), close-to-MSA MPP of verb (yaḥsibūn), lexical items with the MSA lexical enclitic -at (bada?at), MSA negative particle lā + non past tense verb, and the construction mumkin, ?i'rāb occasionally, MSA particle sa + non past tense indicating future tense (whereas BGI would have rāḥ/ rāyiḥ and non past tense), and MSA collocations (l-qunbula dh-dharriyya). The passage also involves stylistic features such as paranomasia in yaḥsibūn ḥisābāt. There are a few BGI elements such as localism wakit and preformative yi- (yitaṣawwarū) which, together with the relative pronoun ?illi, are multilevel and found at higher levels than "plain" BGI.

What follows is a repetition of the same idea (still in MSA) in different terms, "the Zionist entity should revise its position" and Saddam Hussein ends this justification of the Iraqi position by advising Europeans to review their position:

> /yanbaghī ?an yuwadjdjah hādha s-su?āl min qibalkum ?ilā kull il-muta'āṭifīn ma'a l-kiyān iṣ-ṣahyūniy/ wa ?ilā kull iṣ-ṣahāyina fī l-gharb/
> This question should be addressed to all those who sympathise with the Zionist entity and to all the Zionists in the West. *SH1 l.41*

Because he is apparently giving advice to a European audience, Saddam Hussein symbolically distances himself through the use of a formal register. The level is MSA with the cooccurrence of the fixed expression yanbaghī, complementiser ?an and subjunctive, MSA "internal" passive MPP (yuwadjdjah), phoneme q (qibal), agent passive structure (min qibal) and MSA collocation (l-kiyān iṣ-ṣahyūniy).

Extract 3 *SH1 l.87-90*
Parallelism in construction is often used in MSA passages of the discourse to create a dramatic effect of build up and climax:

> /?innu lā yumkin ?an yaḥmi ?istiqlālah/ lā yumkin ?an yaḥmi sharafa/ fī 'ālami l-yawm/ lā yumkin ?an yaḥmi ḥuqūqah/ ?illa 'indama yablugh/ martaba mutawāzina ma'a t-taṭawwur l-'ilmi fī l-'ālam/
> It is not possible to protect independence, honor and law nowadays, without reaching a level of scientific development in balance with that of the rest of the world.

In this bombastic extract, lā yumkin ?an yaḥmi is repeated three times with political concepts and abstract terms: ?istiqlāl "independence", sharaf "honor", ḥuqūq "law", and martaba mutawāzina "balanced level" while the listing adds a sense of inexorability to the content.

Linguistically, MSA elements cooccur, with the negative particle lā and non past verb, phoneme q < OA /q/ (ḥuqūqah), complementiser ?an, phoneme aw (yawm), close-to-MSA MPP of verbs (yaḥmi), maṣdar (taṭawwur) and MSA collocations (martaba mutawāzina).

Extract 4 *SH2 l.6-11*

/1 daraḏjat ṣadāqatna ma'a l-?ittiḥād is-sūfyētī ghayr daraḏjat ṣadāqatna ma'a ?axarīn min id-duwali l-?ishtirākiyya/ wa hāḏha ṣ-ṣadāqa turattibha/ it-taṣawwurāt il-istrātiḏjiyya/ li ḥudūd maṣlaḥati l-?umma wa ṭarīqat xidmatha/ bi l-?iḍāfa ?ila l-?iltiqā? 'ala nuqāṭ markazīyya/ ḍudd 'aduw mushtarak /2 fa l-?ittiḥād is-sūfyētī ṣadīqna/ kān wa mā zāl/ 3 naḥrus 'ala ṣadāqatna ma'ah wa yiḥris 'ala ṣadāqtah wiyyāna/
Our friendship with the Soviet Union is different from our friendship with other socialist countries. And this friendship has been arranged according to strategic considerations of national interest and service, as well as agreeing on central points, against a common enemy. And the Soviet Union is our friend. It has been and still is the case. We are concerned about our friendship with them as they are with theirs for us.

This extract is interesting as it shows MSA used in 1 as Saddam Hussein is recounting historical facts and explaining Iraqi-Soviet relations. The speaker takes this opportunity to justify the alliance with the Soviet Union "we are on friendly terms with them because of our common strategic interests and our common enemy". Although he is here addressing Iraqis, he is merely rehearsing supposedly well-known facts. 2, still in MSA, is a repetition of what has been said before, it is a fixed expression and works as a transition with what follows. 3 is a conclusive statement with a levelling down in the style as the countries are personified and the reciprocal nature of the relationship is stressed. The political and commercial agreement is thus brought to a more conversational and personalised level. The same idea is repeated in BGI further down, ?iḥna ma'a l-?aṣdiqā? mālna "we are with our friends", with the very dialectal use of māl.

Textually, 1 is MSA with elements such as phoneme [q] < OA /q/, diphthong ay (ghayr), close-to-MSA MPP of verb (turattib), ?iḍāfa (ṭarīqat xidmatha), MSA collocations and abstract vocabulary (it-taṣawwurāt il-istrātiḏjiyya). 3 is BGI with elements such as close-to-BGI MPP (yiḥris) and localism (wiyyāna).

Extract 5 *SH2 l.24 to 27*

> /1 lammā ya'djaz il-?ittiḥād is-sūfyētī ?aw li ?asbāb tit'allaq bih/ 2 mā yunṭēna ḥalaqa min ḥalaqāt taslīḥ nrūḥ infattish 'an ?ayyi dawla bi l-'ālam 'an hādhi l-ḥalaqa wa nsalliḥ bihi djayshnā ḥatta yakūn/ 3 mū djaysh 'irāqī faqaṭ wa ?innamā djaysh il-?umma l-'arabiyya/
>
> When the Soviet Union, for reasons of its own, is unable to provide us with armament, we go and look for it in any nation in the world and we provide our army with it so that it becomes not just the army of Iraq but also the army of the whole Arab nation.

This passage is an example of how the speaker organizes his discourse through a "complex" syntax by using framing elements such as lammā "when". Conjunctions such as lammā or kamā and conditional ?idhā exist of course in the dialect, but in our data, they tend to occur in passages where the speaker develops an argument. In 2 and 3, changing from a slow tempo in 1 (1.2 words per second), to a faster one (2.7 words per second), the discourse becomes more direct and familiar with the use of the "we" pronoun, to stress the ordinary aspect of his argument "if they cannot give us what we want, then we go somewhere else". The last sequence (3) is mixed as the speaker switches within it from BGI to MSA, producing a hybrid construction with the correlative coordination (mū faqaṭ wa ?innamā). The passage ends on a grandiloquent note with MSA elements; as Saddam Hussein is speaking now for the whole Arab nation "our army will defend not only Iraq but the entire Arab nation as well", because of the symbolism involved, his style cannot be too local, so he switches to MSA.

Linguistically, 1 is a mixed sequence which starts with MSA elements as conjunction lammā, close-to-MSA MPP of verb (ya'djaz) and ends with BGI preformative ti- and deletion of unstressed vowel (tit'allaq). 2 is BGI with the combination of negative particle mā + non past tense, deletion and prosthetisation of vowel (infattish), complex verb form (nrūḥ infattish, rāḥ indicating futurity) and the dialectal lexical choices of nrūḥ and infattish. 3 is mixed with the hybrid combination of BGI negative particle mū and MSA elements faqaṭ wa ?innamā.

The same idea of trade between countries is repeated again below, where the Soviet Union is personified, and political and commercial transactions are brought down to an everyday conversation between a customer and a shopkeeper in the form of a reported speech with a fast tempo (3 words per second):

> /... l-?ittiḥād is-sūfyētī yigul mā 'indi ?aw mā ?agdar azawwid-kum biha nrūḥ nāxidhha min id-duwal/
> when the Soviet Union says: "I don't have [armament] or cannot provide you with it", we go and take it from [other] countries. *l.31*

Extract 6 *SH3 l.6 to 9*

> /na'taqid ?innu/ hādha l-muxaṭṭaṭ/ ?illi huwa muxaṭṭaṭ kamb dēfid/ ?alḥaqa ?adhā/ kabīr bi l-?umma l-'arabiyya/ wa li dhālik yanbaghī ?an yuṭawwaq/ wa tuqallal l-?āthār in-nafsiyya wa l-fi'liyya/ il-muḍādda li l-?umma l-'arabiyya wa li sh-sha'b/ wa li sh-sha'b il-'arabī/
> We believe that Camp David has caused great damage to the Arab nation and therefore it should be limited to alleviate its psychological and actual effects hostile to the Arab nation and to all the Arab people.

In this passage, Saddam Hussein is criticizing the events at Camp David, putting himself forward as the defender of the Arab nation, and commenting on its morality. Performed in MSA, this formal statement adds authoritativeness to the argument that "since Camp David has harmed the Arab nation, these are the measures that should be taken". The passage is characterized by markedly MSA collocations (?alḥaqa ?adhan "it caused damage", yanbaghī ?an yuṭawwaq wa tuqallal "it should be limited and (its effects) lessened". This extract, uttered slowly (1.6 words per second), combines MSA elements such as phoneme [q], close-to-MSA MPP of verb (na'taqid), passive forms (yuṭawwaq), long nominal phrases (l-?āthār in-nafsiyya wa l-fi'liyya), collocations (l-?umma l-'arabiyya) and lexical choices (yuṭawwaq).

Extract 7 *SH4 l.1 to 3*

> /ba'd ?ittifāq il-djazā?ir/ ?illi ẓurūfa l-xāṣṣa biēnna u bēn ?īrān/ zurit ?īran/ wa ltaqēt ma'a shā ?īrān/ wa gult lah bi wuḍūḥ il-?ān il-'ilāqa biēnna wa bēnak mā 'ādat 'ilāqat ḥarb/
> After the Algiers agreement which had its own circumstances for us and Iran, I visited Iran and met with the Shah and said to him very frankly that the relation between us is no longer that of war.

In this extract, Saddam Hussein recounts a conversation he had with the Shah in a reported speech format, and he levels down his style to BGI to make the content more understandable to the audience. The passage is pitched in the conversational style of a first person narrative (I went to Iran, I said to him). BGI elements concur such as phoneme g < OA /q/, close-to-BGI MPP of verb zurit, long vowel ē for ay, connective u. Moreover, I would like to point out the use of the dialectal feature [ie] in the word biēnna. [ie], a close front gliding, is another dialectal reflex, together with ē < MSA/ OA /ay/, and found in certain "consonant environments".[48] The form ē as in bēn, is a much more widespread, pan-Arabic form than [ie], which would categorize the item as BGI or Mesopotamian in Ingham's terms. Overall, in the Iraqi data, apart from a few cases of [ie], long vowel ē is found since it is more appropriate for this kind of discourse. To go back to our extract, further on, when Saddam Hussein is talking more impersonally of Iran-Iraq bilateral relations, a more distant stance is struck and there is a language shift to MSA:

> /ḥatta wi l-'ilāqāt ith-thunā?iyya suwwiyat bi ṭ-ṭarīqa llati suwwiyat fīh/
> even after mutual relations were straightened out.

with MSA collocations, close-to-MSA passive verbs (suwwiyat). Later on, Saddam Hussein reverts once more to a more direct, anecdotal style, when giving the Shah's answer. This is pitched at an appropriately lower formal level:

> /wa wāfaq shā ?irān 'ala hādhi l-mabādi?/ gāl ?ana l-?ān fawran musta'idd ?awaqqi'/
> and the Shah argued on those principles and said: "I am now prepared to sign immediately".

Finally, the speaker concludes by depersonalising once again and there is a concomitant switch to MSA:

> /yanbaghī ?an tunāqash hādhihi ma'a l-'arab/ fī l-xalīdj/
> This issue should be discussed with the Arabs from the Gulf.

This whole extract, from lines 1 to 21, shows the speaker's desire to present the discourse in a progressive, logical sequence and to underline his role, i.e. "I said this and then he said that and, as a conclusion, this should be discussed among the Arabs". This type of text development is intended to give the audience an insight into "real politics" as if it is all happening in front of them. The story telling in particular, produces a sense of involvement and makes the discourse livelier, and, to a less educated person, more comprehensible.

The following short extracts illustrate further uses of MSA/ BGI for different functions of the language.

Extract 8 *SH2 l.16*

In a line of poetry, MSA is used with homespun philosophy, as in:

> 1 /'idna sha'ār yigūl/2 ?iksib ṣadīqaka bi l-bayyina [...] qabla ?an tafqudhu bi l-ghumūḍ/
> We have a proverb that says: Win your friend with clarity before you lose him with ambiguity.

The first sequence is BGI, as if deliberately the speaker drops the level before giving an MSA sequence, and the "proverb" itself is a levelling up with stressed words at regular intervals and a pause in the middle. Linguistically, 1 is BGI with pronoun 'idna and MPP of verb (preformative yi-, phoneme g in yigūl). 2 is MSA with preformative ta-, phoneme q (tafqud).

Extract 9 *SH4 l.24-25*

Finally, BGI is used as the speaker is asking for feedback and confirmation of his point to the person next to him:

> /fa lammā 'uqid mu?tamar fī 'umān/ mā hīč yā duktūr/ fī 'umān/ fī l-wizārā l-xāridjiyya ṭuriḥat ba'ḍ il-?afkār min hādhā n-nō'/
> And when the conference was held in Oman, isn't it so Doctor, issues of this sort were submitted in the ministry of Foreign Affairs

The BGI aside with the use of the particle mā and phoneme č < OA /k/ contrasts with the rest of the passage which is in MSA (phoneme q < OA /q/ and passive verbs ('uqid, ṭuriḥat)), and adds a more personal aspect to the MSA passage. In order to be more effective, this aside had to be in a different level of formality and the speaker is addressing his neighbour directly. It is interesting to compare the same organisational move occurring in the first extract but in different levels of formality, where a similar statement (?a laysa hādha ṣaḥīḥ), is pronounced in MSA this time after BGI and mixed sequences, so as to engage the audience's attention.

This chapter consisted of an analysis of Arabic political discourse in a press conference, delivered by Saddam Hussein. The first part of the chapter dealt with an analytical description of the data and showed how MSA, BGI and intermediate levels were used in phonology, morphophonology, syntax and lexicon. Examples from the data showed how MSA and BGI elements concurred within items and combined with other features in a sequence. These cooccurrence rules were particularly interesting in cases of hybridization which indicated the limits of overlapping between MSA and BGI in various linguistic systems of morphophonology, syntax and lexicon, as well as the persistence of phonological, morphophonological and syntactic dialectal elements, within more formal levels. The second part of the chapter was concerned with the aims of the speaker in delivering his speech and I looked at language form in relation to functions of discourse. MSA was used when the speaker was distancing himself from the audience and giving authority to his "text", while some passages were explained and repeated in BGI to get the audience committed, involved and unified to the issues discussed.

NOTES

1 Based on an earlier version of this chapter, an article was published in Zeitschrift für arabische Linguistik 30 (1995).
2 see Lakoff 1981: 26.
3 Batatu 1978: 1079; Iraq: A Country Study 1990: xxiv, 58; Karsh and Rautsi 1991: 6. Miller and Mylroie (1990) give Saddam Hussein's birthplace as the village of al-Auja, near Tikrit, and hence an area where gelet Arabic is spoken. We believe nonetheless that the speaker is influenced by his Tikriti connections, and when he resorts to Baghdadi realisations, this is due to the fact that he lived more than 30 years in Baghdad – a gelet spoken area for the Muslim community.
4 Blanc 1964: 5–6.
5 see Batatu 1979: 244; Iraq: A Country Study 1990: 58.
6 Iraq: a Country Study 1990: xiv, Langley 1961: 13.
7 Langley 1961: 14.
8 see note 4 above.
9 Jastrow 1983.
10 Abu Haidar 1987: 41.
11 In an article published previously (see Mazraani 1995), I showed the opposition between prestigious Tikriti vs. dominant Baghdadi. I do not stress this opposition here as this would reinforce the case of convergence, i.e. the speaker imitating his audience's linguistic habits. As will be discussed below in the phonology section, the high occurrences of phoneme [q] from OA /q/ rather than BGI [g] should be linked to the formal level of the press conference, and thus the resort to MSA phonetic realisations in words with an MSA lexico-semantic status, rather than an evidence of qeltu Arabic.

12 Blanc 1964: 14–6.
13 Blanc 1964: 10.
14 Blanc 1964: 164–5; Johnstone 1975: 100–1.
15 Blanc 1964: 98–9, Johnstone 1975: 92–3.
16 see Blanc 1964: 27.
17 Ingham 1976: 72.
18 Ingham 1976: 71–3.
19 Al Ani 1978: 105.
20 Ibrahim 1986: 119.
21 Grotzfeld 1983.
22 Holes 1983a.
23 see note 19 above.
24 Trudgill 1986: 9.
25 Abu Haidar 1988: 75.
26 see El Dash and Tucker 1975: 42.
27 Heath 1989: 10.
28 Abd El Jawad 1986: 24.
29 Abd El Jawad and Awwad 1987: 80.
30 see Owens and Bani-Yasin 1987: 726.
31 see Holes 1995: 57.
32 Johnstone 1975 and Jastrow 1983.
33 Blanc 1964: 62.
34 see also Jastrow's discussion on prefixes ya-, ta-, na- (1983:106).
35 see Altoma 1969: 67.
36 see Erwin 1969: 126, Lecerf 1969: 161, Blanc 1964: 99, McCarthy and Raffouli 1964:47.
37 see Erwin 1969: 260.
38 see Van Ess 1938: 49, 55.
39 Cantarino 1974: 108; Holes 1995: 199.
40 Heath 1989: 225–6.
41 see Owens and Bani-Yasin 1987: 717.
42 see McCarthy and Raffouli 1964: 177 and Erwin 1963: 323.
43 Erwin 1969: 274.
44 see Owens and Bani-Yasin 1987: 711.
45 see Meiseles 1981: 1077.
46 compare similar comments in Owens and Bani-Yasin 1987:729.
47 see Halliday 1978: 31–5 and section 2.5 for a discussion of the concept of involvement.
48 see Ingham 1982: 79–80.

5 Form and Function in the Libyan data

This chapter is an analysis of variation in political speeches delivered by Muammar Al Gaddafi. As in chapters three and four, the first part is a description of linguistic features from the phonology (P), morphophonology (MPP), syntax (S) and lexicon (L), to determine the formal language levels used by Gaddafi. The second part of the chapter will relate language form to language function, and discuss the predictability of this relationship.

5.1 THE DATA AND MACRO-LEVEL CONTEXTUAL FACTORS

The data is based on two speech extracts delivered by the Libyan president Muammar al Gaddafi. The first extract, lasting twenty-four minutes, is set on the occasion of the "Solidarity Day with the Palestinian People" in 1981 (kalimat al-qā?id fī yawm at-taḍāmun al-'ālamī ma'a sh-sha'b al-falasṭīnī). This speech is supposed to be a plea in support of the bravery of the Palestinian people. Gaddafi wants to rally Libyans and all Arabs to support Palestinians and make the audience appreciate the danger of everyday life for the Palestinians facing Israeli aggression. In the presence of leading members of the PLO, the speaker refutes rumours of division between Libya and the PLO, reasserts Libyan support for the Palestinian cause and asks all Arabs to join him: Palestinians cannot fight with Israelis and Arabs at the same time and the latter should unite in common cause. Libya has adopted the Palestinian cause, its conflicts and ideals as its own. Because of its colonial past, Libya identifies with Palestinians as victims of foreign aggressions and Fatah's motives have become Libyan national ones.

The second extract, lasting thirteen minutes, is a sermon and an explanation of a sura of the Quran, delivered in a mosque on 26

May 1978 (xuṭba l-d̲jum'a allatī ?alqāha al-?ax al-qā?id bi masd̲jid mawlāya muḥammad wa s̲haraḥa fīhā sūrat al-qāri'a). The extract deals with a few verses from al-qāri'a, "the Calamity".

The main factors of the first extract consist of a speech delivered by Gaddafi to Libyans and Palestinians assembled in Tripoli (as to setting and participants) and the purpose of the speech is to reinforce and emphasise solidarity links between Libya and Palestinians (as to subject of discourse). The second extract is a sermon delivered in the Mawlāya Muhammad mosque and the speaker, who wants to be seen not only as a politician but also as a religious guide, explains some Quranic verses to a small gathering of Libyans. As will be shown in what follows, the two speech extracts mix levels of formality and display linguistic variation as they fulfill different functions of the language.

Following a description of sociolinguistic pattern in Libya, I will refer briefly to the main differences between the various Libyan dialects as well as to the speaker's linguistic background. The same procedure as in chapters three and four is followed.

5.2 SOCIOLINGUISTIC PATTERN IN LIBYA

Libya consists of three provinces, Cyrenaica, Tripolitania and the Fezzan, and is a conservative society in terms of the strong adherence to tribal values and pride in its Bedouin origin, although over the years the government has tried to settle the nomads. 70% of the population (3,014,100 in a 1978 estimate and 4,380,000 in 1989)[1] lives along the coastline of Tripoli and Cyrenaica. The coastal towns of Tripoli, Benghazi and al-Bayda are large ports which rapidly expanded with the discovery of petroleum in the 1950s, this changed the economy of the country drastically and propelled Libya onto the international stage. Tripoli and Benghazi are important political and economic centres. Finally, these three towns, Tripoli, Benghazi and al-Bayda house the television centres and radio stations.

Linguistically, the dialects spoken in Cyrenaica are the Eastern Libyan dialects, close to Egyptian Arabic, while the dialects spoken in the Fezzan and Tripolitania belong to the Maghribi group.[2] The Libyan linguistic situation can be seen in terms of the contrast between Tripoli Arabic (TA) and Benghazi Arabic / Cyrenaican Arabic (Cyr.A.). Benghazi Arabic represents the dialect generally spoken in Cyrenaica, although there are internal variations (see below). Tripoli Arabic is used in Tripolitania and understood, with the help of broadcasting means, by the majority of the population who lives along the coast. Because of this broadcasting power, Tripoli Arabic represents "Libyan Arabic" on the wider regional stage and can be assumed to be the non-standard standard, pervasive dialect in Libya. Firstly, I will point out the main differences between Eastern Libyan Arabic/ Benghazi Arabic on the one hand and the Maghribi group/ Tripoli Arabic on the other.

5.2.1 Tripoli Arabic and Cyrenaican/ Benghazi Arabic differences

El Fitoury,[3] in the preface of his study, mentions that Tripoli Arabic differs from Cyrenaican Arabic "particularly in its phonology", without however providing any examples. From what can be observed in the studies on Libyan Arabic,[4] there are no major consonantal differences between the two types apart from OA /dh/ which is [d] mainly in Tripoli Arabic and [dh] mainly in Cyrenaican Arabic (as in ?axad in TA and ?axadh in Cyr.A.), and OA /th/ which is [t] mainly in TA (occasionally th) and [th] mainly in Benghazi (Cyr. A.). Phonological differences in the vowels occur however between West and East Libyan Arabic dialects, as mentioned by Owens[5] with, for instance, kammal "he finished" in Benghazi and kammil in Tripoli, where a short vowel is raised in final, closed, unstressed syllables. These phonological features and the morphophonological examples given below, are distinctive from those of East and West Libyan dialects and will be significant later in the analytical description of variation and levels in Tripoli Arabic of the data.

Morphophonologically, variation between Tripoli Arabic and Cyrenaican Arabic occurs in verb formation. For the past tense, Tripoli Arabic has the pattern CCaC whereas Cyr.A. has CiCaC with, however, a resyllabication and an initial prosthetisation at the 3rd person feminine singular, 3rd feminine plural and 3rd masculine plural as in iktibat "she wrote", iktibu "they (m.) wrote" and iktiban "they (fem.) wrote". Resyllabication occurs since a sequence of two short open syllables is inadmissible,[6] and prosthetisation of a high vowel happens when a word starts with two consonants.[7] Hence Cyrenaican Arabic has:

- kitabat (underlyingly)

→ ktibat (deletion of the first unstressed vowel and raising of the second vowel)

→ iktibat (vowel insertion) "she wrote"

These phonological and morphophonological variants place Cyrenaican Arabic typologically in the Bedouin group of dialects which cover a wide area of Eastern Arab world, including places as far removed as the Gulf states.

Lexical enclitics differ as well, Cyrenaican Arabic having for the past tense -at (3rd fem.sg.) whereas Tripoli Arabic has -it. In Tripoli Arabic, with the vowel initiated enclitic (i.e. for the 3rd person singular and 3rd plural), there is a change and a resyllabication in the syllable patterns, with shurbit "she drank" and shurbu "they drank".

For the non-past tense, Tripoli Arabic has the CCvC pattern, with ni, ti, yi as preformatives and Ø, i, u as various endings of the lexical enclitics (see lexical enclitics in the morphophonology section below). As explained below (in the dialectal verbs), v is a or i, the preformative vowel being mainly i, except in cases of vowel harmony. Cyrenaican Arabic forms, on the other hand, show a resyllabication with a vowel initial enclitic in the 2nd feminine singular (tikitbi she wrote), 1st plural (nikitbu we wrote), 2nd masculine plural (tikitbu you wrote), 2nd feminine plural (tikitban you wrote), 3rd masculine plural (yikitbu they wrote) and 3rd feminine plural (yikitban they wrote), the other non-suffixed forms having the ni-ti-yi- CCiC pattern.

Whereas Tripoli Arabic and most dialects have a common gender for the 2nd and 3rd persons plural, Cyrenaican Arabic has different enclitics according to gender, as is the case in most Bedouin dialects[8]:

	Past tense		*Non-past tense*	
	Cyr.A.	TA	Cyr.A.	TA
2nd m.pl.	kitabtu	ktebtu	tikitbu	tiktibu
2nd f.pl.	kitabtan	ktebtu	tikitban	tiktibu
3rd m.pl.	iktibu	ktebu	yikitbu	yiktibu
3rd m.pl.	iktiban	ktebu	yikitban	yiktibu

Variation however occurs not only between East and West Libyan Arabic but also within East and West Libyan dialects.

5.2.2 Internal variation

Owens,[9] taking into account Mitchell's work, mentions distinctive features within the Benghazi area and classifies them as mainly urban vs rural / Bedouin dissimilarities. The main differences concern:

(i) diphthongs -ay, -aw in rural dialects vs monophthongs / long vowels ē, ō in urban dialects (as in lay<u>sh</u> vs lē<u>sh</u> "why");
(ii) vowel raising and palatalization in rural dialects (iktieb "book" and iktibietih "she wrote it") and;
(iii) 3rd person singular suffix pronoun, -ih in rural / Bedouin and -a in Benghazi.

As to lexicon, there are few cases of variation between East and West Libyan Arabic with <u>gh</u>udwa "tomorrow" in Tripoli and bukra in Benghazi.[10] A more extensive analysis of variation within those dialects would involve substantial research on various dialects and would be beyond the scope of this study.

5.2.3 Ethnic groups and religion in Libya

Nearly the entire population is Malikite Sunni Muslim, Arabic speaking and "shares a common Arab-Berber origin", but "what the citizens did not share was a strong sense either of common nationality or of allegiance to the nation state".[11] The non-Arab population consists of Berbers (3% of the population speaks Berber and Arabic and is of the Kharidjite sect of Islam), Tebus (whose language relates to a Sudanic dialect and are Muslim), Tuaregs (1% of the whole population speaks the Tamahek dialect and adheres to Malikite Sunnism mixed with magical elements) and Negroes (whose languages belong to the Chad group and have adopted Islam).[12]

As the population is highly homogeneous given its religious and linguistic components (most of the population being Sunni, Arabic speaking and living along the Tripolitanian and Cyrenaican Coast), the dialect usage in Tripoli is one of minor differentiation.[13]

Gaddafi's background

Muammar Al Gaddafi was born in Sirte, Tripolitania, of a family of Berber stock originally, the Qaddafa tribe.[14] His language, as will be seen from the data, is identifiable as Tripoli Arabic (with however some Bedouin phonological elements), although his education took him from Sirte (Tripolitania), to Sebha (Fezzan), Masrata (Tripolitania) and Benghazi (Cyrenaica). Sirte, in Tripolitania, is a "transitional" area according to Owens,[15] between the West and East parts and shows characteristics of West (Tripoli) and East (Benghazi). Gaddafi's speech however, to judge from the data, does not show any influence of Cyrenaican Arabic.

Gaddafi is seen by his people as a charismatic figure, "possessed of special abilities of rhetoric and persuasiveness"[16] and who cultivates some aspects of his personality:

- from a very early age, Gaddafi was influenced by Nasser's speeches and wished to establish himself as the new paragon of Arab nationalism, and according to El Fathaly and Palmer,[17] he was aware of the power of mixing literary Arabic and the dialect, although he insisted on using "pure", Classical Arabic devoid of any influence from foreign languages.
- Although he was looked down on as a child because of his Bedouin family (and Berber origins as said earlier), Gaddafi has always been very proud of his heritage, and he wished to emphasize the image of a pure Arab, "more Arab than the Arabs", by his origins and devout religiosity. The second extract to be examined here, a sermon in a mosque, is an example of how he arrogates to himself the right to explain Quranic verses to the gathered people, which might be understood in the context of his tribal origins since, among Bedouins, any tribal member may lead communal prayers. His tribal origins do not seem to influence his speech making habits since, in the extracts under analysis, he mixes MSA and Tripoli Arabic features. As Gaddafi switches between MSA and TA, mixes the two codes, and delivers these two speeches in Tripoli, there is no need to consider convergence as a factor, i.e. the process by which a speaker adapts his linguistic habits to those of his interlocutor(s) in crossdialectal discourse, in intercommunal situations.

5.3 ANALYSIS OF THE DATA

The aim of this section is to analyze the data (i.e. the two speech extracts transcribed phonemically) according to phonology, morphophonology, syntax and lexicon, to see how the MSA and TA systems are used, and to examine the predictability of the variation. Finally, this chapter will relate language form and language function.

As was the case for the Egyptian and Iraqi data, the elements of discourse can be divided into major types:

(a) whenever Gaddafi is introducing a subject, building his argument, channeling general understanding, ordering the audience and patronizing them in a process that is a distancing one, MSA is used and the discourse has a impersonal quality;

(b) whenever the speaker is explaining some issues, clarifying his arguments, personalising, specifying, and pleading his cause, dialect is used as well as when he wishes to influence and move the audience, and to build up solidarity links and create a sense of unity.

Data will be analyzed in terms of its MSA use and colloquialness. Chapter two provides a comprehensive description of how elements are categorized according to their level of formality. Items are analyzed according to their lexico-semantic (L-S) and morpho-phonological (MPP) statuses. The L-S status refers to whether an item is MSA, dialectal, or shared in terms of its root meaning combined with its use, and the MPP status refers to the morphophonological rules which operate on it. A sequence will be considered MSA when it combines non-dialectal MSA elements as in:

> *1981 l.122* /mādha yakūnu mawqif al-'ālam law ?aṣbaḥat mi?āt al-mu?tamarāt/ which shows the concurrence of MSA features such as phonemes q < OA /q/ (mawqif), dh < OA /dh/ (mādha), close-to-MSA MPP of verb with ?i'rāb (yakūnu) and MSA lexical enclitic -at (?aṣbaḥat).

An item and a sequence will be considered dialectal when they conform to the TA rules, as described below in the phonological and morphophonological sections. In a dialectal sequence, TA elements cooccur as in:

> *1978 l.17* /wa ?irtajafit 'indama smi'it kalmit l-qāri'a/ where dialectal elements combine: close-to-dialectal MPP of verb with dialectal lexical enclitic (?irtajafit) and deletion of unstressed vowel (smi'it), dialectal feminine ending -it in a possessive construction with deletion of unstressed vowel as well (kalmit l-qāri'a).

In most sequences however, TA and MSA elements cooccur as in:

> *1981 l.142* /zēn al-?ān lā yumkin njī ngūl/ which combines MSA negative particle lā + non-past tense and close-to-MSA MPP of verb yumkin with saliently dialectal elements such as phoneme g < OA /q/, close-to-TA MPP of verb with deletion of unstressed vowel (ngūl) and the purely dialectal lexical item zēn.

5.3.1 Phonology

In this phonological section, lexical items are analyzed according to some distinctive, salient phonemes in which MSA and the dialects differ: OA [q], [th], [dj], [dh], and [ẓ]. Items in this section consist of nouns and adjectives mainly. Verbs are taken into account in the listing of items but they will be dealt with in the morphophonology section.

In the speeches, phonemic variation is related to lexical types: abstract concepts are expressed through MSA lexical items, with a likelihood of MSA phonemes, while concrete entities are often expressed via dialectal lexical items which show dialectal phonemic variants. But this is only a general tendency: there is no exact correspondence between the phonemes and subject matter, and given the constant interaction between MSA and the dialect, MSA elements are found mixing with TA ones.

MSA and TA are similar consonantally apart from these salient phonemes:

1 OA /q/ is [q] in MSA and [g] in TA.
2 OA /th/ is [th] in MSA, [t] mainly and [th] occasionally in TA.
3 OA /dj/ is MSA [dj] and TA [j].
4 OA /dh/ is [dh] in MSA, [dh] occasionally and [d] mainly in TA.
5 OA /ẓ/ is MSA [ẓ]; [ẓ] can be found in TA but often replaced by [ḍ].

These five phonemes will be analyzed according to occurrences found in the data, although phoneme OA /q/ is by far the most fruitful source of examples and variation.

OA /q/

In the Tripoli Arabic dialect, OA /q/ is mainly realized as [g]. [q] occurs however[18] in proper names (qaṭar "Qatar", dimashq "Damascus") and words with religious connotations (qiyāma "resurrection day"), although Griffini[19] gives qur?ān with a [g] phoneme in TA, gur?ān. Our data, however, consisting of the 1978 and 1981 speeches, has mainly occurrences of [q] (284 occurrences of [q] in 75 items) and a few [g] (41 occurrences of [g] in 7 items):

- MSA [q] and TA [q] only 284 tokens (75 items)
- TA [g] only 5 tokens (5 items)
- [q]-[g] variably 45 tokens (2 items)

1. OA /q/ > [q]
[q] < OA /q/ is found in large proportions even cooccurring with dialectal elements. As will be seen from the data, OA /q/ is realized as [q]:

1 in MSA lexical items as in tanāquḍ,
2a in shared verbs, with a close-to-MSA MPP (yuqātil),
2b in shared verbs with a close-to-TA MPP (yiqātil), and
2c in fixed expressions, and collocations such as quwwāt 'arabiyya. The cooccurrence rules regarding verbs will be dealt with in the morphophonology section below.

[q] in MSA lexical items
In the data, there are few MSA lexical items with [q] < OA /q/ that belong to the MSA set of vocabulary of abstract concepts. These items can also be the MSA counterpart of an existing dialectal item (for instance MSA raqam versus dialectal nimra) and have an MSA MPP as in verbal nouns/masdars (tanāquḍ). They typically combine with other MSA features (as in <u>th</u>aqulat with <u>th</u> < OA <u>th</u>) and have an MSA vowel patterning (as in the past participle mutanāqiḍ). Since the 1978 extract deals with a passage from the Quran and is set in a mosque, there are several religious terms found in MSA, mixed and TA sequences (al-qāri'a recurs 54 times). The MSA items are tanāquḍ "incompatibility" and from the same root mutanāqiḍ "contradictory", and natanāqaḍ "we contradict", sā'iqa "lightning", al-qāri'a "the Calamity", qiyāma "resurrection", qur?ān "Quran", ṭāriq "Tareq", raqam "number", quḥḥa "pure", qar'a "blow", <u>th</u>aqulat "it was heavy", yaqḍū "they impose", tuqma' "it is suppressed" and the particles qad and faqaṭ.

These items (82 tokens/ 16 items) occur in MSA sequences mainly as in:

1978 l.6 /wa ka?anna jibrīl illa<u>dh</u>ī ?anzala ha<u>dh</u>ihi s-sūra 'ala n-nabiyy yaqūl mā l-qāri'a/ where phoneme q (in qāri'a and yaqūl) cooccurs with MSA phoneme <u>dh</u>, and close-to-MSA vowel patterning of verbs (?anzala and yaqūl). qāri'a however can be found occurring with dialectal features as in:
1978 l.17 /wa ?irtajafit 'indamā smi'it kalmit l-qāri'a/ where [q] cooccurs with dialectal features such as lexical enclitics (?irtajafit, smi'it), feminine ending -it (kalmit). [q] occurs in qāri'a which is a fixed item, a "quotation" which retain its shape in all contexts.

q in shared lexical items

Shared lexical items are items that are widely used both in MSA and in the dialect and that, in the speeches, retain their MSA MPP as in: masdars (tawaqquf, muqārana, muqāwama), past participle (multaqa), vowel patterning in derived forms (yuqātil, ?a'taqidu, tataḥaqqaq, yuqawwi) and passives (tuqra'). Most of the data is formed of this shared vocabulary since it is public speaking in a formal setting. Some of these items, as part of frozen expressions and MSA collocations (as in quwwāt 'arabiyya and qiyāda 'āma), are not susceptible to internal variation and can occur as such in what are otherwise TA sequences. Adverbs, such as ?iṭlāqan and taqrīban, keep the characteristic MSA case ending and can combine with dialectal elements as they have become multilevel, i.e. can be found at various levels of formality. Given the subject, most of the items from this shared list belong to the military-political terminology:

quwwāt	"forces"	xandaq	"trench"
ḥaqq	"right"	yuqātil	"he fights"
mawāqi'	"position"	muqātilīn	"fighter"
dimuqrāṭiyya	"democratic"	bunduqiyya	"rifle"
?iqlīmiyya	"territorial"	qarrarāt	"decisions"
muqāwama	"resistance"	qabīla	"tribe"
qā?id	"leader"	multaqa	"gathering"
yaḥaqq	"he is right"	muttafqīn	"agreeing"
tawaqquf	"it was determined"	?iqāmat	"establishment"
minṭaqiyyan	"regionally"	yiqṣudū	"they consider"
tqarrar	"it was decided"	tuqra'	"it is hit"

Some of these items are found as such in MSA and the dialect without any morphophonological change (quwwāt, qunbula). Other items have a dialectal phonological counterpart that does not occur in the data as it would probably be felt too dialectally marked for this type of discourse and the speaker makes a choice towards the shared item with q < OA /q/ realization:

shared item	*TA item not occurring in the data*
ḥaqq	ḥagg
xandaq	xandag
waqt/waqit	wagt
bunduqiyya	bindga
qarīb	grīb
qulūb	glūb
fawqa	fōg

In the Egyptian and Iraqi data, we looked at cases of /q/ combining with dialectal elements within the same item: we observed the combination of /q/ and a multilevel element. In the Libyan data on the other hand, we observe a greater variety in the combination of /q/ and dialectal features, since some items of the "shared" list show a variable cooccurrence of /q/ and elements such as: the feminine ending -a (qaḍiyya-qaḍiyyit), preformative (yuqātil-yiqātil), the syllable structure (waqt-waqit, qaṣaf-qaṣf), deletion of unstressed vowel (muttafqīn), resyllabication (yi'alqu), vowel harmony (yuq'ud), and occurring with syntactic elements as a discontinuous negative particle (mā ?a'taqdsh, mā qūltūsh) (see below in the morphophonology section for a discussion of verb formation). These shared items occur mainly in MSA and mixed sequences as in:

> *1981 l.122* /mādhā yakūnu mawqif al-'ālam law ?aṣbaḥat mi?āt al-mu?tamarāt/ where /q/ cooccurs with MSA elements (verbal vowel patterning of a fourth form which is rare in dialect (?aṣbaḥat), ?i'rāb (yakūnu), phoneme dh, particle law).
> *1981 l.16* /li?annahu yuqātil fī nafs il-waqit/ which combines MSA elements such as phoneme [q] < OA /q/, close-to-MSA MPP (yuqātil), and a dialectal feature in the case of a "no-final consonant cluster rule", waqit for MSA waqt.

2. OA /q/ > [g]

There are few occurrences of TA [g] < OA /q/ realized in common, everyday vocabulary as in: guddāmna "in front of us", ḍāyig "annoying", gabil "before", tigdar "you can" and gā'id "staying". gā'id is a common active participle which is frequently used in the dialect instead of finite verbs. These five dialectal items occur in purely TA sequences.

3. OA /q/ > [q]-[g] variably

This variation between [q] and [g] can only be found in qāl-gāl "he said". The verb "to say" (see also morphophonological section) is found frequently throughout the two speeches (9 times with [q] and 34 times with [g]). Dialectal gāl is used to introduce reported speech and is found in mixed and TA sequences as in:

> *1978 l.69* /biywaḍḍaḥ lih bigūl ?arāh l-qāri'a hiya yawmu takūnu in-nāsu ka l-farāsh il-mabthūth/ which is an example of stylistic fulcrum[20] where a level change occurs in one element and spreads to the rest of the sequence as it triggers the

cooccurrence of elements of that level. The first part of the sequence (up to ?arāh) combines dialectal features as phoneme [g] < OA /q/, aspectual prefix bi-, preformative yi-, and where the second part, a Quranic quotation, combines Classical/MSA features such as phoneme [q] < OA /q/ and [th] < OA /th/, ?i'rāb (yawmu), close-to-MSA MPP of verb (takūnu) and collocation (farāsh mabthūth).

The verb "to say" is an example of how elements can adapt their MPP to "fit" in a different level of formality.

1978 l.87 /biygūl xalāṣ mā 'ādsh fīh fayda/ In this dialectal sequence, phoneme g cooccurs with other dialectal elements such as preformative bi-, discontinuous negation (mā -sh) and lexical element (xalāṣ). Within a purely MSA sequence, "to say" is realized as /yaqūl/, with a close-to-MSA MPP as in the example seen earlier:
1978 l.6 /wa ka?anna jibrīl illadhī ?anzala hādhihi s-sūra 'ala n-nabiyy yaqūl mā l-qāri'a/

When we compare the uses of OA /q/ in the Egyptian, Iraqi and Libyan data, we observe that in the Egyptian data, CA [?] is found combining with MSA elements whereas in the Iraqi and Libyan data, dialectal [g] combines rarely with MSA elements. This phenomenon is explained by the fact that BGI/ TA [g] carries more dialectal weight than its Cairene counterpart, [?], which is pan-Arabic and widespread. [g] is also the Bedouin reflex of OA /q/, but, contrarily to the interdentals where the Bedouin reflexes correspond to the MSA realisations, [g] is avoided in this type of discourse because of its dialectal markedness.

OA /th/

Tripoli Arabic has mainly [t] realisation for OA /th/ and occasionally [th]. However, as was the case for the previous phoneme, the data consistently has [th] apart from a few items.

- MSA [th] 77 tokens (14 items)
- TA [t] 2 tokens (2 items)
- [th]-[t] variably 5 tokens (2 items)
- [th]-[s] variably 6 tokens (1 item)

There are 77 realisations of OA /th/ as MSA interdental [th] in items occurring in MSA and mixed sequences.

List of elements with [th] < OA [th]

thawra	"revolution"	ḥadīth	"discussion"
nabḥath	"we examine"	?akthar	"more"
tamthīlīyya	"performance"	tumaththil	"it represents"
nitaḥaddath	"we converse"	ḥaythu	"since"
thaqulat	"it was heavy"	thumma	"then"

Some elements of this list tend to be part of a frame of conceptual reference with which MSA is associated (thaqulat "it was heavy", muba'thara "scattered") while others belong to a more neutral, shared set of vocabulary (mithil "since", ?akthar "more").

Some of these items combine MSA th with dialectal syllable structure (mithil versus MSA mithl), and yi- preformative (nitaḥad-dath). These items are found in mixed and MSA sequences as in:

> *1981 l.134* /yumaththil ash-sha'b al-falasṭīni yigūl ?anni mithil ash-sha'b al-falasṭīni yijību ?ayyu majmū'a/ where [th] < OA /th/ cooccurs on the one hand with MSA elements such as close-to-MSA MPP of verb (yumaththil), collocation (ash-sha'b al-falasṭīni), and on the other hand, dialectal elements such as preformative yi and close-to-dialect MPP of verb (yijību) and phoneme g (yigūl).
> *1978 l.12* /lā yaxtalif ?ithnāni mina l-muslimīn 'ala ?anna hādhihi hiya sūrata l-qāri'a wa 'ala ?annaha nazalat bi makka) In this sequence, th < OA /th/ combines with other MSA features such as phoneme q < OA /q/ (qāri'a), enclitic -at (nazalat), close-to-MSA MPP of derived verb (yaxtalif), negative particle lā and non-past tense (lā yaxtalif).

The reason why there are so many occurrences of th< OA /th/ is due to the fact that Gaddafi is using his Bedouin native speech where OA /th/ is realised as [th].[21] Phonological realisations are usually less amenable to variation, and speakers normally retain phonological characteristics of their own native dialect even after being exposed to another language variety. As to items occurring with dialectal [t], a stylistic levelling down from MSA [th], they concern the numerals and the adverb matalan (which shows, exceptionally, how MSA ?i'rāb can concur with the dialectal segmental feature [t] instead of MSA [th]. Numerals, as one saw in the Egyptian data, tend to be realised with a dialectal phoneme [t] (although the data show 2 cases of thalātha), and TA may be influencing the speaker's speech. The situation of OA /th/ is slightly different from what one saw in the Egyptian data. The Egyptian data showed the emergence of the intermediate sibilant

[s] < OA /th/ to fill the gap between two marked choices. In the Libyan data, [th] is found recurrently as it is part of the speaker's Bedouin native speech and is an MSA realisation as well, suitable for the discourse. There are however some cases of [s] varying with [th] in the item mabsūs/ mabthūth, but I do not have enough data to see whether there could be an emergence of an intermediate [s] < OA /th/ in TA influencing his native Bedouin speech.

OA /dh/

OA /dh/ is realized as [dh] throughout the data, even in dialectal sequences. These results may seem surprising since El Fitoury mentions [d] realizations mainly for OA /dh/ in Tripoli and [dh] occasionally. However, one must bear in mind that, as for the previous interdental, Gaddafi is using his Bedouin native speech which has [dh] < OA /dh/, hence the overwhelming presence of [dh] compared to the previous interdental /th/ which had realisations of TA dialectal [t] < OA /th/ in the case of numerals. Items in which [dh] occurs may have some dialectal features as in tāxudh (instead of ta?xudh, TA has taxud) with deletion of glottal stop. Data has the following items (92 tokens/ 13 items):

dhī	"owner of"	dhāt	"being"
hādha/hādhihi	"this"	?idhā	"if"
?idhan	"then"	dhikra	"memory"
limādhā	"why"	dhull	"humiliation"
tāxudh	"you take"	xudhlān	"disappointment"

Data show MSA items with dh (as in xudhlān) as well as more common words such as ?idhā. To take the case of the demonstrative and relative pronouns since they number high occurrences in the data (70 occurrences of MSA hādha, hādhihi, alladhi where TA has hāda, hādi, illi) they are found in MSA and mixed sequences as in the example cited earlier:

> *1978 l.12* /lā yaxtalif ?ithnāni mina l-muslimīn 'ala ?anna hādhihi hiya s-sūrata l-qāri'a wa 'ala ?annaha nazalat bi makka/ where hādhihi cooccurs with MSA elements such as phoneme [q] < OA /q/ (qāri'a), close-to-MSA MPP of verb (nazalat, yaxtalif), negative particle lā + non-past tense and ?i'rāb as in s-sūrata, and, *1978 l.27* /alladhī bitaḥṣul fī l-?ashyā? al-?ātiya/ where MSA alladhī cooccurs with the hybrid form of aspectual prefix bi and close-to-MSA verbal vowel patterning (bitaḥṣul), and,

1981 l.126 /?anā takallamt fī hā<u>dh</u>a l-makān yōmha/ where <u>dh</u> concurs with dialectal elements: -t 1st person suffix (takallamt) and long vowel ō instead of diphthong aw (yōm).

Relative pronoun ?illi is the dialectal equivalent of alla<u>dh</u>ī, allatī and cooccurs with dialectal features in mixed and TA sequences. However, because of its widespread use (a phenomenon observable in the other data in chapters 3 and 4), ?illi has become multilevel and combines with MSA elements as in:

1981 l.9 /li?annu huwa ?illi yaḥaqq lahu ?an yatakallam/ where multilevel ?illi coocurs with MSA elements such as phoneme [q] < OA /q/, complementiser ?an, verbal vowel patterning (yaḥaqq, yatakallam).

OA /ẓ/

TA, according to the literature, has [ḍ] regularly for OA /ẓ/, but this data, even in non-MSA contexts, show a preponderance of [ẓ]. [ẓ] realisation is explained (as in the two phonemes before) by the speaker's linguistic background (he prides himself on his Bedouin origin), and is simply using his normal dialectal (non-TA) [ẓ] reflex. In the case of phonemes OA /<u>dh</u>/ and OA /ẓ/, there is no instance of sibilants z and Z, i.e. a third phoneme between the MSA and dialectal realizations, between <u>dh</u> and d, ẓ and ḍ respectively. Our data show ẓ < OA /ẓ/ in MSA and in fixed and shared items as in: mu'ẓam "majority", munaẓẓama "organization", yunẓuru "he considers", tunaẓẓim "she organizes", tanẓīm "organization". There are 29 tokens (5 items) occurring in MSA and mixed sequences mainly. Although [ẓ] is the MSA realization of OA /ẓ/, it can cooccur with colloquial elements such as feminine ending -it (munaẓẓamit), dialectal vowel patterning (yunẓuru, with a vowel harmony u-u), and the aspectual prefix bi as in biyunẓiru. Phoneme ẓ cooccurs with MSA and dialectal elements and is found in MSA and mixed sequences as in:

1981 l.127 /mā kān fī niyyatī ?abadan ?innu ?ayyi wāḥid satub'id munaẓẓamat at-taḥrīr al-falasṭīniyya/ where ẓ < OA /ẓ/ cooccurs with phoneme q, collocation (munaẓẓamat at-taḥrīr al-falasṭī-niyya), masdar (taḥrīr), MSA prefix sa- and, on the other hand,
1981 l.96 /biyunẓurū munaẓẓamit at-taḥrīr al-falasṭīniyya ka munaẓẓama faqaṭ/ where ẓ cooccurs with MSA elements such as phoneme q, particle faqat, the same collocation (munaẓẓamit t-taḥrīr al-falasṭīniyya) but with dialectal features prefix bi, dialectal verbal vowel patterning (biyunẓuru with vowel harmony u-u).

OA /d̲j̲/

Libyan Arabic consistently has fricative [j] for OA affricate /d̲j̲/ and the data show [j] throughout in MSA, dialectal and shared items, in MSA, mixed and TA sequences. [j] is found throughout urban/rural dialects and among those settled and nomads in Libya.[22] The following items show how [j] can combine with purely MSA (satajid) and purely dialectal features (nij'il), in lexical items shared by the dialect and MSA:

yajib	"he should"	jibrīl	"Gabriel"
jiddan	"very"	mawjūda	"found"
xijlān	"ashamed"	?iltajat	"she took refuge"
jibāl	"mountains"	al-jamāhīr	"the masses"
yuwajjih	"you turn"	jamī'	"entirety"
yuxrij	"he removes"	taḥtāj	"you need"
bitujāhalū	"you ignore"	lijān	"committees"

The case of [j] < OA /d̲j̲/ is however different from the previous phonemes analyzed since the dialectal variant occurs in 100% of the cases, without any lexical conditioning. Alveo-palatal [j] is a non-standard standard[23] that is never replaced by an MSA counterpart and is the only realization of OA /d̲j̲/ in the data (and in the Libyan dialects as a whole). On the other hand, dialectal phonemes seen earlier such as [t] < OA /t̲h̲/ and [g] < OA /q/ cooccur with their MSA counterparts [t̲h̲] and [q] respectively. The reason why the dialectal variant [j] is persistent throughout our data and the dialect seems to be due to the fact that [j] is a stable variant because of its wide geographical spread, and is only a very slight phonological change from OA /d̲j̲/, so slight, perhaps, that it is less salient and less susceptible to replacement. As will be observed throughout this study, the dialectal elements that are pervasive in more formal styles, are never highly local, extremely marked dialectal features. [g] < OA /q/ for instance is more susceptible than /j/ to replacement as it is found in some dialects only, and is particularly strongly associated with Bedouin speech in a way that /j/ is not.

5.3.2 Morphophonology

This section is concerned with verbs which are classified according to their lexico-semantic (L-S) status and their morphophonological shape (MPP). Verbs are classified into five categories:

			Third level		
L-S:	MSA	**shared**	**shared**	**shared**	TA
MPP:	MSA	**close-to-MSA**	**multivalent**	**close-to-TA**	TA
	1	**2**	**3**	**4**	5

with, in addition, cases of symbiotic and hybrid verbs (see Methodology Chapter). Categories 2, 3 and 4 belong to a third, intermediate level, between MSA and dialectal verbs. MSA and TA verbs are strictly defined. A verb is MSA when its L-S status is MSA and at the same time conforms to MSA morphological rules of verb formation. Similarly, a verb is dialectal when it belongs to the dialectal set of vocabulary and when TA morphological rules are applied to it. The third (shared) level is more difficult to outline since, morphophonologically, a verb can belong to different morphophonological categories (yuqātil is close-to-MSA (MSA yuqātilu) and yiqātil is close-to-TA "he fights"), whereas lexically it is part of the third, intermediate level of the shared set of the lexicon (q-t-l, third derived form "to fight", a shared root). Most of the lexicon in political speaking belongs to this third, intermediate level and thus allows variability in the language form, which can fluctuate between MSA and the dialect depending on (1) the subject matter and (2) the linguistic environment of cooccurrence rules. This section deals with the five verbal categories indicated in the chart above.

As was said, the choice of verb MPP is closely related to its L-S status, for instance:

MSA (level 1)		*dialect* (level 5)	
q-m-'	L-S MSA "to suppress"	sh-f	L-S TA "to see"
tu	MSA preformative	-it	MPP TA enclitic
tuqma'	MPP MSA vowel pattern.	shufit	MPP TA vowel patterning
	passive voice		
	"it is suppressed"		"I saw"

intermediate (level 3)

		q-t-l	L-S shared "to fight" third derived form
yu-	MPP MSA preformative	yi-	MPP TA preformative
yuqātil	MPP MSA vowel pattern.	yiqātil	MPP TA vowel patterning
	close-to-MSA verb		close-to-TA verb

multivalent

k-n	L-S shared
kān	MPP multivalent

symbiotic

j-h-l	L-S shared "to ignore"
tu-	MPP MSA preformative
tujāhalu	MPP MSA vowel patterning (close-to-MSA)
bi-	dialectal aspectual prefix
bitujāhalu	symbiotic form

Distribution of verbs in the Libyan data

(1) L-S and MPP MSA verbs	18 tokens (9 items)
(2) L-S shared and close-to-MSA verbs	201 tokens (77 items)
(3) L-S shared and multivalent verbs	31 tokens (4 items)
(4) L-S shared and close-to-TA verbs	174 tokens (50 items)
(5) L-S and MPP TA verbs	8 tokens (7 items)
symbiotic verbs	8 tokens (5 items)
hybrid verbs	18 tokens (10 items)

MSA verbs

Data show 18 tokens (9 items) of MSA verbs which belong to the MSA set of vocabulary and conform to the MSA rules of verb formation. As noted previously, ?i'rāb is considered an MSA extramarker whose inclusion is unnecessary for a verb to be classified as MSA (see Chapter three for the chart of lexical enclitics for the past and non-past tenses of MSA verbs, and where the non-past plural ending is also -ū(na)).

The MSA list of items consists of: ?istahjanat "it disapproves", yataḥawwal "he changes", nad'imū "we support", tataḥarrar "it becomes free", tatanāqaḍ "it decreases", tuqma' "it is suppressed", tuqra' "it is hit", tudahhimhu "it blackens it", thaqulat "it was heavy". These MSA verbs occur in MSA sequences as in:

> *1981 l.93* /mafrūḍ yataḥawwal yanbaghī ?an yataḥawwal min al-mufīd/ where MSA elements cooccur such as complementiser ?an and MSA verbal vowel patterning in derived verbs as well as lexical choice (yanbaghī ?an yataḥawwal).

MSA verbs and dialectal influence

It can be seen from the MSA list that these verbs do not have ?i'rāb. As was the case in the speeches from the other dialects, absence of ?i'rāb is the only concession to dialect for MSA verbs, and, because of the widespread use of the dialectal endings, verbs are found with ū ending instead of ūna for the non-past tense. In the Libyan data, as in the Egyptian, -ūn(a) in the non-past tense functions as an "extramarker", like verbal ?i'rāb in general. This of course was not the case in the Iraqi data, where ūn is the normal dialectal form, and whose use has no particular stylistic significance. The case of ?i'rāb is different, however, for adverbs where MSA ending -an is a "frozen" feature which can combine with a dialectal phoneme (as in matalan, see OA /<u>th</u>/). These MSA verbs are not found with dialectal features such as (1) phoneme g < OA /q/ *tugra', (2) enclitic -it *?istahjanit, (3) preformative yi- *titanāqaḍ, (4) phoneme s < OA /<u>th</u>/ *saqulat, (5) deletion of unstressed vowel *tudhhimhu, (6) shortening of long vowel *tatanaqaḍ, (7) dialectal prefix bi- *bitatanāqaḍ.

TA dialectal verbs

At the other end of the continuum, we have the dialectal set of vocabulary consisting of common, everyday, specific items, such as tib<u>gh</u>ū "you want", yifarfi<u>sh</u> "he gets flustered", <u>sh</u>ufit "I saw", rāḥ "he went", mā yi'ībā<u>sh</u> "he is not ashamed", biṣīr "it comes out" and bidīr "he is doing" (8 tokens/ 7 items). Verbs are classified as TA when they are part of this dialectal "core" set and, morpho-phonologically, they invariably conform to the TA rules of verb formation, as illustrated below in the TA vowel patterning and lexical enclitic paradigms for the past and non-past tenses of the first and derived forms:

	Past tense	*Non-past tense*
I	CCaC	yiCCaC
	CCiC	yuCCuC/yiCCiC
II	CaCCiC	yiCaCCaC/iCCiC
III	CāCiC	yiCāCiC
IV		
V	tCaCCaC	yitCaCCiC
VI	tCāCaC	yitCāCiC
VII	nCCaC	yinCCaC

VIII	CtCaC	yiCtCiC
IX	—	—
X	staCCiC	yistaCCiC

Lexical enclitics of the first form

	Past	*Non-past tense*
1 sg	stem-t/it	nv-stem
2 m sg	stem-t	tv-stem
2 f sg	stem-ti	tv-stem-i
3 msg	stem	yv-stem
3 f sg	stem-it	tv-stem
1 pl	stem-na	nv-stem-ū
2 pl	stem-tu	tv-stem-ū
3 pl	stem-u	yv-stem-ū/ō

For the past tense, the stem vowel v can be a or i and for the non-past tense, the preformative vowel is mainly i, except in cases of vowel harmony.[24]

The data show very few purely dialectal verbs (only 8 tokens (7 items) in the data), which display dialectal features such as (a) preformative yi- (tibghū), (b) aspectual prefix bi- (bisīr), (c) lack of ?i'rāb (yifarfish), (d) enclitic -it (shufit) and (e) cooccurrence of discontinuous negative particle (mā yi'ībāsh). Other dialectal features (such as deletion of unstressed vowel) will be illustrated with examples from the data in the following section on close-to-TA verbs. Such dialectal verbs do not, and could not, occur with MSA elements such as ?i'rāb *tibghūnā enclitic -at *shufat; prefix sa- indicating future tense *sayidīr. TA verbs occur mainly in sequences as in:

> *1978 l.40* /jāyi min it-tifarfīsh ?inna l-wāḥid yifarfish mish 'ārif kīf yidīr/ which shows a cooccurrence of dialectal morphophonological features such as present participle (jāyi, 'ārif), preformative yi (yifarfish, yidīr), long vowel ī for diphthong ay (kīf), negation (mish) and non-standard lexical items.

Shared verbs with a close-to-MSA morphophonology

Lexically, close-to-MSA verbs are part of the shared set of vocabulary which contains most of the items occurring in the data. This shared set is in between MSA and TA, and has one end closer to MSA and the other closer to TA. By this is meant that some verbs are mainly restricted to the MSA end, have a close-to-MSA morphophonology and are mainly used with this MSA shape. In the list of examples that follows, most of the verbs are part of the complex, abstract, political, journalistic vocabulary which typically show this close-to-MSA morphophonology:

yatakallam	"he speaks"	yuwajjah	"he is directed"
yuqātil	"he fights"	taṭghū	"it dominates"
yubarhin	"he demonstrates"	?a'taqidu	"I consider"
qutil	"he was killed"	quṭi'at	"it was cut"
yu'ātab	"he is blamed"	nuxawwin	"we suspect"
?istaslamat	"she surrendered"	tantashir	"you spread"
yaqḍū	"they spend"	jā?a	"he came"
taḥtāj	"you need"	tatanaffas	"you breathe"
?ibtadat	"she began"	yuṣallū	"they pray"
yuqawwi	"he strengthens"	satantaṣir	"you'll triumph"
tataḥaqqaq	"it is confirmed"	faqadat	"she failed to find"
yughādiru	"they depart"	yushakkil	"he gives shape"
tuwājih	"you face"	yaxḍa'ū	"they surrender"
?āmanū	"they believed"	sallamū	"they surrendered"
duwwinat	"it was recorded"	?adrā	"he informed"
yukattim	"he hides"	yalja?	"he resorts"
?a'ūdhu	"I seek refuge (in God)"	satab'ad	"you'll become distant"

These verbs are shared lexically and close-to-MSA morphophonologically and conform to the MSA rules of verb formation, apart from a few concessions to dialect such as (a) dialectal non-past ending ū instead of MSA extramarker ūna (apart from one case in the data yu?ayyidūna) and, (b) deletion of unstressed vowel (ntakallam) and occasionally deletion of glottal stop and lengthening of the vowel tāxudh for MSA ta?xudh and ?ibtadat for MSA ?ibtada?at. In these two cases, although the glottal stop is missing, the form is still to be considered close-to-MSA because of the (respective) preformative ta- and lexical enclitic -at; preformative ti- and -it ending would cast the forms into the close-to-TA category. In some other verbs however, the glottal stop is kept (jā?a, tabda?). The MSA features of these close-to-MSA verbs are the vowel patterning in the pattern I of the verb as in ḥaṣalat with the lexical enclitic -at (TA has -it), derived forms of the verb (tumaththil), preformative ya- (ya'rif), passive form of the verb (duwwinat), and the verb cooccurs with the future prefix sa- (satab'ad). Some of these verbs occur more frequently than others, because of their all-purpose nature, as for instance yakūn (20 occurrences), ?aqūl (11), yatakallam (6), yuṣbiḥ (11), sami'na (7), ḥaṣalat (7), or because of subject matter as nazalat (8) (in referring to Quranic suras) in the 1978 speech. Some (16 verbs) of these close-to-MSA verbs are however found in the close-to-TA section since the same root can concur with dialectal features. This is part of the flexibility of this third, intermediate level of shared vocabulary, for instance yuqātil is close-to-MSA and yiqātil is close-to-TA and the verb in itself is shared lexically. This flexibility and morphophonological variation concerns the following items:

Morphophonological form:

close-to-MSA	*symbiotic-hybrid forms*	*close-to-TA*
?u?akkid (11)		binakkid (1)
sami'na (8)		smi'it (4)
yatakallam (7)		ntikallimu (2)
yuqātil (2)		yiqātil (5)
yamūt (1)		yimūt (5)
nuxawwin (2)		yixawwin (1)
yushakkil (1)		yishakklū (1)
nazalat (9)	nazalit (4) hy.	tinzil (5)
jā?a (1)		jāt (2)
tas?al (1)	bitas?al (1) s.	yis?al (2)
ya'rif (3)		yi'rif (4)
ḥaṣalat (7)	bitaḥṣul (1) s.	
tudīr(1)	bitudīru (2) s.	
?aqūl (9)	mā qultūsh (1) hy.	yigūl (28)
yakūn (21)		yikūn (12)

Verbs from these three columns belong lexically to a shared set of vocabulary. Morphophonologically, close-to-MSA verbs show MSA characteristics as seen earlier. Morphophonological close-to-TA verbs combine dialectal features as will be described below. Preformative yi- as in close-to-TA verbs is a dialectal marker and will automatically cast the form into the close-to-TA category, so tas?al is close-to-MSA whereas yis?al is close-to-TA. The other verbs in the close-to-TA column show determining dialectal characteristics: prefix bi- and deletion of glottal stop in binakkid, deletion of glottal stop in jāt and vowel patterning and lexical enclitic in smi'it. Forms in the middle column consist of symbiotic verbs (prefix bi and close-to-MSA verb) and hybrid forms (cases of discontinuous negative particle and close-to-MSA verb and dialectal lexical enclitic -it in a close-to-MSA verb). This dialectal influence might be explained by the fact that these verbs are in common usage. In this Libyan data, symbiotic and hybrid forms are lexically part of the shared set of vocabulary (see below).

Although some of these close-to-MSA verbs can be found cooccurring with dialectal elements and part of the close-to-TA list, colloquial influence is limited, and close-to-MSA verbs do not occur with the following elements: (a) phoneme g < OA /q/ *?a'tagidu, *guṭi'at, (b) 1st person singular preformative n- instead of ?a- *nitasā?al. Apart from the 16 verbs which could occur with either MSA or dialectal features, the other verbs of the list are not found with, for instance, -it lexical enclitic instead of -at *fariḥit, and preformative yi- (*yinbaghī) would cast the verb as close-to-TA (in the case of a shared verb but here, the verb is not "shared" in terms of L-S) and TA in the case of a dialectal verb. Close-to-MSA verbs occur in MSA and mixed sequences as in:

> *1981 l.47* /nu?akkidu ?an mustaḥīl taqa' ?azma bayna thawra wa thawra/ where MSA features combine such as phoneme q < OA /q/, phoneme th < OA /th/, verbal vowel patterning of derived verbs (close-to-MSA MPP, nu?akkid), complementiser ?an, diphthong ay (bayna), and
> *1978 l.86* /?ayya wāḥad bijāwib gabil lā yasma' baqiyyata l-?āya/ where MSA elements such as phoneme q (baqiyyata), vowel patterning (yasma'), negative particle lā + non-past tense verb combine with dialectal features such as phoneme [g] in gabil and aspectual prefix bi- (bijāwib).

Shared verbs with a close-to-TA morphophonology

Close-to-TA verbs are verbs which lexically belong to the set of vocabulary, shared between MSA and TA and are not identifiable with either of the two categories. Because of their meaning and their use, these verbs are closer to the TA designation. Ideationally they refer to common, everyday matters or actions and morphophonologically, these verbs conform to the dialectal rules as given earlier and are called "close-to-TA". The list includes:

xāfit	"she feared"	nistab'id	"we set aside"
tishtamū	"you insult"	tiṭraḥ	"you remove"
yifāji?ūn	"they suppressed"	nij'il	"we place"
yitḥāwil	"he tries"	tqarrar	"it was determined"
t'abbir	"you declare"	bīmārsū	"they pursue"

?irtajifit	"it trembled"	?afza'it	"it frightened"
tfakkar	"he considered"	byiḥtimi	"he takes refuge"
yistanid	"he relies"	nfakkir	"we consider"
jāt	"she came"	biywaḍḍaḥ	"he explains"
bitxalxal	"it is shaken"	yifarfish	"he is flustered"

Some of these shared close-to-TA verbs were seen earlier with close-to-MSA characteristics: yixawwin, ntikallimu, yiqātil, yimūt, yisma', yigūl, yi'rif, binakkid, yis?al, jāt, yishakklū, yikūn.

These close-to-TA verbs from the list, exhibit dialectal characteristics: (1) phoneme g (yigūl), (2) deletion of glottal stop/hamza (binakkid, jāt), (3) preformative yi- and vowel patterning in 1st and derived forms (yisma', yistab'id). As said earlier, preformative yi- is a dialectal marker and, in many cases, the only feature to differentiate a morphophonological form as either close-to-MSA or close-to-TA, ya'rif is close-to-MSA and yi'rif is close-to-TA. (4) Absence of ?i'rāb (nij'il) and non-past tense ending ū instead of ūna (tishtamū), (5) TA lexical enclitics such as 3rd fem. sg. -it (xāfit), (6) 1st sg. preformative n- (ngūl), (7) aspectual prefix bi- (byiḥtimi), (8) resyllabication of the syllable pattern with a vowel-initial enclitic (e.g. bi'arfū); resyllabication (bi- yCCvCū → bi- yCvCCū) is an alternative dialectal verb form. (9) deletion of unstressed vowel (bitxalxal), (10) vowel harmony (tutruk).

Most of the lexically shared, close-to-TA verbs do not combine MSA and TA characteristics (apart from those of the list with a shared lexico-semantic status), showing: (a) TA [g] < OA /q/ and MSA verbal patterning *yugātil, (b) ?i'rāb; ūna ending occurs only once in the data with a close-to-MSA verb (yu?ayyidūna) and does not cooccur with a close-to-TA verb and dialectal patterning *yis?alūna. (c) TA phoneme [g] < OA /q/ does not cooccur with a passive *yuxtarag, (d) MSA future prefix sa- with dialectal patterning *sanij'il. The future tense in Libyan Arabic is indicated by a non-past tense verb and an adverb indicating futurity,[25] of which there are few examples in the data, as in: 1981 l.96 /bukrā yunẓuru ?ilā ?abū 'ummār/. (e) MSA lexical enclitics with TA verb stem features, e.g. *smi'tu is a non-occurring form.

Shared verbs with multivalent morphophonology

Multivalent verbs belong lexically to the third level, and have a shared lexico-semantic status. Morphophonologically, multivalent verbs are identical in MSA and the dialect: they tend to be very common verbs, used at all levels of speech and in various settings. Data show 31 tokens (4 items) only of such verbs which are not marked for either MSA or TA, such as kān "he was", ya'ni "that is", mā dām "still", mā zālat "still". Although ya'ni has an MSA preformative and zālat an MSA enclitic, those forms are found as such at formal and dialectal levels. The same verbs used in another tense would be categorized differently: kān is multivalent, but yikūn is close-to-TA and yakūn close-to-MSA. In the following sequence:

> *1981 l.59* /ya'ni l-yōm ma'ak wāḥid bukra yigūluk qutil/ where multivalent ya'ni cooccurs with MSA phoneme [q] < OA /q/ and a passive verb (qutil) and dialectal characteristics such as long vowel ō instead of aw (yōm), phoneme g < OA /q/ and preformative yi (yigūluk).

Symbiotic and hybrid forms

Symbiotic and hybrid verbs in the Libyan data are lexically part of the shared set of vocabulary. In its dialectal inventory, Libyan dialect has the aspectual prefix bi + non-past tense verb. Prefix bi, as in the Egyptian chapter only (since Iraqi dialect does not have aspectual prefix bi), indicates habitual, continuous or repetitive aspects of the verb. Data include 32 tokens (13 items) of bi + close-to-TA verbs and hence combining with dialectal characteristics such as: lack of ?i'rāb and ū ending instead of ūna (bīmārsū), preformative yi and verbal patterning (byiḥtimi), occasionally ō ending instead of ū (bitsammōha), deletion of unstressed vowel (bingūl), vowel harmony (biyunẓurū), resyllabication (by'arfū). Prefix bi and close-to-TA verbs occur in mixed and TA sequences and combine in the data with dialectal elements such as ?illi, <u>sh</u>ū, long vowel ē (ba'dēn, kēf). Prefix bi is also found with some close-to-MSA verbs and forming a symbiotic form.[26] The symbiotic forms found in the data (5 items/8 tokens) combine prefix bi and a close-to-MSA verb with a cooccurrence of MSA vowel patterning in 1st and derived forms as in bītujāhalū, bitudīru, bitas?al, bituṣbaḥ, bitaḥṣul. As said earlier, in the case of close-to-MSA verbs, the only concession to dialect is the lack of ?i'rāb. Since the examples are scarce, it is difficult to draw any conclusion on the combination of bi and close-to-MSA verbs. These symbiotic verbs however should be seen as further evidence of the flexibility of the cooccurrence rules, and more particularly, an example of the change of status of aspectual prefix bi-: it is so widespread that it combines with MSA elements, loses its dialectal markedness and becomes multilevel, i.e. accepted at formal and informal levels. Besides symbiotic verbs, the data include a few examples of hybrid verbs which consist of: (1) dialectal resyllabication but with MSA phoneme q and MSA preformative of a shared verb as in taqublu; (2) lexical enclitic -it with MSA verbal patterning in shared verbs, as in nazalit, fakkarit, and ?afza'it which, in the last case, combines a fourth form unusual in dialect with a close-to-MSA verbal patterning and dialectal -it enclitic.

Hybrid and symbiotic forms concern only a few cases of our data that are significant nevertheless in showing the possible combinations between categories of verbs and the flexibility of the language. Whereas in the Cairene and Iraqi dialects hybrid forms come from lexically MSA verbs mainly, the Libyan data include hybrid forms from lexically shared verbs. The syntactic section below deals with hybrid forms in negative constructions.

Hybrid forms concern nouns as well, with the feminine ending -at which is a hybrid between the MSA contextual -atu/a/i ending and the dialectal ending. As in chapters three and four, we look at cases of noun-pronoun constructions. The examples are interesting in terms of dialectal influence and combinatorial rules. Hypothetically, noun + pronoun could be realized as:

MSA	*hybrid*	*dialect*
-atuhu (0)	-athu (9)	-ithu/ituh (2)
quwwatuhu	quwwathu	quwwithu

In the data, there is no occurrence of MSA ending, 9 examples of hybrid forms as in ḥaqīqathum, ḥurriyatah, ?irādatha, qaḍiyyatha, and 2 cases of dialectal ending -it, in quwwitha and qiyāditha. Results here indicate that the hybrid ending occurs more frequently than the dialectal -it ending.

To conclude on this morphophonological section, we notice, as was the case in the other dialects, that some dialectal elements become multilevel, pervade higher levels of formality and combine with MSA features. These elements are:

1 the non-past tense ending -ū instead of the full MSA ending -ūna (yaxḍa'ū);
2 lexical enclitic -it in hybrid forms (nazalit);
3 aspectual prefix bi + close-to-MSA verbs (bituṣbaḥ);
4 deletion of the glottal in close-to-MSA verb (?ibtadat);

5 deletion of unstressed vowel in close-to-MSA verb (ntakallam);
6 In the case of feminine endings, we have the emergence of a hybrid ending -at pervasive in noun-pronoun constructions;
7 relative pronoun ?illi is preferred to its MSA counterparts in most cases.

5.3.3 Some syntactic features

The previous sections were concerned with phonology and morphophonology. We illustrated examples from the MSA, dialectal and various types of mixed systems. This section deals with syntactic structures: the influence of elements on one another and the cooccurrence of syntactic and morphophonological features. Syntactic elements can have a style-raising (e.g. in the case of complementiser ?an and MSA negative particles) or a style-lowering effect (e.g. with dialectal negative particles and complementiserless verbs). The syntactic constructions analyzed are the negative system, complementiser ?an and the asyndetic verb strings.

The negative system

The following chart presents the MSA and dialectal systems at the disposal of the speaker and examples from the data will show how much the speaker uses the MSA, TA or a mixture of the two with occasional hybrid forms:

TA system

1) completed past action
   mā + past tense verb -sh
   + adverb indicating futurity

2) present action
   mā + non-past tense -sh
   mish + non-past tense

3) equational sentences
   mish / mū + adj./prep
   ghēr + adj/noun
   mā + pronoun -sh

4) negation of future
   mā + (bi-)non-past tense -sh

5) negative command
   mā + non-past tense -sh

The data show that Gaddafi uses both the MSA and dialectal systems. But apart from a few hybrid forms, there is no general overlap between the two systems: MSA negative particles are used with close-to-MSA verbs mainly and dialectal particles with close-to-TA verbs essentially. But the totality of this syntactic structure (i.e. negative particle + verb), whether basically MSA or TA, cooccurs with features of various levels in mixed sequences. Again, the indications are that certain sorts of syntagmatic relationships (particle + verb) are stronger, and less amenable to between-code variation than others.

A. The MSA system

The MSA examples consist of particles mā, lā, laysa, lan cooccurring mainly with MSA elements from the phonology, morphophonology, syntax and lexicon. On the whole, MSA particles occur more frequently than their dialectal equivalents, with 42 occurrences of MSA particles and 21 occurrences of dialectal ones. This does not mean however that the whole material is "rather" MSA since, as pointed at, most sequences are mixed, MSA linguistic elements combining with dialectal ones, and it is the total effect of this mixing which defines style at any particular point in the speech.

1 Completed past action: Data show 10 occurrences of particle mā + past tense (and no cases of lam + jussive apart from one case of hybrid form lam tinzil, see below) in mixed and MSA sequences as in:

   1981 l.127 /mā kān fī niyyatī ?abadan ?innu ?ayyi wāḥid satub'id munaẓẓamat at-taḥrīr al-falasṭīniyya/ where mā cooccurs with ?i'rāb occasionally (?abadan, ?ayyi), prefix sa and close-to-MSA verbs (satub'id) and collocation (munaẓẓamat at-taḥrīr al-falasṭīniyya, this time with the -at hybrid ending).

Although mā + non-past tense historically existed also in the classical system, it has become rather rare in MSA and tends to be avoided as it is now tainted as a "purely dialectal" feature. We notice from the data that mā + past tense, a shared MSA-TA feature, is preferred to the high-flown and markedly MSA particle lam (and lā and lan, see below).

2 Present action

Particle lā + non-past tense occurs 14 times with close-to-MSA verbs, in MSA sequences mainly, combining with MSA elements, but also in a few cases in mixed sequences as in:

1981 l.142 /zēn al-?ān lā yumkin njī ngūl/ where lā cooccurs with close-to-MSA MPP of yumkin and MSA lexical item al-?ān and dialectal features such as zēn, and the close-to-TA verb string njī ngūl.

As said earlier, particle mā + non-past tense is rare in MSA and tends to be avoided in the literary style since mā is commonly used in the colloquial.[27] The data however show examples of particle mā + non-past tense and a close-to-MSA verb twice in the data and found in mixed sequences as in:

1981 l.192 /nibghī l-jamāhīr al-falasṭīniyya mā yakūn 'alayha 'asaf/ where mā + close-to-MSA MPP of yakūn combines with dialectal preformative ni- and vowel patterning (nibghī) and two-syllable word 'asaf for MSA 'asf (with the no final consonant cluster rule). This use of mā is probably to be seen as due to dialectal, rather than MSA influence, however, given the concurrent dialectal features.

3 equational sentences: laysa is found with an adjective (1 occurrence), a noun (4), a preposition (1). Particle lā is found with a noun (8 times) in mixed and MSA sequences as in:

1981 l.177 /lammā tuṣbiḥ al-jamāhīr ḥurra tattajih ḥatman ?ilā tanẓīm nafsahā fī mu?tamarāt sha'biyya ḥaythu lā dīmuqrāṭiyya wa lā mu?tamarāt sha'biyya/ where lā + noun cooccurs with other MSA elements such as MPP of verb (tuṣbiḥ, tattajih), and collocations (mu?tamarāt sha'biyya).

Particle lan with a non-past tense verb and a close-to-MSA verb occurs only once in the data, in /lan nuxawwin/. lā, laysa and lan, like lam represent MSA choices which are mainly found with other MSA choices in MSA or close-to-MSA sequences.

B. The dialectal system

In the dialectal system, particles mā -sh, mish and mū combine with dialectal features from the P, MPP, S and L, in mixed and TA sequences.

1 completed past action: mā + past tense with a close-to-TA verb is found once in the data, and discontinuous mā + past tense -sh occurs 4 times in mixed and TA sequences as in:

1978 l.56 /hiyya mā zaltshi l-qāri'a/ where mā -sh cooccurs with the shortening of ā to a, and the deletion of unstressed vowel.

2   present action: mā + non-past tense -s̲h̲ occurs (7 times) in the
    data, in mixed sequences:

> 1981 l.11 /wa mā yiʻībās̲h̲ al-kalām ?idh̲ā kān yatakallam/ where
> mā cooccurs with a TA verb and close-to-TA MPP (yiʻībās̲h̲), a
> close-to-MSA MPP verb (yatakallam) and multivalent kān.

Particle mis̲h̲ with a close-to-TA verb occurs once in the data (mis̲h̲
yigūl).

3   equational sentence: particle mus̲h̲ is heavily marked for the
    dialect and occurs with a pronoun (2 occurrences), an active
    participle (1) and a noun (2) in TA sequences mainly, as in:

> 1978 l.40 /jāyi min it-tifarfīs̲h̲ ?inna l-wāḥid yifarfis̲h̲ mis̲h̲ ʻārif
> kēf yidīr/ which combines a whole string of dialectal features:
> active participles (jāyi, ʻārif), lexicon (tifarfīs̲h̲), preformative yi
> (tidīr, yifarfis̲h̲), particle mis̲h̲, long vowel ē for ay.

Discontinuous particle mā -s̲h̲ occurs twice, with a pronoun, in
mixed sequences as in:

> 1978 l.37 /an-nās tabda? mfarfas̲h̲ in-nās mā hīs̲h̲ ʻarfa/ which
> combines close-to-MSA MPP of verb (tabda?) on the one hand,
> and dialectal elements on the other hand, with discontinuous
> negative particle mā -s̲h̲ and active participle (ʻarfa).

mū occurs once with a passive participle and once with an adverb
(dā?iman):

> 1981 l.186 /yaʻnī ḍughūṭ ?aqṣud mū dā?iman ḍughūṭ yiqṣudū
> bihā/ this mixed sequence combines multivalent yaʻnī, MSA
> MPP (?aqṣud), phoneme q < OA /q/ and close-to-TA MPP
> (yiqṣudū).

It can be seen here that the dialectal particles tend to collocate
mainly with other dialectal elements, in dialectal or mixed
sequences.

C. Hybrid forms
The data show a few occurrences of hybrid negative forms such as:

1   MSA particle lam occurring with a close-to-TA verb, /lam tinzil/
    with preformative ti.
2   mā + close-to-MSA verb -s̲h̲: discontinuous particle mā -s̲h̲ is a
    dialectal particle: it is expected to have an informalising effect

and to cooccur with dialectal features. However, in this hybrid combination, mā -sh cooccurs with MSA features such as close-to-MSA MPP (mā yaṭla'sh, mā yaxḍa'sh) and phoneme q (mā ?a'taqdsh, mā qaltūsh).

3 particle mā cooccurring with close-to-TA verb without -sh as in mā yiqātil and mā tigdar where the discontinuous particle is expected (and occurs in other cases (mā yiqātilsh)). These forms occur in mixed sequences as in:

1981 l.64 /wallah mā nistab'id bukrā yigūlū wāḥid minhum qatalūh al-yahūd/ where mā cooccurs with dialectal preformative, dialectal ū ending and close-to-TA MPP (nistab'id, yigulū) and MSA phoneme q (qatalūh).

Results from the data concerning the negative system used by the speaker suggest (1) the emergence of multilevel and flexible particle mā -sh which is originally colloquial but cooccurs with MSA features. As said before, we witness a penetration of dialectal elements that have become multilevel at higher levels of formality. (2) The speaker seems to be avoiding the formal particle lam which usually combines with high-flown elements in formal sequences – perhaps too formal for Gaddafi's purposes here. The particle lam is minimally flexible and does not combine with colloquial elements as a rule (apart from one hybrid case lam tinzil). (3) mā (+ either past or non-past tense) seems to occupy a neutral position which may occur in any type of sequence.

Complementiser ?an + verb

?an is an MSA marker and has a style-raising effect on what follows it. It is followed in literary Arabic by a verb in the subjunctive. The Libyan equivalents of ?an (+ subj) (as in the Egyptian dialect) are asyndetic verb strings together with ?inn followed by a pronoun. Iraqi data on the other hand showed the multilevelness of ?an in MSA and BGI sequences. The Libyan data show one case of ?an with a MSA verb in MSA sequence, 12 cases of ?an with close-to-MSA verbs (10 in MSA sequences and 2 in mixed sequences), and finally 4 examples with close-to-TA verbs in mixed sequences. Among ?an + close-to-MSA verbs, it is significant to see the cooccurrence with MSA passive forms such as ?an yuqtal and ?an tuqma' with MSA q which is a further indication of its association with a "higher" style. Verbs, realized without ?i'rāb, have preformative ya and a close-to-MSA MPP (?an yatakallam), and glottal stop is kept (?an ?u?akkidhu). However, ?an combines as well with dialectal characteristics such as deletion of unstressed vowel (?an tkūn), preformative yi- (?an yixawwinūhā) and with a hybrid negative form (discontinuous negative particle and a close-to-MSA verb in ?an mā yasma'ū<u>sh</u>). As seen in the following sequence, ?an combines with the close-to-MSA MPP of derived verbs (yataḥawwal) and the lexical choice of yanba<u>gh</u>ī

> *1981 l.93* /mafrūḍ yataḥawwal yanba<u>gh</u>ī ?an yataḥawwal min al-mufīd/

?an occurs in mixed sequences as in:

> *1981 l.12* /maksūfīn ?an ntakallam li ?an naḥna mā nqātil<u>sh</u> il-ḥaqīqa baqiyyat il-'arab/ where complementiser ?an combines with discontinous mā -<u>sh</u> and close-to-MSA verb (nqātil), phoneme q (ḥaqīqa, baqiyyat), close-to-MSA MPP of verb (ntakallam).

Asyndetic verb strings and complex verb form

Dialectal syntax is also characterized by asyndetic verb strings from which the complementiser ?an is missing. The verbs tend to be TA or part of the shared set of vocabulary with a dialectal MPP as in / mā nigdru<u>sh</u> nim<u>sh</u>u/ "we cannot go".[28] Our data however yield different results: there are 7 cases of asyndetic verb strings showing some dialectal features such as deletion of unstressed vowel (lā yumkin njī), deletion of glottal stop (lāzim tāxu<u>dh</u>) and cooccurring with a hybrid negative form (of discontinuous negative particle and close-to-MSA verb, yajib mā yaxḍa'<u>sh</u>). But what is salient in other cases is that, although complementiser ?an is missing, other MSA characteristics are kept, and hence we have a complex hybrid structure from which ?an is missing, but which contains verbs having MSA MPP, particle lā + non-past tense, phoneme q and glottal stop, as in lā yumkin yaqa', lāzim tatanaffas, mumkin yalja?:

MSA	hybrid	dialect
lāzim ?an tatanaffas(a)	lāzim tatanaffas	lāzim titnaffis

We observe from the syntactic features analysed cases of hybrid forms such as the negative constructions mentioned earlier together with preformative yi- combining with MSA complementiser ?an (?an yikūn, ?an yixawwinūha) and cases of asyndetic verb strings, normal in the dialect, but combining with MSA elements mainly.

5.3.4 Lexical features

This section is concerned with describing the lexicon in MSA and TA sequences. MSA sequences are characterized by fixed expressions and collocations which are of a political, journalistic nature, given the subject matter of the speeches:

quwwāt 'arabiyya	Arab forces
ath-thawra l-falasṭīniyya	the Palestinian revolution
al-?umma al-'arabiyya	the Arab nation
al-jabha ash-sha'biyya	the popular front
l-qiyāda l-'āmma	the general leadership
mu?tamarāt sha'biyya	popular conferences
al-?arḍ al-muḥtalla	the occupied territory
al-qaḍiyya al-falasṭīniyya	the Palestinian case
al-lijān ath-thawriyya	the revolutionary committees
l-?irāda l-'arabiyya	the Arab will

in the 1978 speech:

l-farāsh al-mabthūth	the scattered moths (Quran)
l-'ihni l-manfūsh	the carded wool (Quran)

These collocations are fixed expressions, found in oral and written modes, and do not necessarily have a formalizing effect on the passage in which they occur. They display MSA characteristics such as phonemes [q] and [th]. As far as their agreement pattern is concerned, the nature of these expressions, dealing with abstract concepts and hence the MSA set of vocabulary, is associated with an MSA noun-adjective agreement system[29] which has the following combinations: an impersonal plural noun and a feminine singular adjective (ḥukūmāt 'arabiyya), and a feminine plural human noun and a feminine plural adjective.

The Libyan dialectal system however would have a plural adjective following a plural noun not referring to human beings, as in kalmtēn gwiyyāt "two strong words", brarik kbar "big huts", dyar milyanat "full rooms".[30] All examples from the data however show application of MSA rules with no influence of the dialect and a strong resistance from the MSA system to mixing and hybrid forms between the MSA and dialectal systems.

Whereas phonology, morphophonology and syntactic phenomena such as negative systems, complementiser ?an and verb strings show examples of dialectal influence on MSA systems, the agreement system shows the prevalence of MSA rules in a lexically "MSA" context.

TA passages on the other hand are characterized by:

(a) TA lexicon which includes TA verbs (with phonological and morphophonological characteristics) as seen earlier, tibghū "you want", shufit "she saw", rāḥ "he went", yidīr "he does", mā yi'ībāsh "he is not ashamed", biṣīr "it comes out";
(b) dialectal phonemes, long vowel ō instead of diphthong aw as in yōm "day", mōt "death", and long vowel ē instead of diphthong ay, bēna "between", kēf "how", 'alēhum "on them", zēn "good", wēn "where";
(c) cases of "no final consonant cluster rule" as in waqit (MSA waqt) "time", ḥizib (MSA ḥizb) "group", libis (MSA labs) "confusion", faham (MSA fahm) "understanding", gabil (MSA gabl) "before", 'asaf (MSA 'asf) "tyranny", sha'ab (MSA sha'b) "people";
(d) localisms such as guddāmna "in front of us", bass "only", tintēn "two", talāta "three", negative particles (mū and mish) as seen earlier mā fīsh "there isn't", relative pronoun ?illi which is multilevel and can combine with MSA elements in mixed sequences.

The dialect, moreover, makes frequent use of active participles instead of finite verbs[31] such as: gā'id "staying", shāyif "seeing", jāyi "coming", bāgi "remaining".

As observed in chapters three and four, fixed MSA lexical elements tend to pervade even lower levels of formality. MSA collocations remain as such and are found in dialectal sequences since, on the one hand, there is no equivalent to such expressions in dialectal terms, and on the other hand, fixed collocations of a journalistic, political nature are widely used and kept unaltered. The noun-adjective agreement system which applies to such fixed elements is MSA, as dialectal variants would be too marked for such a formal setting.

5.4 LANGUAGE FORM AND LANGUAGE FUNCTION

The previous sections were concerned with important aspects of the formal description of the two speeches (1978 and 1981) from the point of view of phonology, morphophonology, syntax and lexicon. It appears that Gaddafi is using elements from the MSA and dialectal systems, frequently resulting in mixed elements and sequences belonging to both systems as a result of the flexibility of cooccurrence rules. Linguistic variation does not occur randomly: at a macro level, choice is related to language function; at the micro level, there are certain relatively fixed local linguistic rules (an MSA negative particle is likely to be followed by a close-to-MSA verb, as seen earlier). This section will relate language function and language form in the Libyan data. Various functions would involve language variation which is the result of ideational, interpersonal and textual aspects.[32] The basic aims of such political discourse is to inform the public of government actions and its new policies, and persuade them of the validity of its decisions. These objectives hold for most political discourses. Moreover, on the basis of these two speeches, one can derive further functions. The 1981 and 1978 speeches are however very different in nature and they will be analysed respectively although there are some common functions involving similar language forms, such as distancing, in MSA, and specifying, in dialect.

In the 1981 speech, ideationally, whenever Gaddafi is introducing a subject, preparing the ground, channeling general understanding, advising (and at times patronizing) the audience, and discussing divisive lines of action, he distances himself from the public, depersonalises the discourse and makes it abstract. The discourse is characterized ideationally by abstractness, compactness, formality, detachment, planning and integration (see Involvement section in chapter two). The interpersonal relation is a neutral one (with impersonal 3rd person) and as the discourse is abstract, the linguistic form is MSA with a cooccurrence of characteristics such as:

- phonemes [q] < OA /q/ and [th] < OA /th/;
- MPP of verbs, complementiser ?an, prefix sa- indicating future tense;
- long nominal phrases, verbal nouns (masdars), negative particles;
- lexically abstract nouns and items of the MSA set of vocabulary (see above), collocations and MSA lexicon triggering an MSA agreement system.

Tripoli Arabic, however, is used when Gaddafi is personalising, specifying his discourse by supplying examples to which the audience can relate; when the speaker is pleading his cause and invoking loyalty to Libya or rousing support from the crowd. In all these cases, dialectal elements are heavily used. There is also a stylistic downgrading when Gaddafi reasserts links between different parties, justifying the support provided and levelling down his speech to make it more understandable. Interpersonally, there is a direct address to the public to get it involved and 1st and 2nd person pronouns (I and you) are used. Ideationally, the discourse is characterized by involvement, personalisation, specificity and spontaneity. Textually, detailed speech is accompanied by dialectal features such as:

- phoneme g < OA /q/, t < OA /th/;
- MPP of verbs, lack of ?i'rāb, resyllabication, aspectual prefix bi, deletion of short vowel and glottal stop;
- syntactically, dialectal negative particles, asyndetic verb strings;
- lexically, everyday items (of the dialectal set of vocabulary), localisms.

In the 1978 speech, in MSA passages, the speaker repeats some verses and extracts from the Quran with various explanations. He distances himself from the audience using an authoritative tone to guide the public into understanding the text. The sermon shows the discrepancy between, on the one hand, text, i.e. passages from the Quran which are fixed, unalterable and in Classical Arabic, and, on the other hand, exegesis,[33] i.e. an explanation of text, in dialect (see MSA characteristics before, with the occurrence of ?i'rāb added to the list).

Dialect is used in passages where the speaker provides explanatory examples and uses images as he wishes the audience to relate to the various points and understand the message of it all. As Gaddafi wants the public to be more involved, he involves them in his explanations (use of "I" and "you" forms). Exegesis provides a precise explanation of text, and interpretations are given "in other words" or at different levels of formality. Whereas in MSA passages, the speaker is often judging and guiding, in dialectal (and mixed) passages, he has a more modest role, more human ("one-of-us") in his desire to unify people.

In this section we will provide examples from the 1981 and 1978 speeches that display various functions.

5.4.1 Extracts: The 1981 speech

In the 1981 speech, Gaddafi starts by saying that everyone is tired of listening to empty words, while Palestinian camps are being bombed, and it would be useful to listen to Abu Ammar (Yasir Arafat). The introduction, from lines 1 to 9, has many MSA features, as he prepares and introduces the subject.

(1) /lākin kāna min/ min al-muhimm/ ?anna sami'nā kalām qā?id a<u>th</u>-<u>th</u>awra l-falasṭiniyya l-?ax ?abu 'ummār/ clap/ (2) li?annu huwa ?illi yaḥaqq lahu ?an yatakallam/ al-falasṭīni al-ḥaqīqa huwa ?illi/ yiqātil wa yimūt/ wa mā yi'ībā<u>sh</u> al-kalām ?i<u>dh</u>ā kān yatakallam/

(1) But it is important for us to listen to the words of the leader of the Palestinian revolution, Brother Abu Ammār.(2) Because he has the right to talk. The true Palestinian is the one who is fighting and dying and he should not be ashamed of talking if he has to. *1981 l.8 to 11*

This passage shows the duality between language form and function. In (1), Gaddafi is advising and, maybe moralising. In so doing, he distances himself from the crowd, and the tone is neutral, impersonal ("it is important that"). The passage is in MSA with features such as phonemes [q] < OA /q/ (qā?id) and [<u>th</u>] < OA /<u>th</u>/ (<u>th</u>awra), collocation (<u>th</u>awra falasṭiniyya) and close-to-MSA MPP of verb (sami'na). As the first section deals with some advice, the second one shows a gradual downgrading to a more specific level, as Gaddafi is talking personally about Abu Ammar and justifies his action (he has the right to talk). (2) starts with MSA elements such as phoneme [q] and close-to-MSA MPP of verb (yaḥaqq), preposition lā, complementiser ?an and dialectal features combine such as relative pronoun ?illi, preformative yi, lexical item and discontinuous negative particle (mā yi'ībā<u>sh</u>).

Rumours have circulated about putative differences between Libya and the PLO and the speaker wishes to refute these stories. To add weight to his argument, he depersonalises his discourse, and uses MSA, which gives an air of axiomatic inevitability:

l.39 /... lā yumkin tūjad ?azma ../
"a crisis cannot be found"
l.42 /... lā yumkin yaqa' tanāquḍ bayna humā bayna <u>th</u>-<u>th</u>awra wa <u>th</u>-<u>th</u>awra/
"It is impossible that an incompatibility occurs between the two, between a revolution and a revolution"
l.47 /... mustaḥīl taqa' ?azma bayna <u>th</u>awra wa <u>th</u>awra/
"It is impossible that a crisis should occur between a revolution and a revolution"

Gaddafi uses impersonal verbs and expressions to create distance (mustaḥīl, lā yumkin), and other MSA features such as phoneme q, close-to-MSA MPP (yaqa'), negative particle lā + non-past tense, MSA verbal noun (tanāquḍ).

In lines 146 to 148, Gaddafi is insisting on the support that should be provided to Palestinians:

> /?idhā lā budda min al-ḥifāẓ 'alēha wa da'mahā wa ta?yīdaha ?a'laniyan ḥatta l-'ālam ya'rif ?anna hādhihi l-mumaththil ash-shar'ī wa l-waḥīd li sh-sha'b al-falasṭīni/
> It is necessary [to provide the PLO] with protection, support, public assurance so that the whole world knows that it is the sole and legitimate representative of the Palestinian people.

As Gaddafi wishes to give a serious message, influence and persuade the audience, he speaks in the third person, by the use of lā budda min "it is necessary" (rather than "we must"), and by the use of verbal nouns al-ḥifāẓ wa da'mahā wa ta?yīdaha (rather than personalised finite verbs "that we protect, support and assure"). The whole proposition is impersonal. The level used is consequently MSA with MSA features at all levels: close-to-MSA MPP (ya'rif); phoneme th (mumaththil); verbal noun (ta?yīd); expression of necessity (lā budda min, dialect has lāzim); collocation (l-mumaththil ash-shar'ī) and long nominal phrases with few finite verbs.

But Gaddafi also wants to plea, personally, for the Palestinians and stress the real-life insecurities and dangers encountered in their daily lives. To move the audience and rouse their sympathy, he levels down his speech, making it more vivid and human-scale, with details of actual or imagined persons:

> *l.59* /ya'ni l-yōm ma'ak wāḥid bukra yigūlūk qutil/
> "I mean, one day someone is with you, the next day they tell you he is dead"
> *l.61* /u kān mumkin in-nās yi'allaqu yigūlū ?innu hawlā? in-nās wēn qaḍiyyathum/ wa ba'd kam yōm qutilū/
> "and people could be commenting, saying about these people "so what about their cause" and a few days later, Palestinians are killed
> *l.63* /... kān ma'āya bassām ash-shak'a/ al-?ān quṭi'at rijlayh t-tintēn/
> One day Bassam Shakaa was with me ... and now his legs are amputated
> *l.64* /an-nās ?illi mawjudīn guddāmnā/ wallah mā nistab'id bukrā yigulū wāḥid minhum qatalūh al-yahūd/ hādha l-yōm ma'akum bukrā yimūt/

"People who are in front of us now... we couldn't rule out the possibility that tomorrow they say "one of them has been killed by the Jews" – here today, dead tomorrow"

Interpersonally, Gaddafi wishes to involve his audience, he addresses them directly (he is among "you", people in front of "us"). Although there are a few MSA characteristics (phoneme q and close-to-MSA MPP of verb qutilū), dialectal features predominate: phoneme [g] < OA /q/ (yigūl); [t] < OA /th/ (tintēn); long vowel ō for diphthong aw (yōm) and long vowel ē for diphthong ay (wēn); close-to-TA MPP of verb (nistab'id); connective u (MSA has wa); absence of ?i'rāb (ū ending for MSA ūna); hybrid feminine ending (qaḍiyyatkum); relative pronoun ?illi; lexical localisms (guddāmna, tintēn); negative particle mā and non-past tense verb. All of these features figure prominently.

Once he has invoked pity for the Palestinians' fate, Gaddafi wants to endorse solidarity between Palestinians and Libyans, and emphasize the Libyan loyalty rather than that of other Arab states and, at the same time, justify political support being provided to the Fatah. To do so, he gives an account of a discussion he had with two leaders:

l.71 to 73 /...wa l-?ams gult li ?abu 'ummār wa ?abu ?iyyād/ gultilhum/ ?in ḥad ḍāyigkum min al-'arab wa tibghū tishtamū ḥadd ?ishtamū lēna ?iḥna li?annu ?iḥna/ masāmḥīnkum/ wa mā nuwāxizkum/

And yesterday, I said to Abu Ammār and Abu ?iyyād/ I said to them/ "If someone among the Arabs annoys you and you want to insult someone, insult us because we are tolerant and we won't hold it against you.

This report lightens the tone and makes the discourse livelier by turning it into a reported conversation involving 1st and 2nd persons singular ("I said to them, if you .."). Dialectal features occur as a consequence of this, e.g. phoneme g < OA /q/ (gult, ḍāyig), verb string (tibghū tishtamū), MPP of verb (tibghū), long vowel ē for ay (lēna, ?ilayna).

5.4.2 Extracts: The 1978 sermon

The 1978 sermon in a mosque displays various functions of the language involving code-switching. The salient features of the discourse are the repetitions of some verses from the surat al-qāri'a and the constant interplay between these verses and their interpretation. The presentation of the analysis is somewhat different from the earlier case: we will proceed through the discourse gradually so as to exemplify the full impact of these repetitions and "litany" effects as well as showing the relations between language forms and different functions.

The speaker recites the first two verses of the sura (al-qāri'a, mā l-qāri'a) with long pauses of 5 to 6 seconds to stress the words, and presents the facts known about the sura (it has the number 101, and was revealed in Mecca). This introduction is repeated as in the following passage (*lines 11 to 14*):

> /wa lā yaxtalif 'alayha ?i<u>th</u>nāni mina l-muslimīn/ min d-dār al-bayḍā? ḥatta jakarta/ lā yaxtalif ?i<u>th</u>nāni mina l-muslimīn 'ala ?anna hā<u>dh</u>ihi hiya s-sūrata l-qāri'a wa 'ala ?annaha nazalat bi makka/ wa 'ala ?annaha taḥmilu raqam miyya u wāḥad fī l-qur?ān/ wa haka<u>dh</u>ā duwwinat 'indamā nazalat/
> And two Muslims would not disagree on this/ from Casablanca to Jakarta/ two Muslims would not disagree that it is the surat al-qāri'a and that it was revealed in Mecca/ and that it holds the number 101 in the Quran/ and this is how it was recorded when it was revealed/

Ideationally, by repeating the different facts, the speaker gives credibility (these are the facts, this is what is known about the sura and everybody agrees on this). The approach is one of distancing which is part of the authoritative tone (this is what is known, no point questioning it). The whole passage is set in MSA with features such as phonemes q (qāri'a, raqam), <u>th</u> (?i<u>th</u>nāni), verbal vowel patterning (yaxtalif) and enclitics (nazalat), ?i'rāb occasionally (taḥmilu), diphthong ay ('alayha instead of dialectal ē), negative particle lā plus non-past tense verb.

Throughout the speech, the speaker organises his discourse as in l.16 where he introduces the next verse:

> l.16 <u>th</u>umma ya?ti su?āl ?āxar/**wa mā ?adrāka mā l-qāri'a**/
> Then comes another question "what will convey onto thee what the Calamity is" (Picktall 1976:818)

Discourse organizing moves in the discourse, however, can be in MSA as in this case or in dialect as in the example below (see l.28). Moreover, the speaker wants the audience to respond, and to understand the issue. Hence, he uses an image to give an idea of the scale of the destruction and says the Calamity was like a bomb (*l.15*

/al-qāri'a/ wa kānat mithil qunbula/ and the three verses were like three explosions (*l.21* /thalāth ?infijarāt warā? ba'ḍuh/ (the same idea will be illustrated below). The speaker wants involvement and commitment of his audience. To this effect, he levels down his speech and gives examples which are readily understood:

> (*lines 21 to 22*) /?idhā simi'at in-nās hādhi kalām li ?awwil marra/ lā budda ?annaha tkūn/ mundahisha/ mashdūda li hā l-kalimāt/ l-qawiyya/
> If people hear these words for the first time, no doubt they will be astonished, taken by such powerful words

The speaker tries to impress his audience and win support. The sequence is mixed with MSA features such as phoneme q (qawiyya), the MSA negative form (lā budda) and dialectal elements cooccur, such as verb close-to-TA MPP (simi'at), and deletion of unstressed vowel (tkūn).

The above signals a change in direction: Gaddafi drops his initial authoritative tone and the discourse now becomes a constant switch and interplay between the text, i.e. the verses from the Quran, repeated over and over and set in MSA, and at a slow pace (with on average 1.5 words per second) and, on the other hand, he explains and interprets, increasing the pace (3.5 words per second on average). As will be seen, there can be a repetition of the explanation, or the same interpretation at another level of formality. The functional switch is accompanied by a language switch: text is in MSA and exegesis in dialect or mixed level. Dialectal forms may also be used in discourse organising moves to introduce and quote verses from the Quran as in the following passage:

> (*l.28 to 31*) (1) /gāl l-qur?ān/ (2) **yawma yakūnu n-nāsu ka l-farāsh al-mabsūs/ wa takūnu l-jibālu ka l-'ihni l-manfūsh**/(3) ?a'ūdhu bi llāh/ hādhihi l-qāri'a allati ?afza'itna/ yabdū ?innahā muxīfa fi'lan 'indamā nazalit bi hādhihi l-kalimat l-qawiyya/ yabdū hiya qawiyya bi l-fi'il/
> (1) The Quran says/ (2) the day when men will be like scattered moths/ and mountains will be like carded wool/ (3) God forbid! This calamity that frightens us/ it seems to be very frightful as it was revealed with this powerful word / and it seems that it is powerful indeed.

In (1), gāl, in its dialectal morphophonological shape, introduces (2), quotations from the Quran, in Classical Arabic. In (3), there is level downgrading and a more personal tone as the speaker makes a personal intervention and then relates the message to "us", i.e. people in general, and shows the discrepancy between the Calamity (al-qāri'a), unknown, frightening, distant, in the MSA level, and specific "us" (?afza'itna) in a mixed level. In (3), the speaker speaks more modestly, as "one of us". With dialectal forms, he attempts to unify people's reactions vis-à-vis this frightening threat. The dialectal elements that appear are the lexical enclitic -it (?afza'itna, nazalit), the two-syllable word as a result of the "no final consonant cluster" rule (fi'il for MSA fi'l).

As can be seen from the transcription of the 1978 sermon, Quranic passages are printed in bold characters to highlight the repetitions. Occasionally, there will be words from the Quran that are not in bold, as when they are part of the exegesis of the text and not the text itself (as al-qāri'a in (3) in the passage just given).

The same Quranic verse is then repeated and an explanation of that verse is given:

> (*lines 36 to 41*) (1) **yawma yakūnu n-nās ka l-farāsh al-mabsūs**/ (2) (a) an-nās tabda? hā?ija wa mā?ija wa muxarriba/ mithil il-farāsha/ (...) mfarrash mish yigūl lik l-?insān mfarfash/ tabda? mfarfash in-nās mā hīsh 'arfa kēf ta'mal/ (b) bi ẓ-ẓabṭ/ hādhi wārda bi l-lugha l-'arabiyya bi hādha n-naṣṣ/ wa ḥatta kalimat imfarfasha hiya kalmat 'arabiyya quḥḥa/ jāyi min it-tifarfīsh ?inna l-wāḥid yifarfish mish 'ārif kīf yidīr/ (c) kulli n-nās mish shaxaṣ wāḥad/ wa lā sha'ab wāḥad/ wa lā qabīla waḥda/
> (1) The day when men will be like scattered moths, (2) (a) people will start to be agitated, tumultuous and destructive, like moths, they will get flustered ... this does not mean to you that people are flustered, people will become agitated as if they don't know what to do (b) this is it exactly; this is an Arabic word which comes in the text, and even the word imfarfasha is a pure Arabic word and comes from "agitation", someone is agitated when he does not know what he is doing (c) everybody, not just one person or one people or one tribe.

In this passage, Gaddafi aims again to interpret the verses and make the message simpler:

1 is the MSA Quranic verse as seen earlier; (2) is an interpretation of the verse "people will become like scattered moths". The passage (from lines 36 to 41) shows:

   (a) the image of people behaving like moths, not knowing what to do. As the speaker is carried away, he hesitates (...). The tempo is very fast (4 words per second). This imagery is repeated further down in the text, on l.38 /... mā hī<u>sh</u> 'arfa/ kēf ta'mal/ and l.40 /... mi<u>sh</u> 'ārif kēf yidīr/, and l.54 (mā hum<u>sh</u> 'arfīn kēf ya'milu).

(b) is introduced by a conversational adverbial expression, and is delivered at a fast pace (3.33 words per second); people are "flustered" and Gaddafi attempts to explain this term etymologically.

(c) kulli n-nās means all people, everybody, the speaker and his audience. "all people" is uttered in three paraphrases and repeated again in lines 41 and 42: (1) **yawma takūnu n-nāsu/** (2) ya'ni kull n-nās/ (3) **ka l-farā<u>sh</u> l-mabsūs/** These three sequences provide a good example of the duality text-exegesis with a rapid change of tone: (1) is uttered at a slow pace (two words per second) and a monotonous tone of voice, whereas (2) is delivered at a fast pace (three words per second) and with a conversational contour, and (3) is at a slower pace again (1.4 words per second).

The whole passage, from lines 36 to 41, shows how language form and function interrelate; the Quranic verses (*l.36 and 42*) are set in fixed Classical Arabic, whereas the rest of the passage, being a more personal explanation, combines dialectal elements, such as phoneme [g] < OA /q/ (yigūl), long vowel ē for diphtong ay (kēf), verbal vowel patterning (yifarfi<u>sh</u>), no final consonant cluster rule (mi<u>th</u>il for MSA mi<u>th</u>l), negative particle mi<u>sh</u>, present participles ('arfa, jāyi), deletion of unstressed vowel (ka<u>l</u>mat), and lexical item (yidīr).

A new verse is introduced l.43, following a pause: /**wa takūnu l-jibālu ka l-'ihni l-manfū<u>sh</u>/** and deals with the horror and effect of such calamity, so destructive that mountains will become like carded wool. Gaddafi gives a detailed account of a catastrophe (*l.42 to 53*). Mountains, which are so solid and offer a shelter for people in case of attacks, will be turned into wool. On l.54 onwards, the speaker goes back to the previous verse n-nās mi<u>th</u>il farā<u>sh</u>a "people will be like moths" where similar explanations to the ones before are given (see l.34 to 41) and repeated in different words as in l.54 /... mā hum<u>sh</u> 'arfīn kēf ya'milu) or in juxtaposition at a different level of formality as in l.57 /in-nās bitkūn mi<u>th</u>il farā<u>sh</u> **wa takūnu in-nās ka l-farā<u>sh</u> l-mabsūs**,/ "people will be like moths, people will be like scattered moths" where the first part shows dialectal features such as preformative bi, deletion of unstressed syllable (bitkūn) and mithil for MSA mithl, whereas the second part is the Quranic extract with ?i'rāb and close-to-MSA verbal MPP (takūnu).

Similar explanations of the verses are repeated, but this time in the form of a vicarious conversation so as to give the discourse more variety:

> /?ayy wāḥid minna yagulūn al-qāri'a yawm il-qiyāma tkūn in-nās ka l-farāsh il-mabsūs/ yigūl ṭayyib/ wēn il-malja/ ṭayyib fī jibāl ya'ni mumkin ?insān yalja?/ li l-jibāl/
> All of us are told that on the day of the last judgement, people will be like scattered moths/ anyone can say "OK, where is the shelter?" "OK it's in the mountains", which means that people can take refuge in the mountains. *(lines 59 to 61)*

This passage is set in a conversational tone: "Do you realize this?" he seems to be saying to the audience "on the day of the Calamity, if someone is confronted with these words (men will be like moths), he could say "OK, where is the refuge?" I am going to hide in the mountains". Well no, because here comes another verse:

> *l.61* (1) jāt il-?āya u gālat lah/ (2) **wa takūnu l-jibālu**/ (3) willi ?inta tfakkar taḥta mā biha/ (4) **ka l-'ihni l-manfūsh**/
> This is a verse that tells him/ and the mountains will become - and you think about this- like carded wool

This passage shows another example of code-switching at short intervals (as seen before on l.41) with, in (1), the use of the dialect in orienting the audience to a Quranic verse, which is in slowly-delivered Classical Arabic (2). (3) is an exhortation, with Gaddafi speaking directly to the audience ("try to think about this"), at a conversational pace (4 words per second) and with dialectal elements such as deletion of unstressed vowel (tfakkar), lexical items (willi, mi). And (4) is a return to the end of the verse.

Lines 62 to 71 provide another explanation of the effect of the destruction of mountains with a summary of the sura so far and a repetition of the explanation. He repeats the theme and, for emphasis, specifies the names of mountains, listing examples (*l.74 to 79*) of actual mountains known to the public (the Himalayas, the Atlas, the Alps, the Everest), finishing with a further direct address, teacher-style, to the audience:

> *l.76* /kull il-jibāl ?illi bta'arfūha bi jughrāfyā wa lli yi'arfūha l-jughrāfya ?illi hi mawjūda bi l-'ālam/

All the mountains that you know through geography and that are known in the geography of the world

with dialectal elements such as relative pronoun ?illi, aspectual prefix bi, resyllabication and preformative yi (yi'arfū). As illustration, Gaddafi makes a comparison with a bomb explosion: everything will be destroyed, even mountains, as if a bomb exploded in a building (1.81) /miṯẖilma tunfujaru l-qunbula fī mabna/, turning it into ashes by the scale of the explosion (1.81) /min ṣẖiddati l-?infijār yitfattat il-mabna/ yiṯẖawwal ilā trāb/. As Gaddafi tries to engage the crowd, the level becomes informal with dialectal elements such as preformative yi and deletion of unstressed vowel (yitfattat, yiṯẖawwal).

Gaddafi repeats the bomb simile a third time, in a conversational style, with intensifier "very" repeated three times (1.83) qunbula daxma jiddan jiddan jiddan, which sounds as if it is part of an ordinary chit-chat. The passage ends with a reiteration on the topic of destruction.

In this speech, we have tried to show the importance of the interplay of text and exegesis, and the function of repetition of the same message, at different linguistic levels in order to attain maximum impact. The text was in Classical Arabic / MSA and the explanation was delivered at a faster pace, sometimes in an anecdotal style, in what we have termed mixed and dialectal sequences. The text was seen as authoritative, intimidating and distant, whereas the exegesis was meant to explain by an easily understood context: "We are all in the same boat" Gaddafi seems to be saying, on the day of the last judgement.

NOTES

1 Quarterly Economic Review of Libya. The Economist Intelligence Unit Annual supplement 1978: 2; Unesco Statistical Yearbook 1991: 1–6.
2 Area Handbook for Libya 1973: 96; Rosenhouse 1984: 6.
3 El Fitoury 1976.
4 for Tripoli Arabic, see El Fitoury 1976; El Gadi 1986; Griffini 1913; Cesaro 1939. For Cyrenaican Arabic, see Mitchell 1952, 1960; Panetta 1943; Owens 1984.
5 Owens 1984: 239–43.
6 see Mitchell 1960: 384.
7 see Owens 1984: 13.
8 see Rosenhouse 1984: 27.
9 Owens 1984: 2–3; Mitchell 1960.
10 see Owens 1984: 239 and Griffini 1913: 93.

11 Area Handbook for Libya 1973: 1.
12 see Harris 1986: 26; Area Handbook for Libya 1973: 97–9.
13 Blanc 1964: 14–6.
14 Harris 1986: 45.
15 Owens 1984: 243.
16 El Fathaly and Palmer 1980: 60–7; Harris 1986: 43.
17 El Fathaly and Palmer 1980: 67.
18 see El Fitoury 1976: 5.
19 Griffini 1913: 66.
20 see Mitchell 1980: 102.
21 see Rosenhouse 1984: 8.
22 as well as in Tunisia and Morocco, see Cantineau 1960: 59.
23 see Holes 1986: 19.
24 with cases of yiCCiC, yuCCuC, see Rosenhouse 1984: 28, Singer 1980: 261–2.
25 see Owens 1984: 148–9.
26 see Meiseles 1981: 1077, and the Methodology Chapter.
27 Cantarino 1974: 108.
28 El Fitoury 1976: 136.
29 see Owens and Bani-Yasin 1987: 717.
30 El Fitoury 1976: 128.
31 see El Fitoury 1976: 110, Rosenhouse 1984: 39.
32 see Halliday 1978: 31–5.
33 see Holes 1993.

6 Forms and Functions: shared tendencies in the data

This chapter is concerned with a comparison of the three sets of Arabic data so as to examine the functional and linguistic parallels in the Egyptian, Iraqi and Libyan material collated.

6.1 COMPARISON OF THE THREE SETS OF DATA

6.1.1 Language functions

As we consider the three sets of data, we notice that they share a certain number of functions and strategies associated with a particular language level:

- In all three sets of data, MSA is particularly likely to be used whenever the speaker is constructing an abstract argument, recalling historical events, expanding new political ideas, and axioms. General and abstract concepts are presented as if they were unquestionable text, as opposed to exegesis. As the speaker distances himself from the audience, he tends to depersonalise the discourse. The speaker may also want to act as a spokesman or third party. Because in these cases the speaker is instructing his audience, the tone is authoritative, that of superior to inferior, and MSA is the expected code for such purposes. Accompanying paralinguistic features such as slow delivery and pauses are employed to give full emphasis to some words and to signal the "weight" of the message.
- On the other hand, the dialect, whether Cairene, Baghdadi or Tripoli Arabic, tends to be used when the speaker, for instance, explains and specifies his political programme, his conversations with various leaders, or his personal experience. Abstract concepts (in MSA) are repeated and paraphrased in the dialect to make sure

> that the audience understood them. This involves the establishment of a more "equal" personal relationship with the audience, in which the speaker "levels" with them. Typically such moves involve a switch to the dialect. In dialectal passages, the speaker wishes to establish a sense of solidarity and get the audience involved. The tone is more familiar and personal ("we", "you" and "I" pronouns to create a sense of communion, a "one-of-us" feeling of the speaker with the audience). Whereas in MSA passages the politician is often vicariously judging and guiding, in dialectal passages, he plays a more modest role, more "human" in his desire to create unity and understanding. The dialect is used in asides, narrative accounts, and in the relating of anecdotes. Paralinguistic features such as the use of conversational intonation patterns and a more rapid rate of speech are used. The tone in such passages can be argumentative to show emotion and commitment (see below for a comparison with English speeches). Specific examples are resorted to, to elicit deep feelings of sympathy or pity from the audience and to unite behind the speaker's views.

As to the speech functions associated with the dialect, there are more idiosyncrasies than in the case of MSA, in the extracts which form the subject of this study: these idiosyncrasies are related to each speaker's linguistic habits, but also to his political and rhetorical aims in the speeches examined:

- Nasser uses it to insist on a sense of common solidarity and unity (all Egyptians together, all Arabs united).
- Saddam Hussein wants to appear relaxed, friendly and confident, very much at ease in the debate: he recounts the detail of political negotiations in a conversational style with reported speech and (presumably invented) repartees ("the Shah of Iran said this, then I said this and then he said that..."). Moreover, to bring politics on to a more specific level, he even personifies countries ("the Soviet Union went and said this..").
- Gaddafi presents himself in the role of a national guide and uses specific examples and colourful imagery to explain concepts and to provoke a reaction of indignation, pity or sympathy.

I am not dealing in this chapter with the dialectal peculiarities specific to each dialect and country. Rather, I am concerned with the functions associated with a switch from MSA towards dialectal forms in the speeches under study. However, I would like to point out the fact that, overall, in Nasser's speeches, the switches between MSA and the dialect are much more marked and drastic: by this I mean that the speaker is able to maintain an MSA level consistently and sound very formal, and then, as the function changes within the same stretch of discourse, the level descends to basic, authentic Cairene, with all its localisms.

In Saddam Hussein and Gaddafi's speeches, the MSA and dialectal passages are not as sharply defined as in Nasser's: MSA patches can be found, but interspersed most of the time with dialectal features which produce more of a mixed linguistic level, rather than a clearcut MSA versus dialect differentiation. Nasser seems at ease and fluent in both styles and manages to use these shifts fully for dramatic and rhetorical effects. As explained in chapter three, Nasser was a populist politician and the first to make deliberate use of switches, between MSA and Cairene, in his speeches. As Abd El Jawad[1] says, "the late President Nasser of Egypt used what is called "the language of the masses" in his speeches to be closer to the audience, to stress his principles and to convey his messages to a wider audience, e.g. peasants and workers".

Despite the differences in time, background, political stance and aspirations, Saddam Hussein and Gaddafi seem to have been influenced by Nasser's style in their imitation of the call to the Arab nation and in their mixing of MSA and dialectal levels for the achievement of their rhetorical aims.

Whether other politicians in the Arab world with similar political aspirations are found using comparable language shifts is worthwhile investigating but would be beyond the scope of this study.

To sum up, variation in language level is related to the following major factors:

(1) discourse functions and strategies: where the function is didactic and "legislative", speakers are led to use MSA; where the function is exegetical, the dialect (or at least a more dialectalised MSA) is usual.

(2) throughout the discourse, the speaker might want to claim different statuses and roles:[2] the politician may wish to associate himself with the connotations of fuṣḥā prestige, authority, power and respect. On the other hand, he may wish to emphasise solidarity with his listeners – hence he will use dialect.

6.1.2 Linguistic comparison of the three sets of data

Although I said earlier that I am not concerned with a comparison of linguistic features as such since the three dialects are different, I will look at parallels in the linguistic "adjustments" which occur in code-switching in the three sets of data. By this I mean that when a speaker switches from dialect to a more formal language level, some obvious dialectal elements may be retained within his speech and mixed with MSA features; one asks, are the same types of dialectal elements retained ? The following general points are offered for consideration:

1 In order to understand the mechanisms, I look at code-switching from dialectal to mixed sequences to find persistent dialectal elements. As dialect is the native language of Arabic speakers, I analyze the process of movement from what feels "natural" in the language system (the dialect) to what feels "less-natural" (MSA) and I look at the dialectal elements that are not eliminated in the process.
2 These dialectal elements that are still pervasive in more formal discourse may be significant in terms of their salience and their particular status. The fact that they combine with MSA features suggests that they may have undergone a change of status: they have lost their dialectal markedness and become multilevel. Although originally dialectal, these elements are not too "dialectally marked" otherwise they would tend to occur with other dialectal elements only.
3 The dialectal-multilevel elements that I will be looking at below belong to phonology, morphophonology and syntax, and they are hence all non-referential, non-meaning bearing features. Even if the speaker is aware of the non-referential dialectal elements, these tend to be more immune to conscious suppression or change than lexical items. This point is illustrated in Lavendera's[3] article where she demonstrates that the elements best suited for a study on variation are non-referential, or more precisely "need not have referential meaning", and in her article, are phonemes. Phonemes, together with the morphemes and syntactic elements which are considered in this study, all fill the condition of being non-referential and non-meaning bearing elements; the latter is an important condition set by Labov[4] for the study of variation, in which the varying segments should be integral units of larger structures. In our case, the phonemes are consonants forming part of the root of an item. Morphemes, such as preformative yi- and aspectual prefix bi- for example, are affixed to the verb, and in the case of syntactic elements, the negative particle mā is placed before the verb. When I consider

mā + verb and very often -sh (see below), I notice that, from the point of view of stress assignment, mā is phonologically part of the verbal unit and not an independent segment, as in mastaṭa'nāsh.

In the next part, I will look at commonly recurring types of dialectal elements in the three sets of data within each category of phonology, morphophonology and syntax. Since dialects are different, I cannot expect elements to be identical across the three dialects. Occasionally, there are common elements in two dialects (generally Cairene (CA) and Tripoli (TA) which are relatively close) with the third dialect diverging. But despite these local differences, the basic mechanisms seem to be the same in the three sets of data in terms of which types of categories of features are integrable into MSA elements.

Phonology

In the case of individual segments, there is generally a substantial difference between the MSA realisation and the dialectal one. Two phenomena occur: either the dialectal realisation is scarcely used at all in combination with MSA elements (apart from the frequent item ?āl/ gāl), or there is an emergence of a third phoneme, intermediate between MSA and the dialect.

a) Scarce dialectal realisation: the case of OA /q/

In the case of OA /q/, there is no third phoneme intermediate between MSA and the dialect. The Iraqi and Libyan data, with dialectal [g] realisation for OA /q/, have very rarely [g] cooccurring with MSA features, apart from the case of the item gāl which is so widespread that it is "accepted" in more formal levels and in the numerous passages of reported speech. In the following example, gāl introduces a case of reported speech in MSA:

> *BGI SH4 l.15* /gāl ?ana l-?ān fawran musta'idd ?uwaqqi'/ where g cooccurs with MSA phoneme q and MPP (?uwaqqi') in the reported clause.

The reason for the scarcity of [g] in more formal levels is that [g] (as well as Iraqi [č] < OA /k/) is felt to be too local, dialectal and hence inappropriate for public speaking.

The Egyptian data on the other hand show more cases of [?] cooccurring with MSA elements. [?] is found in items such as ḥa??, wa?t, musta?bal, ?āl, ?ām. The higher frequency of Egyptian [?] compared to Iraqi and Libyan [g] might be explained by the fact that [?] has acquired pan-Arabic acceptability as it is typical of Cairo, the largest population centre, and also in the urban centres of the Levant. On the other hand, [g] is typical of Bedouin speech in the area and smacks of the countryside. Moreover, as we commented in chapters one and three, Egyptians feel confident and proud of their dialect, and rarely change it in making speeches or in cross-dialectal conversations,[5] retaining many Egyptian localisms which are understood outside Egypt. Mixed MSA-dialect passages with [?] include:

> *CA 1957 l.90* /kullu wāḥad fīkum ?ām yuqātil/ and
> *CA 1957 l.103* /kuntu fī nafsi l-wa?t ?ash'ur bimā qāsaytum/ where [?] cooccurs with MSA elements such as MSA phoneme q, MPP (yuqātil) and ?i'rāb (kullu).

b) Emergence of a third phoneme: the case of the interdentals

Reflexes of the OA interdental /th/ (in Egyptian and Libyan), and /dh/ and /ẓ/ (in Egyptian), show the emergence of third, intermediate phonemes: [s] between MSA [th] and dialectal [t] (sawra in CA and mabsūs in TA), [z] between MSA [dh] and dialectal [d], and [Z] between MSA [ẓ] and dialectal [ḍ]. The sibilants represent a slight downgrading from MSA and are found occurring in mixed and what are otherwise purely MSA passages.

It is interesting to notice that the Libyan data has the MSA realisation of OA /dh/ and OA /ẓ/ but no occurrence in the data of a dialectal ([d], [ḍ]) or a third phoneme. The literature on the Libyan dialect however does not mention any case of intermediate phonemes. Phonemes /th/, /dh/ and /ẓ/ are also dialectal reflexes of a typically Bedouin dialect; hence, in the case of interdentals, Bedouin dialect (i.e. the speaker's native speech) and MSA coincide. And one can speculate that this absence of dialectal phonemes [d] and [ḍ] is due to the fact that the speaker is using his native speech (which in this case corresponds to MSA). The fact that TA [t] < OA [th] occurs in the dialect in the case of numerals can be seen as an influence of TA on the speaker's native speech.

In the Iraqi dialect, interdentals /th/, /dh/ and /ẓ/ are multivalent and found combining with MSA and dialectal features (hence interdentals have a different stylistic significance in BGI than in CA and TA).

In the Libyan data, there is an interesting case of dialectal phoneme which occurs throughout dialectal and MSA passages:

alveo-palatal [j] is the general Libyan dialectal realisation of OA /dj/ and is found consistently throughout the Libyan data apparently without any lexical conditioning. The fact that the dialectal variant is only at a very slight phonetic distance from OA /dj/ has perhaps made it less salient and therefore acceptable. At any rate, it is realised as such in MSA passages. A similar phenomenon is found in Syria/ Lebanon, where /j/ is also consistently used in high level MSA, and, of course in Cairene, where [g] < OA /dj/ is used.

Morphophonology

The common mechanism by which dialectal morphophonemes consistently pervade the MSA system (contrarily to phonemes) is easier to observe since morphophonological features are homogeneous and similar to a certain extent across the three sets of data. When switching to MSA, all three speakers have in their language systems the following elements:

1 a non-standard non-past tense plural ending: -ū in CA and TA and -ūn in BGI. These occur in dialectal, mixed and MSA sequences. The full ?i'rāb ending -ūna is apparently felt too formal to be occurring in these speech contexts. As said before, -ūna is an MSA extramarker and would only be used at very high levels of stylistic formality. There is however a stylistic significance in -ū in CA and TA that is not found in BGI -ūn. Since -ūn is closer to MSA -ūna than CA and TA are, it does not carry as much dialectal weight as -ū. Despite this difference, the -ū and -ūn endings have become multilevel in formal usage.
2 In all three sets of data, the mixed passages reflect the dialectal deletion of unstressed short vowels, as exemplified in the following tokens which are in other respects of their morphophonology, MSA: CA yughādrū "they abandon", BGI yat'āmal "he trades" and TA nḥāwil "we try"; here, CA, BGI and TA refer to the different data.
3 The relative pronoun ?illi is all pervasive in the three sets of data, since the MSA choices alladhī, allatī, alladhīna are felt too formal.
4 The Egyptian and Libyan data show the persistence of the dialectal lexical enclitic -it (third feminine singular) cooccurring with MSA elements, CA badhalit, TA nazalit.
5 The Iraqi data has the dialectal lexical enclitic -it for the 1st person singular combining with MSA elements such as: BGI ?a'lanit, baḥathit.

6 The sixth point shows an interesting division (and parallel in the language system) between dialects. The Egyptian and Libyan data show the frequency and multilevelness of the prefix bi-, originally dialectal, and combining with MSA elements in mixed sequences. The form produced is a symbiotic verb (see chapters 3, 4, 5) of prefix bi + the non-past tense of a close-to-MSA verb such as CA binaḥtafil "we are celebrating" and TA bitas?al "you are asking". Prefix bi- is extremely widespread and routinely cooccurs even with markedly MSA elements in mixed sequences as in: CA (*1957 l.47*) /kān kulli wāḥad fīkum biyastaṭī' ?an yuqābil al-mu'tadīn waghan li wagh/ where bi combines with MSA features such as phoneme q, MPP (yastaṭī', yuqābil), complementiser ?an, ?i'rāb (kulli, wagha).

The Egyptian data also has a few cases of the future tense prefix ḥa-, which behaves exactly as bi- in that it combines with close-to-MSA verbs to produce symbiotic verb forms, as in ḥaya<u>sh</u>tariku "they will cooperate" and ḥanantaṣir "we will triumph".

The BGI dialect does not have prefix bi- but the data show a similar mechanism to bi- in CA and TA: in the Iraqi data, preformative prefix yi- is found recurrently combining with the non-past tense of a verb with MSA features such as phoneme [q] in tit'allaq "it relates" or combining occasionally in hybrid forms with MSA negative particle lā (lā yiḥsinūn). Preformative yi- occurs in mixed sequences as in: *BGI SH3 l.25* /hā<u>dh</u>i l-mas?ala mumkina walākin lā yumkin ?an yitḥaqqaq natī<u>dj</u>ata l-mutawaxxayāt/ where yi- combines with MSA elements such as phoneme q, MPP (yumkin), negative particle (lā), and ?i'rāb (nati<u>dj</u>ata).

7 This seventh point concerns the feminine ending in noun-pronoun constructions (see examples in chapters 3, 4 and 5) where one has the possibility of an intermediate, hybrid form between the MSA and the dialectal choices (as was the case for the interdentals).

Feminine endings in Egytian and Libyan data (Iraqi data)

MSA	*Hybrid*	*Dialect*
atu/a/i	-at	-it
(atu/a/i)	←————————	(-at)

Egyptian and Libyan endings are similar; Iraqi endings are different and put into parentheses.

One observes the following phenomena:

(a) in the Egyptian data, although one notices the emergence of a hybrid ending -at, the dialectal option nonetheless recurs throughout the data.
(b) In the Libyan data, hybrid endings in noun-pronouns are pervasive, as in quwwathu.
(c) The Iraqi data is different in the sense that the dialectal ending for noun-pronoun construction is -at which is a hybrid ending in the two other dialects. Since the Iraqi dialect has an acceptable, not "too" dialectally marked ending, there is no need or indeed real possibility for a hybrid form to emerge in this construction, and the dialectal endings are found to pervade. It is as if the language system maintains a balance between not too dialectally marked elements and not too MSA marked features in this kind of public speaking.

Syntax

As far as the negative system is concerned, one observes in the three sets of data the fact that the MSA and dialectal systems are kept separate. Apart from a few hybrid forms with mā (in CA and TA), dialectal particles occur with dialectal features (close-to-dialect and dialectal verbs), and MSA particles occur with MSA elements (close-to-MSA and MSA verbs). The three sets of data share a considerable frequency in the use of the negative particle mā with a non-past tense verb. This use of mā is common in Classical Arabic and is attested in MSA but it is overwhelmingly regarded as a "dialectal" feature, occurring in virtually all Arabic dialects. It has become so much part of the native's language system that it is found cooccurring with MSA as well as dialectal features. When mā combines with MSA verbal elements it forms a hybrid construction. The Egyptian and Libyan data show cases of:

(a) mā and close-to-dialect verb without -<u>sh</u> where -<u>sh</u> would be expected as in CA mā nikallim, mā niṭla' and TA mā yiqātil.
(b) Cases of mā + close-to-MSA verb and -<u>sh</u> this time as in CA mastaṭa'nā<u>sh</u> and TA mā yaxḍa'<u>sh</u>.

In the Iraqi data, one does not have cases of hybrid constructions of mā + close-to-MSA verb since mā + non-past tense occurs with BGI and close-to-BGI verbs only. Some hybrid forms occur however, but concern mainly MSA particle lā combining with close-to-BGI verbs (as in lā yiḥsinūn) which is explained by the pervasiveness of preformative yi- at higher levels of formality. Hence, in the Iraqi data, as seen earlier, preformative yi- is a multilevel element and combines with MSA particle lā and complementiser ?an.

In the case of complementiser ?an, the Egyptian data show that MSA ?an combines with MSA and close-to-MSA verbs (?an tu?ammin, ?an tuwāgihha). There is no dialectal influence on ?an and its complement although ?an + verb can occur occasionally with dialectal elements in mixed sequences. In the Libyan dialect, ?an occurs mainly with MSA features (MSA and close-to-MSA verbs) and very occasionally with dialectal elements (TA ?an yixawwinūhha). ?an is multivalent in the Iraqi dialect and can be found combining with MSA and dialectal features (as in ?an yikūn).

Asyndetic verb strings, on the other hand, are dialectally marked in the three sets of data and combine dialectal elements of MPP as in (TA yumkin yi'allaqu, BGI yiḥāwlūn yiṭfunha) and tend to occur in dialectal sequences as in:

CA 1962 l.68 /mā kānitsh ti?dar ta'mil hāga ?abadan/

When one deals with the lexical category of language, purely dialectal items are too local (and hence salient, such as CA barḍu, ?izzay) to concur with MSA elements (apart from some rare Egyptian cases such as 'alashān, due again to the particular privilege associated with the Cairene dialect. 'alashān can occur with MSA features as in:

CA 1957 l.112 /'alashān yukammil 'amaliyyāt/
CA 1957 l.152 /wa 'alashān yudāfi' 'an ḥurriyyituh wa 'an ?istiqlāluh/ where 'alashān occurs in mixed sequences and combines with MSA elements such as close-to-MSA MPP (yukammil, yudāfi'), phoneme q (?istiqlāluh) and dialectal ending -it (ḥurriyyituh). However, one finds that MSA lexical items, particularly fixed collocations, occur in dialectal passages as well, because there is no dialectal equivalent for such fixed expressions. Examples include:
BGI SH1 l.11 /likay itgūl ?inna l-'irāq garrab yintidj qunbula nawawiyya/ where the collocation qunbula nawawiyya combines with dialectal elements such as deletion and prosthetisation of vowel (itgūl), phoneme [g] < OA /q/ (garrab), close-to-BGI MPP (yintidj); and in:
CA 1957 l.144 /wa faransa il-baladēn ?illi byu'tabaru min il-bilād al-'uẓma/ where the collocation (il-bilād al-'uẓma) with the MSA phoneme /ẓ/ combines with dialectal elements such as relative

pronoun ?illi, preformative bi (byu'tabaru), long vowel ē (baladēn).

In the three sets of data, one observes that the noun-adjective agreement system is lexically determined, and conforms to the MSA rules; given the formality of the setting, dialectal rules would be too marked for this kind of discourse.

In conclusion, one finds that some phonological, morphophonological and syntactic dialectal features rise up the stylistic cline and progress into higher levels of formality, combining with MSA elements. These dialectal elements lose their "dialectalness" in the process, and become multilevel, neutral features. They are non-referential and as such are embedded in the language system, use of which may be largely unconscious. Parallel to these dialectal features which penetrate higher levels, there are some hybrid forms which fill a gap between the MSA and dialectal choices, where the former is felt to be "too formal" and the latter "too informal" for the speech context examined.

Hence, when switching up, the speakers keep dialectal phonemes, morphemes and some syntactic elements, but when they switch down, MSA lexical items remain. This process produces a form of Arabic reminiscent of what some authors have described as part of ESA (see chapter one).

NOTES

1 Abd El Jawad 1986: 24.
2 see Holes 1993.
3 Lavendera 1978.
4 Labov 1966: 49.
5 see also El Hassan 1978: 42.

7 The political speech as a textual genre

This chapter consists of a comparison of functions in Arabic and English political discourse, as well as an analysis of the universality of the functions and the effects of code-switching. The chapter is divided into three: firstly, a comparison of functions in Arabic and English political oratory. Secondly, shared rhetorical tactics in Arabic and English political discourse are illustrated so as to point out the widespread nature of those rhetorical tactics. The last section is a comparison of the strategies used, not only in political discourse but in conversation as well. Arabic and non-Arabic conversational studies are analysed, and several issues are brought up for attention which have relevance to this study. I look notably at constraining factors in the choice of a level, which vary according to community, are linked to language functions, topic of discourse, participants, role-playing, etc. I will consider male and female attitudes towards language as well as the effects of stigmatized and prestigious dialects.

7.1 UNIVERSALITY OF FORM-FUNCTION RELATIONSHIPS: COMPARISON OF ARABIC AND ENGLISH POLITICAL DISCOURSE

I have made the point that there is a clear division of form between the dogmatic and didactic style (MSA) and the expressive, emotional and argumentative style (the dialect). A similar distribution of functions can be found in some kinds of English political oratory – by English one means speeches in the English language delivered by British or American speakers. In such discourse however, one looks at variations between standard English and a non-standard form (when there is one) which is the functional equivalent of Arabic dialect as opposed to MSA.

Although an analysis of political discourse in the English language is beyond the scope of this study, it would be interesting to see whether similar relationships exist between language functions and variation in language form -given the linguistic and paralinguistic properties of the English language. This chapter does not aim to be a detailed analysis of English oratory; rather one uses Gumperz's examples (see below) to point out the linguistic and functional similarities between English and Arabic political speeches.

Gumperz[1] provides a good example of form function variation in English usage in his analysis of a political speech delivered by a Black American leader. This example bears numerous interesting sociolinguistic aspects worth considering, but the one directly relevant to this study, deals with a significant use of linguistic and paralinguistic features related to changes in speech function. When the black speaker wishes to grab the audience's attention, appeal for their cooperation, fire them up with enthusiasm and involvement, he resorts to some words and expressions that belong to the Black English Vernacular (BEV). This use of non-standard forms to get the audience's attention and co-opt them to support the speaker's aims is reminiscent of one of the uses of Arabic dialect in political discourse, especially that of Nasser

The speech analyzed by Gumperz was delivered in the late 1960s, at a San Francisco public meeting, organised to protest against the United States policy in Vietnam. The speaker is a controversial Black community leader and the audience is mainly white. To show his disagreement with American policies, his commitment and wish to take some actions, the speaker used a BEV expression "we will kill Richard Nixon" which is a BEV metaphor for "we will destroy his influence". The white audience however did not share the same ethnic values and certainly was not aware of the BEV interpretation of the statement. As a consequence, misunderstanding occurred and the public reacted violently to what they perceived as an offensive and criminal statement. The use of a minority code in this instance was ineffective because of a mismatch between the speech norms of speaker and audience – in fact it was counterproductive.

Studies have shown that speakers from minority groups, when in discussion with speakers from dominant communities, vary their native, local speech, adapt it and imitate features of the dominant group. This accommodation is resorted to in order to avoid the negative associations of speaking the stigmatized dialect, and may happen even if this change implies abandoning forms that are objectively closer to the standard language.[2]

Amongst themselves, speakers from minority communities, indulge in their native dialect as a sign of belonging to the same community and sharing in the same social values and identity (see discussion below, section 7.3). Such strategies are appropriate within the community but are commonly misunderstood elsewhere, e.g. in interactions where all speakers do not share the same values. To go back to our case of BEV, the Black leader should have avoided using non-standard expressions with a white audience if he wished -as he did- to persuade and convince. In this example, one observes a gradual linguistic and functional switch. Before the controversial passage with the expression "we will kill Richard Nixon", the speaker resorts to abstract concepts, uses general statements ("All power to the people/ black power to black people), and depersonalises his discourse (no I and you pronouns). The speaker is exposing facts and gives the background to the political situation he is discussing. He then starts to give his personal opinion but rather formally, "We believe/ that black people should not be forced/ to fight in the military/ to defend the racist government/ that does not support us/". Linguistically, in the more formal passages, we observe the use of "kill" in the standard English meaning, the use of third person ending on the verb, and no BEV contraction of the -ing ending. But, according to Gumperz, the "speaker's argument met with considerable scepticism from the audience". He then attacks Nixon's administration and, to achieve effectiveness, he resorts to the BEV controversial expression and to paralinguistic devices, associated with BEV. Hence, as in our Arabic data, when the speaker wishes to catch the audience's attention, he switches levels accordingly, relating form and function. The BEV passages in the speech were accompanied by paralinguistic features such as voice rising, increasing intensity for the delivery, and short pauses which give the passage the impression of a series of hammer blocks. In such passages, BEV lexical items combine with black phonology such as the vowel elongation in [mæn], and [kīdz], use of "ain't", the vowel in cain't [keynt]; morphology with the lack of third person endings on the verbs, contracted -ing endings as in cursin, counterin, recognizin, and syntax with the use of double negation. This example is significant since it shows a parallel with the Arabic data in the way function of discourse is related to language form. The end result, however, is different in the sense that the black speaker does not achieve his objective because of the fact that the listeners do not empathise with the message or its associated linguistic medium. Although one does not have a similar case of misunderstanding occurring after a code-switching in our Arabic data, this example was important in order to stress the parallels and variation of form and function variation in Arabic and English discourse.

7.2 RHETORICAL TACTICS IN ARABIC AND ENGLISH POLITICAL SPEECHES

This section is concerned with the similarities in rhetorical tactics used by politicians in general. The term "tactics" is used here to refer to stylistic features which are intended to move the audience by appealing to them on a "poetic" level, to obtain their feedback, and perhaps win their applause, or at least grab total attention.

Atkinson[3] provides a good analysis of the devices used by English and American politicians to achieve successful speeches. It may seem difficult to evaluate how a speech can be termed successful. Obviously a good way of judging would be by (a) quantifying any feedback e.g. clapping, cheering, chanting slogans as opposed to booing, heckling, etc., and, (b) by delayed feedback, i.e. comments and press coverage.

Atkinson analyses systematically some of the most renowned speeches and slogans that made an impact on the public for some reason, such as those of John.F. Kennedy, Martin Luther King, Winston Churchill, Margaret Thatcher among others. Atkinson observes that climactic moments, such as general applause, are all part of well-thought and organized rhetorical tactics. Some of these devices consist of: listing elements in threes, in contrasting pairs, and references to "us". There are other devices which trigger involvement in conversation and in political oratory, as those discussed by Tannen:[4] use of repetition, imagery, detail, and constructed dialogue with reported speech and dialogue. These devices maintain attention and often trigger applause, or at least positive audience feedback. Moreover, they give the public the feeling that the argument is well organized and, therefore work well in holding the audience's attention.

What is interesting is that these devices are also found in the three Arabic sets of data, suggesting that these may have multiple cultural appeal in political oratory. I will show these devices in use, from speeches in the English language and from the Arabic data. In this section, I will not take feedback into account, i.e. feedback in terms of applause. The three Arabic sets of data differ in the circumstances of their delivery, and cannot be compared with audience feedback: for instance, the Iraqi data is used as an international press conference, and one part of the Libyan data is a sermon in a mosque where no direct feedback is possible.

Listing three elements

As Atkinson[5] says, "one of the main attractions of three-part lists is that they have an air of unity or completeness about them". Atkinson gives an example of a passage in the speech of M.Thatcher (Conservative Party Conference 1980) in which she lists three elements showing the unity of her party, and "she is able to expand the scope of the boast while simultaneously amplifying its strength".

1 "This week has demonstrated that we are a party united in
- purpose
- strategy
- and resolve."

A further example found in the written press is an account of a passage of a speech made by H.Kohl:[6]

2 The German chancellor, Helmut Kohl, after talks with President François Mitterrand on Tuesday, said Brussels had become
- "too powerful,
- constantly expanding,
- and exterminating national identities".

The three-element listing is widely used in the written mode as well, in the political field and beyond. Moreover, these stylistic strategies are not exclusively English or Arabic, but are found in other languages too such as French.

3 Mais, pour les religieux, l'heure est à présent
- aux démarches collectives,
- à l'investissement associatif et
- à un certain raidissement des discours.[7]

4 In a speech given by Marguerite Yourcenar at her reception at the Académie Française:
Jusqu'au bout, il [Rimbaud] restera fidèle à cette formule, et cela d'autant plus que les objets que fixeront, non ses délires, mais ses suprêmes méditations, seront

- les plus concrets,
- les plus denses,
- les plus immobiles que nous offre le paysage terrestre...

The three sets of Arabic political discourse provide numerous examples of this listing of three elements that strengthen the argument (without necessarily adding much to the argument) and, at the same time, moves the audience emotionally by the repetition and symmetry of the phrase structure. These stylistic features are intended to pander to the audience's poetical sense and co-opt their commitment and involvement in the discourse. There are some typical examples from the data illustrating three-element listing; some items are repeated and the effect of repetitions will be discussed below.

5 (Nasser *1957 l.4*)
naḥtafil bi 'īd in-naṣr
/'ala siyāsati l-quwwa/
/wa 'ala siyāsati l-'udwān/
/wa 'ala siyāsati l-ghadr/

6 (Nasser *1957 l.23*)
/tunādi bi l-ḥurriyya/
/wa tunādi bi l-?istiqlāl/
/wa tunādi bi l-qawmiyya l-'arabiyya/

7 (Nasser *1957 l.32*)
/daxalna ma'ārik muta'addida/
/ma'ārik ṭawāla/
/wa ma'ārik marīra/

The three-element listing can also be more elaborate and structured as in (8) where the first three elements are opposed by another three, that are in turn contrasted with another list of three:

8 (Nasser *1957 l.87*)
/qātaltum bi sharaf/
/wa qātaltum bi ?imān/
/qātaltum min ?agli maṣr/
/lā min agli l-maṣlaḥati il-xāṣṣa/
/?aw min ?agli il-maksab il-mādcī/
/?aw min ?agli maṣlaḥatin zātiyya/
/qātaltum min ?agli l-musul l-'ulyā/
/qātaltum min ?agli l-ḥurriya lli ḥaqqaqtūha/
/wa qātaltum min ?agli l-?istiqlāl illi sabbittūh/

The Iraqi data provide an example of an argument in three parts without repetitions this time:

9 (Saddam Hussein *SH1 l.7*)
/wa ?innu dōl il-'arab nās lā yuḥsinūn
?illā rukūb il-d̲jimāl/
/wa l-bukā? 'ala l-?aṭlāl/
/wa n-nawm bi l-xiyām/

The Libyan data present examples of such listings, with the repetition of elements as in:

10 (Gaddafi *1981 l.87*)
/?aw yikūn ḍudd al-jamāhīr as̲h̲-s̲h̲a'biyya
?aw ḍudd al-mu?tamarāt as̲h̲-s̲h̲a'biyya
?aw ḍudd al-lijān at̲h̲-t̲h̲awriyya/

11 (Gaddafi *1981 l.195*)
- /wa ?innamā yaxḍa'ū li l-?irāda al-lībiyya
wa lā l-?irāda l-jazā?iriyya
wa lā l-?irāda l-maṣriyya/

The following is another example of the point the speaker is making in three steps:

12 (Gaddafi *1978 l.12*)
/lā yaxtalif ?it̲h̲nāni mina l-muslimīn
'ala ?anna hād̲h̲ihi hiya sūrata l-qāri'a
wa 'ala ?annahā nazalat bi makka/
wa ?annahā taḥmilu raqam miyya u wāḥad fī l-qur?ān/

Repetition of words or clauses in the examples of the above type has been discussed by several authors.[8] Repetition of an item highlights it, helps its comprehension by providing greater textual redundancy and less dense discourse. Rhythmically, repetition provides a musical aspect to language and may create a rhetorical crescendo and captures audience attention. Patterned repetition is a technique of persuasion. According to Koch,[9] the grammatical structure of Arabic makes repetition a strategy available especially to Arabic speakers, and, she says, is the key to linguistic cohesion of many Arabic texts, and to understanding their rhetorical effectiveness. The effects of repetition in English oratory are illustrated in Tannen.[10]

Besides repetitions, the Arabic data show examples of rhyme as in the (11) case above and in a passage from Jackson's[11] speech (1988):

13 Dream. Of doctors who are concerned more about public health than private wealth.

Contrasting pairs

Contrasting pairs of items (words, phrases or whole clauses) is a device used by speakers, by which they introduce the element of conflict into the discussion, as if the point argued by the speaker is being criticised, or challenged by the audience. Hence it makes the discourse livelier by, firstly, imitating an argumentative conversation, or a "two-way conversation" with the audience. Secondly, strengthening and giving more weight to the argument since the impression is that the issue has been fully, logically and rationally, discussed. Atkinson[12] provides the following example of a contrasting pair in the speech of the Liberal Party leader David Steel at the 1979 general election:

14 The truth is beginning to dawn on our people that there are two conservative parties in this election, one is offering the continuation of the policies we've had for the last five years, and the other is offering a return to the policies of forty years ago.

and Tannen[13] gives the following example where Jackson uses a chiasmus to surprise the audience and attract their attention:

15 (Jesse Jackson 1988):
I was born in the slum but the slum was not born in me.

Contrasting pairs of items were also found in our Arabic data:

16 (Nasser *1957 l.68*)
/win<u>sh</u>ūf lēh ?intaṣarna/ fī hāzihi l-fatra/ wa lēh mā kunnā<u>sh</u> binantaṣir fī l-māḍī/

17 (Nasser *1957 l.68*)
/li?anna maṣr/ milki li ?abnāha/ mi<u>sh</u> milki li fi?a minna n-nās/

18 (Saddam Hussein *SH1 l.98*)
/... u rāḥ yilgāha ba'da xamsa sanawāt/ bi ḥāla mutaqaddima wa laysa bi ḥāla muta?axxira/

Memories – Images – Details

A rhetorical device used by English-speaking politicians is the recounting of (a) personal memories, which give the impression that the speaker is being open, frank and involved personally, and,

(b) specific images and details to make a concept or situation more understandable, and better accepted by the audience. Tannen[14] has stressed the importance of details and images in creating involvement: "Images, like dialogue, evoke scenes, and understanding is derived from scenes because they are composed of people in relation to each other, doing things that are culturally and personally recognizable and meaningful". Details make a concept understandable and strengthen the issue. Tannen[15] comments again: "the accurate representation of the particular communicates universality, whereas direct attempts to represent universality often communicate nothing. Particularity allows the audience to imagine a scene, and this participation in sense-making is emotionally moving. Generality does not trigger this process and therefore leaves audiences unmoved".

In the following example, the Reverend Jesse Jackson delivers a speech in which he wants to share his personal memories and he gives details of his childhood that create images and convey the feelings of the time:[16]

19 Jesse Jackson (1988):
> I wasn't born in the hospital. Mama didn't have insurance. I was born in the bed, at house. I really do understand. Born in a three room house, bathroom in the back yard, slop jar by the bed, no hot and cold running water, I understand. Wallpaper used for decoration ? No. For a windbreaker.

In the following passage, Nasser describes a particular episode in which he tries to bond with the audience as he acknowledges them "I saw you, I remember you". But at the same time, the audience is given the opportunity to remember the scene, recall emotions and the atmosphere of the previous occasion.

20 (Nasser *1957 l.92 to 98*)
> /ana fī hāza l-waqt ?ayyuha l-?ixwā/../ kuntu <u>sh</u>āyif kullu wāḥad fīkum fī balakunāt wa fī <u>sh</u>-<u>sh</u>awāri'/ fī l-ma'raka/ kuntu <u>sh</u>āyif kullu wāḥad fīkum/ zayyi mā kuntu <u>sh</u>āyif yōm tamantā<u>sh</u>ar yunyu/ fī balakunāt wa fī <u>sh</u>-<u>sh</u>awāri'/ wa kunt ?u?min bi n-naṣr/ li ?innu l-wugūh ?illi kuntu ba<u>sh</u>ūfha/ hiya l-wugūh ?illi kānit bitihtif bi l-gala? yōm tamantā<u>sh</u>ar yunyu/ yōma rafa'na l-'alam al-maṣrī/ mā kān al-'alam al-briṭāniy 'ala mabna l-baḥriyya/ bōr sa'īd/

In the second extract, Nasser recalls childhood memories and the general feelings towards politics at the time:

21 (Nasser *1962 l.74 to 78*)

/?ana ?azkur min ?awwil/ ?ayyām iṭ-ṭufūla/ kullama nikkallim fī ?ayyi ḥāga/ yi?ūlak bittikallim fī ?ē sa'd bāsha ?āl mā fīsh fayda/ mā fīsh fayda fi hāza l-kalām/

The (20) and (21) examples illustrate the matching of language form to rhetorical purposes. As the speaker recounts his personal memories, the level drops to the dialect, and linguistically CA elements combine such as: phoneme [z] < OA /dh/ (hāza), [?] < OA /q/ (y?ulak), long vowel ō for aw (yōm), use of the active participle, favoured in the dialect instead of a verb (shāyif), close-to-TA MPP of verb (nikkallim, kānit), aspectual prefix bi (bashūfha), discontinuous negative particle mā -sh (mā fīsh). A similar parallel between language form and function of discourse is observed in the preceding example (19), where Jackson uses short, clipped sentences, typical of conversational English.

References to "us"

Atkinson[17] has stressed the importance of the favourable references to "us" since these references to "us" "convey positive or boastful evaluations of our hopes, our activities or our achievements". References to "us" have been referred to throughout the analyses of the three sets of data as examples of the creation of speaker-audience solidarity in the discourse and combining in most cases with a language form which is dialectal or "mixed".

22 (Nasser *1957 l.67*)

/nubuṣṣu li nafsina/ winshūf lēh ?intaṣarna/ fī hāzihi l-fatra/ wa lēh mā kunnāsh binantaṣir fī l-māḍī/

23 (Nasser *1962 l.10*)

/bidūn shu'ūrnā bi l-mas?ūliyyā mā kunnāsh ni?dar nu?ūm bi ?ayyi 'amal min al-?a'māl/

These examples of references to "us" are all in the dialect and display CA features as in (22) and (23) above. As Nasser is addressing the audience directly and involving them in his speech, he speaks as "us, Egyptians", and uses dialect as in: phoneme [z] < OA /dh/ (hāza), [?] < OA /q/ (ni?dar, nu?ūm), verb MPP (nubuṣṣu), long vowel ē in the lexical form (lēh for limādha), aspectual prefix bi (binantaṣir), discontinuous negative particle mā (mā kunnāsh), verb string (ni?dar nu?ūm).

Direct and reported speech and dialogue in political discourse

Constructed dialogue and direct/ reported speech are additional devices used by a politician to make his discourse livelier and maintain audience rapport. The next two examples are from Atkinson and Tannen[18] who analyze the use of constructed dialogue more specifically in conversations:

24 (Thatcher, at the 1983 general election)
The Russians said that I was an Iron Lady. They were right. Britain needs an Iron Lady.

25 (Jesse Jackson, 1988)
I'm often asked, "Jesse, why do you take on these tough issues. They're not very political. We can't win that way".

Chapters three, four and five illustrated similar cases of actual speech and "constructed" conversations in the analysis of the dialectal data. The Iraqi data, in particular, provides numerous examples as in:

26 (*SH2 l.57*)
/li?annu bi s-sābiq kānu yigulūn ?innu niḥin shū nigdar insawwi/ wa tnāqashna/ tnāqashna ma'a ba'ḍ il-'arab/ bi mshakil mubāshir/ gulnā lkum lā tidjibūn ?ilna l-?amrikān tunṭūnhum il-qawā'id l-?adjnabiyya/

and the passage is full of instances of actual speech.

27 (*SH2 l.31*)
/... l-?ittiḥād is-sūfyētī yigul mā 'indi ?aw mā ?agdar ?azawwidkum biha../

The cases of actual/ reported speech/ dialogue are in a relatively "dialectal" form of Arabic and (26) and (27) report speech in dialect with elements such as: phoneme [g] < OA /q/ (yigulūn, nigdar), morphology of the pronoun niḥin for MSA niḥna, localism (tunṭūn), close-to-BGI MPP of verb (yigulūn), verb string (nigdar insawwi), lexical items (shū), negative particle mā + non-past tense (mā ?agdar). The English (25) and Arabic examples (26, 27) are cases of "actual speech" to enliven the discourse.

The passionate plea

This device is different from the previous rhetorical tactics in that it deals with the tone of a speech, which can convey numerous emotions depending on the function of the discourse: anger, passion, ridicule, among others. One that is particularly interesting in political speeches is the passionate tone as in some of Nasser's speeches, in Martin Luther King and John F. Kennedy's for instance. Atkinson[19] observes that in King's and Kennedy's speeches, while the public is clapping, the speaker would continue talking through the clapping, implying that the point he has to make is more important than acknowledging the clapping and waiting for it to stop: "he will appear to be passionately committed to the business of getting his point across, as well as reluctant to accept praise". This device conveys a sense of honesty and involvement of the speaker, pleasing to his audience, and presents the politician as sincere and human too.

In the Arabic data, one has cases of the politician talking "through the clapping". The following passage, from Nasser's speech, is an interesting example of build up of tension:

28 *1962 l.76* /mā fīsh fayda fī hāza l-kalām/ l-?inglīz mush mumkin yiṭla'u min maṣr/ di shi'arāt ?inhizāmiyya? xarag nās min ?abnā? hādhihi l-?umma/ li yaqḍū 'ala hadhihi sh-shi'arāt āl-?inhizāmiyya/ wa yuqīmū shi'arāt thawriyya/ yarfa'u shi'arāt thawriyya/ tanba' min hādha sh-sha'b/ wa min rūḥ hādha sh-sha'b/ wa min nafsi hādha sh-sha'b/ clap.../ xarag min hāza il-gīl/ xarag ?ē/ nās ?amnum bi l-mustaqbal/ kullu wāḥid minhum/ 'amal fī niṭāquh ?igābiyyan/

In this dialectal passage, Nasser has roused the audience's emotions and built up his argument ideationally and rhythmically. Despite the defeatist feelings, Nasser remarked that some people exhibited revolutionary feelings. The argument reaches a climax after two sets of lists of threes with a repetition of items and regular stress on words. As tension builds up, people start clapping:

/li yaqḍū 'ala hadhihi sh-shi'arāt al-?inhizāmiyya/	
/wa yuqīmu shi'arāt thawriyya/	
/yarfa'u shi'arāt thawriyya/	clapping starts
/tanba' min hādha sh-sha'b/	clapping
/wa min rūḥ hādha sh-sha'b/	clapping
/wa min nafsi hādha sh-sha'b/	climax

The audience is still clapping when Nasser starts his next point; then clapping fades away, but you can hear the audience chanting and repeating slogans. This way of talking before the clapping is over has the effect of stopping the audience from clapping, but shows also the speaker's involvement. Gaddafi uses a similar device of talking through the clapping (in 1981 line 167 for instance).

7.3 UNIVERSALITY OF POLITICAL STRATEGIES

Here one is concerned with the universality of discourse strategies, which means one needs to consider not just political oratory, but also, outside the political arena, conversations. People, because of their background, occupation and extensive social networks may employ a wide variety of speech strategies within their daily conversations. The strategies used in political discourse are merely a particular sub-set of the common strategies used by speakers in more everyday interactions.

Conversational discourse involves a very complex framework of interactions in which interlocutors who wish to communicate with one another use numerous speech functions: they persuade, criticize, show anger, tease, influence others, justify their actions, inform and advise the interlocutor, tell jokes, cajole, appear friendly, etc. A political speech is an act of persuasion of an audience and, like a conversationalist, the politician mobilises a certain array of communicative skills to get his message across and to influence his listeners. He can count on their subconscious knowledge of how convention works in the language which he shares with them, and exploit this knowledge from a position of power.

This section shows the use of functions in political discourse and makes comparison across data, as well as functions in conversational discourse with examples from various studies – in Arabic and other languages. I believe that political and conversational discourses are closely linked and interrelated, and Tannen[20] points out that conversational discourse provides the source for strategies which are taken up by other, including literary genres, both spoken and written, and deliberately composed genres such as political speeches.

In what follows, I will list some of the functions found in political oratory together with the aims of the politicians. I will then discuss these strategies with those found in Arabic and non-Arabic conversational studies, looking, firstly, at functions which motivate a more formal level of language, and, secondly, at functions that are associated with a dialectal, local, or otherwise non-standard level of language. Finally, I will discuss the effects of such switches and the conditions required to achieve effective communication.

A formal, standard (MSA) form of language, as said earlier, is generally used whenever the politician's aim is to inform and educate the public, recall history, articulate and announce policy, or otherwise present himself as a powerful figure; and, to achieve such effects, a standard form of language is, in the Arab world, culturally appropriate as a signal of authority and seniority. But, at the same time, politicians want and need to appear friendly, to establish a sense of contact, solidarity and shared goals with the public. For these purposes, the use of dialect is more effective, because this is the normal vehicle for the expression of such affective layers of meaning in everyday life. Politicians may want their ideas to have an impact on the public, and use the dialect to make some abstract concepts more readily understood.

7.3.1 Code-switching as strategy

Thus, MSA and the dialect are used as the means for particular types of communication. But what is important to stress is that, once the politician has finished appealing to the emotions of his audience and established solidarity with them through the dialect, he reverts to MSA – associated speech functions again so as to re-establish his authority and regain formality. The main motive behind this recurrent code switching is to keep the audience's attention, and this is an essential strategy in large gatherings, and in long speeches, where the audience's attention can wander. A speech in MSA requires a lot of concentration on the part of the public for whom MSA is not the native language, and may sound monotonous. A speech in the dialect on the other hand would not fulfil the criteria for a "serious" speech and would lose the politician his credibility as a figure of authority. Hence one device would be to avoid using long monotonous sentences and to vary functional strategies together with linguistic switches and accompanying paralinguistic features.

This strategy holds as well for speeches in the English language despite the lack of a language level difference in English which equates to the MSA-dialect dichotomy in Arabic. By a change in intonation and the use of a conversational style in a formal setting for example, a speaker can surprise his audience and keep the discourse livelier. Moreover, a conversational style and direct / reported speech in a discourse give the audience the impression that they are being addressed individually, or being included in the circle of the speaker's intimates. It is as if they are being given the opportunity of answering back or being seen as equals. Eventually, by keeping the audience's attention, the speaker hopes to cajole and persuade.

Keeping the audience's attention is obviously a necessity in general conversation just as it is in political oratory: one can imagine the strategy of constant code switching applying in conversation as the topic, the attitude of the interlocutor to it, and his immediate conversational aims, change. These changes are often not the result of conscious decisions, but a good speaker will intuitively do whatever is needed to keep his interlocutors's attention. Nasser's discourse is a case in point: he seems to have been well aware of the effect of mixing Cairene and MSA and, throughout his career, switched levels, purposefully.

Keeping the audience's attention is one motivation for varying rhetorical tactics, which results in code switching. Another motivation can be detected in Gumperz and Hernandez's[21] study. They observed that while discussing her problems to quit smoking, a woman was alternating between Spanish and English. Spanish was used to express emotions, convey intimate and personal feelings while English was used for expressing facts; it was more neutral in contrast and had connotations of distance and clinical detachment. This particular language switching and vacillation between English and Spanish shows precisely the woman's ambivalence towards her problem. Hence, the coexistence of alternate forms conveys additional information, and code switching, say the authors, is meaningful in much the same way as is lexical choice.

Gumperz and Hernandez give several conversational examples where one language carries emotional feelings and conveys personal experiences, while another is used when conversation has no reference to speakers and to their minority status, and when the subject is treated in a generally detached manner. In their article, the authors look at cases of Spanish and English among Mexicans, Spanish and English among Puerto Ricans in Jersey City, and Standard English and Black English in Afro American homes. Some cases of code-switching between English and Spanish for example show a change (to Spanish) in interpersonal relationship, towards greater informality. In other examples, English is used to introduce new information, while Spanish provides "stylistic embroidering to amplify the speaker's intent". Hence code switching will bring out contrasts between the two levels and emphasize the feelings of involvement, anger, excitement, etc.

according to the language, community and situation. In the following, I will be looking at the similarity of the relationship between forms and functions in Arabic and non-Arabic conversational studies.

7.3.2 Arabic conversational studies

A research programme, carried out in the 70s, aimed at describing the extempore speech of groups of educated Arabs in unprepared conversation and examined, among other things, the use of MSA in speech. The conversations usually involved speakers from a single country, or even several. The research was carried out at the department of Linguistics and Phonetics, University of Leeds, and was conducted by a team of researchers led by T.F. Mitchell.

Two long conversational extracts from that Leeds project were examined to see the extent of variation. The first extract deals with a housing crisis and involves three Jordanians (male), one Egyptian (male) and one Syrian (female). The second one deals with the structure of the Arabic language and the principles which lie behind its teaching, and involves an Egyptian (male), two Syrians (one male, one female) and one Jordanian (male). The first discussion presents several advantages for language level analysis, since it consists of a cross dialectal conversation, involving men and women, and treats a "neutral" topic, as opposed to the one on the Arabic language where participants may, by the very nature of the topic, be more conscious of their speech. The setting in both cases is relatively formal since all participants are aware that they are being recorded. I will look at factors in these conversations which seem to be consistently associated with a more-MSA or a more-dialectal speech style.

As to factors triggering an MSA-style, when the interviewer sets the topic – housing problems in Damascus – one of the male Jordanian interviewees starts a long monologue, using a style which is quite close to written MSA. He seems to think that he has a didactic role to fulfil, and that he has to inform the group of the current situation. The other Jordanian man then joins him in this lecture-like discussion, making a similarly lengthy diatribe. Both of them seem at ease throughout their speeches. Typical examples of MSA-like syntax are al-wāqi' ?innu .., ?astaṭī' ?an ?aqūl, dual forms occur (qawlān mutaḍāribān) and ?i'rāb as in yaltaḏji?ūna. In the second extract, the language level matches, as expected, the topic of conversation which is the problem of using the Arabic language as a means of instruction in Arab schools. Although there are some fluctuations, one of the participants, a Syrian professor of Arabic, uses a consistently MSA-like style.

More dialectal passages occur in these extracts, however. In the first one, after a long tirade by the two Jordanian speakers, the Jordanian interviewer tries to draw the Syrian woman into the discussion, by inviting her opinion; at first she is very hesistant, the speed of delivery is slow, and there are many false starts. She seems unable to maintain the "high" level established by the previous two male speakers. Her speech exhibits dialectal features such as, in phonology, deletion of short vowel frūgh for MSA furūgh, and morphophonologically, dialectal verb forms such as in biyḥibbū. However, she seems aware of her lack of MSA fluency and tries awkwardly to raise the language level by choosing MSA lexical items and "correcting" dialectalisms she had uttered in the previous breath (yarghabūn instead of yuḥibbu, as well as use of the choice of mahmā kān and likay). At a given point, the Egyptian interviewer cracks a joke which has the effect of releasing the considerable tension, after which the Syrian woman relaxes and speaks naturally, at a high speed with many dialectal features. Significantly, in this, she deals with the question of "housing problems" from a personal, anecdotal point of view, compared with the more abstract treatment given by the men. But as the formal setting reasserts itself, she tries again to raise the language level, and the delivery gets slower and more hesitant.

This incident shows some of the complexity in analyzing conversational interaction. Language level can vary, depending on numerous factors – mainly on the particular role a participant wishes to play or feels she/he has to in the given context. Speakers may then fulfil very different roles and some will have greater resources of linguistic competence and experience to draw on than others, depending on their background and occupation. According to Heller,[22] code-switching is seen as a boundary-levelling or boundary-maintaining strategy which contributes to the definition of roles and relationships at a number of levels, to the extent that interlocutors bear multiple interrelationships. It is an important part of social network and boundaries. Abd El Jawad[23] comments that through language usage and choice, speakers desire to perform one or more of a set of overlapping communicative functions.

Discourse organization

In the second extract from the Leeds project, on the subject of the Arabic language itself, the Syrian (male) speaker gives a long answer, mostly in MSA, but uses English for such technical terms as "phonological differences". When he has finished, but wishes the discussion to continue, he elicits the other speakers's participation with a dialectal invitation: mā ba'rif ya'ni shū ra?y il-?ixwān "I don't know what other people's views are". A second type of discourse "move" associated with the dialect is by way of a parenthetical, personal comment, e.g. ya'ni baddī ?a'ṭī mulāḥaẓa "I'd like to make an observation", bZinn ?an "I think that" and kut 'āyiz "I wanted". I discussed similar cases of overtly personal involvement in our Arabic political discourse where the speaker uses the dialect to make a comment on the developing text of his speech. In BGI *SH4 l.24* /mā hīč yā duktur/ "Isn't that right, doctor?" Saddam Hussein addresses his neighbour in an aside in plain BGI dialect, with the use of dialectal negative particle mā, phoneme č < OA /k/ to get some feedback. This aside is even more striking as it occurs in the middle of an MSA passage. Other examples from the Egyptian material are the following, which help to give the discourse a more personal dimension:

1962 l.56 /wa ana ?innahardā wa ana batadhakkar hādhihi l-?aḥdās/
1962 l.64 /ana mā ba?sudsh bi hāza.../
1957 l.103 /kuntu fī nafsi l-wa?t ?ash'ur bimā qāsaytum/
1962 l.74 /?ana ?azkur min ?awwil ?ayyām iṭ-ṭufūla/ These sequences display dialectal elements such as: phoneme s < OA /th/ (?aḥdās), ? < OA /q/ (wa?t), aspectual prefix bi (batadhakkar), lexical item (?innahardā).

Competence in MSA

As said earlier, the Syrian woman is very hesitant in participating and keeping up with the MSA level established by previous speakers. She makes greater use of the dialectal features than the males, and the male speakers address her in the dialect. Male and female language levels were discussed earlier (see chapter one), and I mentioned that women, in some cases, given their generally narrower social network (i.e. more limited sets of contacts and roles), do not show the same ease as male participants in using MSA[24]. Linguistic insecurity may be felt if the speaker is unsure as to the correctness of his or her use of MSA and also of his or her use of dialect which might be stigmatized compared with more prestigious dialect such as the Egyptian one.

Prestige and dialect

Throughout the two extracts, it is interesting to notice the use of language by the Egyptian male speaker who consistently uses markedly dialectal features (in some cases purely Egyptian) such as 'āyiz, s̲h̲āyif, bititkallam, barḍū, mabitḥibbis̲h̲ despite the fact that he is the only Egyptian present. This suggests security in dialect use. The tendency of Egyptians to speak more dialectally than other Arabs, all things being equal, has been commented on by El Hassan[25] of the Leeds Project.

Another interesting point is that after the Syrian woman is asked by the Egyptian speaker to participate, she responds by borrowing some Cairene features such as ?awi "very". Used with other Syrian interlocutors, an Egyptian feature would sound artificial but it seems appropriate in this crossdialectal conversation: a case of convergence towards a prestigious, widely understood dialect. By using such features, the Syrian wishes to show that she is equal to the Egyptian who has just finished talking, and achieve some kind of solidarity with him. As Abd El Jawad[26] says, speakers may shift their speech styles to become more similar to those with whom they are interacting, in an attempt to gain favorable appraisal, social acceptance and give an impression that they are trying to respond positively. This problem of pleasing listeners while conveying a message is particularly acute for politicians and this aspect was discussed in the data analyses. By using the dialect, politicians wish, among other things, to establish a better understanding and keep communication lines open to their audience. Occasionally, we have cases of convergence or accommodation where the speaker imitates the dialect of his audience. This similarity between Arabic political discourse and Arabic conversation is part of the most general image of code switching that I observed in Arabic and non-Arabic types of discourse, and used to fulfil communicative purposes.

7.3.3 Relevant non-Arabic conversational studies

In the following, I will look briefly at more general conversational studies and consider factors that occasion use of a standard form of a language, similar to those seen earlier in political oratory and in Arabic conversation, and, strategies which use the dialect. As will be seen, use of dialect is very complex, more than the use of standard language, since it depends on factors specific to each country and their respective sociolinguistic frameworks. The use of a variety is affected by factors such as topic, participants and setting amongst others, but these factors have varying importance according to each sociolinguistic community.

Blom and Gumperz's[27] study in Hemnesberget, a small town in Northern Norway, shows that the standard language (Bokmål) and the dialect (Ranamål) were used to symbolize the differing social identities which members may assume. Use of Bokmål, associated with official transactions, religion and the mass media is subject to social constraints and is used for certain authoritative roles: for instance, when a speaker wants to validate his status as an intellectual and to convey meanings of officialdom, expertise, and politeness towards strangers, since the presence of a foreign participant would formalize a conversation and elicit the use of the standard. The dialect, Ranamål, on the other hand, enjoys great prestige among Hemnesberget's inhabitants and symbolizes relationships based on shared identities involving the local culture. It is used at home, in workshops and other public places. However, at university for example, where lectures are delivered in Bokmål, free discussions are encouraged in Ranamål. And dialect can be heard even at official meetings when the group of participants all know each other well and when they are talking about business.

In Hemnesberget, the most important constraining factors that affect the use of the dialect are thus topic and speaker-role. According to Blom and Gumperz,[28] the social significance of the dialect can only be understood by contrast with that of the standard speech, the language of non-local activities. The standard is associated with education and power at national level and carries connotations of differences in rank, which are unacceptable in the realm of informal, local relations.

The phenomenon of role-switching operates below the level of consciousness and speakers have a tacit knowledge of which variety to use and when, and a speaker, who uses the standard format where the dialect is appropriate, violates commonly accepted norms.

Blom and Gumperz discuss the effects of metaphorical switching in conversations and show that the use of Ranamål in a normally Bokmål discussion can "add a special social meaning of confidentiality or privateness to the conversation", and Ranamål is used as well to provide "local color, indicate humor, etc". These social meanings are reminiscent of the different functions of code-switching seen earlier in Gumperz and Hernandez's conversational study. Similar instances of metaphorical switches were observed in our Arabic data:

(a) in the aside quoted earlier, BGI *SH4 l.24*
/fa lamma 'uqid mu?tamar fī 'umān/ mā hīč yā duktūr/ fī 'umān/ fī l-wizāra l-xāridjiyya ṭuriḥat ba'ḍ il-?afkār min hadhā n-nō'/

In this passage, Saddam Hussein reminds the audience of the circumstances of the conference and gives information; the BGI aside, addressed to his neighbour to obtain some feedback, adds intimacy and lightens up the otherwise monotonous MSA passage.

(b) Conversely, in a less formal setting, MSA can be used in an expected dialectal situation to achieve different purposes. When used in conversations, MSA adds authoritativeness and knowledge, and establishes a superior-inferior perspective in the conversation. Such is the case in the Leeds extracts, which by their environment, are less formal than political speeches. Nonetheless, the two Jordanian male speakers referred to earlier, feel they have to inform the others on the topic discussed – housing problems in Syria- and adapt a very MSA/ didactic style so as to add authority to their views.

Gumperz[29] shows how by code switching and the choice of a dialect, a speaker is able to show his identity values and his solidarity with his community peers, as in the example:

> Following an informal graduate seminar at a major university, a black student approached the instructor, who was about to leave the room accompanied by several other black and white students, and said:
> – Could I talk to you for a minute? I'm gonna apply for a fellowship and I was wondering if I could get a recommendation?
> The instructor replied:
> – O.K. Come along to the office and tell me what you want to do.
> As the instructor and the rest of the group left the room, the black student said, turning his head ever so slightly to the other students:
> – Ahma git me a gig! (Rough gloss: I'm going to get myself some support.)

This incident shows how, at first, the black student chooses the standard language to talk to his instructor. The standard is appropriate in this case as he awaits a positive reply and to establish clear communication. His next statement, however, is uttered in BEV as he wants to emphasise his identity values and links with his friends. Moreover, the "sing-song" rhythm marks the utterance as stereotypically "black" from which his friends may infer that he is maintaining his distance from the "white" values associated with the situation, that he is still in control, and knows what he is doing.

Gal's[30] study provides many good examples of language use affected by social factors. The study was conducted in Oberwart, a small Austrian village on the Hungarian border. The "standard" language here is German but the "local" language is Hungarian. Constraining factors for the use of either variety are different from Blom and Gumperz's study in Norway. While in Hemnesberget factors affecting the use of the dialect were primarily topic and role-playing, in Oberwart, the constraining factors are the setting and the participants. In Oberwart, German, the "standard" language, is associated with work, knowledge and cultural sophistication. It is used in official settings and business. What is particular about Oberwart is that the "local" language, Hungarian, lacks prestige (contrarily to the prestigious Ranamål in Norway) and is stigmatized for being "old-fashioned and related to peasant life". Young people increasingly use mainly German in all circumstances, although they understand Hungarian. At home, however, where Hungarian is mainly used, Gal discovered that German was indeed used to show authority and anger, and in the "expression or assertion of expertise and knowledgeability", and for emphasis of the statement. When spoken among native Hungarian speakers, German would also convey a feeling of social distance.

Local people feel embarrassed about their dialect, and would avoid using it with strangers even when the subject of conversation would, in other circumstances, require it. Gal recounts an anecdote where she interviewed some Oberwart women, who, despite the fact that they were recounting emotional memories and were even crying, they were nonetheless aware of the formality of the interview, due to the presence of the foreign interviewer and as a result, German was used. Hence, despite the emotion of the topic, the primary factors that triggered the use of German were the setting and the interviewer, a foreigner.

These political and conversational studies have shown the importance for a speaker in conversations, to be "in tune" with the norms of his community and share the local values. And in political discourse particularly, to be aware of the participants and the need to be on linguistic common ground in discussing issues. Referring back to the example given by Gumperz[31], if the black leader had realized the inappropriateness of using BEV with a mainly white audience, none of the misunderstandings would have occurred. As Gumperz says, it is easier to get things done when everyone concerned has the same background than when it differs.

Moreover, most political speeches and conversations are concerned primarily with maintaining communication and establishing solidarity, since it is the sharing of strategies that creates the feeling of satisfaction.[32]

Good communication requires speakers to find a common and appropriate way to approach the interlocutor:

(a) the speaker, particularly in public speaking, has to be aware of the "connotations" the use of his local dialect might have on the audience in the event that they might not share the same values. Rather than reinforcing solidarity links, there might be a serious breakdown in communication.
(b) The speaker might have to borrow phonological forms that are not part of his native speech as is the case in Bahrain[33] where Shi'is borrow, imitate features from the dominant Sunni dialect when in conversation with Sunnis.

To conclude the discussion on language levels in public speaking, one has to stress the importance of a speaker's communicative competence, i.e. the grammatical and sociocultural knowledge in knowing what language to use and in which context. And Blom and Gumperz[34] say, the determinants of this communicative process are the speaker's knowledge of the linguistic repertoire, culture and social structure, and his ability to relate these kinds of knowledge to contextual constraints.

Finally, the results on form and function in the Arabic data find echoes in other research in different languages (Norwegian, German/Hungarian and Black English Vernacular). Despite diverging social constraints inherent to each country and speech community, one can observe some parallels in the use of a standard or dialectal language, in Arabic and non-Arabic discourses, given the aims of the speaker, his interlocutors and the environment. The phenomenon of code-switching may endow the speaker with a different status, enabling him to play different roles and convey various feelings. The speaker, whether a politician or not, speaking dialectal Arabic, Ranamål or Hungarian, can resort to code-switching to achieve persuasion and communication.

7.4 GENERAL CONCLUSION

To my knowledge, this is the first attempt to examine linguistic variation and persuasive strategies through language, and more precisely through code-switching in Arabic political discourse. To this effect, I related language form to function in discourse.

Language form:
In order to determine exactly the type of language the politician is using, I carried out a detailed analysis of the data in different linguistic levels of phonology, morphophonology, syntax and lexicon. My refinement of the concept of a continuum has the advantage of providing an accurate interpretation of the speaker's grammar as well as throwing new light on the flexibility of the language and on the limits of combinatorial rules.

Language functions:
As I related language form to functions of discourse in each set of data and compared them crossdialectally, I stressed the commonality of persuasive strategies in Arabic and English political speeches, but also in Arabic and non-Arabic conversational discourses which form the invisible but ever-present background to political discourse. One found parallels in the way speakers from diverging backgrounds, different languages and in various settings, were manipulating language to convey different messages and achieve their objectives.

NOTES

1 Gumperz 1982.
2 as in the case of Bahrain, Holes 1983b: 446. See also Al-Khatib 1995.
3 Atkinson 1984.
4 Tannen 1989.
5 Atkinson 1984: 57.
6 from the Guardian, 26 September 1996, p. 12 article by J. Carvel.
7 in an article by P. Bernard, "France, terre d'Islam", Le Monde, 17 November 1992, p. 12.
8 Tannen 1989; Koch 1983; Johnstone 1987.
9 Koch 1983: 47-48.
10 Tannen 1989: 82-5, 175-94.
11 Tannen 1989: 176.
12 Atkinson 1984: 74.
13 Tannen 1989: 178.
14 Tannen 1989: 135-6.

15 Tannen 1989: 92.
16 Tannen 1989: 182.
17 Atkinson 1984: 37.
18 Atkinson 1984: 118; Tannen 1989: 180.
19 Atkinson 1984: 99-105.
20 Tannen 1989: 2.
21 Gumperz and Hernandez 1971; see also Gal 1979: 91.
22 Heller 1988: 1.
23 Abd El Jawad 1986: 21.
24 see Bakir 1986.
25 El Hassan 1978: 42.
26 Abd El Jawad 1986: 24.
27 Blom and Gumperz 1971.
28 Blom and Gumperz 1971: 433.
29 Gumperz 1982: 30.
30 Gal 1979.
31 Gumperz 1982: 187-203.
32 Tannen 1982b: 217.
33 see Holes 1983b.
34 Blom and Gumperz 1971: 422.

Appendix A

NASSER 1957

xiṭāb ir-ra?īs gamāl 'abdu n-nāṣir fi l-?insiḥāb min bōr sa'īd (23 December 1957)

?ayyuha l-muwāṭinūn/ clap../ laqad kāna l-liqā? il-?axīr/ ma'akum/ hunā fī bōr sa'īd/ yōm tamantāshar yunyō sanat sitt u xamsīn/ wa kunna fī hāza l-yōm/ naḥtafil/ bi galā? ?axir 'askariy ?inglīziy 'an maṣr/ ba'd ?iḥtilāl ?arba'a wa sab'īn sana/ clap../ ?innahardā/ naltaqī marra ?uxra/ hunā/ fī bōr sa'īd/ li naḥtafil bi 'īd in-naṣr/ 'ala siyāsati l-quwwa/ wa 'ala siyāsati l-'udwān/ wa 'ala siyāsati l-ghadr/ naltaqi fi bōr sa'īd/ al-yōm/ ba'd 'āmin/ min galā?/ ?āxir 'askariy/ ?inglīziy firinsi/ 'an hāzihi l-?arḍ aṭ-ṭāhira/ clap../ yōm talāta wa 'ishrīn dīsimbir min al-'ām al-māḍi yōma xaragu l-?inglīz min bōr sa'īd/ kuntum btaḥtafilum bi hāzihi l-?a'yād ?illi kānat natīgit kifaḥkum/ wa samarat qitalkum wa kān biwiddi ?ayyuha l-?ixwa ?an ?aḥtạfila ma'akum bi hāza l-yawm/ fīlwa?t/ ?illi kuntu bash'ur fī bi mashā'irkum/ wa basma' fī l-?izā'a/ il-?iḥtifalāt wa l-hutāfāt wa ?aghāni n-naṣr/ wa r-rūḥ il-'āliya ba'da xurūg il-?inglīz min maṣr/ kuntu ?ash'ur/ ?inni bēnkum/ walākinni fī hāza l-waqt/ lam ?akun ?astaṭī'/ ?an ?aḥtafila ma'akum/ li?an/ kān fī guz?i/ min ?arḍ al-waṭan/ lā yazāl yuqāsi min al-?iḥtilāl/ fī sīna/ kāna l-yahūd yaḥtallu guz?i min sinā?/ wa ghazza kānat tuqāsi/ min al-?iḥtilāl al-yahūdi/ wa mā kānsh in-naṣr bi n-nisba li maṣr yu'tabar naṣr kāmil/ wa ?innahardā/ ba'da ?an ?aṣbaḥa hāza n-naṣr naṣr kāmil/ ?atawāgad bēnkum li ?aḥtafil ma'akum bi 'īd in-naṣr/ clap.../ ?ayyuha l-muwāṭinūn/ lam tantahi ma'ārikna/ bi sabīl ?istiqlālna/ wa fī sabīl tasbīt hāza l-?istiqlāl/ bi l-'udwān/ wa l-kifāḥ wa l-qitāl wa l-?insiḥāb min bōr sa'īd wa min sinā? wa min ghazza walākin/ hāzihi l-ma'ārik/ ?istamarrat/ bi ṭarīqa qad takūn ?ashadd 'unf/ wa ?ashaddu quwwa/ bada?at ma'rakat al-'azl wa bada?at ma'rakati t-tagwī'/ wa bada?at ma'ārik al-?a'ṣāb/ wa kāna li hāzihi l-ma'ārik gamī'an hadaf wāḥid/ huwa l-qaḍā?/ 'ala l-fikra/ ?illi ?inba'athat min maṣr/ tunādi bi l-hurriyya/ wa tunādi bi l-?istiqlāl/ wa tunādi bi l-qawmiyya l-'arabiyya/ il-fikra ?illi ?inba'athat min maṣr/ tunādi/ bi ?an lā makāna li manāṭiq an-nufūz/ wa ?innanā lan naxḍa' li manṭiqati nufūzi ?aḥad wa lan naxḍa' li sulṭān ?aḥad/ il-fikra lli ?imba'athat min maṣr/ tunādi/ bi ?annana ?aḥrār fi biladna/ nuqarrar siyasitna fi biladna/ wa nuqarrar siyasitna min ḍamirna/ wa ni'mil ?illi ḥna na'taqidu ?innu l-xēr/ wa lā na'mal ish-sharr/ li?annahu/ yi'gib balad min al-bilād l-kubra/ ?aw li?annahu raghbat ?iḥda l-bilād il-kubrā/ ba'da hāza l-?insiḥāb/ bada?at ma'ārik muttaṣila/ ma'ārik mutawāṣila/ min ?agli l-qaḍā? 'ala hāzihi l-fikra/

wa min ?agli l-qaḍā? ‘ala hāzihi r-rūḥ/ wa ba‘d ?insiḥāb bōr sa‘īd yōm talāta u ‘ishrīn disimbir/ daxalna ma‘ārik muta‘addida/ ma‘ārik ṭawīla/ wa ma‘ārik marīra/ min ?agli tasbīt ?istiqlalna/ wa min ?agli tasbīt ?intaṣārna/ wa ?idhā kunna ?innahardā binaḥtafil bi n-naṣr/ ‘an/ il-?insiḥāb illi ḥadas yōm talāta u ‘ishrīn disimbir fī l-‘ām l-māḍi/ wa l-?insiḥāb ?illi ḥaṣal min ghazza/ wa l-?insiḥāb ?illi ḥaṣal min sinā?/ fa naḥnu ?ayḍan/ naḥtafil/ bi n-naṣr fī ma‘rakati l-?a‘ṣāb/ wa fī ma‘rakati ḍ-ḍaghṭ al-?iqtiṣādi/ wa fī ma‘rakati t-tagwī‘/ wa fī l-ma‘raka llati kānu yahdifūn biha ?ixḍā‘na wa ?izlālna/ naḥtafil bi n-naṣr/ wa naḥnu nash‘ur ?annana ?a‘izza? kuramā fī bilādna/ wa ?inna siyāsitna/ tuqarrar min ḍamirna/ clap.../ ?ayyuha l-?ixwa/ fī far?i kbīr/ bēna l-ma‘raktēn/ ma‘rakat il-udwān/ wa ma‘rakat il-‘azl wa l-?ixḍā‘/ ma‘rakat il-‘udwān kānat bitistaxdim/ al-qanābil/ iṭ-ṭayārāt/ ?asāṭīl ad-duwal al-‘uZma/ brīṭāniya u faransa/ rigāl il-muZallāt/ ?intu kuntu ‘arfīnhum ṭab‘an hinā fī bōr sa‘īd/ clap.../ wa ish-shayāṭīn il-ḥumr willa al-‘afarīt al-ḥumr/ barḍu ?intu shuftuhum hina fī bōr sa‘īd/ clap../ btistaxdim id-dabbabāt/ wa kunna nastaṭī‘ ?an nuwāgihha wagha li wagh/ wa kan kull wāḥid fīkum biyaxud silāḥuh/ wa yiṭla‘ ‘ashān yuqābil al-mu‘taḍīn/ u yudāfi‘ ‘an baladuh/ wa yudāfi‘ ‘an waṭanuh/ wa yi?til il-mu‘tadī/ wa yaqḍi ‘alēh/ kān kulli wāḥad fīkum biyastaṭī‘ ?an yuqābil al-mu‘tadīn waghan li wagh/ clap.../ ?ayyuha l-?ixwa/ ?amma ma‘rakati l-‘azl/ fa kān silaḥha silaḥ muxtalif/ kān silaḥha ?a‘wān il-?isti‘mār fi l-manṭiqa lli bin‘īsh fīha/ ?a‘dā? il-qawmiyya l-‘arabiyya/ kānit hāzihi l-ma‘raka ma‘raka muxtalifa/ kānat ma‘raka qāsiya/ wa kānat ma‘raka marīra/ fī l-ma‘raka l-?ūla ?illi kunna binwāgih fīha ṭ-ṭayyarāt wa l-bawārig wa d-dabbabāt/ kunna nastaṭī‘ ?an nuwāgiha ḍ-ḍarba bi ḍarba ?uxra/ wa kunna nastaṭī‘ ?an nuqābil al-‘udwān bi l-‘udwān/ wa nastaṭī‘ ?an nuqābil il-qatli bi l-qatl/ walākin il-ma‘raka t-taniya/ kānat/ ma‘raka/ ?aṣ‘ab/ mā kānshi min is-sahil ‘alēna ?in niḥna nuwāgih ḍ-ḍarba/ bi ḍarba ?uxra/ walākinna kunna nanẓur/ min ḥawlina/ li narā hāzihi ḍ-ḍarabāt/ allati tuwaggahu ?ilayna/ li ta‘zilna/ wa li tuḥaqqiq ?ahdāf il-musta‘mirīn/ ?illi mā ?idrūsh yuḥaqqiqūha bi l-qanābil wa d-dabbabāt wa ṭ-ṭayyarāt/ wa kunna nanZur ?ila hāzihi l-ma‘raka/ wa nuḥārib fīha/ walākin mā kunnāsh bini?dar niḍrab iḍ-ḍarba bi ḍarba/ kān is-silāḥ al-?asāsiy/ ?a‘wān il-?isti‘mār/ al-‘arab wa ?a‘dā? il-qawmiyya l-‘arabiyya/ l-‘arab/ clap../ walākin/ .../ Zaharat mashārī‘/ wa xiṭaṭ/ li l-qaḍā? ‘ala l-qawmiyya l-‘arabiyya/ wa li ‘azli maṣr/ wa l-qaḍā? ‘ala fikrat il-ḥurriya/ ‘amal ?a‘wān il-?isti‘mār/ bi kulli ṭāqithum/ muta‘āwinīn fī hāza ma‘a l-?isti‘mār/ walākinnahum fashalū/ wa ?intaṣarna ?ayḍan fī hāzihi l-ma‘raka/ clap.../ ?innahardā/ .../ wa ?ana baltaqi bīkum fī bōr sa‘īd/ wa naḥnu nash‘ur bi n-naṣr/ wa naḥmadu llāh ‘ala hāza n-naṣr/ wa naḥtafil bi hāza n-naṣr/ in-naṣr fī l-ḥarb il-musallaḥa ḍiddi d-duwal il-kubra/ in-naṣr ‘ala l-‘udwān/ in-naṣr ‘ala l-quwwa l-ghāshima/ in-naṣr ‘ala siyāsati l-quwwa/ nubuṣṣu li nafsina/ winshūf lēh ?intaṣarna/ fī hāzihi l-fatra wa lēh mā kunnāsh binantaṣir fī l-māḍī/ ?intaṣarna ?innahardā/ li?anna maṣr/ milki li-?abnāha/ mish milki li fi?a minna n-nās/ maṣr ibta‘itku kullukum/ bita‘it kullu wāḥid fīkum/ bita‘it ?abnā?kum/ maṣr ?illi intu dāfi‘tu ‘anha/ clap.../ maṣr ?illi intu dāfi‘tu ‘anha/ wa ?abnā?kum wa ?ixwatkum wa ?ixwāti yistashhidum fīha/ bita‘itkum/ mish bita‘it nās ma‘dūdīn/ mish bita‘it il-xidēwi/ wa lā bta‘it al-‘ēla ?ila l-malka/ wa lā bta‘it fi?a qalīla mina l-mullāk/ maṣr ?ibta‘it kullu wāḥid min ?abna?ha/ kullu wāḥid kān biyuqātil u huwa yash‘ur bihāza sh-shu‘ur/ kan biyudāfi‘/ ‘ala illi ksibnāh ba‘da thawra yōm talāta wa ‘ishrīn yulyu/ ‘ādat maṣr ?ila ?abnā?ha/ kullu wāḥid kan biyuqātil li maṣr ibta‘tu/ li-l-?arḍi bta‘tu li waṭanuh/ wa li hāza/ kullu wāḥid kān biyshīl is-silāḥ/ ish-shubbān wa sh-shuyūx wa n-nisā?/ ?intu hinā fī bōr sa‘īd kuntum/ fī ‘izzi l-ma‘raka/ bituqatlu ‘ala l-?istiqlāli lli ḥaqqaqtūh/ bituqatlu fī sabīl al-galā? ?illi ḥaqqaqtuh ba‘da xamsa u sab‘īn sana min il-?istiqlāl/ maṣr ?amma ṣbaḥit/ milk li ?abna?ha/ maṣr ?amma ṣbaḥit/ milki li kulli wāḥid min ?abna?ha/ ?istaṭa‘na ?an nuḥaqqiq hāza n-naṣr/ wa ?istaṭa'na ?in niḥna nihzim id-duwal l-kubra/ wa l-?asaṭīl ?illi gat hāgmitkum hina/ ba'di mā rig'it/ ?a'lanu ?innuhum bybī'ūha li ?an mā lihāsh fayda/ maṣr/ clap.../ ?intaṣarna ya ?ixwāni/ li?innukum kullukum ?intum taḥti s-silāḥ/ wa ?ana 'ārif/ ?izzay kuntu btuqatlu/ wa ?izzay il-madaniyyīn hina fī bōr sa'īd kānu byaḥmilu s-silāḥ/ wa ?izzay ish-sha'b kulluh ?ām taḥti s-silāḥ/ yuqātil fī sabīl maṣr/ fā sabīl baladuh/ kuntum ?antum ya ?ahla bōr sa'īd/ ṭalī'ati l-ma'raka/ talī'ati l-ma'raka fī hāza l-qitāl l-marīr/ qātaltum bi sharaf/ wa qātaltum bi ?imān/ qātaltum min ?agli maṣr/ lā min ?agli l-maṣlaḥati l-xāṣṣa/ ?aw min ?agli il-maksab il-māddī/ ?aw min ?agli maṣlaḥatin zātiyya/ qātaltum min ?agli l-musul al-'ulyā/ qātaltum min ?agli l-ḥurriyya lli ḥaqqaqtūha/ wa qātaltum min ?agli l-?istiqlāl illi sabbittūh/ kullu wāḥad fīkum ?ām yuqātil/ wa kānat bōr sa'īd tumassil ṭalī'at il-ma'raka/ wa kānat maṣr kullaha taḥta s-silāḥ/ ana fī hāza l-waqt ?ayyuha l-?ixwā/ kuntu ma'akum daqīqa bi daqīqa/ wa kuntu ?arākum fī tamantāshar yunyu/ sanat sitt u xamsīn ?amma zurtu bōr sa'īd/ kuntu shāyif kullu wāḥad fīkum fī balakunāt wa fī sh-shawāri'/ fī l-ma'raka/ kuntu shāyif kullu wāḥad fīkum/ zayyi mā kuntu shāyif yōm tamantāshar yunyu/ fī balakunāt wa fī sh-shawāri'/ wa kunt ?u?min bi n-naṣr/ li ?inni l-wugūh ?illi kuntu bashūfha/ hiya l-wugūh ?illi kānit bitihtif bi l-gala? yōm tamantāshar yunyu/ yōma rafa'na l-'alam al-maṣrī/ makān al-'alam al-briṭāniy 'ala mabna l-baḥriyya/ clap../ bōr sa'īd/ clap../ ?ayyuha l-?ixwa/ clap / ?ayyuha l-?ixwa/ kuntu mu?min/ zayyukum/ bi llāh wa bi 'awn illāh/ kuntu mu?min ?ayḍan zayyukum/ bi baladi/ maṣr/ wa kuntu mu?min ?ayḍan/ zayyukum/ bi ?abnā? baladī/ bīkum/ bi kulli fardi fī maṣr/ wa kuntu wāsiq/ ?in iḥna ḥanantaṣir/ 'ala d-duwal al-kubra wa d-duwal al-'uZma/ kuntu fī nafsi l-wa?t ?ash'ur bimā qāsaytum/ wa ?a'lam ?innukum tash'uru ?innuh di ḍaribit il-waṭan/ wa ?ult ?innama bōr sa'īd/ fādit maṣr kullaha/ ?ult bi shahr nōvimbir/ ?ult ?inna bōr sa'īd fādit il-'arab ?agma'īn/ zayyima ?ult ?ilkum/ kuntum ṭ-ṭalī'a/ wa/ mādarsh ?a?ūl bōr sa'īd il-bāsila/ bōr sa'īd ish-shugā'a/ bōr sa'īd il-mugāhida/ li?anni ?ayyu waṣf ?a?ūlu/ yaqill 'anni l-wāqi'/ wa ?ayyi kalām ?a?ūlu/ lā yu'abbir 'anni l-ḥaqīqa/ ?anna ba?ūl ?innuku kuntu ṭ-ṭalī'a/ ?illi ta'arraḍit li l-'udwān/ li tuḥaqqiq in-naṣr/ wa ?istaṭā'at hāzihi ṭ-ṭalī'a/ ?an tuḥaqqiq in-naṣr/ ?istaṭā' al-mu'taḍūn/ id-duwal il-?isti'māriyya ?innaha taḥtall bōr sa'īd/ hal ?iḥtilāl bōr sa'īd/ kān maṣr li ?ingiltira wa faransa d-duwal al-'uZma/ kullina na'lam/ ?in ?ayyi gēsh mihāgim/ lāzim yāxud rās gisr/ 'alashān yukammil 'amaliyyāt/ wa kullina na'lam/ ?innu byixtār rās il-gisr/ min ?ayyi makān/ wa kullina na'lam ?ayḍan/ ?inni dā?iman/ hāzihi l-'amaliyyāt/ 'amaliyyāt al-?inzāl kānat/ taṣil ?ila natīgitha/ li?annaha bitatarakkaz fīha/ gamī' al-quwwa/ bōr sa'īd/ kānit ḍaḥiyya li-l-'udwān il-brīṭāni l-firinsi/ bi ?asāṭīl briṭāniya wa faransa/ wa ṭayyarāt briṭānya wa faransa/ wa fī yōm ?āl balāgh rasmī ?in/ xarag min al-baḥriyya al-?inglīziyya/ tultumiyya u sab'īn ṭal'it ṭayarān/ mafrūḍ ?innu ṭal'it iṭ-ṭayarān tib?a talāt ṭayyarāt/ ya'ni ḥawāliy ?alf ghara 'ala bōr sa'īd/ ?istaṭā' al-?inglīz bi tarkīz hāzihi l-quwwa 'ala bōr sa'īd/ ?innuhum yu?amminu li nafsahum/ rās kūbri/ wa ?ālu/ ?innuhum nizlum fī bōr sa'īd/ walākin minna n-nāḥya l-'askariyya/ kulli dawla ?arādit ?innaha tuhāgim dawla ?uxra wa ti'mil ras kubrī/ ?istaṭā'at ?innaha ti'mil rāsi kubrī/ walākin/ l-'ibra binatīgit il-ma'raka/ ?iḥna kunna binantaZir/ al-'udwān min bōr sa'īd/ kunna binantaZir il-'udwān min ?iskindiriya/ kunna binantaZir il-'udwān min lībyā/ u kānat xiṭaṭna l-'askariyya/ ?in niḥna nastaṭī'/ ?an nattagih/ ?ila al-'udwān/ fī l-makān ?illi yō?a' fīh/ walākin ḥaṣal il-ghadr wa l-xiyāna/ hagamit ?isra?īl/ wa kān/ taqdīrna ?inna l-ma'raka r-ra?īsiyya ma'raka ma'a ?isra?īl/ u mā fakkarnāsh ?in ad-duwal al-kubrā/ tighishsh ar-ra?yi l-'ām al-'ālami/ wa ti?ūl ?innaha ḥati'mil bulīs/ bēn maṣr wa ?isra?īl/ 'ashān tuhāgim maṣr/ il-djinirāl kitli/ ?illi huwa kān qā?id al-'udwān/ ?āl ?innu kān 'āyiz/ yuhāgim maṣr min libyā/ wa ?āl ?ayḍan ?in il-malik ?idrīs is-sinūsī malik lībyā/ haddid/ ?idhā ?istaxdamat

?ingiltira libyā li l-'udwān 'ala maṣr/ wa bi hāza lam yatamakkanu/ wa da ṭab'an natīga/ min n-natā?ig il-qawmiyya l-'arabiyya wa t-taḍāmun al-'arabiy wa l-quwwa l-'arabiyya/ clap.../ it-taḍāmun il-'arabiyya wa l-qawmiyya l-'arabiyya/ mana'it ?ingiltirā/ raghm mu'āhaditha ma'a lībyā wa raghmu qawā'idha fī libyā/ min ?innaha tastaxdim lībyā li l-'udwān/ 'ala dawla 'arabiyya ?uxra/ dā mawqif musharrif li l-malik ?idrīs is-sinūsi malik libyā/ wa hagamit ?ingiltira 'ala bōr sa'īd/ wa ?istaṭā'at ?ingiltira/ ?an tu?ammin/ ra?su kubri fī pōr sa'īd/ ?abli l-hugūm bi yōmēn/ lamma l-?isra?īl/ daxalit min il-ḥidūd/ wa taqaddamat fi sinā?/ kunna barḍū binantaZir/ 'udwān/ fī makān min il-?amkina ?illi ?ultha/ yā?imma 'ala minṭaqati l-qanāl/ yā?imma fī ?iskindiriya/ yā?imma min libyā/ wa kunna bnuwaggih quwwātna ?ila/ gabhati l-qitāl/ fī ṣaḥrā? sina?/ guz?i min il-quwwāt ?illi kānit mawguda 'andukum hīna fī bōr sa'īd/ taḥarrakit 'alashān tu'azziz quwwāt il-'arīsh/ il-guz? illi fiḍil / 'alashān/ yatawallā iddifā'/ ṭab'an lam yakun/ bi l-quwwa ?illi tumakkinuha tiwāgih ḥāga briṭāniya l-'uZma/ wa faransa il-baladēn ?illi byu'tabaru min il-bilād il-'uẓma/ walākin l-gēsh qātil/ wa sh-sha'b qātil ?ayḍan/ ma'a l-gēsh/ ish-sha'bu kulluh/ ?aṣbaḥ taḥti s-silāḥ/ wa ?anā ?arēt/ fi ?aḥad il-kutub ?illi katbīnuh il-firansawiyyīn/ wāḥid saḥafi faransāwi katab kitāb u ?āl/ ?innu shāf fi bōr sa'īd/ ba'da mā nizil ma'a l-quwwāt al-mu'tadiyya fī bōr sa'īd/ ?in sh-shabāb al-miṣrī kān yuqātil bi 'inād/ wa ?innu sh-shabāb fī sana ḥadāshar sana u tnāshar sana/ kān shāyil is-silāḥ/ wa kān biyuqātil wa ?istaṭā' ?an yuwa??if id-dabbabāt il-?inglīziyya wa ?istaṭā'a/ ?in yuwa??if il-quwwāt il-muqtaḥima/ il-?ingliziyya/ ish-sha'b kullu ?ām taḥti s-silāḥ 'alashān/ yuqātil/ wa 'alashān yudāfi' 'an ḥurriyyituh wa 'an ?istiqlāluh/ wa sh-sha'b kulluh ?aṣbaḥ gēsh/ il-quwwāt il-musallaḥa/

Appendix B

NASSER 1962

xiṭba 'abdun-nāṣir fī 'īd th-thawra (23 July 1962)

?ayyuha l-?ixwatu l-muwāṭinūn/.../ ?ayyuha l-ixwa/.../ ?ayyuha l-?ixwatu l-muwāṭinūn/.../?ayyuha l-?ixwatu l-muwāṭinūn/.../kull sana wa intu ṭayyibīn/ kulli sana/ min ḥaqqi kulli fardi fīkum/.../ min ḥaqqi kulli muwāṭin/.../ min ḥaqqi kulli muwāṭin/ .../ al-yōm/ ?an yaḥtafil bi hādha l-'īd al-'āshir/ li th-thawra/ .../min ḥaqqi kulli ragul/ 'ala hādhihi l-?arḍ il-magīda/ ṣāni'ati l-ḥaḍāra wa ṣāni'ati t-tārīx/.../ min ḥaqqi kulli ?imra?a/.../ min ḥaqqi kulli shayx/.../ min ḥaqqi kulli shābb/.../ min ḥaqqi hādha l-gīl/... kulluh/ alladhī wā'adahu l-qadar/ ?an yataṭalla'a warā?ahu ?ila mā qāma bihi min ?a'māl/ izzayyi mā binbuṣṣu warāna winshūf ?ēh il-?a'māl illi 'amalnāha / min ḥa?? hādha l-gīl ?ayḍan/ ?innu yubuṣṣ ?amāmuh wa yataṭalla' ?amāmuh ?ila mā yantaẓiru min mas?ūliyyāt/ li ?an niḥna/ bidūn shu'ūrnā bi l-mas?ūliyya mā kunnāsh ni?dar nu?ūm bi ?ayyi 'amal min al-?a'māl/ walākin shu'ūrna bi l-mas?ūliyya / xallāna n-nahārdā ḥīnamā nataṭalla' ?ila l-warā?/ narfa' ir-ra?s bi l-'izza wa s-siqa/ narfa' r-ra?s/ bi l-'izza wa s-siqa/ fī n-nafs/ wa l-?īmān bi-llāh/ wa l-?īmān bi l-mustaqbal / min ḥa??ina n-nahārdā/ wa ?iḥna binataṭalla' ?ilā s-sinīn il-'ashara ?illi fātit/ ?in niḥna nattagih ?ila l-masal il-?a'la / wa ḍamirnā murtāḥ/ min ḥaqqina l-yōm/ ?an nash'ur bi l-faraḥ il-'amīq / wa ?an nadhkur ?ayḍan az-zikrayāt al-?alīma l-bākiya/ wa ?an na'rif ?ayḍan wa nataṣawwar il-mas?ūliyyāt al-kubra l-mulqā 'ala 'ātiqna/ kuntu tamalli ba?ulluku/ ?inna hādha l-gīl min sha'bi miṣr 'ala maw'idin ma'a l-qadar/ ?innahardā ba'da 'ashri sanawāt mina s-sawra/ ?a?dar ?a?ūl/ ?inna hādha l-gīl gā?a fī maw'idihi ma'a l-qadar/ lam tamna'u 'awā?iq/ lam taṣuddahu 'aqabāt/ wa ?innamā gā?a fī maw'idihi tamāman/ wa lāqa l-qadar/ wa sāra bihi mutaxaṭṭiyyan kulla ṣ-ṣu'ubāt/ mugābihan kulla l-?axṭār/ ḥatta ?istaṭā'a hādha l-gīl/ ?an yamlika li nafsih/ makānan/ yaqdiru minhu thawriyyan 'ala taghyīri ḥayātina wa ?i'ādati ṣun'iha min gadīd/ hādha huwa l-?asās/ taghyīru l-ḥayā/ ?i'ādatu ṣun'i l-ḥayā min gadīd/ ?inna hādha l-gīl min sha'bi miṣr al-'arabiy/ ?istaṭā'a/ ?an yuḥaqqiqa fī 'umrih/ kulla mā kānat tataṭalla'u ?ilayhi ?agyālun sābiqa/ fī l-māḍi bada?a li-laḥaZāt/ ?anna t-tārīx/ yushīru ?ila hādhihi l-?agyāl/ walākinnaha/ raghmi l-guhūd ?illi badhalitha/ lam tastaṭi' ?an tuwāfi? l-qadara ḥaythu ?ashāra laha/ fī ?awwal il-qarn it-tis'atāshar/ kāna sh-sha'b fī miṣr bi ta?sīr ?afkār 'asr in-nahḍa/ allati shāraka fī ṣun'iha qabla ?an yaḍghiṭa 'ala ?arḍiha ẓallām 'ahdi l-mamālik/ wa l-'ahdi l-'uthmāni/ yafūr/ wa ka?annahu bada?a ḥarakatuhu l-kubra / walākin/ limādha/ limādha lam naltaqi ma'a l-qadar fī hādhihi l-?ayyām/ maṭāmi' d-duwal il-?isti'māriyya/ fī dhālika l-waqti fī ?ūrūbā/ mutaḥālifa ma'a 'anāṣiri l-?istighlāl iṭ-ṭufayliyya/ fī ḥukm ?usrit muḥammad 'ali/ 'arqalat il-ḥaraka/ wa mana'at liqā?iha ma'a l-qadar/ fī ?awāxiri l-qarn it-tis'atāshar/ bada?a sh-sha'b ba'da fatra ṭawīla min it-ta?ahhub ith-thawri/ yasta'iddi li l-'amal ith-thawri/ walakinna l-xiyāna/ ḍarabat ith-thawra min il-xalf/ wa lam taṣil sawrat 'irābi ?ilā ḥaythu kānat tastaṭī'/ law lam taḍribha l-xiyāna l-mutaḥālifa ma'a l-?isti'mār/ ?izan ish-sha'bu hunā/ ish-sha'bu bi baladnā/ lam yastakīn ?abadan bi ?ayyi ḥālin mina l-?aḥwāl/ wa lam yataqabbal 'uhūd aZ-Zallām bi ?ayyi ḥālin mina l-?aḥwāl/ walākinnahu kāna dā?iman yata?ahhabu li th-thawrati wa yanṭaliqu ?ilayhā/ walākin/ 'āqat ḥarakatuhu l-mu?āmarāt il-?isti'māriyya/ summā 'anāṣiru l-xiyānati l-mutaḥālifati ma'a l-?isti'mār/ ba'd ?intihā? il-ḥarb il-'ālamī l-?ūla/ taḥarraka sh-sha'b/ alladhī kāna yata?ahhabu li-th-thawra/ yuḥāwilu ?ayḍan marratan ?uxra/ ?an yumsika l-qadar bi yadih/ walākinna l-furṣa ?aflatat/ ḥīna tamakkanat ar-rag'iyyatu l-miṣriyya l-mutaḥālifa ma'a l-maṣāliḥ ar-ra?simāliyya/ al-maḥalliyya wa l-?agnabiyya/ min tabdīdi ṭāqātin thawriyyatin 'adīda/ ba'da kida/ ?istaṭā'at taḥwīla n-niḍāl ith-thawrī l-gamāhīri/ ?ila makāsiba shaxṣiyya/ wa maghāhim wa maṭāmi'/ kullina bna'raf hāza t-tarīx/ kullina bna'raf hāzi n-nakasāt/ kullina bna'raf ?inna sh-sha'b lam yastakīn bi ?ayyi ḥālin min al-?aḥwāl/ walākinnahu kāna yurīdu ?an yashuqqa ṭarīqa/ li yughayyira ḥayāta/ wa li yughayyira mustaqbalah wa li yaṣna' ḥayātahu min gadīd/ walākin hādhihi l-muḥāwalāt fī l-māḍi lam tafläḥ/ lam yumkin li sh-sha'bi ?an yaltaqī ma'a l-qadar/ ḥatta gā?a hādha l-gīl/ gilkum ?intum/ il-gīl illi ḥna na'īshu l-?ān/ hādha l-gīl lāqa l-qadar fī maw'idih/ wa ?irtafa' ?ila mustawa maṭālib ?ummatu l-ḥayawiyya/ wa fī nafsi l-waqt/ ?istaṭā'a hādha l-gīl/ bi nagāḥiha ?an yukallila bi n-naṣr/ tārīxa n-niḍāl ish-sha'bī l-?ummatih/ gīlan ba'da gīl/ wa ana ?innahardā wa ana batadhakkar hādhihi l-?aḥdās/ lā ?ashukk ?anna ?agyāl min sha'bina tataṭalla' al-?ān min 'ālamha l-lānihā?i/ faxūra/ mu'tazza bi hāza l-gīl/ alladhī kāna fī tārīxu ?ummatih ṭalī'a sawriyya/ ghayyarata l-maṣīr taghyīran ḥāsiman wa taghyīran ?asāsiyyan/ wa ?ana ?ayḍan/ ?asiq ?anna ?agyālan qādima/ muqbila/ min sha'bina/ mā zālat il-?ān/ fī l-ghaybi l-ba'īd/ sawfa tanZur/ faxūra mu'tazza ?ayḍan bi hādha l-gīl/ hādha l-gīl/ illi ?iḥna na'īsh fīh/ li?annahu makkanaha bi qudratihi 'ala th-thawra/ min ṣun'i ḥayātin gadīdatin 'ala hādhihi l-?arḍi l-xālida/ hādha l-gīl ?ayyuha l-?ixwatu l-muwāṭinūn/ alladhi na'īshu/ kāna ṭalī'atan thawriyyatan fī ḥayāti l-?umma/ wa ?innamā ba?ūl ṭalī'a sawriyya/ ?ana mā ba?sudsh bi hāza ?illi ṭil'u l-yōm talāta wa 'ishrīn yulyu/ magmū'it ish-shabāb ?illi xaragū yōm talāta wa 'ishrīn yulyu/ li/ li yaruddū 'ala nidā?i sh-sha'bi l-mulihḥi min ?agli t-taghyīr/ hādhihi l-magmū'āt min ash-shabāb/ lam takun tastaṭi' shay?an/ clap.../ magmū'āt ish-shabāb ?illi ṭil'it fī sawra yōm talāta wa 'ishrīn yulyu sana tnēn u xamsīn/ mā kānitsh ti?dar ta'mil ḥāga ?abadan/ law lam yakun al-gīl kulluh/ musta'idd li ḥtimalāt as-sawra/ iṭ-ṭalī'a s-sawriyya/ fī ra?yi/ hiya kulli n-nās ?illi ?amnum bi ?imkāniyyāt it-taghyīr/ kull ?illi ṭaraḥū sh-shi'arāt il-inhizāmiyya s-sābiqa/ bi ?annahu lā fā?ida wa lā ?amal/ ?iḥna ṭli'na wa kunna bnisma' ?ēh/ kunna ?amma nikkallim fī ?ayyi ḥāga ?alūlina sa'd bāsha ?āl mā fīsh fā?ida/ lēh ish-shi'arāt dī/ shi'arāt ?inhizāmiyya kānū biḥāwlu bihā ?innuhum / yabussu fī nufusna l-ya?s/ wa yaqḍū 'ala l-?imān fī qulubna/ ?anā ?azkur min ?awwil ?ayyām iṭ-ṭufūla/ kullama nikkallim fī ?ayyi ḥāga/ yi?ūlak bittikallim fī ?ē sa'd bāsha ?āl mā fīsh fayda/ mā fīsh fayda fī hāza l-kalām/ l-?inglīz mush mumkin yiṭla'u min maṣr/ di shi'arāt ?inhizāmiyya/ xarag nās min ?abnā? hādhihi l-?umma/ li yaqḍū 'ala hadhihi sh-shi'arāt al-?inhizāmiyya/ wa yuqīmū shi'arāt thawriyya/ yarfa'u shi'arāt thawriyya/ tanba' min hādha sh-sha'b/ wa min rūḥ hādha sh-sha'b/ wa min nafsi hādha sh-sha'b/ clap../ xarag min hāza l-gīl/ xarag ?ē/ nās ?amnum bi l-musta?bal/ kullu wāḥid minhum/ 'amal fī niṭāquh ?igābiyyan/ likay yataḥaqqaq ?amaluh fī l-mustaqbal/ dōl kulluhum ṭalā?i' sawriyya/ ba'ḍuhum mā sma nāsh ?ismuh/ bēnhum ẓubbāt wa bēnhum gunūd/ lam tutaḥ lahum il-furṣa 'alashān yashtarikū fī talāta wa 'ishrīn yulyu/ bēnhum shabāb kān ya'nīh ?amr waṭanuh/ wa lā yaqif minhu mawqif salbī/ bēnhum fallāḥīn lam yughadrū ḥuqulhum/ walākin ḍarabāt fu?ūshum 'ala l-?arḍ/ kānat tashuqqu ṭ-ṭarīq li t-taghyīr is-sawri/ bēnhum 'ummāl lam yatruku maṣāni'ahum/ lākin ?aydīhim kānat taḥmil al-maṭāriq allati tahāwat ?amāmaha kulli l-mawāni'/ bēnhum magmu'āt min al-muthaqqafīn/ ?illi hum tharwa 'aẓīma hā?ila li waṭanihim/ ḥāfila bi l-?imkaniyyāt il-qādira 'ala xidmat qaḍiyyat it-taghyīr/ li ṣāliḥi l-gamāhīr/ wa kānatu ẓ-ẓurūf/ tubā'idu baynahum wa bayna ḥaqqihim fī l-xidmati l-waṭaniyyat il-ḥaqqa/ kulli dōl kānū ṭalā?i' sawriyya/ kulli dōl yu'tabarū min il-gīl illadhi kāna ṭalī'a sawriyya fī ?ummatihum/ kulli ha?ulā?i ḥaqqaqū maw'id sha'bahum ma'a l-qadar/ kulli ha?ūlā?i rāwadathum il-?aḥlām/ shaddahum il-?amal/ dafa'athum il-?irāda ṣ-ṣalbatu l-kāminati fī ?a'māqi sha'bihim/ likay yaqifū fī 'inād/ yōm talāta wa 'ishrīn yulyu/ thummā yaqūlūna fī yaqīn/ hādha bid?u tārīxin gadīd/ clap../ ba'dēn mā ?ālūsh kida u sakatum/ bal ?inṭalaqū li yuḥaqqiqū qawlahum ba'da dhālik/ bi kulli l-?a'māl al-kabīra/ bi kulli t-taḍḥiyāt al-bāsila/ bi kulli ṣ-ṣabr sh-shugā'/ bi kulli l-?iṣrār al-'anīd/ ?innahardā ?ayyuha l-?ixwa/ ba'da 'ashri sanawāt/ min dhālika l-yawm al-'aẓīm/ 'ala daw? at-tagrubati wa l-wāqi'/ naqifu hunā gamī'an/ wa ?idhā mā qālu/ kulli shi yit?āl/ fī hādha l-yōm/ ḥaqīqa wāqi'a/ ?innanā l-yawm nastaṭī'u ?an nanẓura ?ila hādhihi s-sanawāt al-'ashr/ binbuṣṣ li s-sinīn il-'ashara/ wa n?ūl/ laqad kāna talāta u 'ishrīn yulyu sanat itnēn u xamsīn/ bid?u tārīxin gadīdin li hādhihi l-?ummati th-thā?irati l-munāḍila/ clap../ ?ayyuha l-?ixwatu l-muwaṭinūn/ 'alashān ni?dar ni'raf/ wa nudrik ?ab'ād hādha t-tārīx/ lāzim nunẓur naẓra ?ila l-māḍi/ wa nu?af 'inda l-ḥāḍir/ wa nataṭalla' ?ila l-mustaqbal/ binshūf ?ēh il-'ashra sinīn illi ?abli s-sana tnēn u xamsīn/ nishūf il-fatra min sanat itnēn u ?arb'īn li sanat itnēn u xamsīn/ il-fatra min itnēn u xamsīn ?ilā ?itnēn wa sittīn/ thumma namuddu baṣarnā ?ilā l-fatra min itnēn u sittīn/ ?ila itnēn u sab'īn/ hādhihi l-fatra hiya 'umr gīl/ ?ammā nikkallam 'ala l-fatra min sana itnēn wa ?arb'īn ?ila itnēn u xamsīn/ ?adhkur yōm itnēn wa 'ishrīn yulyu sana tnēn u xamsīn/ zay ?innahardā min 'ashar sanawāt/ ish-sha'bu kulluh kān musta'idd li th-thawra / ish-sha'bu kulluh kān fī ḥālit ghalayān/ al-gēsh kān yatagāwab ma'a sh-sha'b li?anna l-gēsh guz?i min ish-sha'b/ fī hādha l-yōm min 'ashra sanawāt/ ?adhkur/ ?in niḥnā/ ṣammimnā 'ala ?an naqūm bi 'amal wa ?an naqūm bi 'amal thawrī ṭalī'i/ fī hādhi l-fatra/ kānat fatra tanaqqulāt l-quwwāt/ bēn il-bilād il-muxtalifa/ ?amma ?ista'raḍnā quwwātna fī hādhihi l-?ayyām yimkin ?abl talāta u 'ishrīn yulyu bi talat ?arb'at ?iyyām/ mā kān shi l- Z-Zubbāṭ il-?aḥrār/ quwwāt kāfiya fī l-qāhira/ kānat quwwātna fī l-qāhira/ quwwāt qalīla/ walākin/ kān/ ?inṭalaq ish-sha'b is-sawri/ wa kānat al-?ayyām al-baghīḍa llatī 'ishnāha qabla hādha/ ḥāfiz kabīr/ yad'ū ?ilā ?allā budda min il-qiyām bi shēy/ ba?ūl ?in naḥna yimkin ?abla mā ṭitla' is-sawra yōm talāta wa 'ishrīn yulyu ?aw yōm tnēn u 'ishrīn yulyu lēla talāta u 'ishrīn yulyu/ law kunna nu?'ud niḥsib il-'amaliyya bi wara? u ?alam/ fa kunna nagid ?inna n-nagāḥ yimkin ?iḥtimāluh ḍa'īf/ walākin / kān kullu wāḥid min iZ-Zubbāt il-?aḥrār kullu wāḥid min in-nās ?illi ?ishtarakū fī s-sawra/ fī hādhihi l-?ayyām/ kān biy?ūl/ ?iza mā ?istaṭa'nāsh ?in niḥna ningaḥ/ fī l-qaḍā 'ala hādha ẓ-ẓulm wa 'ala hādha l-?isti'bād/ fa laysa ?aqall min ?an nuḍaḥḥi/ wa nuthbit li-l-?agyāl il-qādima ?in il-gīl ?illi kān 'āyish fī sanat itnēn u xamsīn/ marḍish yiskut 'ala ẓ-ẓulm walākinnu qāma wa qātal/ ḥatta istushhid/ clap.../ iZ-Zubbāṭ ?illi kānū mawgudīn sanat itnēn u xamsīn yōm itnēn u 'ishrīn yulyu zayy ?innahardā/ min ?agli l-qiyām bi s-sawra/ kānū ḥawālī/ tis'īn Zābiṭ/ fī hādhihi il-manṭiqa/ il-quwwāt ?illi kānat ma'āna kānat quwwāt qalīla/ il-xiṭṭa ?illi kānat mawḍū'a yimkin lam takun qad bullighat li kull/ in-nās/ illi ana badhkuru yimkin zayy dilwa?ti yōm itnēn u 'ishrīn yulyu sanat itnēn u xamsīn/ kunt bamurr 'ala

Z-Zubbāt/ min iṣ-ṣubḥ/ ?illi hayashtariku fī s-sawra/ wa kān kulli siqa wa ?īmān fī llāh wa fī hādha sh-sha'b/ iḍ-ḍuhr ?igtama'na u ba'da ḍ-ḍuhr ?igtama'it il-qiyāda/ wa tuqarrar fī hādha l-yōm ?an tunaffaz is-sawra/ kān mafrūḍ ?anna s-sawra tunaffaz fī llēh ?illi fātit walākin ?ugīlat as-sawra li?anna al-xiṭṭa lam takun kāmila/

Appendix C

SADDAM HUSSEIN 1980

Press conference held in Baghdad, 20 July 1980
ḥadīth fī l-qaḍāya l-'arabiyya wa d-dawliyya

Question 1

sayyid ir-ra?īs/ hunāka su?āl/ yata'allaq bi t-tiknōlūdjiyā n-nawawiyya/ wa fī mādha kān il-'irāq yas'a ?ila ṣun' il-qunbula n-nawawiyya/ wa l-marāḥil ?allati qaṭa'aha li taḥqīq hādha l-hadaf/ wa mā huwa hadaf it-ta'āwun/ al-'irāqi al-firansi/ fī madjāl it-tiknōlūdjiyā n-nawawiyya/ xāṣṣatan wa ?inna l-'irāq mina l-buldān al-muwaqqi'a 'ala haẓr ?intishār il-?asliḥa in-nawawiyya/ wa mā hiya ?ahdāf al-'irāq/ min al-ḥuṣūl 'ala hādhihi t-tiknōlūdjiyā/ wa hal nadjaḥat ?isrā?il fī 'arqalati djuhūd il-'irāq fī hādha l-madjāl/

Saddam Hussein's answer (SH1)

?inqaḍa 'adad min as-sanawāt mā ?aẓunn/ 'adad/ kathīr min il-?ān/ fī l-?awsāṭ iṣ-ṣahyūniyya fī li l-shā?idīn wa ?aktharhum min ?ūrubbā/ al-?awsāṭ iṣ-ṣahyūniyya bi stimrār ittrawwidj fī /.../ ?awrubbā/.../ fī buldān yikūn fī firansa fī ?ingiltrā fī ?almāniyā l-gharbiya/ fī d-danimark/ is-swīd/ fī ?iṭāliyā/ ?ila ?āxirihi/ tigūl ?inna l-'arab dhōl nās mutaxallifīn/ mā yifhamūn il-'ilim/ mā hum muthaqqafīn/ mā yidirkūn mas?uliyāthum tidjāh nafishum/ wa lidhālik/ maṭlūb ?an yikūn 'alēhum waṣiyy u hādha l-waṣiyy lam/.../ yat'āmal wiyyāhum bi l-'aṣa l-ghalīẓa/ wa ?innu dhōl il-'arab nās lā yuḥsinūn ?illā rukūb il-djimāl/ wa l-bukā? 'ala l-?aṭlāl/ wa n-nawm bi l-xiyām/ ?alaysa hādha ṣaḥīḥ/ wa fudji?atan/ wa tiṭla' iṣ-ṣahyūniyya wa sana bi sana il-kiyēn iṣ-ṣahyūniy min/ sanatēn bi barnāmidj ?i'lāmi siyāsi mutaṣā'id/ fī ?asālībah wa fī nawayāh/ likay itgūl ?inna l-'irāq garrab yintidj qunbula nawawiyya/ fā n-nās ?illi lā yiḥsinūn ?illā rukūb il-djimāl kēf mumkin ?innu yintidj qunbula nawawiyya / 'ala ?ayyati ḥāl/ 'abdun-nāṣir ?allah yirḥāmu ḥakam tis'atāsh sana/ wa 'abdun-nāṣir mā kān muwaqqi' 'ala 'adam ?intishār il-?asliḥa n-nawawiyya/ kamā huwa shāni l-'irāq/ il-'irāq muwaqqi' 'ala 'adam ?intishār il-?asliḥa n-nawawiyya/ wa ma'a dhālika tis'atāsh sana wa 'abdunnāṣir ?allah yirḥamah mā gdar yintidj qunbula nawawiyya/ likay yuwādjih l-qunbula n-nawawiyya li l-kiyān iṣ-ṣahyūniyy il-muntidja ?aw fī ṭarīqha ḥasab taṣrīḥāt/ il-?awsāṭ iṣ-ṣahyūniyya wa ḥasab taṣrīḥāt ?awsāṭha r-rasmiyya/ wa qarība min il-?awsāṭ ir-rasmiyya fī l-gharb ʻumūman/ wa fī ?ūrubbā/ hādha l-ḥamla tinṭaliq min il-?iʻtiqād wa hādha l-?iʻtiqād ṣaḥīḥ/ ?innu qīmatu l-?insān fī ʻilmah/ fī l-ʻaṣr il-ḥadīth wa l-?umma ?illi/ itkūn ḍaʻīfa fī ʻilimha/ qābila ?an tuhzam ?akthar min il-?umma l-mutamakkina ʻilmiyyan/ wa li dhālik yuḥāwilūn kull ʻēn ʻarabiyya tkūn imfatḥa yiḥāwlūn yiṭfūnha/ wa hum yidirkūn ?innu ʻēn il-ʻirāq imfatḥa li ṣāliḥ il-?umma l-ʻarabiyya wa li ṣāliḥ karāmatha wa li ṣāliḥ siyādatha wa li ṣāliḥ ?istiqlālha/ wa hum yaʻrifūn tamām il-maʻrifa ?inna barnāmidji l-ʻirāq wa lā sirra fīh/ ?innuhu yurīd yistaxdim/ il-mafāʻilāt/ ?illi yitʻāqad ʻalēha maʻa faransa/ ?aw il-?adjhizat yitʻāqad ʻalēh maʻa ?iṭāliya/ li l-?aghrāḍ is-silmiyya/ ?idh-dharra ?il-?ān tustaxdam ʻala niṭāq wāsiʻ wa bi l-?asās li l-?aghrāḍ is-silmiyya/ ?amma kawnha tustaxdam li l-?aghrāḍ il-ʻaskariyya fa hādhi ?illi yaqūm bihi d-duwal il-kubrā l-maʻrūfa/ fa ?idhan is-su?āl nuwadjdjihah ?ila l-kiyān iṣ-ṣahyūniy hal yaʻni hādha ?innu mā ʻādu l-ʻarab rākibi l-djimāl wa/ mutaxallifīn/ wa lā yaḥtādjūn ?ilā l-waṣiyy ?illi yaḍrubhum bi l-ʻaṣā/ ?idha kāna l-?amr hakadhā limādha lā/.../ lā tuʻīdi n-naẓar fī nawayāha l-ʻudwāniyya ḍiddi l-?umma l-ʻarabiyya/ ?idhā kānat/.../ ?idhā kānat l-kiyān iṣ-ṣahyūniy yuqaddir ?inna l-?umma l-ʻarabiyya bada?at marḥalat in-nuhūḍ/ limādhā n-nās il-ʻuqqāl fī hādhā l-kiyān lā yaḥsibūn ḥisābāt daqīqa li l-mustaqbal/ kayfa mumkin ?an yitaṣawwarū ?innu mumkin ?an yaʻīshū fī/ dāxil l-?umma/ tanhaḍ ʻilmiyyan ?ilā l-ḥaddi ?illi ṣāru yatḥaddathu ʻanhā/ bi?annaha satamtalik l-qunbula dh-dharriyya fī wakit qaṣīr/ fī sana ?aw sanatēn ?aw thalātha ?aw fī ?arbaʻa ?aw/ ?ila ?āxirihi/ ?a lā yistaṭīʻ hādha badal mina t-tahwīsh/ ʻala l-barnāmidji n-nawawiy/ ʻala l-barnāmidj il-?istixdām dh-dharra li l-?aghrāḍ is-silmiyya fī l-ʻirāq/ ?an yuʻīdu naẓar fī nawayāhum il-ʻudwāniyya ḍiddi l-?umma l-ʻarabiyya/ yanbaghī ?an yuwadjdjah hādha s-su?āl min qibalkum ?ilā kull il-mutaʻāṭifīn maʻa l-kiyān iṣ-ṣahyūniy/ wa ?ilā kull iṣ-ṣahāyina fī l-gharb/ yuqāl ?ilhum ?idhā kānat il-?umma l-ʻarabiyya fī waḍaʻ/ sārat tuḥsin it-taʻāmul maʻa/ dh-dharra/ wa ṣāru tithāwwashūn ʻalēha/ wa ?in kān hādhā t-tahwīsh mafhūma dawāfʻah/ walākin hādhā yaʻni ?innu bada?tum tishʻurūn ?inna l-?umma l-ʻarabiyya sataṣbaḥ qādira ʻala t-taʻāmul maʻa l-ʻilm taʻāmul ṣaḥīḥ/ ?idhā kāna l-?amr hakadhā limādha tughmuḍ ʻuyūnkum ʻala ḥuqūq il-?umma il-ʻarabiyya/ wa tistamirru timʻinu fī ʻudwānkum ḍiddi l-?umma l-ʻarabiyya/ kāna l-kiyān iṣ-ṣahyūni wa mā zāla/ wa kull il-mutaʻāṭifīn wiyyāh wa l-mutaʻāwinīn maʻah/ yibnūn ḥisābāthum ʻala ?asās il-fadjwa l-ʻilmiyya bēn il-kiyēn iṣ-ṣahyūniy wa bēn il-?umma l-ʻarabiyya/ wa ʻala hādha l-?asās taghdu kathīr min malayīn it-tafawwuq/ bi l-bishir/ li ṣāliḥ il-?umma ?aṣfār/ wa naḥnu naʻrif hādhā/ wa hum ʻala ḥaqq fī hādhihi l-ḥisābāt/ walākin hādhihi l-ḥisābāt hiya laysat ḥisābāt thābita/ ʻala l-kiyēn iṣ-ṣahyūniy wa kull il-mutaʻāwinīn wiyyāh wa l-mutaʻāṭifīn maʻah/ ?an yudriku ?inna l-?umma l-ʻarabiyya bada?at tanhaḍ wa laysa hunālik man huwa qādir ʻala ?īqāf nuhūḍha/ wa sawfa tuḥsin it-taʻāmul/ maʻa dh-dharra li l-?aghrād is-silmiyya wa tuḥsin ?istiʻmāl is-silāḥ/ wa tuḥsin ?istiʻmāl iṣ-ṣināʻa/ wa sawfa yataxarradj bi l-malayīn min ?afwādj il-ʻarab min il-maʻāhid wa l-kulliyyāt wa l-madāris/ sanawiyyan/ ?idhan ʻalēhum ?an yuʻīdu n-naẓar fī r-ru?yi li l-?umma l-ʻarabiyya wa ?ila mustaqbal il-?umma l-ʻarabiyya wa ?ilā ḥuqūq il-?umma l-ʻarabiyya/ wa ʻala hādha l-?asās badal min ?an yuṣṣawwaru ?innu bi ?imkānhum ?an yufshilū/ barnāmidji l-ʻirāq fī ?istixdām idh-dharra li l-?aghrāḍ is-silmiyya bi hādhā ṭ-ṭarīqa taḥat ?aghṭiya/ ?inna l-ʻirāq yurīd ?an yuntidj qunbula nawawiyya/ ʻalēhum ?idha kānu ḥarīṣīn ʻala mustaqbal ʻumūm mustaqbal il-?insāniyya/ ?an yuʻīdu n-naẓar fī mawāqifhum il-ʻudwāniyya/ wa fī ?arāhum il-maghlūṭa tidjāh il-?umma l-ʻarabiyya/ ?antum fī ?ūrubbā/ il-?ixwān ?illi yisālūn/ taqūlūn ?innu ?ūrubbā balad ḥaḍāriy ?aw qārrā/ mutaṭawwirā/ ḥaḍāriyyan fī l-mustawa l-?insāniy wa l-?idjtimāʻi wa l-?iqtiṣādī wa th-thaqāfī ?ilā ?āxirih/ wa qawlkum hādhā ?ila ḥadd kabīr ṣaḥīḥ ?inna ?ūrubbā mutaṭawwira/ walākin maṭlūb ?an takūn ?ūrubbā ?insāniyya/ lā yakfī ?an it-taṭawwur fī maydān il-‘ilim/ wa ?an nizīd min watīrat/ numūna l-?iqtiṣādiy/ wa ?an nizīd min daxala l-qawmi li l-?afrād/ wa ?innamā l-maṭlūb ?an nakūn ?insāniyyīn/ wa lā yakfī ?an takūn ṣuḥufkum fī buldānkum tatakallam bī ḥurriyya/ wāfaq manṭiq id-dimuqrāṭiyya l-librāliyya wa ?innama yanbaghī ?an yuḥtaram il-?insān fī kull makān/ lā yumkin il-?insān ?an yakūn ?insān fī balada wa yantahik il-?insāniyya fī makān ?āxar ?aw yuskut ‘ala ?intihākha/ wa l-maṭlūb min il-?aqlām il-ḥurra fī ?ūrubbā ?an tarfa‘a ṣawtha ‘ālī/ wa ?in itgūl ?innu hādhi/ hādhi l-ḥamla yanbaghī ?an tuwadjdjihha ḍuddi n-nās ?illi humā il-mughtaṣṣ id-dīn/ ḍuddi n-nās il-mu‘taddīn/ ḍuddi n-nās ?illi yastaxdimūn idh-dharra li l-?aghrāḍ il-‘askarriyya/ mū ḍiddi n-nās ?illi yistaxdimūn idh-dharra li l-?aghrāḍ is-silmiyya/ wa fī barnāmidj mutawāḍi‘ wāḍiḥ/ li l-djamī‘/ il-qaṣid fī hādhā wāḍiḥ/ il-qaṣid fī hādhā huwa ?an yi‘aṭṭal ḥarakati l-?umma fī nuhūḍha l-‘ilmi/ walākin mā bistaṭā‘at/ lā l-kiyān iṣ-ṣahyūni wa lā ghayr il-kiyān iṣ-ṣahyūniy ?an yi‘aṭṭal/ ḥarakat nuhūḍ il-?umma fī maydān il-‘ilm/ li?annaha l-?umma ?imtalakat/ ḥaqīqat nafisha/ wa ?inna fī hādhā lā ?ataḥaddath ‘ani l-ḥukkām/ fī ḍiminhum ?ana/ wa ?innamā ?ataḥaddath ‘an ish-sha‘ab/ ?illi ?a‘arfah tamām il-ma‘rifa/ sha‘b il-?umma l-‘arabiyya fī kull makān/ fī l-‘irāq wa fī l-?urdun/ wa fī s-sa‘ūdiyya wa fī/ sūriyā wa fī l-djazā?ir wa fī maṣr/ wa fī kull makān/ ?imtalak/ bi t-taṣawwur wa l-ma‘rifa l-‘āmma/ ?imtalak nafsah/ ya‘ūzha tadābīr ‘amaliyya/ fī t-ta‘bīr ‘an hādhā/ fa hādhā zaman li hādhā/ wa min ḍimin hādha ?adrak/ ?innu lā yumkin ?an yaḥmi ?istiqlālah/ lā yumkin ?an yaḥmi sharafa fī ‘ālami l-yawm/ lā yumkin ?an yaḥmi ḥuqūqah/ ?illa ‘indama yablugh/ martaba mutawāzina ma‘a t-taṭawwur l-‘ilmi fī l-‘ālam/ ?illi bilghōh l-?axarīn/ u min ḍiminhum ?a‘dā? u fī muqaddamat ?a‘dā? l-kiyān iṣ-ṣahyūniy/ ?illi kān yunquṣna mū ?innu/ mā nigdar ?in fardiyyan indāfi‘ ‘an nafisna/ bi ḥayth nuqtul ka ?afrād/ ?illi kān yunquṣna huwa/ qaḍāya ?asāsiyya/ ?inna ?awwalan mā miktashfīn nafisna/ min naḥin/ wa mā huwa dawrna fī tārīx wa mā maṭlūb min ‘idna l-?ān/ wa ba‘dēn mā nsawwi rabaṭ ṣaḥīḥ bēn hādhā/ wa bēn l-‘ilm wa ?ahammiyyatah fī ‘asr il-yōm/ wa hādhā ḥaṣal/ wa li dhālik/ ?illi yirīd yiṣādiqna rāḥ bi stimrār yadjid ?aṣdiqā?/ muqtadirīn fī t-ta‘āmul ma‘a ḥaqā?iq siyāsa d-dawliyya fī taṭawwurha r-rāhin wa fī l-mustaqbal/ wa ?illi yirīd yi‘ādīna xallih yitwaqqa‘/ ?inna l-?umma ?illi yi‘ādīha rāḥ yishūfha l-yōm bi shakil/ u rāḥ yilgāha ba‘da xamsa sanawāt/ bi ḥāla mutaqaddima wa laysa bi ḥāla muta?axxira/.

Question 2:

hunāk ‘iddat ?as?ila ḥawla l-‘ilaqāt il-‘irāqiyya is-sūfyētiyya wa ta?thīr t-tadaxxul is-sūfyētiy fī ?afghānistān/ ‘ala t-ta‘āwun l-‘irāqi s-sufyētiy wa xāṣṣatan fī l-madjalāt l-‘askariyya l-?iqtiṣādiyya/ wa l-?imkānāt il-‘irāq taqlīl ?i‘timādihi ‘ala l-?ittiḥād is-sūfyētiy/ wa hal min il-muḥtamal ?an yas‘a is-sūfyēt ?ila ta‘zīz tawādjudihum fī ba‘ḍ al-?aqṭār al-‘arabiyya/ wa mādha sayakūn mawqaf l-‘irāq ?athnā? dhālik/ wa hal ?atharat ?aḥdāth l-?afghanistān ‘ala ‘ilāqāt l-‘irāq ma‘a d-duwal l-?ishtirākiyya

Saddam Hussein's answer (SH2)

bi s-su?āl/ ?illi sama‘nā ?illih bi ?intibāhi kalimat/ ta‘tamidūn/ naḥna lā na‘tamid ‘ala ḥadd/ naḥna lā na‘tamid ‘ala l-‘irāq wa ‘ala l-?umma l-‘arabiyya/ wa nuṣādiq fī l-‘ālam/ wa min ?aṣdiqā?ana fī l-‘alam/ l-?ittiḥād is-sūfyētī/ faransa/ kūba/ l-yūghūslāfiyā/ iṣ-ṣīn/ ?ila ?āxirihi/ qā?ima ṭawīl mina l-?aṣdiqā?/ walākin li ṣ-ṣadāqa daradjāt/ daradjat ṣadāqati faransa ghayr daradjat ṣadāqat il-?axarīn fī ?ūrubbā/ hādhihi ḥaqā?iq ?aḥna lā yaz'al ?aḥad minha/ daradjat ṣadāqatna ma'a l-?ittiḥād is-sūfyētī ghayr daradjat ṣadāqatna ma'a ?axarīn min id-duwali l-?ishtirākiyya/ wa hādha ṣ-ṣadāqa turattibha/ it-taṣawwurāt il-istrātidjiyya/ li ḥudūd maṣlaḥati l-?umma wa ṭarīqat xidmatha/ bi l-?iḍāfa ?ila l-?iltiqā? 'ala nuqāṭ markazīyya/ ḍudd 'aduw mushtarak/ fa l-?ittiḥād is-sūfyētī ṣadīqna/ kān wa mā zāl/ naḥrus 'ala ṣadāqatna ma'ah wa yiḥris 'ala ṣadāqtah wiyyāna/ wa ?āxar hādhihi l-mabādi? ?akkadnāh fī liqā?na yawm ?ams/ mā ?adri ?awwal ?ams walla yawm ?ams/ yawm ?ams ma'a/ l-wazīr is-sūfyētī 'inda l-ladjna l-markazī ?illi/ zurna fī baghdād bi mushārak ?iḥtifālāt tamūz/ wa s-sufyēt yiḥrasūn 'ala 'ilāqathum ma'a 'irāq wufuq hadhihi mafāhim ?illi a'lanitha/ ?amamhum/ ḥakyēnhum ḥakyēna ma'ahum/ ?iḥna ma'a l-?aṣdiqā? mālna/ 'idna sha'ār yigūl/ ?iksib ṣadīqaka bi l-bayyina qabla ?an tafqudhu bi l-ghumūḍ/ mawḍū' il-?asliḥa/ ?inta ti'arfūn ?inna ?akthar silāḥna min il-?ittiḥād is-sūfyētī/ wa bidūn qaḍiyyat it-tanwī' il-?asliḥa/ ?illi marāt li yiṭraḥa wāḥid yirūḥ/ yiṣṣawwar li tarafa ṣadīq byēnah wa huwwa ṣār ?ibnah ?aw ?abūh ?aw ?axūh/ wa ba'd fatra lamma yaddi tarafa muqābil muwādjibāt il-?ubuwwa ?ilah/ kamma yanbaghi/ yu'lin 'an nadama wa yirudd yirdja' yifattish 'an ?āb djidīd/ ?iḥna/ mā/ ya'ni/ mā kunna ?aṣdiqā? ?ittiḥād is-sūfyētī mā kān ?abūna/ wa lā kunna taba' 'alah/ ḥatta naktashif yawmanmā ?annana kunna 'ala xaṭa? bi taqdīr/ kunna ?aṣdiqā? wa mā zilna ?aṣdiqā?/ lammā ya'djaz il-?ittiḥād is-sūfyētī ?aw li ?asbāb tit'allaq bīh/ mā yunṭēna ḥalaqa min ḥalaqāt taslīḥ nrūḥ infattish 'an ?ayyi dawla bi l-'ālam 'an hādhi l-ḥalaqa wa nsalliḥ bihi djayshnā ḥatta yakūn/ mū djaysh 'irāqī faqaṭ wa ?innamā djaysh il-?umma l-'arabiyya/ ḥatta l-?ān mā 'adna shakwa min/ taṣlīḥ min il-?ittiḥād is-sūfyētī/ ya'ni marāt yasīr ṣu'ubāt/ fī ?ixtiyār hādha nō' min is-silāḥ wa min nāḥyati l-kammiya/ min nāḥyati l-naw'iyya/ yisīr niqāsh yisīr fī widjhāt in-naẓar tabāyun/ lākin bi shakil 'ām mā 'idna ṣu'ūbāt nishkū minha fī mawḍū'/ tazwīdna bi s-silāḥ/ wa ba'ḍ il-ḥalaqāt ?illi l-?ittiḥād is-sūfyētī yigul mā 'indi ?aw mā ?agdar ?azawwidkum biha nrūḥ nāxidhha min id-duwal/ ?illi ẓurūfha/ ?aw ?imkaniyātha/ l-muhayya?a ?illi zawwadna bi mithli hādha s-silāḥ wa qad fa'ilna/ wa xadhna silāḥ min faransa/ wa xadhna silāḥ min ?iṭālyā/ fī nafsi l-wakit/ silāḥ il-?asāsī min il-?ittiḥād is-sūfyētī/ ṭab'an niḥna muxtalifīn niḥna wa l-?ittiḥād is-sūfyētī ḥawl taqīmna li taṣarrufhu fī ?afghnistān wa mā zilna/ wa waḍḍaḥna mawqifna wa ?iḥna waḍḍaḥnahum mawqifna walākin/ mā zāl huwa lahu fihim li hādha l-mawḍū' iḥna 'inna fihim ?āxar nu'lin huwa l-fihim ?illadhi 'ālināh huwwa lā taghiyir 'alēh/ ka mabādi? ?asāsī/ ?amma 'ala su?āl ?ittiḥād is-sufyētī lā / il-ḥuṣūl 'ala ta'zīz it-tawādjidhum fī ba'ḍa l-?aqṭār il-'arabiyya/ xalna ngūl/ xalna ngūl bi shakil mubāshir/ ?iḥna na'taqid/ il-'irāqī 'indu kul dawla kubrā/ tithaya ?amāmha ẓrūf/ li ?inthawwal 'ilāqat iṣ-ṣadāqa ?ila ṣiyaghin ?uxrā/ sawfa tataṣarraf mudjib sīgha djadīda/ kul wāḥad yiqbal li ?an yikūn taba'/ ?ayya dawla kubra ?ayya dawla kubra bi l-'ālam lā tarfuḍ hādha/ fa hādhihi ta'tamid 'ala man sayakūn it-taba'/ ?iḥna lā na?mal ?an lā yakūn fī l-?umma l-'arabiyya taba' lā li l-?amerikān wa lā li s-sūfyēt wa lā li firansa wa lā li l-?inglīz/ wa lā l-?iṭālīn/ wa lā ?ayya dawla ?uxra/ lākin/ ?iḥna mā nlōm is-sūfyēt ?aw il-?amerikān ?akthar mimma nlōm in-nās ?illi yiḥimlūn il-djinsiyya l-'arabiyya lamma yaqbalūn .../ ?idha kānat il-?istiqlāliyya hiya laysat mabādi? fa ḥasab fa ?innama hiya mathalat ?imkanāt/ fa l-?i'lān il-qawmi/ fī l-mabādi? l-wāḍaha/ liman yurīd il-?istiqlāl 'ala ?asās ?imkanāt/ yuwaffir lahu l-?imkanāt wa yu'azziz il-?istiqlāl/ lākin man tanquṣuhu l-?irāda/ ?aw il-mabda?iyya/ fa ?aḥna/ yuṣ'ab 'alēna ?an nuwaffira ?ila l-mabādi?/ wa nishḥana bīha kamā yishḥan huwa nafsa bīh/ wa yuṣ'ab 'alēna ?innu yuwaffir li l-?abā? li l-?irāda kamā yanbaghi mithli mā/ lamma huwa yi'āwina wa yanxa nafsah ?ayḍan/ fā ?aku nās taba'/ li hādha ṭarafa dawliyya ?aw dhāk fī l-waṭani l-'arabiyya/ walākin 'alēna ?an lā nṣubb mas?uliyya 'ala l-?adjnabi/ fī daradja l-?asās wa ?innama nṣūbbha ʻala l-ʻarabī fī daradja l-?asās wa l-?adjnabi ka ḥāla thāniya/ nṣubbha ʻala tabaʻ wa laysa ʻala matbūʻ/ il-lōm yuwadjdjah li l-tabaʻ/ wa laysa li l-matbūʻ/ li?annu bi s-sābiq kānu yigulūn ?innu niḥin shū nigdar insawwi/ wa tnāqashna/ tnāqashna maʻa baʻḍ il-ʻarab/ bi mshakil mubāshir/ gulnā lkum lā tidjibūn ?ilna l-?amrikān tunṭūnhum il-qawāʻid l-?adjnabiyya/ wa ?idh tgulūn/ nxāfū min is-sūfyēt wa nrīd nḥuṭṭ il-?amrikān ?amāma s-sūfyēt/ tara ?intu tssahilūn li s-sufyēt/ il-ḥuṣūl ʻala ?atbāʻ fī l-waṭan il-ʻarabī ʻindama tanṭūn wi l-qawāʻid/ il-ʻaskariyya l-?amrikān/ u gulnālhum/ shwakit mā djit il-djyūsh is-sūfyētiyya/ itrīd taḥtall ?arāḍīkum/ ?iḥna ngulkum mina l-?ān mustaʻidīn nsarrab biha djyūshha sāʻ mā yismaʻūnī/ yatadhakkarūn hādha l-kalām/ wa ?ana gul ?ilkum/ gulnālkum ?innu ?idha djit il-djyūsh is-sūfyētiyya wa mā saddatha l-djyūsh il-ʻarabiyya/ ʻandkum bi mūdjiba l-?iʻlān il-qawmī/ ?illi ?iqtaraḥnā ʻalēkum/ djībū djaysh il-?amrīkī yaqafu djaysh is-sūfyētī/ widhāk djaysh ?amrikī ?iqtarāb mū baʻīd/ mawdjūd bi safkum/ bi l-maḥyēṭāt wa l-biḥāra/ bass tighumzūlu bi ṭaraf ʻaynku yidjī wara fatra/ wa ?aḥna naʻtaqid/ bi tadjarrud/ bi maʻna ?innu l-?iʻlān laysa li l-ʻirāq/ laysa li maslaḥa ʻirāqiyya/ min naẓra maʻa l-?asaf il-?iqlimiyya min maslaḥa ?illi/ sārat mawdjuda ʻanda l-baʻaḍ/ il-?iʻlān mā bih shī? li l-ʻirāq/ lā nrīd mini l-ʻarab djuyūshhum/ humma yismaʻūna/ kaththar ?allah xayrhum/ ?idha djāna ?adjnabī ?iḥna min is-sāʻa ngūl lkum/ ya?xudhūn rāḥathum lēy yikallifūn nāfishum fī ?annu/ yifzaʻūni/ tara ?iḥna gādrīn inwādjih il-?adjnabī ḥatta lō kān/ ?amrika/ bi kull djayshha/ ḥatta lō kān il-?ittiḥād is-sūfyētī bi kull djaysh/ bi gāʻna/ xāridj ?arḍna mā nigdar nuwādjih il-djaysh il-?amirikī/ xāridj ?arḍna mā nigdar nuwādjih il-djaysh is-sūfyētī wa lā nigdar nuwādjih il-djaysh il-firansi/ walākin dāxili l-ʻirāq/ dāxili l-ʻirāq ?iḥna mhay?īn nafisna ?akbar il-djyūsh bi l-ʻālam nuwādjih min qātilna/ fa/.../ ?idha yissawwarūn ?iḥna ṭaraḥna l-?iʻlān li?innu xāyifīn min il-?adjnabi faḥna wallah bi daradja ?asās/ xāyifīn ʻalēhum/ wa ?aqṣad ʻalēhum xāyifīn ʻala ?arḍna l-ʻarabiyya wa shaʻbna l-ʻarabī wa karāmatna l-ʻarabiyya wa tārixna l-ʻarabiy/ wa mabādi?/ il-?umma l-ʻarabiyya fī t-taḥarrur wa fī l-?istiqlāl/

Question 3:

hunāk ʻiddat ?as?ila ḥawla ittifāqiyya kamp dēfid wa dawr l-ʻirāq fī muwādjahāt l-mu?āmara illati taʻarraḍ laha l-qaḍiyya il-filisṭīn/ wa mā huwa shuʻur l-ʻirāq/ ʻan xiṭṭaṭi l-ʻamal al-ʻarabi l-mushtarak li muwādjahat al-mu?āmara wa ?imkāniyat ʻadhl as-sadāt/ wa hal hunā fi?a ʻarabiyya tuḥāwil ḥarb muqāṭaʻa ʻala kamp dēfid/ wa mā huwa ya sayyid ir-ra?īs taqīmutuh bi ẓurūf taṣʻīd l-ʻudwān iṣ-ṣahyūniy/ wa ḥtimāl ?an yadjirra dhālik minṭaqa ?ila ḥarb djadīda/ wa dawr al-ʻirāq il-muntaẓar fīha/

Saddam Hussein's answer (SH3)

?ana ?aʻtaqid ?innu/ illi yixdamu l-?umma l-ʻarabiyya wa/ djumāʻiyyan/ huwa l-?iltizām bi muqarrarāt qimmat baghdād wa bi l-?iltizām illati rasamathu qimmat baghdād / fī taṭwīq wa muḥāṣarat/ ʻamal is-sadāt/ wa fī taṭwīqha wa muḥāṣarat/ ʻumūm il-muxaṭṭaṭ il-mushtarak bayna l-?amrīkān wa ṣ-ṣahyūnī wa s-sadāt/ wa illi naʻtaqid/ wa ?iʻtaqad maʻanā kull il-ru?asā? wa l-mumaththilīn id-duwal il-ʻarabiyya illi waqaʻat/ wa wāfaqat ʻala/ muqarrarāt qimmat baghdād/ naʻtaqid ?innu hādha l-muxaṭṭaṭ/ illi huwa muxaṭṭaṭ kamb dēfid/ ?alḥaqa ?adhā/ kabīr bi l-?umma l-ʻarabiyya/ wa li dhālik yanbaghī ?an yuṭawwaq/ wa tuqallal l-?āthār in-nafsiyya wa l-fi'liyya/ il-muḍādda li l-?umma l-'arabiyya wa li sh-sha'b/ wa li sh-sha'b il-'arabī/ ṭab'an ba'ḍa l-?aqṭār il-'arabiyya lam tuṣādiq 'ala hādha l-muqarrarāt/ wa taḥāfaḍat 'alēyh/ fī baghdād thumma ṣaḥabat taḥaffudhha fī tūnis/ thumma 'iddat tata?ardjah bēyna hādha wa dhāk/ walākin 'ala ?ayyati ḥāl illi himna huwwa/ il-muṣādaqa bi l-qanā'a/ mū l-muwāfaqa l-shakliyya wa t-taṣarruf bi l-'aks/ fa hunālik ba'ḍa l-?aqṭār il-'arabiyya tataṣarraf/ xāridj ?iṭār wa rūḥ qimmat baghdād/ wa minha/ ṣ-ṣūmāl/ wa minha 'umān/ wa s-sūdān/ ḥatta l-?ān/ bi daradja ?aw bi ?uxra wa li sababin ?aw li ?āxar/ walākin fī ṭaqīmna wa ḥādha l-kalām ?aḥna gulnā lahum bi l-wadjih/ ?aḥyānan ?izīdu t-taṣarruf/ ?illi yiftaraq ma'a qimmat baghdād wa ?aḥyānan tqill zāwita/ lākin 'ala l-'umūm huwa laysa xaḍ qimmat baghdād/ li?annu s-sādāt yanbaghī ?an yu'zal/ wa huwwa mā ṭarḥīn hādha t-taṣarruf/ ḥatta lammā yaḥdjum ba'aḍhum min idh-dhihāb ?ila l-qāhira/ yaḥdjum rubbamā li ?asbāb tit'allaq bi waḍ'a dāxila/ mū bi l-qanā'a l-qawmiyya/ wa l-mabda?iyya/ bi qarārāt qimmat baghdād wa ?ahammiyyat ?iltizām bīh/ wa l-wādjib huwa yaqtaḍī ?an niṣ'a li ?an hādha l-qisma muta?ardjih ya?ti ?illa/ rūḥ qimmat baghdād/ ?aw yufḍah/ wa 'ala niṭāqin wāsi'/ wa l-maslaḥa huwa bi ta'zīz manhadj qimmat baghdād wa l-?irtiqā? bi ḥaythumā tawwafarāt il-furas/ wa ḍuminat il-?aghlabiyya/ li ?annu ?irtiqā? bi ?ayya xuḍwā/ bi l-qilla/ hādhi l-mas?ala mumkina walākin lā yumkin ?an yitḥaqqaq natīdjata l-mutawaxxayāt/ li 'amal wa l-fa'la l-kuthra/ li dhālik mā zilna/ hārīṣīn 'ala l-kuthra/ li muwādjahat il-qilla/ wa kulna na?mul ?an yubqa sādat li waḥda/ wa ?an lā yata?ardjaḥ bēyna baghdād/ bēyna qimmat baghdād wa/ mawqif kamb dēvid/ 'adad min il-?ashiqā? il-'arab/ walākin lā budda ?an naqūl ?innu ba'aḍhum walākin hādha l-ba'aḍ/ mā zāl ḍumin l-qilla/ sāra yata?ardjaḥ bēyna/ qarārāt qimmat baghdād wa bēyna/ mawqif kamb dēvid ?aw li nagul/ fī ḥaqēqta ma'a kamb dēvid wa ?an ?aẓhar ?innahu humma ma'a qimmat baghdād/ ?amma shū yikūn mawqif l-'irāq law ?isrā?īl tit'arraḍ ?ila ?āxirihi ?ila 'udwān/ mā ?aẓunn ?intu shū daraytu 'an il-'irāq/ il-'irāq qabla mā nidjih niḥna/ qabla mā nidjih niḥna/ min il-'ahdi malik yiqātil difā' 'an il-filisṭīn fī 'ām thamāniya wa ?arb'īn/ wa fī 'ām sab'a u sitīn ?arsal il-djaysh/ wa qātil bi sharaf 'ala djabhatayn fī 'ām talāt ?ū sab'īn/ qātil 'ala djabha miṣriya bi silāḥ ṭayarān/ wa qātil 'ala djabha s-sūriyā bi kul ṣunuf il-?asliḥa/ wa ḥamā dimashq min is-suqūṭ ma'a shirafā? min ?abnā? is-sūriyā/ ḥamāha min is-suqūṭ bi yadd il-kiyēn iṣ-ṣahyūnī/ wa ?aẓunn ?anna ṭ-ṭā?irāt il-'arabiyya il-waḥīda ?illi siqṭat 'ala l-?arḍ ?illi yuqām 'alēh il-kiyān iṣ-ṣahyūnī hiya l-'irāqiyya/ ba'da l-ḥarb l-ḥarb sab'a ?u sitīn/ fa ?iḥna 'inna mabādi? thābta ?u gulnālkum ?iḥna dā?iman wiyya l-'arabi u ḍidda l-?adjnabī/ wa min is-sīr l-ḥarb bēna l-'arab wa l-?adjnabī mā nis?al man huwa l-muqassar/ ḥatta il-ḥadd xall al-?ixwān/ il-gharbiyīn yaxdhūn 'alēna hādha l-kalām/ ya'ni yidjūz nlūma/ ba'd ?intihā? dh-dharf/ lākin mā nidjī musabbaqan nitraddad nigūl xalli nshūf ?awwil marra/ man muqassar il-'arabī/ wa l-?adjnabi/ lā ra?san inshūf wiyya l-'arabi thumma ba'dēn dhālik lūma ?idha 'adna lōm/ hādhihi mabādi? thābita fī/ manāhidjna/

Question 4:

hunāk 'iddat ?as?ila ḥawl ?amn minṭaqt il-xalīdj il-'arabi/ ?innu hunāk shu'ūr 'ām bēn ba'ḍ id-duwal/ duwal ?ilēha hadaf li 'amaliyāt taghrīb/ qarārāt ta'rīḍ istiqrāriha wa 'urūbatiha li maxāṭir/ kamā ?innu hunāk muḥāwalāt li taṭwīqihā bi l-qawā'id wa l-?aḥlāf il-'askariyya/ mā hiya xuṭṭaṭi il-'irāq li muwādjahat it-taḥaddiyāt illatī tuwādjihu il-xalīdj il-'arabiyya wa l-?aṭmā' il-?adjnabiyya fīh/ wa mā huwa l-mawqif min id-duwal illati taqūm/

tuqaddim tashīlāt baḥriyya ?aw djawwiyya li l-quwwa d-dawliyya l-kubra/

Saddam Hussein's answer (SH4)

ba'd ?ittifāq il-djazā?ir/ ?illi ?ilah ẓurūfa l-xāṣṣa biēnna u bēn ?īrān/ zurit ?īrān/ wa ltaqēt ma'a shā ?īrān/ wa gult lah bi wuḍūḥ il-?ān il-'ilāqa biēnna wa bēnak mā 'ādat 'ilāqat ḥarb/ ?aw ḥāfat ḥarb/ walākin lāzim yikūn 'indak taṣawwur ?innu fī ?ayy laḥdha mumkin ?an taqūm bēnna ḥarb/ ḥatta wi l-'ilāqāt ith-thunā?iyya suwwiyat bi ṭ-ṭarīqa llati suwwiyat fīh/ ?idha mā kān taṣarrufak ?i'tidā?i ḍidd ?ayy 'arabī fī l-xalīdj/ ?idhā tkūn itaḥriṣ/ 'ala ?istimrār al-'ilāqa/ 'ala l-ḥadūd al-mudjāwira/ fa 'alayk ?an it'ālidj il-'ilāqa/ l-muxṭi?a/ fī l-xalīdj/ wa bi shakil wāḍiḥ lāzim tisḥab quwwātik min/ 'umān/ hiya tigūl/ ?iḥna 'idna masāliḥā wa/ 'umān/ tiqa' 'ala madxal al-xalīdj wa fī maḍīq hirmiz/ u xuṭūṭ muwāṣalātna min hnāk/ fa ?iḥna/ naṭraḥ/ naqtariḥ/ 'alēk ?an yiṣdar ?i'lān/ ?aw bayān/ wa naqtariḥ ?anna l-?i'lān tikūn il-iṣdār hādhihi l-?afkār bi ṣighat ?i'lān li?annah ?aqwa/ ingūl biha iḥna kull duwal al-xalīdj ma'an/ nu'lin ?innuh ?amn il-xalīdj min mas?ūliyyatna l-mushtaraka/ bi ma'na ?innu l-milāḥa biha ḥurra/ wafq il-qawānīn id-dawliyya/ wa ?idhā mā ṣār taṣarruf yighliq il-milāḥa fī l-xalīdj fa djamā'iyyan/ nabḥath/ kayfiyyat ?i'ādat il-?umūr ?ila madjrāha l-ṭabī'i/ wa wāfaq shā ?irān 'ala hādhi l-mabādi?/ gāl ?ana l-?ān fawran musta'idd ?uwaqqi'/ hādha l-mawḍū' ?amma mawḍū' quwwāt fī/ 'umān fa hādhihi binā?an 'ala ṭalab/ qābūs/ fa gulnā lah/ walākin hādha/ yabqa l-ḥāla/ il-'afū/ il/ quwwātik fī 'umān wa djuzur il-'arabiyya th-thalātha/fa huwwa nāqash niqāsh ṭawīl 'ala l-djuzur il-'arabiyya th-thalātha u gāl ?innuh/ quwwāt fī 'umān binā?an 'ala/ ṭalab qābus/ wa ?ana l-?ān musta'idd ?uwaqqi' 'ala hādhihi l-mabādi?/ wa gulna lēh lā/ yanbaghī ?an tunāqash hādhihi ma'a l-'arab/ fī l-xalīdj/ wa ?in hiya ṣ-ṣīgha ?ilha/ bi hadhihi l-mafāhim/ ma'a l-?asaf/ ?inna huwa wu ba'ḍ al-'arab/ kānu yiṣṣawwaru bi ?imkānhum djarr il-'irāq ?ila ghēr hādha ṣ-ṣūra/ ?ila/ ṣūra qarība min ṣīghati l-?aḥlāf/ fa lammā 'uqid mu?tamar fī 'umān/ mā hīč yā duktūr/ fī 'umān/ fī l-wizārā l-xāridjiyya ṭuriḥat ba'ḍ il-?afkār min hadhā n-nō'/ fa wugaf il-'irāq u gāl bi wuḍūḥ mawqifah/ wa bī l-?aḥlāf ?aḥnā ḍidd il-?aḥlāf/ bi?ayy shakl min il-?ashkāl/ u ?iḥna hadhihi l-mabādi? ?illi musta'iddīn insawwi/ biha ?i'lān u mā ṣārat/ wa l-?ān il-'irāq ṭaraḥ fī shbāt il-māḍī/ mabādī? il-?i'lān il-qawmi/ wa fī taṣawwurnā/ ?innu ?iltizām duwalu l-xalīdj bihā ka ?iṭār 'ām li 'ilāqāthā/ hādha yiḥaqqiq ?amn il-xalīdj wa ?amn il-xalīdj lāzim yikūn/ yiḥāfaẓ 'alēh min ?abnā? wa duwal al-xalīdj li waḥda/ wa fī mabādi? il-?i'lān il-qawmi mabda wāḍiḥ/ huwa l-ḥirṣ 'ala 'adam/ il-ludjū? ?ila s-silāḥ ma'a d-duwal al-mudjāwira li l-waṭan al-'arabi/ wa hināya 'āladj qaḍiyyat ?īrān/ ba'da ?an tu'ālidj ?īrān/ bi wāqi'iyya/ wa bi djur?a/ il-mawḍū' il-ḥuqūq il-'arabiyya/ wa tansaḥib 'ani l-djuzur il-'arabiyya th-thalāth/ wa tuqīm 'alaqātha ma'a l-'irāq/ wa ma'a duwal al-xalīdj 'ala ?asās ?iḥtirām ḥuqūq is-siyāda bi l-kāmil/ wa mu'āladjat kulla ?axṭā? ish-shāh fī hādhā l-mawḍū'/ ba'ḍ id-duwal il-'arabiyya mumaththil id-duwal il-'arabiyya/ yigūlūn ?innu lēsh / hal sakatu 'ala l-djuzur ith-thalātha/ bi l-waqt al-wāqi'/ biyēn ?ādhār 'am xamsa u sab'īn/ ?ila l-waqt l-ḥāḍir/ ?ila ?an ?uzīḥa sh-shāh/ wa lēsh ?āthartum hal/ dūn ?an yis?alūn nafishum ?innu lēsh siktaw humma sab'a sinīn il-'irāq yiṣtari' ma'a shāh ?īrān/ wa yaṣtari' wiyyāh min il-wāḥid wa sab'īn ?ila xamsa u sab'īn 'ala qaḍiyyati l-djizir/ lēsh siktaw hum/ thumma hal yidjūz ?an niskut 'ala ?iḥtilāl il-?arḍ/ tidjāh/ tidjāh sīn wa lā hādha yiskut 'alēh tidjāh ṣād/ ?iḥna mū sakatna/ lākin ḥawwalna taṣarrufnā fī maṭālib bi djizir bi ṭarīqin ?āxar wa hadhihi wāḥid minha/ ?anā ba'd il-?ittifāq mubāsharatan zurit ?īran wa baḥathit hadhā l-mawḍū' ma'a shāh ?īrān/ wa gulnā lah bi wuḍūḥ mā lam yit'āladj/ kul qaḍāya is-siyāda fī l-xalīdj/ w-?intihākātik ?ilha/ tara ?ittifāq il-'irāq il-?īrān il-mu'arruḍ ?ila ?an yinfidjir fī ?ay wakit/

Question 5:

/hunāk ?arba'ata ?as?ila ḥawla mawqifa l-'irāq min djabhati ṣ-ṣumūd wa t-taṣaddi/ wa ṭabī'ata l-'ilāqāt il-qā?ima bayna l-'irāq wa duwal hadhihi l-djabha/ wa xāṣṣatan sūriyā/

Saddam Hussein's answer (SH5)

djabhat iṣ-ṣumūd wa t-taṣaddī humā shunhum wa thumma 'aqīda ya'ni/ madjmū'a d-duwal kull wāḥad minhum 'indu qaḍīthu/ multaqīn fī tabādul li l-masāliḥ bīh/ ?iḥna hādhi lā yaz'alūn minha/.../ kull wāḥad minhum ?ilah nidhāmu yaxtalif 'ala ?āxar/ kul wāḥad ?ilah tafkīru yaxtalif 'ana l-?āxar/ lākin multaqīn ḥawl ?umūr mu'ayyana/ .../ ?idha kān it-taṣawwur ?annahum multaqīn ḥawl il-qaḍiyya l-filasṭīn ?akthar min ghayrhum il-djawāb lah/ ba'aḍhum maxluṣ li qaḍiyyat filasṭīn ?u ba'aḍhum yanẓar il-qaḍiyyat filasṭīn mithil qaḍiyya fī djunūb sharqiya ?āsiya/ li ?an huwwa ?aslan li ?umūra lā yu?min bih/ wa ba'da l-?āxar ṭab'an muḥtalla ?arḍa/ wa li sā'a kull wāḥad muḥtalla ?arḍa wa yaqif ḍudd iṣ-ṣahyūnī wa lī sā'a lā nadri mawqifa hādha ?iqlīmi wa lā qawmi/ ?illa ba'd mā yistardji' il-gā'/ wa yiruddi yiẓall ḍudd iṣ-ṣahyūnī ?alla ngūl bih hādha l-gawmi/ wa l-?irtiqā? bī/ ?aw/ mā inmīl ?ila mahwariya/ il-mahwariya mā tqaddim shi/ wa bi dalīl/ ?innu ṣ-ṣumūd wa t-taṣaddi mā ṣār ?ila čam sana/ lā ṣ-ṣumūd wa lā t-taṣaddī/ ya'ni min shakkil ḥatta l-?ān ya'ni shū huwwi ?illi ṣār/ mā ṣār shi/ lākin min ṣārat qimmat baghdād hazzat il-'ālam kullah/ fī muqararātha wa ?awqafat fawran it-tadā'ī n-nafsī ?illi kān mawdjūd bi wa ?aṣgha ?ila sh-sha'b/ ?innu sādāt taṣarraf il-'arab sāktīn/ lā l-'arab djawwu muwaḥḥadīn yirafḍūn/ wa djawwu muwaḥḥaddīn yid'amūn il-xaḍḍ il-?amāmi il-djighrufiyyan/ wa yiḥawlūni ḥawlūh ?in yakun xaḍḍ ?amāmi fi'liyyan/ lākin ḥatta l-?ān ?ana mā ?adri/ ya'ni/ 'ala ḥadd ma'lūmāt naḥna fī l-'irāq lam yaḥṣal shay/ ya'ni mundhu tashkilāt/ il-qimma il-musammāt bi djabha ṣ-ṣumūd wa t-taṣaddī/

Appendix D

MUAMMAR AL GADDAFI 1978

Sermon in a mosque (mawlāya muḥammad), 26 May 1978

bismi llāh ar-raḥmān ar-raḥīm/ ?inna llāh wa malā?ikathu yuṣallūn ʻala n-nabiyy ya ?ayyuha alladhīna ?amanū ṣallu ʻalēhi wa sallumū taslīman/..../ bismi llāh ar-raḥmān ar-raḥīm/ **al-qāri-a**/ **mā l-qāriʻa**/ hakadhā nazalat hadhihi s-sūra/ wa ?ibtadat bi hādhihi l-kalima/ bi kalimat l-qāriʻa/ ḥatta kāna lisān ḥāl kull wāḥad/ yaqūl **mā l-qāriʻa**/ ka?anna n-nabiyy ʻindamā nazalat ʻalayh hādhihi is-sūra yaqūl **mā l-qāriʻa**/ wa ka?anna jibrīl alladhī ?anzala hādhihi s-sūra ʻala n-nabiyy yaqūl **mā l-qāriʻa**/ wa ka?anna kull wāḥad minnā/ ḥatta hādha l-yōm wa ?ilā yōm l-qiyāma/ yaqūl **mā l-qāriʻa**/ ʻindamā yakūn lā yaʻlim maʻna l-qāriʻa/ lam tinzil qabal hādhihi al-kalima ?ayyi muqaddimāt/ kamā huwa wāḍiḥ min as-sūra l-mawjūda fī l-qur?ān/ taḥmilu raqam miyya u wāḥad min as-suwar/ wa mudawwana fī al-qur?ān ʻala ?annahā nazalat fī makka/ wa lā yaxtalif ʻalayha ?ithnāni mina l-muslimīn/ min d-dār al-bayḍā? ḥatta jakarta/ lā yaxtalif ?ithnāni mina l-muslimīn ʻala ?anna hādhihi hiya sūrata l-qāriʻa wa ʻala ?annahā nazalat bi makka/ wa ?annahā taḥmilu raqam miyya u wāḥad fī l-qur?ān/ wa hakadhā duwwinat ʻindamā nazalat/ wa hakadhā nazalat bi ?awwul/ ?awwul mā nazalat nazalat bi hādhihi l-kalima/ **al-qāriʻa**/ wa kānat mithil qunbula/ ḥatta kāna radd il-fiʻl/ **mā l-qāriʻa**/ thumma ya?ti su?āl ?āxar/ wa **mā ?adrāka mā l-qāriʻa**/ ka?anna l-?āya taqūl/ yā man tas?al ʻan al-qāriʻa/ wa ?irtajafit ʻindamā smiʻit kalmit il-qāriʻa/ **mā ?adrāka mā l-qāriʻa**/ ka?anna al-?āya taqūl hakadhā/ min ʻarrafak l-qāriʻa/ mā hiya l-qāriʻa/ hakadhā nazalat al-kalima il-?ūla bi kalimat al-qāriʻa mithil ?infijār/ thumma kāna radd il-fiʻl/ **mā l-qāriʻa**/ thumma kāna su?āl ?āxar/ **wa mā ?adrāka mā l-qāriʻa**/ thalāth ?infijarāt warā? baʻḍuh/ ?idhā simiʻat in-nās hādhi k-kalām li ?awwil marra/ lā budda ?annaha tkūn/ mundahisha/ mashdūda li hā l-kalimāt/ l-qawiyya/ **l-qāriʻa mā l-qāriʻa wa mā ?adrāka mā l-qāriʻa**/ mā hādhihi allatī ?atā bihi al-qur?ān tuqraʻ/ wa tufziʻ/ baʻḍha il-?as?ila l-muḥayyira/ wa l-murʻiba ?ayḍan/ li ?an tas?al ʻan shay muxīf nazal bihā l-qur?ān bidūn muqaddimāt/ **l-qāriʻa**/ jā?a l-jawāb fī l-qur?ān nafsih/ ka?anna biygūl l-qāriʻa hādhī/ ?illi ?irtajifit liha l-qulūb/ wa li kull wāḥad baʻd yis?al ʻan mā hiya l-qāriʻa/ ka?annahā/ hiya/ bal hiyya/ shay/ alladhi bitaḥṣul fī l-?ashyā? al-?ātiya/ gāl l-qur?ān/ **yawma yakūnu n-nāsu ka l-farāsh al-mabsūs/ wa takūnu l-jibālu ka l-ʻihni l-manfūsh**/ ?aʻūdhu bi llāh/ hādhihī l-qāriʻa allati ?afzaʻitna/ yabdū ?innahā muxīfa fiʻlan ʻindamā nazalit bi hādhihī l-kalimat l-qawiyya/ yabdū hiya qawiyya bi l-fiʻil/ ?illi biyis?al ʻan al-qāriʻa/ lammā nazalit al-qāriʻa gāl/ **mā l-**

qāri'a/ ka?annu bigūl **wa mā ?adrāka mā l-qāri'a**/ l-qāri'a hādhi rāhi/ **yawmu yakūnu n-nāsu ka l-farāsh al-mabsūs**/ **wa takūnu l-jibālu ka l-'ihni l-manfūsh**/ in-nās fī hādhi/ 'indamā taqa' al-qāri'a 'indamā ta?ti al-qāri'a/ 'indamā yakūn hādha l-yawm huwa l-yawm l-qāri'a/ hakadhā yaqūlu l-qur?ān/ hādhihi laysat min ta?līf ?ayyi ?insān/ **yawma yakūnu n-nās ka l-farāsh al-mabsūs**/ an-nās tabda? hā?ija wa mā?ija wa muxarriba/ mithil il-farāsha/ mfarrash (...) mish yigūl lik l-?insān mfarfash/ tabda? mfarfash in-nās mā hīsh 'arfa/ kēf ta'mal/ bi ẓ-ẓabṭ/ hādhi wārda bi l-lugha l-'arabiyya bi hādha n-naṣṣ/ wa ḥatta kalimat imfarfasha hiya kalmat 'arabiyya quḥḥa / jāyi min it-tifarfīsh ?inna l-wāḥid yifarfish mish 'ārif kēf yidīr/ kulli n-nās mish shaxaṣ wāḥad/ wa lā sha'ab wāḥad/ wa lā qabīla waḥda/ **yawma takūnu n-nāsu**/ ya'ni kull n-nās/ **ka l-farāsh al-mabsūs**/ ya'ni l-yawmu ?illi bitfarfash fīh kulli n-nās/ rāḥ hādha huwa yawmu l-qāri'a/ yalli bitas?al **mā l-qāri'a/ wa takūnu l-jibālu ka l-'ihni l-manfūsh**/ l-jibāl/ l-?asamma/ al-jibāl/ ash-shāhiqa/ tuṣbiḥ ka l-'ihni l-manfūsh/ ka?anna ṣ-ṣūf nāshfīnna yatatāyir/ ?idhā kāna l-jabal/ ?illi byiḥtimi bihi l-?insān fī l-?arḍ/ ?āxar hāja byiḥtimi biha l-?insān fī l-?arḍ hiya l-jibāl/ ?iltajat in-nāsu ?ila jibāl min shiddati l-qaṣaf/ ?idhā qaṣafāt iṭ-ṭayarāt wa sawārīx in-nās tutruk mumkin il-mudun wa/ ?amākinha l-'ādiyya wa tattajih ila l-jibāl/ ?iltajat in-nās ?ila l-jibāl/ min quwwati is-suyūl/ ?ila s-suyūl jārifa fī il-widyān/ laysa hunāka ma?wā li l-?insān illa l-jabal/ ?iltajat in-nāsu ?ila l-jibāl min shiddati l-ḥarr/ ?idhā shtadd ?ayy shay/ yabḥath l-?insān 'an ma?wā fī al-?arḍ/ laysa hunāka fī n-nihāya/ fawqa l-?arḍ/ ?illā l-jabal/ al-jibāl dā?iman yistanid 'alēha l-?insān/ 'indamā tudahhimhu/ musība ?akbar min ?ayyi shay mawjūd/ ?aqall min/ min il-jibāl/ ... /lamma gāl/ al-qāri'a hādhihi huwa l-yawm illi biyitkūn fīhi n-nās mithil/ farāsha/ mfarfashīn mā humsh 'arfīn kēf ya'milu/ mumkin ?awwal hāja/ nfakkir fīha hādha l-?insān alladhi bi su'uq/ bi l-qāri'a ?illi mā zālat warāh/ hiyya mā zaltshi l-qāri'a/ kull wāḥid minnā/ warāh al-qāri'a/ ?awwal mā yagulūn/ in-nās bitkūn mithil farāsh **wa takūnu in-nās ka l-farāsh il-mabsūs**/ mumkin ?awwal mā yifakkar mā dām hiyya min shiddat ḥawlha ḥatta tuṣbaḥ in-nās/ ka l-farāsh il-mabsūs/ ?innah yiltiji li l-jibāl/ mumkin yuxturuq 'alayhi l-jibāl/ ?ayy wāḥid minna yagulūn al-qāri'a yawm il-qiyāma tkūn in-nās ka l-farāsh il-mabsūs/ yigūl ṭayyib/ wēn il-malja/ ṭayyib fī jibāl ya'ni mumkin ?insān yalja?/ li l-jibāl/ jāt il-?āya u gālat lah/ **wa takūnu l-jibālu**/ willi ?inta tfakkar taḥta mā biha/ **ka l-'ihni l-manfūsh**/ ḥatta l-jibāl ?illi hiyya ?aqwa hāja fī l-?arḍ/ wa hiya r-rawāsi ?illi/ mawḍū'ha fī l-?arḍ/ wa ?illi bitfakkar fī l-?iḥtimā biha/ rāḥi il-jibāl nafisha bituṣbaḥ/ kēf ṣ-ṣūf il-minashshaf/ iṣ-ṣūf ?illi nashfīnna/ yataṭāyir/ hādhā/ hādhihi s-sūra/ nazalit mithil aṣ-ṣā'iqa/ nazalit mithil ?infijār/ bidat l-qāri'a/ wa min shiddit ḥawlaha u shiddit/ hādhihi l-kalima/ u ma'nāha/ illi byisma'ha/ yigūl mā l-qāri'a/ byigūl luh fi'lan wa mā ?adrāka mā l-qāri'a min 'arrafak mā l-qāri'a wa ?inta t'arif al-qāri'a al-qāri'a / wa l-qāri'a hādhi ḥāja xaṭīra/ hādhi ḥāja mur'iba/ biywaḍḍaḥ lih bigūl ?arāh l-qāri'a hiya **yawmu takūnu in-nāsu ka l-farāsh il-mabthūth**/ wa ?idhā fakkarit fī ?ayyi ḥāja bitaḥtimi bihā wa rāhā ḥatti l-jibāli ḍ-ḍaxma hādhi l-waḥda yukattima fī n-nihāya/ il-jibāl hādhi **wa takūnu il-jibālu ka l-'ihnu l-manfūsh**/ min shiddit/ al-qar'a/ min l-qāri'a hādhihi yataḥaddath 'anha l-qur?ān wa illi mā zālat warāna/ il-jibāl/ bituṣbaḥ ka ṣ-ṣūf/ ?illi mnashfīnna tataṭāyir/ jibāl al-hamalāya/ ?aḍxam ?a'la qimma bi l-'ālam/ tuṣbaḥ ka?anna juzit iṣ-ṣūf n-nashfīnna/ jibāl al-?alb/ jibāl l-?aṭlas at-tall/ jibāl al-hārūj/ jibāl al-blāj/ kull il-jibāl ?illi bta'arfūha bi jughrāfyā wa lli yi'arfūha l-jughrāfya ?illi hi mawjūda bi l-'ālam/ mā hiyyash ?istithnā?āt/ mā gāl qimma ?afrist hiyya ?a'la qimmata bi l-'ālam/ wa ?aḍxam l-jabal jabal il-himalāya/ hādha bass rāhu gā'id mā tigdar shī 'ala l-qāri'a/ bitxalxal bass bi yaq'ad/ gāl **wa takūnu jibālu** bidūn ?istithnā?/ kullu il-jibāl/ bituṣbaḥ kēf aṣ-ṣūf li nashf/ ish-shi lli yixallīh bi hādha sh-shakil/ min shiddat al-qar'a/ min ḥawl al-qāri'a/ mithilmā tunfujaru l-qunbula fī mabna/ min shiddati l-?infijār yitfattat il-mabna/

yiṯhawwal ilā trāb/ al-qāri'a bi ḍ-ḍabaṭ/ byishabbahha al-qur?ān ka?annahā qunbula ḍaxma jiddan jiddan jiddan lammā tāti/ min quwwitha l-jibāl tuṣbaḥ mithl iṣ-ṣūf/ u tuṣbaḥ mithl is-sarāb/ ṭayyib/ mā dām 'arafna hādhihi l-qāri'a bykūn in-nās fī 'ala hādhihi l-ḥāl wa bijāwib btikūn hadhihi l-ḥāl/ wa ba'dēn shū biṣīr/ ?ayya wāḥad bijāwib gabil lā yasma' baqiyyata l-?āya/ baqiyyata s-sūra/ biygūl xalāṣ mā 'ādsh fīh fayda/ hādhi n-nās ?aṣbaḥat/ mithil l-farāsh/ l-farāsh/ wa l-jibāl ?aṣbaḥat mithil iṣ-ṣūf mutaṭayira/ mithil is-sarāb/ in-nās ?asbahat mithil il-jarād/ ?idhan xalās mā 'ādsh fīh [..] fayda/ biyiji s-sūra bitigūl lih lā/ mā zāl fīh/ shay ?āxar/ **fa ?amma man thaqulat mawāzīnuhu/ fa huwa fī 'īshatin rāḍiya/ ?amma man thaqulat mawāzīnhu fa huwa fī 'īshatin rāḍiya**/ hunā bidi tafṣīr jidīd/ bidi l-wāḥad yasma'/ yasma' fī s-sūra yasma' fī l-qur?ān/

Appendix E

MUAMMAR AL GADDAFI 1981

kalimat l-qā?id fī yawm at-taḍāmun al-'ālamī ma'a sh-sha'b al-falasṭīnī ma'a taḥiyyāt qism al-marākiz ath-thaqāfiyya al-xārijiyya

?ayyuha l-?ixwa/ raghma ?inna/ ?aghlabiyya kabīra/ min ir-ra?y al-'ām al-'arabiy/ millit al-kalām/ wa ?istahjanat al-xuṭub/ li?annuhu fi'lan bi l-muqārana/ bi fā'liyyāt al-'aduw al-māddiyya wa taṣā'udiha/ yuṣbiḥ al-kalām li l-wahlat al-?ūla ghayr dhī/ jadwa/ fī s-sā'āt allatī/ tughīru fīha ṭ-ṭā?irāt al-?isrā?iliyya/ l-?amrikiyya ḥaqīqa/ bidūn tawaqquf 'ala l-muxayyamāt al-falasṭīniyya 'ala l-mudun al-lubnāniyya wa 'ala l-quwwāt/ al-'arabiyya/ raghma hādha walākin/ muḍṭarrīn ntikallimu/ wa fī l-badi?/ kāna l-kalima/ wa ?anā min alladhīna/ yu?ayyidūna hādha r-ra?y wa huwa ?annanā/ qad malilnā l-ḥadīth/ clap/ lākin/ kāna/ lākin kāna min/ min al-muhimm/ ?anna sami'nā kalām qā?id ath-thawra l-falasṭiniyya l-?ax ?abu 'ummār/ clap/ li?annu huwa ?illi yaḥaqq lahu ?an yatakallam/ al-falasṭīni al-ḥaqīqa huwa ?illi/ yiqātil wa yimūt/ wa mā yi'ībāsh al-kalām ?idhā kān yatakallam/ lākin al-'arab baqiyyat al-'arab/ ?iḥnā willī maksūfīn u muxz.../ maksūfīn ?an ntakallam li ?an naḥna mā nqātilsh il-ḥaqīqa baqiyyat il-'arab/ ?illi yiqātil al-?ān ash-sha'b al-falasṭīni/ wa ?illi ta'arruḍ min warāh li d-damār ash-sha'b al-lubnānī/ wa t-tahdīd ?illi yuwajjah al-?ān li sūriyā ?āxir xandaq/ fī l-jabha sh-shamāliyya/ al-falasṭīni min ḥaqqah yatakallam/ wa yarfa' ṣawtah/ li?annahu yuqātil fī nafs il-waqit/ wa yamūt fī kull yōm/ fa kān min al-muhimm jiddan ?anna sami'nā ṣawt/ al-?ax yāsir 'arafāt/ fī hā s-sā'āt/ kān muhimm fī hadhihi s-sā'āt ?illi taṭghū fīhā/ al-ghārāt al-?isrā?iliyya 'ala/ 'ala al-?arāḍī al-'arabiyya/ wa 'ala l-mawāqi'/ al-falasṭīniyya wa 'ala l-muxayyamāt al-falasṭīniyya wa l-mudun al-lubnāniyya/ ?inna yisma' fī hādhi s-sā'āt/ ṣawt ?abu 'ummār/ li?anna kull mā kān hādha ṣ-ṣawt qawiyy/ kullmā/ qawiyat 'azā?im al-muqātilīn/ wa yajib ?an yakūn/ ṣ-ṣawt al-falasṭīni 'ālī wa ghayr xāfit hādhi s-sā'āt ḥatta yubarhin/ clap/ ḥatta yubarhin 'ala ?an al-'azīma ?ayḍan qawiyya/ wa ?illi fī idih bunduqiyya yuqātil bīha/ 'inda ḥaqq yarfa' ṣawtah/ ?amā ?illi yatakallam faqaṭ/ hādha huwa ?illi yakūn maksūf l-ḥaqīqa/ ?anā shā?if/ ?anni/ l-bilād al-'arabiyya l-?umma l-'arabiyya sh-shu'ub l-'arabiyya ḥukūmāt 'arabiyya tisammīha kamā tisammīha/ hādha l-kamm/ hādha huwa ?illi/ al-wāḥid xijlān yatakallam li?annah mā yiqātil/ al-'arab mā yiqātilu l-?ān/ ?anā sa'īd ?inna fī/ hādhi/ l-waqit yikūnu ma'āna/ lastu sa'īd bi dh-dhikra t-talāta t-talatīn li ?iḥtilāl falasṭīn walākin fī hādha l-waqt yikūn ma'āna al-?ax ?abū 'ummār/ wa ?abu wiyād/ wa ?abu ṭāriq min qiyādit/ fataḥ/ clap/ wa ma'nā/ wa ma'nā l-?uxwa qādat al-?umanā? al-jabhāt/ al-falasṭīniyya/ clap/ al-jabha sh-sha'biyya wa l-jabha l-dimuqrāṭiyya/ wa l-jabha sh-sha'biyya l-qiyāda l-'āma wa ṣ-ṣā'iqa/ fī ḥadd ?axar mā qultūsh ?ana/ clap/ al-ḥaqīqa bi n-nisba li libiyyīn/ bi ṣūra xāṣṣa/ wa li l-'arab kulluhum bi ṣūra 'āmma/ al-muhimm jiddan hādha l-multaqā l-yōm/ ma'a qādat ash-sha'b al-falasṭīnī/ qādat ath-thawra al-filisṭīniyya ?illi 'ala rāshum ?abu 'ummār/ clap/ ?awwalan/ min nāhiyat ḥarakat/ taḥrīr/ falasṭīn fataḥ/ wujūd qiyāditha bēna l-yōm/ fī tarāblus fī lībya/ fīha radd/ ḥaqīqī/ 'ala l-mawāqif ?ash-shāmita/ allati qad fariḥat bi wujūd/ ?azma mufta'ila/ fī yawman mā/ ?a'taqidū bi wujūd ?azma bayna/ lībyā u fataḥ/ walākin fī l-ḥaqīqa lā yumkin tūjad ?azma bēn/ thawra/ bēn thawrat al-fātiḥ/ wa bēyna th-thawra l-falasṭīniyya/ clap/ li?anna/ li?anna mā fīsh ?imkāniyya lījād/ lījād ?ayyi tanāquḍ/ bayna thawra wa thawra/ ya'ni th-thawra l-falasṭīniyya wa th-thawra l-lībiyya/ manṭiqiyyan lā yumkin yaqa' tanāquḍ bayna humā bayna th-thawra wa th-thawra/ lākin limādhā ḥaṣalat ?azma/ 'ala ?ayy ḥāl ?anā ?ayḍan ?atasā?al 'an wujūd ?azma ḥaṣalat fī yawmin mā/ 'ām summiya bi hādha/ li?an ubwatkum takūn fī yad bayḍā wa yad sūdā kēf bitsammōhā/ madsūsa kānat warā? hādha l-mawqif alladhi ḥaṣal/ 'ala kullin/ ?illi ?urīd ?an ?u?akkidhu/ huwa ?inna nḥāwil nabḥath 'an 'ibārāt ṣarīḥa mā takūnsh fīha libis/ nu?akkidu ?an mustaḥīl taqa' ?azma bayna thawra wa thawra/ clap/ ?idha kān/ ?idhā waqa'at ?azma ma'nāha ḥaṣal ?inḥirāf fī ?iḥda th-thawratayn/ law ḥaṣalat ?azma bayna thawra wa thawra/ mi'nāha ?inḥirāf/ 'an xaṭṭ th-thawriyyīn/ fī waḥda/ ?annī l-ḥaqīqa ?aqūl ?inni/ lā/ lā ?a'tarif ?abadan fī wujūd ?inḥirāf fī th-thawra l-falasṭīniyya ?iṭlāqan li?anna n-nās hadhāma/ li?anna/ li?anna n-nās/ ḥaqīqathum n-nās/ bīmūtū/ gabilnā/ wa ?akthar minnā/ ya'ni l-mas?ala laysat mas?alat la'ab bi n-nisba li l-falasṭīnīn/ mumkin mu'ẓam al-ḥukkām al-'arab/ 'āmlīn/ kull wāḥid 'āmil kēf bus'adiyya wa 'āmil/ sawlajān muzayyif wa 'āmil bahraja/ wa 'āmil tamthīlīyya muzayyifa 'āmil sha'b/ wa 'āmil 'alayh sulṭān/ malik/ ra?īs/ u ra?īs madda l-ḥayāt u malik ghayr mutawwij/ wa tamthīlīyyāt bi hādha sh-shakil tumaththil al-?ān 'ala s-sāḥa l-'arabiyya waḥad/ xijlān yikūn fī wasṭ s-sāḥa al-'arabiyya/ lākin bi n-nisba li l-falasṭīnī al-ḥaqīqa al-?ūla al-?ān fā/ al-lubnānī wa/ s-sūrī/ al-qaḍiyya mā hiya mithil baqiyyat al-'arab/ al-qaḍiyya qaḍiyyit ḥayāt ?aw mōt fi'lan/ ya'ni l-yōm ma'ak wāḥid bukra yigūlūk qutil/ bi l-?ams kān ma'anā/ zuhēr/ al-?ān waynuh qutil/ kān ma'āna majmū'a min qādat l-falasṭīniyyīn/ u kān mumkin in-nās yi'allaqu yigūlū ?innu hawlā? in-nās wēn qaḍiyyathum/ wa ba'd kam yōm qutilū/ bi l-qarīb wa bi l-?ams kān ma'āyā bassām ash-shak'a/ al-?ān quṭi'at rijlayh t-tintēn/ al-qaḍiyya mā hiya qaḍiyya sahlah bi n-nisbah li?anna/ clap/ an-nās ?illi mawjudīn guddāmnā/ wallah mā nistab'id bukrā yigūlū wāḥid minhum qatalūh al-yahūd/ hādha l-yōm ma'akum bukrā yimūt/ hādha qātil ?aw maqtūl fi'lan/ ?idhā l-falasṭīnī ḥaqīqa/ huwa ?illi bīmūt bi l-fi'il/ ya'ni al-mōt ?amāmah warāh/ ?amāmah u warāh/ wa kam marra kān yiqātil/ ?ila l-?amām wa ?ila l-xalf bunduqiyya 'arabiyya warāh wa bunduqiyya ?isrā?iliyya ?amāmah/ hādhi ḥaṣalat/ clap/ ?idhan/ mahmā taqa' min ?axṭā? al-ḥaqīqa/ yajib ?alla yu'ātab al-falasṭīnī min al-'arab yakūn ?uqṣud/ wa lā yuḥāsab 'alē shay/ balā il-yōm wa l-?ams gult li ?abu 'ummār wa ?abu ?iyyād/ gultilhum/ ?in ḥad ḍāyigkum min al-'arab wa tibghū tishtamū ḥadd ?ishtamū lēna ?iḥna li?annu ?iḥna/ masāmḥīnkum/ wa mā nuwāxizkum/ clap/ ?idhan/ ?ana bingul ḥatta li l-libyyīn lāzim/ yuḍa' hādha fī l-ḥisbān/ al-falasṭīnī mahmā 'amal fīkum/ lāzim/ taqublūh/ li?annah lā yumkin ?an/ ?an yuqtal min/ al-'aduwu min/ aṣ-ṣāhib/ wa hādha ?iltizām al-ḥaqīqa minni li ?abad/ ?anni ?awwalan/ lan nuxawwin/ qiyāda falasṭīniyya ?illa ?an yixawwinūha al-falasṭinīyyūn/ clap/ ?ana/ ?ana/ ?abu 'ummār al-?ān yaqūd/ fī 'iddit jabhāt/ min al-yaṣār ?ila al-yamīn/ huwa qā?id al-quwwāt al-falasṭīniyya/ huwa ra?īs munaẓẓamat at-taḥrīr al-falasṭīniyya/ mīnu minnā bīkūn/ nāyif ḥawātma ?akbar min nāyif ḥawātma ?aw ?aḥmad jibrīl ?akthar min ?aḥmad jibrīl/ ?a hum n-nās hādha mawjudīn ma'a ?abū 'ummār/ ash-sha'b al-falasṭīnī wa munaẓẓamit at-taḥrīr al-falasṭīniyya/ naḥnu ma'ahum/ yōm/ ?ana gult li ?abu 'ummār/ gult lih l-yōm ash-sha'b al-falasṭīnī yuxawwanak/ satajidni ma'a sh-sha'b al-falasṭīnī mush ma'ak li?anni ?anā ma'ak li?ann kunt ma'āk ash-sha'b al-falasṭīnī/ clap/ il/ il/ illi kān mustaghrab ?innu lā yumkin ?ayyi wāḥid min hawlā?/ ?illi ma'āna al-yōm/ min qādat ash-sha'b al-falasṭīnī/ ?an yakūnu ḍudd ath-thawra ḍudd al-'amil ath-thawrī/ li?annu nāfishum thawra/ hum bīmūtū bi th-thawra yawmiyyan/ ?aw yikūn ḍudd al-jamāhīr ash-sha'biyya ?aw ḍudd al-mu?tamarāt ash-sha'biyya ?aw ḍudd al-lijān ath-thawriyya/ lā yumkin/ wa xāṣṣa ḥarakat fataḥ bi dh-dhāt allatī hiya laysat ḥizib/ kān/ mustab'ad wa mustaghrab/ ?an tkūn mutanāqiḍa ma'a ḥarakat/ al-mu?tamarāt ash-sha'biyya ?aw al-lijān ath-thawriyya/ al-falasṭīniyya/ bi l-'aks/ naḥnu wa l-?ams nitaḥaddath/ ma'a ?abū 'ummār wa ?abū ?iyād u jamā'a/ gulnā/ ?in al-mu?tamarāt ash-sha'biyya al-mafrūḍ tantashir/ fī jamī' al-jamāhīr al-falasṭīniyya wa ash-sha'b al-falasṭīnī/ mafrūḍ yataḥawwal yanbaghī ?an yataḥawwal min al-mufīd/ ?an yataḥawwal kulla l-mu?tamarāt ash-sha'biyya/ li?anna ḥatta ?amāmi l-'ālim bukrā tiṭraḥ qaḍiyya/ bukrā yunẓurū ?ilā ?abū 'ummār/ faqaṭ wa ka ?abu 'ummār/ biyunẓurū munaẓẓamit at-taḥrīr al-falasṭīniyya ka munaẓẓama faqaṭ/ li ha?ūlā? al-qāda ka qāda/ lākin humā yifāju?ūn bi sha'b/ lahu ra?y lahu ?irāda/ munaẓẓam fī mu?tamarāt sha'biyya/ al-'ālam bukra ya'rif ?inna/ ?innuh warā? ka al-qiyāda hādha sha'b/ al-?ān shū yigūlū bigūlū hādhā mā/ ṣa'ālīk 'iṣāba mish sha'b wayn ash-sha'b al-falasṭīnī/ ash-sha'b al-falasṭīnī kānū bāghī wa rāḍī bi l-?iḥtilāl/ al-baqiyya ?urduniyyīn wa l-baqiyya lubnāniyyīn al-baqiyya muwazzi'īn fī l-'ālam/ hakadhā al-?a'idā? yaqulūn/ bītujāhalū ḥaqīqat ash-sha'b al-falasṭīnī li yaqḍū 'ala al-qaḍiyya l-falasṭīniyya/ lākin hum by'arfū ?innu fī sha'b falasṭīnī/ lākin kēf naḥnu nrudd 'alēhum/ ?innu nij'il ash-sha'b al-falasṭīnī/ mawjūd/ ash-sha'b al-falasṭīnī yuxrij ?ila hayz al-wujūd yirā al-'ālim/ bukrā tu'qid mu?tamarāt sha'biyya falasṭīniyya fī l-kwēt matalan/ fī nuṣf milyūn falasṭīnī fī l-kuwēt yithāwilu ?ilā mu?tamarāt sha'biyya/ bukra mu?tamarāt sha'biyya fī al-falasṭiniyyīn l-jamāhīr al-falasṭīniyya fī l-?urdun fī lubnān fī sūriyā fī libyā/ fī ?ayy makān ?āxar/ fī ?awrūbbā fī ?amrīkā/ hādhi kulla mawjūda fīha falasṭīniyyīn/ tu'qud mu?tamarāt sha'biyya falasṭīniyya wa tqarrar/ tqarrar al-qitāl/ tqarrar ar-rafaḍ/ tqarrar kadhā tqarrar kadhā/ yi'rif al-'ālim ?innu fi'lan hā l-qiyāda hādhī nqūd fī sha'b/ wa ?in hal al-?arḍa al-muḥtalla li falasṭīn/ warāha sha'b/ hādha huwa sh-sha'b al-mawjūd/ mā huwa kuweiti mā huwa ?urdunī mā huwa lībī mā huwa lubnānī/ hādha falasṭīn min an-nāḥiya/ al-?iqlīmiyya dāxila l-waṭan al-'arabī l-wāḥid/ ?uqṣud ?innu/ kullna/ muttafqīn taqrīban 'ala ?ahamiyyat/ l-mu?tamarāt ash-sha'biyya/ wa al-lijān ath-thawriyya bal ?akkadūlī gālū ?iḥnā 'indamā lijān sha'biyya/ lijān sha'biyya/ tudīr ?ila l-muxayyamāt/ fa naḥna 'andunā al-lijān ash-sha'biyya bitudīr al-muxayyamāt/ mithil il-lijān ash-sha'biyya ?illi bitudīru l-baladiyyāt fī lībyā/ bāqi l-jamāhīr al-falasṭīniyya ?anā shāyifah bi hādha sh-shakl wa hiya muba'thara/ tunaẓẓim fī mu?tamarāt sha'biyya/ hādha min jinb al-qaḍiyya al-falasṭīniyya/ 'inda l-mu?tamar l-waṭan al-falasṭīnī/ al-'ālam dā?iman yunẓur ?ila qarārāt al-mu?tamar al-waṭanī al-falasṭīnī bi 'tibāra/ jibha sha'biyya/ ?idhan/ mādhā yakūnu mawqif al-'ālam law ?aṣbaḥat mi?āt al-mu?tamarāt/ ash-sha'biyya/ ?aw 'asharāt l-mu?tamarāt sh-sha'biyya al-falasṭīniyya/ ?illi/ al-xaṭ ?illi ḥaṣal ?u'tuqid fī l-bidāya/ ?inna tashkīl al-mu?tamarāt ash-sha'biyya wa l-lijān ath-thawriyya/ ma'nāha/ ghiyāb munaẓẓamit at-taḥrīr al-falasṭīniyya/ ?anā takallamt fī hādha l-makān yōmha/ yōm t-taḍāmun ma'a sh-sha'b al-falasṭīnī/ mā kān fī niyyatī ?abadan ?innu ?ayyi wāḥid satub'id munaẓẓamat at-taḥrīr al-falasṭīniyya/ clap/ munaẓẓamit at-taḥrīr/ clap/..../ hunna wujudnā sīgha li qiyām al-mu?tamarāt ash-sha'biyya wa l-lijān ath-thawriyya/ taḥta maẓalla munaẓẓamit at-taḥrīr al-falasṭīniyya wa munaẓẓamit at-taḥrīr al-falasṭīniyya/ munaẓẓamit at-taḥrīr al-falasṭīniyya/ hiya fī kull makān/ natakallam ʻanha/ wa nadʻimūhā wa baynu l-ʻālam wa hiya ?innahu hiya l-mumaththil al-waḥīd/ li sh-shaʻb al-falasṭīnī ḥatta mā yaṭlaʻsh/ ?ayy/ tājir ?āxar u baʻdu s-sādat/ mithil mā yafʻalu s-sādāt al-?ān fī mu?amarāt al-ḥukm adh-dhātī/ yumaththil ash-shaʻb al-falasṭīni yigūl ?anni mithil ash-shaʻb al-falasṭīni yijību ?ayyu majmūʻa/ wa fī/ xawana yigūlū hādha ash-shaʻb al-falasṭīnī ?iḥnā kull al-ʻarab muttafqīn wa mutmaskīn/ bi/ ta?kīd shaxṣiyyat munaẓẓamit at-taḥrīr al-falasṭīniyya ʻala l-?aqall fī marḥala al-kifāḥ/ al-kifāḥ at-taḥarrarī/ ?ila ?an tataḥarrar falasṭīn wa baʻda dhālik kayfa yaqūm ash-shakil al-jamāhīrī ?aw ash-shuyūʻi ?aw al-librālī ?aw hadhī ?ashyā?/ ta?tī fī waqatna/ lākin/ marḥaliyyan al-?ān kullnā binakkid ?ahamiyyat wa munaẓẓamit at-taḥrīr al-falasṭīniyya/ u ?uʻtuburat ?ana shufit ?aqṣa qāda l-falasṭīn taṭarrufan/ bigūl lī munaẓẓamit at-taḥrīr al-falasṭīniyya hiya al-hāwiyya/ an-niḍāliyya/ li l-falasṭīni/ zēn al-?ān lā yumkin njī ngūl/ munaẓẓamit at-taḥrīr al-falasṭīniyya tistabʻad/ mā dām al-falasṭīnī al-mutaṭarrif/ mutamassik/ bi munaẓẓamit at-taḥrīr al-filisṭīniyya/ mā dām al-falasṭīn kullhum bi ?aydū munaẓẓamit at-taḥrīr al-falasṭīniyya fī al-?arḍ al-muḥtalla wa xārijah/ man lahu l-ḥaqq ?an yustabʻad munaẓẓamit at-taḥrīr al-falasṭīniyya/ ?idhā lā budda min al-ḥifāẓ ʻalēha wa daʻmahā wa ta?yīdaha ?aʻlaniyan ḥatta l-ʻālam yaʻrif ?anna hādhihi l-mumaththil ash-sharʻī wa l-waḥīd li sh-shaʻb al-falasṭīni/ clap/ wa d-dalīl ʻala wa d-dalīl ʻala/ ?annahu lā yujad/ thamma tatanāqaḍ bayna munaẓẓamit at-taḥrīr al-falasṭīniyya/ wa l-ḥarakat al-ḥurra li l-jamāhīr al-falasṭīnī/ fī tashkīl l-mu?tamarāt ash-shaʻbiyya/ ?inna fī libyā al-?ān/ ?uqīmat al-mu?tamarāt ash-shaʻbiyya al-?ān mawjūda al-mu?tamarāt ash-shaʻbiyya al-falasṭīniyya wa lijān thawriyya falasṭīniyya/ ?ahuwa bū ʻummār maʻānā ra?īs munaẓẓamit at-taḥrīr al-falasṭīniyya ?ahamm al-qāda al-falasṭīnīyya mʻāna ?ahiya munaẓẓamit at-taḥrīr al-falasṭīnī maʻāna/ mā yuʻad tanāquḍu fī hadhihi s-sāḥa bēn qiyāda al-muqāwama al-falasṭīniyya/ bēn munaẓẓamit at-taḥrīr al-falasṭīniyya/ bēn bū ʻummār dhāta/ wa bēn al-mu?tamarāt ash-shaʻbiyya wa l-lijān ath-thawriyya/ yaʻni al-qaḍiyya taḥtāj ?ila fahm faqaṭ/ wa ?illā/ sanatanāqaḍ maʻa l-jamāhīr natanāqaḍ maʻa ḥurriyyat al-jamāhīr natanāqaḍ maʻa d-dimuqrāṭiyya/ ?anā dā?iman mawqifī wāḍiḥ/ ?anā maʻa sh-shaʻb al-falasṭīn ?anā maʻa l-jamāhīr al-falasṭīniyya maʻa ḥurriyyatah lā ?urīdu lahā ?an tuqmaʻ/ fī ad-dāxil wa fī al-xāriji hiya kifāya dhull/ u ʻasaf fī al-?arḍ al-muḥtalla/ fiʻlan lāzim tatanaffas aṣ-ṣaʻdā? fī al-?arḍ ghayr al-muḥtalla fī al-?arḍ al-lugha al-ʻarabiyya/ fī ?arḍ al-ḥurra fī ?arḍ mithil lībyā/ clap/ ?idhan fī sāḥa mithil as-sāḥa al-lībiyya l-jamāhīr al-falasṭīniyya lāzim tāxudh ḥurriyyatha/ tʻabbir ʻan ?irādatha/ bimā yadʻam munaẓẓamat at-taḥrīr al-falasṭīniyya bimā yadʻam bu ʻummār nafsah bimā yadʻamu qiyāda al-muqāwama al-falasṭīniyya bimā/ yuqawwi/ clap/ al-mawquf al-falasṭīnī/ mā ?aʻtaqdsh ḥurriyya al-jamāhīr/ bitkūn xaṭar ʻala qaḍiyyatha/ fī al-ʻaks al-jamāhīr lammā tkūn ḥurra/ satantaṣir li qaḍiyyathā/ lākin al-jamāhīr al-maghlūba ʻala ?umrha/ hiya ?illi qaḍāyaha taxṣar/ ?ini yaʻni ?adʻū ?ila ?an al-jamāhīr al-falasṭīniyya tūdī kull fāʻliyyatha/ al-mādiyya wa l-maʻnawiyya/ warā? al-qiyāda al-falasṭīniyya/ warā? bū ʻummār warā? munaẓẓamat at-taḥrīr al-falasṭīniyya/ warā? ath-thawra al-falasṭīniyya/ wa mā shāyif ?inna hādhī al-fāʻiliyyat tataḥaqqaq ʻindamā turfaʻ kull aḍ-ḍughūṭ ʻan al-jamāhīr wa tuṣbiḥ al-jamāhīr ḥurra/ lammā tuṣbiḥ al-jamāhīr ḥurra tattajih ḥatman ?ilā tanẓīm nafsahā fī mu?tamarāt shaʻbiyya ḥaythu lā dīmuqrāṭiyya wa lā mu?tamarāt shaʻbiyya/ wa l-lijān ath-thawriyya hiya l-muḥarrik li l-jamāhīr ash-shaʻbiyya ?ana/ ?āsif ?innu ʻadad min shabāb fataḥ/ qad ghādarū/ as-sāḥa/ wa faqadathum al-jamāhīr/ min xilāl sū? al-faham/ fī l-waqt ?illi kān/ kān al-mafrūḍ hum yishakklū/ al-lijān ath-thawrī maʻa baqīt shabāb al-falasṭīnī ath-thawrī/ fī l-jabhāt al-?uxrā/ mā kān fī mubirr/ li shabāb fataḥ ?annahum yughādirū as-sāḥa bi l-ʻaks al-mafrūḍ hummā ?awwal min yushakkil al-lijān ath-thawriyya/ wa yiḥarraḍū al-jamāhīr al-falasṭīniyya ʻala ?iqāmat al-mu?tamarāt ash-shaʻbiyya ʻala/ rafʻ ?ayy ḍghūṭ ʻala l-

jamāhīr al-falasṭīniyya/ yaʿnī ḍug͟hūṭ ?aqṣud mū dā?iman ḍug͟hūṭ yiqṣudū bihā/ ?inna
ḍug͟hūṭ min qiyāda al-muqāwama ʿala al-falasṭīniyyīn ḍug͟hūṭ ḥatta lībīh/ al-?ān al-
jamāhīr al-falasṭīniyya tuwājih fī ḍug͟hūṭ ʿarabiyya/ tuwājih fī ḍug͟hūṭ ʿarabiyya
li?anna/ as-sayṭara/ li l-ḥukkām al-ʿarab al-?ān/ wa humā mā bi'īs͟hū bi s-sayṭara ʿala l-
190   jamāhīr wa kabt jamāḥḥā wa g͟hulbha/ u takbīlha/ u xudḥlānha/ u ?iḥbāṭhā humma
hād͟hi ?illi bīmārsū al-ḥukkām al-ʿarab/ al-jamāhīr al-falasṭīniyya hiya ḍ-ḍaḥiyya al-
?ūla/ al-?ān bīmārsū ʿalayhā l-?asaf/ nibg͟hī l-jamāhīr al-falasṭīniyya mā yakūn ʿalayha
ʿasaf/ wa gult min hād͟ha l-makān fī d͟hālik l-xiṭāb ?inna/ ʿala l-falasṭīniyyīn/ ?an mā
yasmaʿūs͟h ?ayy ṣawt ?illa ṣawt ḍamīrhum qaḍiyyathum/ wa ?allā yismaʿ minhum
195   ?ayy ṣawt ?illa ṣawt al-bunduqiyya ṣawt al-qaḍiyya/ wa ?innamā yaxḍaʿū li l-?irāda l-
lībiyya wa lā l-?irāda l-jazā?iriyya wa lā l-?irāda l-maṣriyya/ lammā yaxḍaʿū li l-?irāda
l-ʿarabiyya tantahi l-qaḍiyya l-falasṭīniyya/ ?ahiya l-?irāda l-ʿarabiyya/ ?iḥda l-?irādāt
al-ʿarabiyya l-?irādāt al-maṣriyya/ ?a hiya ?istaslamat/ law yaxḍaʿha al-falasṭīnī/ wa
rubbamā juz? min al-falasṭīn waqaʿū l-?ān fī dā?irat al-?istislām/ dāxil maṣr/ al-falasṭīn
200   yajib mā yaxḍaʿs͟h li l-?irāda l-ʿarabiyya/ bukra yaḥṣil al-?istislām fī makān ?āxar/

References

Abd El Jawad H. (1981) *Lexical and Phonological Variation in Spoken Arabic in Amman*, Unpublished PhD Dissertation, University of Pennsylvania.

Abd El Jawad H. (1986) "Social functions of language variation", *AlAbhath* 34, pp. 21–37.

Abd El Jawad H. (1987) "Cross-dialectal variation in Arabic: Competing prestigious forms", *Language in Society* 16, pp. 359–68.

Abd El Jawad H. and Awwad M. (1987) "Reflexes of Classical Arabic Interdentals: A Study in Historical Sociolinguistics", *AlAbhath* 35, pp. 75–102.

Abdel Massih E.T., Abdel Malek Z.N., Badawi M. (1979) *A Comprehensive Study of Egyptian Arabic* 3, Ann Arbor, University of Michigan.

Abu Haidar F. (1987) "The treatment of the reflexes of /q/ and /k/ in the Muslim dialect of Baghdad", *Zeitschrift für arabische Linguistik* 17, pp. 41–57.

Abu Haidar F. (1988) "Speech variation in the Muslim dialect of Baghdad – Urban vs Rural", *Zeitschrift für arabische Linguistik*, 19 pp. 74–80.

Abu Haidar F. (1991) "Language and sex: The case of expatriate Iraqis" in Kaye A.S. (ed) (1991) *Semitic Studies* 1, Wiesbaden, Otto Harrassowitz, pp. 28–38.

Abul Fadl F. (1961) *Volkstümliche Texte in arabischen Bauerndialekten der ägyptischen Provinz Sharqiyya*, Diss, Münster, Westfalen.

Al Ani S. (1978) "The development and distribution of the qaaf in Iraq" in Al Ani S. (ed) *Readings in Arabic linguistics*, Bloomington Indiana University Linguistics Club, pp. 103–12.

Al Khatib M. (1995) "The impact of interlocutor sex on linguistic accommodation: a case study of Jordan radio phone-in programs", *Multilingua* 14:2, pp. 133–50.

Altoma S.J. (1969) *The problem of Diglossia in Arabic: a Comparative Study of Classical and Iraqi Arabic*, Cambridge Mass., Harvard Middle Eastern Monographs XXI.

Area Handbook for Libya (1973) The American University. Washington DC, Library of Congress.

Atkinson M. (1984) *Our Masters' Voices. The language and body language of politics*, London, Methuen.

Badawi A.(1973) *mustawayāt al-'arabiyya l-mu'āṣira fī miṣr*, Cairo, dār al-ma'ārif.

Bakir M. (1986) "Sex differences in the approximation to Standard Arabic: A case study", *Anthropoligical linguistics* 28:1, pp. 3–9.

Batatu H. (1978) *The old social classes and the revolutionary movements of Iraq. A study of Iraq's old landed and commercial classes and its communists, Bathists and Free Officers*, Princeton, New Jersey, Princeton University Press.

Batatu H. (1979) "Class analysis and Iraqi society", *Arab Studies Quarterly* 1:3, pp. 229–244.

Beaman K. (1984) "Coordination and subordination revisited: syntactic complexity in Spoken and Written narrative Discourse" in Tannen D. (ed) *Coherence in spoken and written discourse*, Norwood, N.J., Ablex, pp. 45–80.

Beeston A.F.L. (1983) "The role of parallelism in Arabic prose" in Beeston A.F.L., Johnstone T.M., Serjeant R.B. and Smith G.R. (eds) *Arabic Literature to the end of the Umayyad period*, Cambridge, Cambridge University Press, pp. 180–5.

Behnstedt P. and Woidich M. (1985,1985,1987,1988) *Die ägyptisch-arabischen Dialekte*. Bd1: Einleitung und Anmerkungen zu den Karten; Bd2: Dialektatlas von Ägypten; Bd3: Texte II: Niltaldialekte, III: Oasendialekte, Wiesbaden, Ludwig Reichert.

Bell A. (1984) Language style as audience design, *Language in Society* 13, pp. 145–204.

Benrabah M. (1994) "Attitudinal reactions to language change in an Urban setting" in Suleiman Y. (ed) (1994) *Arabic Sociolinguistics: Issues and Perspectives*, pp. 213–26.

Biber D. (1988) *Variation across speech and writing*. Cambridge, Cambridge University Press.

Bishai W. (1966) "Modern Inter-Arabic", *Journal of the American Oriental Society* 86, pp. 319–23.

Blanc H. (1960) "Style Variations in Spoken Arabic – A sample of Interdialectal Educated Conversation" in Ferguson CA (ed) (1960), pp. 79–156.

Blanc H. (1964) *Communal Dialects in Baghdad*, Cambridge, Mass., Harvard Middle Eastern Monographs X.

Blanc H. (1974) "The nekteb-nektebu imperfect in a variety of Cairene Arabic", *Israel Oriental Studies* 4, pp. 206–26.

Bloch A. (1971) "Morphological doublets in Arabic dialects", *Journal of Semitic studies* 16, pp. 53–73.

Blom J.P. and Gumperz J.J. (1971) "Social Meaning in Linguistic Structure: Code-switching in Norway" in Gumperz J.J. and Hymes D.H. (eds) (1972) *Directions in Sociolinguistics: The Ethnography of Communication*, New York, Holt, Rinehart and Winston, pp. 407–34.

Britto F. (1986) *Diglossia: a study of the Theory with application to Tamil*, Washington, D.C., Georgetown University Press.

Cadora F.J. (1965) "The Teaching of spoken and written Arabic", *Language Learning* 15, pp. 133–6.

Cairo fact book (1963) Social research center, American University of Cairo.

Cantarino V. (1974) *Syntax of modern Arabic prose* 1, Bloomington, Indiana University.

Cantineau J. (1960) *Etudes de linguistique arabe*, Paris, Klincksieck.

Cesaro A. (1939) *L'arabo parlato a Tripoli*, Milano, A. Mondadori.
Chafe W.L. (1979) *Integration and involvement in spoken and written language*. Paper presented at the Second Congress of the International Association for Semitic Studies. Vienna.
Chafe W.L. (1982) "Integration and involvement in speaking, writing and oral literature" in Tannen D. (ed) (1982b). pp. 35–53.
Chafe W.L. (1983) "Integration and involvement in spoken and written language" in Borbe T. (ed) *Semiotics unfolding*, Proceedings of the Second Congress of the International Association for Semitic Studies, Vienna, July 1979, vol II Semiotics in text and literature. Linguistics and Semiotics, pp. 1095–102.
Chambers J.K. and Trudgill P. (1980) *Dialectology*, Cambridge, Cambridge University Press.
Chen G.M. and Starosta W.J. (1996) "Intercultural Communication Competence. A Synthesis", *Communication Yearbook* 19, pp. 353–83.
Cowan W. (1968) "Notes toward a definition of Modern Standard Arabic", *Language Learning* 18, pp. 29–34.
Diem W. (1974) *Hochsprache und Dialekt im Arabischen. Untersuchungen zur heutigen arabischen Zweisprachigkeit*, Wiesbaden, Kommissionsverlag Franz Steiner.
Dil A.S. (1971) *Language in Social Groups*, Essays by John J. Gumperz, Stanford University Press.
Discours de Réception de Madame Marguerite Yourcenar à l'Académie Française et réponse de Monsieur Jean d'Ormesson (21 janvier 1981) Paris, Gallimard.
Dittmar N. (1976) *Sociolinguistics: a Critical Survey of Theory and Application*, London, Arnold.
Doss M. (1987) "Further remarks on the use of b- imperfect in Spoken Literary Arabic", *Zeitschrift für arabische Linguistik* 17, pp. 93–5.
Egypt Meri Report (1985) Middle East Research Institute. University of Pennsylvania, Croomhelm.
Eid M. (1988) "Principles for code-switching between standard and Egyptian Arabic", *Al-'Arabiyya* 21, pp. 51–79.
El Dash L. and Tucker G.R. (1975) "Subjective reactions to various speech styles in Egypt", *Linguistics* 166, pp. 33–54.
El Fathaly O. and Palmer M. (1980) *Political development and social change in Libya*, Lexington, Mass., Heath.
El Fitoury A.B.A. (1976) *A descriptive grammar of Libyan Arabic*, PhD Dissertation, Georgetown University.
El Gadi A.S. (1986) *Tripolitanean Arabic phonology and morphology*, Ann Arbor, MI, University Microfilms International 1987.
El Hassan S.A. (1977) "Educated Spoken Arabic in Egypt and the Levant: a Critical review of Diglossia and related concepts", *Archivum Linguisticum* 8:2, pp. 112–32.
El Hassan S.A. (1978) "Variation in the demonstrative system on Educated Spoken Arabic", *Archivum Linguisticum* 9:1, pp. 32–57.
Erwin W.N. (1963) *A Short Reference Grammar of Iraqi Arabic*, Washington D.C., Georgetown University Press.
Erwin W.N. (1969) *A Basic Course in Iraqi Arabic*, Washington D.C., Georgetown University Press.

Fairclough N. (1995) *Media Discourse,* London, Edward Arnold.
Fellman J. (1973) "Sociolinguistics problems in the Middle Eastern Arab World. An Overview", *Anthropological linguistics* 15, pp. 24–32.
Ferguson C.A. (1959) "Diglossia" reprinted in Ferguson CA (1971), *Language structure and language use,* Stanford, Stanford University Press, pp. 1–26.
Ferguson C.A. (ed) (1960) *Contributions to Arabic Linguistics,* Cambridge Mass., Harvard Middle Eastern Monographs III.
Ferguson C.A. (1963) *Problems of Teaching Languages with Diglossia,* Georgetown University Monograph Series on Languages and Linguistics: Monograph No15, Report of the Thirteenth Annual Round Table Meeting, Washington DC, Georgetown University Press, pp. 165–77.
Fischer W. und Jastrow O. (1980) *Handbuch der arabischen Dialekte,* Wiesbaden, Harrassowitz.
Fishman F.A. (1969) "The Sociology of Language" in Giglioli P.P. (1972), pp. 45–58.
Gal S. (1978) "Variation and Change in Patterns of Speaking: Language shift in Austria" in Sankoff D. (ed) (1978) *Linguistic Variation Models and Methods,* New York, Academic Press, pp. 227–38.
Gal S. (1979) *Language Shift. Social Determinants of Linguistic Change in Bilingual Austria,* New York, Academic Press.
Gibbons J. (1987) *Code-Mixing and Code Choice. A Hong Kong Case Study,* Clevedon, Philadelphia, Multilingual Matters.
Giglioli P.P. (1972) *Language and social context,* Harmondsworth, Penguin Books.
Griffini E. (1913) *L'arabo parlato della libia,* Milano, Hoepli Libraio della Real Casa.
Grotzfeld H. (1983) "Language hierarchy and speaking Arabic: Language constancy, variation and tolerance in an Arabic dialect area", *AlAbhath* 31, pp. 85–97.
Gumperz J.J. (1958) "Dialect Differences and Social Stratification in a North Indian village" in Dil A.S. (1971), pp. 25–47.
Gumperz J.J. (1964) "Hindi-Punjabi Code-Swiching in Delhi" in Dil A.S. (1971), pp. 205–19.
Gumperz J.J. (1968) "The speech community" in Giglioli P.P. (1972), pp. 219–31.
Gumperz J.J. (1982) *Discourse strategies,* Cambridge, Cambridge University Press.
Gumperz J.J. and Hernandez-Chavez E. (1971) "Bilingualism, bidialectalism and classroom interaction" in *Language in social groups*: Essays by J.J. Gumperz, Stanford, Stanford University Press.
ḥadīṯ al-baṭal al-za'īm gamāl 'abdunnāṣir ʔila l-ʔumma. Cairo, dār al-taḥrīr, (1970), 5 vols in 4.
Halliday M.A.K. (1978) *Language as a social semiotic,* London, Arnold.
Halliday M.A.K. (1989) *Spoken and written language,* Oxford, Oxford University Press.
Harrell R.S. (1957) *The Phonology of Colloquial Egyptian Arabic,* New York American Council of Learned Societies.
Harrell R.S. (1960) "Egyptian Radio Arabic" in Ferguson C.A. (ed) (1960), pp. 1–77.

Harris L.C. (1986) *Libya. Qadhafi's Revolution and the Modern State*. Colorado, Westview Press, Croomhelm.

Hartmann M. (1899) *Lieder der libyschen Wüste*... nebst einem Exkurse über die bedeutenderen Beduinenstämme des westlichen Unterägypten von M. Hartmann (Abh. für die Kubde des Morgenlandes. XI, 3), Leipzig.

Havelock E.A. (1963) *Preface to Plato*, Oxford.

Heath J. (1989) *From code-switching to borrowing: foreign and diglossic mixing in Moroccan Arabic*, London, Kegan Paul International.

Heller M. (1982) "Bonjour, hello?: negotiations of language choice in Montreal" in Gumperz J.J. (ed) *Language and Social Identity*, Cambridge, Cambridge University Press, pp. 108–18.

Heller M. (ed) (1988) *Codeswitching. Anthropological and Sociolinguistic Perspectives*, Berlin: Mouton de Gruyter.

Hinds M. and Badawi el S. (1986) *A Dictionary of Egyptian Arabic: Arabic-English*, Beirut: Librairie du Liban.

Holes C.D. (1980) "Phonological variation in Bahraini Arabic: the [j] and [y] allophones of [j]", *Zeitschrift für arabische Linguistik* 4, pp. 72–89.

Holes C.D. (1983a) "Bahraini dialects: sectarian differences and the sedentary/ nomadic split", *Zeitschrift für arabische Linguistik* 10, pp. 7–38.

Holes C.D. (1983b) "Patterns of communal language variation in Bahrain", *Language in Society* 12, pp. 433–57.

Holes C.D. (1986) "Communicative Function and Pronominal Variation in Bahraini Arabic", *Anthropological linguistics* 28:1, pp. 10–30.

Holes C.D. (1993) "The uses of variation: a study of the political speeches of Gamal Abd Al-Nasir", *Perspectives on Arabic Linguistics* 5, pp. 13–45.

Holes C.D. (1995) *Modern Arabic. Structures, functions and varieties*, London, Longman Linguistics Library.

Hymes D.H. (1971a) "Competence and Performance in Linguistic Theory" in Huxley R. and Ingram E. (eds) *Language Acquisition: Models and Methods*, London, Academic Press, pp. 3–23.

Hymes D.H. (1971b) *Pidginization and Creolization of Languages*, Cambridge, Cambridge University Press.

Ibrahim M.H. (1986) "Standard and prestige language: A problem in Arabic sociolinguistics", *Anthropological linguistics* 28:1, pp. 115–26.

Ingham B. (1973) "Urban and rural Arabic in Khuzistan", *Bulletin of the School of Oriental and African Studies* 36:3, pp. 533–53.

Ingham B. (1976) "Regional and social factors in the dialect geography of southern Iraq and Khuzistan", *BSOAS* 39:1, pp. 62–82.

Ingham B. (1982) *North East Arabian Dialects*, London, Kegan Paul International.

Iraq: A Country Study 1990. Chapin Metz H. (ed), Federal Research Division, Research completed May 1988, Washington DC, Library of Congress.

Jastrow O. (1983) "Tikrit Arabic verb morphology in a comparative perspective", *AlAbhath* 31, pp. 99–110.

Johnstone B. (1987) "An Introduction. Perspectives on repetition" in Johnstone B. (ed), special issue of *Text* 7.3, pp. 205–14.

Johnstone B. (1991) *Repetition in Arabic Discourse. Paradigms, syntagms and the ecology of language*, Amsterdam, Benjamins.

Johnstone T.M. (1975) "The spoken Arabic of Tikrit", *Annuals of Leeds University Oriental Society* 3, pp. 89–109.

Jomier J. (1964) *Manuel d'arabe égyptien* (Parler du Caire), Paris, Klincksieck.

Karsh E. and Rautsi I. (1991) *Saddam Hussein, a political biography,* London, Brassey's.

Kay P. (1977) "Language evolution and speech style "Elaborated" vs "Restricted" speech style" in Blount B.G. and Sanches M. (eds) *Sociocultural dimensions of language change,* New York, Academic Press, pp. 21–33.

Kerswill P.E. (1985) *A Sociolinguistic study of rural immigrants in Bergen, Norway,* Unpublished PhD dissertation, Cambridge University.

Khalafallah A.A. (1969) *A Descriptive Grammar of Sa'īdī Egyptian colloquial Arabic,* The Hague, Mouton.

Koch B. (1983) "Presentation as proof: the language of Arabic rhetoric", *Anthropological linguistics* 25:1, pp. 47–60.

Kroch A.S. (1978) "Toward a theory of social dialect variation", *Language in Society* 7, pp. 17–36.

Labov W. (1966) *The Social Stratification of English in New York City,* Washington, Center for Applied Linguistics.

Labov W. (1971) "The notion of "System" in Creole Studies" in Hymes D.H. (1971), pp. 447–72.

Labov W. (1972a) *Language in the Inner City,* Philadelphia, University of Pennsylvania Press.

Labov W. (1972b) *Sociolinguistic Patterns,* Philadelphia, University of Pennsylvania Press.

Lakoff R.T. (1979) "Stylistic strategies within a grammar of style. Language, sex and gender" in Orasanu J. et al. (eds), Annals of the New York Academy of Sciences, 327, New York, pp. 53–78.

Lakoff R.T. (1981) "Persuasive discourse and ordinary conversation, with examples from advertising" in Tannen D. (ed) (1981), pp. 25–42.

Landsman D.M. (1989) *Theories of diglossia, linguistic variation and speaker attitudes, with special reference to recent developments in Modern Greek,* Unpublished PhD dissertation, Cambridge University.

Langley K.M. (1961) *The Industrialisation of Iraq,* Harvard Middle Eastern Monographs.

Lavendera B. (1978) "Where does the sociolinguistic variable stop?", *Language in Society* 7:2, pp. 171–82.

Lecerf J. (1969) "Structure syllabique en arabe de Baghdad et en accent de mot en arabe oriental", *WORD* 25, pp. 160–79.

Mahmoud Y. (1986) "Arabic after Diglossia" in Fishman J.A. (ed et al) *The Fergusonian Impact* 1, Berlin, Mouton de Gruyter, pp. 239–51.

Mansfield P. (1969) *Nasser,* London, Methuen.

Mansfield P. (1982) "Saddam Husain's political thinking: the comparison with Nasser" in Niblock (ed) (1982) *Iraq: the contemporary state,* London, Croomhelm for the Centre for Arab Gulf studies, pp. 62–73.

Marçais W. (1930–31) "La diglossie arabe", 3 articles in *L'Enseignement Public*: 12 (Dec. 1930), 13 (Jan. 1931), 14 (Feb.1931).

Matar A. (1967) *lahadjat al-baduw fī ?iqlīm sāḥil maryūṭ* (The Bedouin Arabic Dialects in the territory of Maryut Coast) Cairo, Ministry of culture.

Mazraani N. (1995) "Functions of Arabic Political Discourse: The Case of Saddam Hussein's Speeches", *Zeitschrift für arabische Linguistik* 30, pp. 22–36.

Mazraani N. (1995) "Style Variation and Persuasion in the Speeches of Gamal Abdel Nasser", *Proceedings of the Second International Conference of AIDA*, 10–14 Sept. 1995, Cambridge, pp. 141–50.

McCarthy R.J. and Raffouli F. (1964) *The spoken Arabic of Baghdad*. Beirut, Publ. of the Oriental Inst. of al-Hikma Univ., Linguistic Ser., I.

McGuirk R. (1986) *Colloquial Arabic of Egypt*, London, Routledge & Kegan Paul.

Meiseles G. (1980) "Educated Spoken Arabic and the Arabic language continuum", *Archivum Linguisticum* 11:2, pp. 118–43.

Meiseles G. (1981) "Hybrid versus symbiotic constructions: a case study of contemporary Arabic", *Linguistics* 19, pp. 1077–93.

Miller J. and Mylroie L. (1990) *Saddam Hussein and the Crisis in the Gulf*, New York, Times Books, Random House.

Milroy L. (1976) "Phonological correlates to community structure in Belfast", *Belfast Working Papers in Language and Linguistics* 1 (August).

Milroy L. (1980) *Language and Social Networks*, Oxford, Blackwell.

Mitchell T.F. (1952) "The active participle in an Arabic dialect of Cyrenaica", *BSOAS* 14, pp. 11–33.

Mitchell T.F. (1960) "Prominence and syllabication in Arabic", *BSOAS* 23:2, pp. 369–89.

Mitchell T.F. (1980) "Dimensions of style in a grammar of Educated Spoken Arabic", *Archivum Linguisticum* 11:2, pp. 89–106

Mitchell T.F. (1986) "What is educated spoken arabic", *International Journal of the Sociology of Language* 61, pp. 7–32.

Mitterand F. (1980) *Ici et maintenant*. Conversations avec Guy Claisse, Paris, Fayard.

Murray D.E. (1988) "The context of oral and written language. A framework for mode and medium switching". *Language in Society* 17, pp. 351–73.

Ochs E. (1979) "Planned and unplanned discourse" in Givón T. (ed) *Syntax and semantics*, Vol 12 Discourse and syntax. New York, Academic Press, pp. 51–80.

Olson D.R. (1980) "Some social aspects of meaning in Oral and Written language" in Olson D.R. (ed) *The social foundations of language and thought*, New York, Norton, pp. 90–108.

Owens J. (1984) *A short reference grammar of Eastern Libyan Arabic*, Wiesbaden, Harrassowitz.

Owens J. and Bani-Yasin R. (1987) "The lexical basis of variation in Jordanian Arabic", *Linguistics* 25, pp. 705–38.

Palva H. (1969) "Notes on Classicization in Modern Colloquial Arabic", Helsinki *Studia Orientalia* 40:3, pp. 1–41.

Pandit I. (1986) *Hindi English Code Switching. Mixed Hindi English*, Delhi, Datta Book Centre.

Panetta E. (1943) *L'Arabo Parlato a Bengasi*. Roma, La libreria dello stato.

Pfaff C. (1979) "Constraints on Language Mixing", *Language* 55, pp. 291–318.

Picktall M. (1976) *The Glorious Koran*. A bilingual edition with English translations, introduction and notes, London, George Allen and Unwin.

Poplack S. (1980) "Sometimes I'll start a sentence in English y termino en Español; towards a typology of code-switching", *Linguistics* 18, pp. 581–618.

Quarterly Economic Review of Libya. The Economist Intelligence Unit Annual Supplement 1978.

Rosenhouse J. (1984) *The Bedouin Arabic Dialects*, Wiesbaden, Harrassowitz.

Schmidt R. (1974) *Sociolinguistic Variation in Spoken Egyptian Arabic: a re-examination of the concept of diglossia*, Brown University Dissertation.

Selim G.D. (1967) "Some contrasts between Classical Arabic and Egyptian Arabic" in Stuart D.G. (ed) (1967) *Linguistic Studies in memory of Harrell R.S.*, Washington D.C., Georgetown University Press, pp. 133–52.

Shouby E. (1951) "The influence of the Arabic language on the psychology of the Arabs", *Middle East Journal* 5, pp. 284–302.

Singer H.R. (1980) "Das Westarabische oder Maghribinische" in Fischer W. und Jastrow O. (1980), pp. 249–265.

Statistical Pocket Year Book 1962 Department of statistics and census. Cairo, General Organisation for Government Printing Office 1963.

Suleiman Y. (1993) "The language situation in Jordan and code-switching: a new interpretation" in Serjeant R.B., Bidwell R.L. and Rex Smith G. (eds) *New Arabian Studies I*, Exeter, University of Exeter Press, pp. 1–21.

Suleiman Y. (ed) (1994) *Arabic Sociolinguistics: Issues and Perspectives*, Richmond, Curzon Press.

Tannen D. (1980) "Spoken/written language and the oral/literate continuum", Proceedings of the Sixth Annual Meeting of the Berkeley Linguistic Society. Feb 16–18, 1980 Berkeley Linguistics Society, Cal., pp. 207–18.

Tannen D. (ed) (1981) *Analysing discourse: Text and Talk*, Georgetown University Round Table, Georgetown University Press.

Tannen D. (1982a) "Oral and literate strategies in spoken and written narratives", *Language* 58:1, pp. 1–21.

Tannen D. (ed) (1982b) *Spoken and written language: exploring Orality and literacy*, vol IX in the Series Advances in Discourse Processes, Norwood, N.J., Ablex.

Tannen D. (1988) "Hearing voices in conversation, fiction and mixed genres" in Tannen D. (ed) (1988), *Linguistics in context: connecting observation and understanding*, Lectures from the 1985 LSA/TESOL and NEH Institutes, Norwood, N.J., Ablex, pp. 89–113.

Tannen D. (1989) *Talking voices. Repetition, dialogue and imagery in conversational discourse*, Cambridge, Cambridge University Press.

Trudgill P. (1972) "Sex, covert prestige and linguistic change in the urban British English of Norwich", *Language in Society* 1, pp. 179–95.

Trudgill P. (1974) *The Social Differentiation of English in Norwich*, Cambridge, Cambridge University Press.

Trudgill P. (1986) *Dialects in contact*, Oxford, Blackwell.

Unesco: *Statistical Yearbook 1990*, Paris, Unesco.

Unesco: *Statistical Yearbook 1991*, Paris, Unesco.

Van Dijk T.A. (1981) "Episodes as units of discourse analysis", in Tannen D. (ed) (1981), pp. 177–95.

Van Ess J. (1938) *The Spoken Arabic of Iraq* (repr.1975), Oxford, Oxford University Press.

Wardhaugh R. (1986) *An Introduction to Sociolinguistics*, Oxford, Blackwell.

Widdowson H.G. (1979) *Explorations in Applied Linguistics*, Oxford, Oxford University Press.

Wise H. (1972) "Concord in Spoken Egyptian Arabic", *Archivum Linguisticum* 3, pp. 7–17.
Woidich M. (ed) (1990) *Amsterdam Middle Eastern Studies*, Wiesbaden, Dr. Ludwig Reichert Verlag.
Woodward P. (1992) *Nasser*, London, Longman.
Wright W.A. (1859, repr.1962) *A Grammar of the Arabic language*, 2 vols Cambridge, Cambridge University Press.

Index: Authors

Index 2: General

www.ingramcontent.com/pod-product-compliance
Lightning Source LLC
Chambersburg PA
CBHW061921130726
47908CB00016B/701
* 9 7 8 1 1 3 8 9 6 3 9 9 3 *